618   1·99

GOODWILL ON FIRE

BRIAN FROST

Goodwill on Fire: Donald Soper's Life and Mission

Hodder & Stoughton
LONDON SYDNEY AUCKLAND

British Library Cataloguing in Publication Data
A record for this book is available from the British Library

ISBN 0 340 64283 1

Typeset by CentraCet, Cambridge
Printed and bound in Great Britain by
Mackays of Chatham PLC, Kent

Hodder and Stoughton Ltd
A Division of Hodder Headline PLC
338 Euston Road
London NW1 3BH

Dedicated to William Edwin Frost (1904–1991)

CONTENTS

The love of Christ was goodwill on fire, indefatigable, undefeated.

Donald Soper, *The Advocacy of the Gospel*, p. 115.

Goodwill on fire, goodwill lit by the love of God, and its glow maintained by fellowship with Jesus. I know of no better description of the Christian life.

Donald Soper, *Popular Fallacies about the Christian Faith*, p. 52.

What God requires of me is that which He perfectly received from Jesus – the performance of goodwill, the persistent intention to seek the good of others.

Donald Soper, *All His Grace*, p. 80.

. . . the Gospel of redemption is the practice of love, not as a pleasant emotion but as goodwill on fire.

Donald Soper, *Morning Star*, 27 October 1979.

PREFACE

Many people have contributed material for *Goodwill on Fire* – members of the Christian Socialist Movement and the Labour Party, the Methodist Peace Fellowship, the Methodist Sacramental Fellowship, the Order of Christian Witness, and Christians from many backgrounds, including former members of Kingsway Hall, and some from Hinde Street and other Methodist Churches.

I am particularly grateful to those who wrote to me with specific details and also those who allowed me to interview them, particularly Lord Soper's colleagues in the House of Lords.

In researching material on Lord Soper's life I am grateful to the BBC Written Archives Centre, Caversham, and the British Library (National Sound Archive), and to the Fellowship of Reconciliation, the Methodist Archive (John Rylands Library, University of Manchester), the staff of the League Against Cruel Sports, the Marx Memorial Library, the *Methodist Recorder*, the Peace Pledge Union, the *Jewish Chronicle*, the *Morning Star*, and *Tribune*, for help received.

I would also like to thank the Rev. Dr Leslie Griffiths, whose initial idea the biography was; the Rev. Dr Gordon Wakefield, who helped me work through the material; and Miss Kath Humphreys, Lord Soper's secretary, who was a model of helpfulness and resourcefulness, as was Mrs Lilly Massicott, who typed out the eighteen special interviews I did with Lord Soper, which are to form the basis of the Soper Archive being set up at John Rylands Library. I was also helped by writings on evangelism and the secular mind by the Rev. George Hunter III, Dean of the E. Stanley Jones School of Evangelism, Asbury Theological Seminary, Kentucky.

Above all, I wish to thank Lord and Lady Soper, and their four daughters, for their help and interest at various stages as the work proceeded. I am well aware, however, that in a life as complex and varied as Lord Soper's I have been able only to cover the main themes, leaving readers to explore in greater detail later other aspects which have been hinted at rather than described in detail.

Thanks are due to the following for permission to use photographs: *Methodist Recorder/E W Tattersall* – Methodist Conference early 1930s; Trafalgar Square c. 1946; Drs Sangster, Weatherhead and Soper; Trevor Huddleston at Central Hall 1956. *Methodist Recorder/ Roy Cook* – Christian Socialist gathering 1971. *Methodist Recorder/ Fleet Fotos* – Launch of Fellowship, Freedom and Equality 1990. *Methodist Recorder* – Ninetieth birthday Eucharist 1993; National Children's Home Caring 1972 meeting. *Roy Cook* – Lord Soper with George Thomas, etc, 1993. *Mrs Noel Wilkinson (nee Rutter)* – Order of Christian Witness team, Risca Valley 1949. *North West London Press* – Fernhead Road Methodist Church 1985. *Tyne Tees Television/ Jack Cutter* – In the hot seat. *Peter Dawe* – County Hall 1985. *Nancy Grey* – group photo and poster for Dorchester Peace Rally 1936. Poster photographed by *Alan Coney*. *Hulton Deutsch Collection/Picture Post* – With Joan Middleton Murry 1950. *RF Rowley/League Against Cruel Sports* – With Eric Heffer MP 1968. *Greater London Records Office* – Campaigning for nuclear disarmament 1984. *Morning Star/ Nigel Tanburn* – Fellowship of Reconciliation delegation to Downing Street. *West London Mission* – St Luke's Centre 1990. *Tomas Jaski* – Diamond Wedding 1989.

Brian Frost,
London,
March 1995.

INTRODUCTION

THERE WERE VERY few people about in Green Park on 31 January 1993, as I walked across it from my flat near Buckingham Palace to my church in St Marylebone. It was a warm, sunny day, just right for the celebration I was about to enjoy. I crossed Piccadilly by the Ritz and was soon through Mayfair and crossing Oxford Street. Cutting through an alleyway, I arrived at Hinde Street Methodist Church by 9.35 a.m. to find fifty people already gathered for the ten o'clock Communion Service.

This, however, was no ordinary Sunday, as the TV cameras outside the church indicated. It was, in fact, Donald Soper's ninetieth birthday and when he began the Eucharist instead of the usual twenty-five or so there were 200 people present. By eleven it was standing room only, as over 600 people crowded into the church, including Lady Soper, the Sopers' four daughters and their families, M.P.s Tony Benn and Peter Brooke, Methodist leaders and Michael Foot, a family friend.

Who were they? Mostly people from different parts of Dr Soper's complex life – from the Christian Socialist Movement, the League Against Cruel Sports, the Order of Christian Witness, which he founded, the Methodist Peace Fellowship and from the Labour Party, as well as members of the congregation where Dr Soper found a home after retirement, or 're-treading' as he termed it, when Kingsway Hall, his base in London for over forty years, closed.

Dr Soper's sermon on 'Faith, Hope and Love', ('One of the best sermons I've ever heard,' Tony Benn was later to say) was most appropriate. So, too, was the inscription on the stained-glass window behind Lord Soper which read 'Glory to God in the highest and on earth peace', for they were the two main themes which had formed Donald Soper's life since he left Cambridge University in 1926.

I

After the service there were greetings from Michael Foot and the Rev. Dr Kenneth Greet among others and the cutting of the birthday cake. The children presented red roses, red not only for politics but for passion, too, the minister of the church, the Rev. David Cruise, declared, causing loud laughter, as he explained they were pacifist roses – their prickles had been removed!

At lunch there was time to greet special guests, before Dr Soper moved on to Hyde Park for 3.00 p.m., as he had done most Sundays since the 1940s. Many of the crowd were regulars, but on this occasion it was swollen to 400 by some of the morning congregation, who had followed him to Speaker's Corner. At four o'clock Lord Soper returned to Hinde Street Methodist Church for a rest; then prepared for the live *Songs of Praise* on BBC TV at 6.25 p.m., as more guests, including Bishop Huddleston, Paul Boateng, M.P., Dr Pauline Webb, Bruce Kent, Lord Murray and the Bishop of London, arrived.

The programme was seen by millions. Pre-filmed were tributes from Sir David Steel, Tony Benn, Lord Archer, Michael Foot, Cardinal Hume and Lord Runcie. There were also shots of Dr Soper in Hyde Park and of the social work of the West London Mission, which he had done so much to support. In between were hymns chosen and introduced by Dr Soper himself. It was a tiring day, but through it all Donald Soper had maintained a dignity and modesty which were most appealing. To cap it all, though it was pre-recorded, at 11.45 p.m., he was part of a Yorkshire TV panel discussion on when, if ever, it is permissible to take the life of another human being.

How had a Methodist minister, the first ever to become a member of the House of Lords, a socialist of radical views, come to receive such affection and acclaim, as indicated in the newspapers the following morning? 'At 90, Soper disarms hecklers in the name of God and socialism,' said *The Independent*. 'Lord Soper, 90, puts down the birthday hecklers and uplifts his soapbox fans,' added the *Daily Telegraph*. Why, indeed, had both radio and TV noted his birthday, sometimes with interviews, during that weekend?

In this biography I try to explain how from a secure, middle-class home in Wandsworth as this century began, Donald Soper became the socialist to whom millions have listened, and also a pacifist, a sacramentalist and Christian controversialist and campaigner. I explain, too, his complexity and explore his emotional and intellectual roots, and the reason for his ongoing open-air ministry, which started on Tower Hill in 1927. I also try to show how Dr Soper has responded to Britain's changing role this century by describing the themes which have preoccupied him.

Because Lord Soper has lived both a public and a private life I start and end this biography with chapters which set him in the context of his family from whom he has gained such strength. I examine, too, his involvement with the Labour Party and also how he has tried to refashion Christianity for 'our terrible times', as Gordon Wakefield has called them. For Dr Soper has been at pains always to help people find, then keep, a faith which is credible. He is, and always has been, one of John Wesley's travelling preachers, but one who sees the need to communicate through radio, TV and the press, channels of communication which enabled so many to share his ninetieth birthday celebrations.

Donald Soper has always been first and foremost a Methodist parson and on that birthday his Church really seemed to claim him as one of its own, even though in an often turbulent ministry it had not always agreed with his vision. This biography, therefore, roots him in Methodism, in its sacramental life, as on 31 January 1993, and in Methodist preaching, with its strong sense of the need to reach outside the walls of the church. It tries, too, to reveal the man behind the legend, capable not only of strong views, but also of strong emotions and responses, a facet of Donald Soper's personality visible both in Hyde Park on Sundays and in the House of Lords and elsewhere during the week.

On that birthday Sunday and in his life Donald Soper has played many roles, so varied probably no single person has seen them all, or agreed with all his views. Most, nevertheless, have been attracted by Dr Soper's courage and goodness, courage seen that Sunday as he walked with difficulty because of his arthritis. They have been attracted, too, by his humour and charm, but Dr Soper would not want adulation for he is acutely aware we all do wrong. This biography, therefore, examines the need he feels people have for penitence in their lives.

Despite his flaws, which Donald Soper acknowledges, as a 'would-be Christian', to use one of his many catch phrases, he has tried to generate goodwill, and distil Christian love in society. It is this quality which has enabled him to reach out to thousands in open-air speaking across Britain and elsewhere as well as to many millions through the media. *Goodwill on Fire*, therefore, ends up, as did Dr Soper's ninetieth birthday, with the celebration of a life open to the modern world in all its doubts, ferment and anguish, and open to a God who can tolerate through forgiveness our many mistakes, wrong turnings and ambiguities.

Chapter 1

PUPIL

'CHRISTIANITY IS REVOLUTIONARY,' Donald Soper said on Tower Hill in December 1986, a view he had expressed for six decades. By January 1993, when he was ninety, he had proclaimed it to well over a million people in every continent, though he was denied permission to speak in Red Square in Moscow in 1954. On Tower Hill from 1927 and in Hyde Park regularly from 1942, he probably addressed three-quarters of a million people, both regulars and passers-by, including three Prime Ministers – James Callaghan, who in the 1930s heard Donald Soper give a philosophical critique of capitalism when working in the City of London; Jomo Kenyatta, a student in London in the 1950s, who remained strangely silent at the back of the crowd in Hyde Park; and David Lange, who implemented some of Donald Soper's peace concerns as Prime Minister of New Zealand in the 1980s.

On Tower Hill and in Hyde Park Donald answered over a quarter of a million questions, mostly about how Christianity affects personal and social life. In market places and city centres and also in a few village squares, as in Northern Ireland, where Ian Paisley heckled him, Donald Soper faced audiences in their hundreds, and on the Galle Face Green in Colombo, Sri Lanka, he spoke to over 4,000, his largest open-air meeting ever. The achievement which made him a 'legend in his own lifetime'[1] is even more considerable if you include the millions who heard him on radio and television as he tried, as an evangelist, to reach them in what he called 'the first secular age'.[2]

How did Donald find the courage to become addicted to his soapbox, whatever the weather conditions? Here his mother's influence was critical. 'One of my earliest memories,' he recalled, 'is that of being taken by my mother . . . to a suffragette meeting.'[3] He knew his mother first in her public role when he accompanied her to

5

Swaffield Road Junior School in Wandsworth. Here she taught English, maths and religious studies and here he received his first lessons. But in this suffragette meeting Donald saw his mother anew and discovered 'she was a most militant person'.[4]

Caroline Amelia Pilcher, the daughter of a builder, a small and intense lady of dynamism and energy, a trait Donald inherited, came from a Congregational background in West Hartlepool, though when married she fitted happily into Wesleyan Methodism. Active in the London Teachers' Union, she was one of the early headmistresses, first of Swaffield Road Junior School and then of other south London schools.

Donald always went to his mother with his troubles.[5] 'She was,' wrote Grace Pugh, who met Mrs Soper in the 1930s, 'an elegant lady always ready to listen to any problems ... lively and full of compassion for others.'[6] Indeed, in 1919 she took in a young boy whose mother had died in the flu epidemic.[7] Most importantly Mrs Soper was a teacher whose aim was to help children, including her own, develop. Initially she had emphasized education as nourishment. Later, however, she saw education as the drawing out of what was latent, 'encouraging people to criticize what was offered', Donald once explained.[8]

Caroline Pilcher was born in 1877 and had married Ernest Frankham Soper, six years her senior, in 1900. They had three children, Donald, born in 1903, Millicent in 1905 and Meredith Ross in 1907. 'I think of my mother and the natural way in which she would give to us, without any question of bargain,' Donald reflected later, 'and without any assessment of her own need.'[9] One aspect of this caring, which proved seminal, was teaching Donald how to project his voice for speaking.[10] However, there was an astringent element in her make-up, too. When Donald was made a Life Peer in 1965, for example, she urged him to remember he was still a Methodist minister, neither more nor less.[11] Once, when Donald was six, her local church sent a deputation to discuss a piece of work with Mrs Soper. 'There was,' Donald remembered, 'a dramatic touch about her response.' Pointing to her children she said, 'Gentlemen, there's my church work. Good afternoon!'[12]

Despite work pressures Mrs Soper was aware of community needs, though 36, Knoll Road, SW 18, where they lived, was a prosperous, middle-class area, the Sopers' house itself epitomizing this, with its view of Wimbledon Common from one of the three floors. Once Mrs

Soper took part in a survey of what was happening in public houses at midnight on Saturdays. 'She found 143 children below the age of ten,' Donald reported, 'either asleep in corners or left outside the doors.'[13]

Caroline Soper was not always serious, however. 'My mother was spontaneously funny,' Donald remembered.[14] Indeed, his humour came more from her than from his father, who used to collect jokes to tell at Christmas, which he recounted whether the family thought they were funny or not.[15] 'I think he had a sense of humour,' Millicent said of him, 'but it was a controlled one, and the little things of life which were, to us, very funny, he didn't see.'[16] Certainly there was in the family background a sense of fun, for Donald's grandfather used to travel up the Thames with Jerome K. Jerome, whose whimsical account of a boat trip from Kingston to Oxford, *Three Men in a Boat*, had become famous, and Donald used to hear from him of their various meetings and discussions.[17]

When Donald's father died in 1962 aged ninety-one he was described as 'a Christian gentleman, whose quiet courage, strong convictions and delightful sense of humour impressed all who knew him',[18] so an obvious mellowing had occurred for this Londoner, one of whose parents had been born within the sound of Bow Bells, which enabled Donald to claim he was part cockney. A considerable linguist, Mr Soper was an average adjuster in marine insurance where he assessed the monies to be paid out when ships came to grief. Starting as an office boy he ended up with considerable authority in Charles Cooper and Sons in Leadenhall Street EC 3. 'I never, I think, was very close to my father,' Donald Soper has conceded. 'I admired and respected him and I know he cared for me, but . . . we were never comrades on a common path.'[19]

The son of a tailor, Ernest Soper, was shaped by a mixture of Primitive Methodism and its more Anglicized Wesleyan form. He was a committed Nonconformist, spending his spare time between a Salvation Army mission and his superintendency of the Sunday School at St John's Wesleyan Methodist Church in East Hill, Wandsworth. Mr Soper himself was, according to one eyewitness, an excellent open-air speaker, good with hecklers, and those who heard him could well understand 'how it is that his son is so gifted in that direction. It was born in him.'[20]

As a boy Donald used to boast of his father, and still did so in middle age, arguing in the playground about his family's wisdom.

'Between us, my father and I knew everything,' he would maintain 'and the difficult questions were the questions my father could answer.'[21] A first-class athlete, whom Donald tried to emulate,[22] Mr Soper was addicted to the novels of Dickens which meant that Donald read them, too.[23] His father also taught Donald to do the breast stroke as he lay over a stool and simulated swimming movements.[24] Once in the water Donald soon learned to swim and in 1912, when he was nine, he received the London County Council's Elementary School Swimming Certificate for forty yards. Donald's father also insisted Donald should become a fast bowler, as he was himself, and took him to Streatham Common to practise.[25]

His father's Puritanism also influenced Donald, for he was a pristine example of the Protestant work ethic, exemplifying John Wesley's dictum 'Gain all you can, save all you can, give all you can.'[26] A piece of homely advice geared to help poor people, by 1900 it had become a clear moral guide shaping the lives of thousands, producing disciples who were earnest and hard-working. 'I can remember promising my father when I was a small boy,' Donald Soper wrote in 1961, 'to work harder. It didn't last very long; sometimes it never began. But from time to time, I think it did.'[27] Like many other boys who misbehaved Donald was sent upstairs to cool off. Sometimes, too, his father would also use corporal punishment to control him. Despite this sternness Donald accepted automatically his father's approach to thought and truth until 1914.[28] 'My father, above all,' he reflected, 'was concerned not to sin.'[29] He got ten out of ten in Donald's eyes but he also felt he did not understand his form of sinfulness. Ernest Soper regarded the supreme sin as failure to do your duty, which Donald emulated 'rather than the Methodism of Wesley'.[30] He also gave entertaining and edifying lectures for the Band of Hope Union,[31] which were given an added impetus because on many Saturday nights Mr Soper would be called out to retrieve one of his own relations from the pub.[32]

Ernest Soper's convictions included care for those in trouble. A Liberal in politics, though the subject was never discussed, Mr Soper was involved in the early days of the Police Court Mission.[33] Sabbatarianism was also part of his faith, though here he was inconsistent for he did not object to buying a Monday paper. 'Everything was either black or white,' Millicent once observed of her father. 'We weren't allowed to go to theatres. We were allowed to go to the cinema, occasionally, but not to dances when we were very young, although as we got older we were . . .'[34] Donald himself only first went to the theatre when he was twenty-one, though he indulged his passion for dancing, which appealed to his flamboyant side, when he wished.[35]

Religion even enveloped breakfast-time as the children listened 'all uncritically, and yet with a strange wonder, to the words of Jesus or the music of the Psalms or the perils of St Paul'.[36] Even at Christmas, by breakfast they were playing a tune on the musical instrument they found in their stocking. 'No doubt,' Joan Clifford observes, 'this initiation paved the way for the near-legendary recitals'[37] given later by Donald Soper on his tin whistle at National Children's Home gatherings. There was, however, another side to the Sopers when they held young people's parties in their Streatham home, with games like sardines to enliven the proceedings.[38]

As Donald grew he developed relations with his brother Meredith Ross (known as Sos to rhyme with Dos), with whom he felt much affinity and with his sister, Millicent, with whom there was less intimacy. She was plump as a girl, her height and vivaciousness made her noticed as she entered a room and she liked sport as well as music. Sometimes she felt Donald was arrogant and found herself resisting his seemingly effortless superiority.[39] She could never understand, for example, why, although he rarely appeared to work, he usually passed his examinations. He would read, but as she and Meredith Ross poured over their homework, Donald seemed uninvolved. She decided he worked on the train, helped by what soon became apparent, that besides his handsome appearance he was gifted with a 'blotting-paper' memory, too. Moreover, like his mother, he was prepared to argue and now his outspokenness was noticed, as he showed himself prepared to speak about anything.[40] Donald himself felt he got 'most of the plums' and that it was wrong to have left Millicent 'out in the cold',[41] so there seems some justification for her antipathy.

Because Mrs Soper worked, her children were in the care of Aunt Liza – Miss Woollard – who took charge of family matters the year after Mrs Soper's wedding, at which she had been bridesmaid. She was very strict indeed. In addition another lady, Miss Watson, called Aunt Nellie, a colleague of Mrs Soper's, also lived with the family. Both women were as closely involved with the growing children as were their parents.[42] At one point his mother was also Donald's headmistress, his father his Sunday School superintendent and Aunt

Nellie his Sunday School teacher. 'I didn't take too kindly to it, got into trouble very often,' Donald has remarked.[43]

Donald was devoted to his younger brother, Meredith Ross, who followed his path – captain of school, good, indeed better, at cricket and certainly better at soccer. He had a similar sensitivity to people in distress, often taking out on his motorbike the motherless boy who lived with them in Forest Hill. Both Sos and Dos had a like inquisitiveness and their voices were so akin that on the phone Mrs Soper could not guess who was speaking. At home Donald played the piano and his brother the violin. Millicent recalls, 'They would go on playing tunes until just before bed. And often the three of us (I used to sing, too) would do Negro spirituals and Donald would give a talk about them, and we would illustrate them.'[44] The brothers would share jokes, too, understood only by them, as each slightly raised an eyebrow. Once at a concert Donald announced 'one of the lesser-known works of Järnefelt,' which they made up as they went along, not falling out of tune because they 'had that sense of fellowship, if you like, call it telepathy,' Donald has explained.[45]

There was a period in Wandsworth when the family went out every Saturday to Wimbledon Common. Here they played, had tea and then returned home.[46] Later, as their horizons expanded, though Donald grew up entirely oblivious of the inner London slums nearby,[47] like many prosperous families they had holidays by the coast. Mr Soper took time off when his wife, for whom he had and showed great affection, was on school holidays. For her part she was devoted to her husband and seemed to Donald in retrospect 'to obey him rather than be conjoined with him in a corporate effort'.[48]

The holidays started on a Saturday with a train journey. Previously Donald's mother had filled the boxroom trunk: swimming trunks, one cricket bat only, Donald's ('then we needn't put your brother's in') passed her test, but not the roller-skates. 'You can leave those at home,' she would say firmly.[49] 'When I look back to those days, I still discern the heartbeat of the socialist faith I hold,' Donald subsequently observed. 'The environment, with its unity and group spirit, largely engineered my own conviction about society.'[50]

Minehead, Heacham, near Hunstanton in Norfolk, Bognor or Worthing, were favourite spots. Once settled in they were off to the beach where vigorous bathing was obligatory, often followed by tennis and a long walk. If the walk was rapid enough, there was time for another bathe, then perhaps cricket on the sands or even a second walk.[51] Donald thought sun-bathing was a waste of time – too much relaxing was involved for the noisy and inquisitive though endearing boy he was, known in Wandsworth as adept at jumping over the forms in the Sunday School room.[52] Indeed, such was his energy not only on holiday but at home that once, in Forest Hill, he took a carving knife out of the kitchen table drawer and played with it as a sword. Aunt Lizzie told him to put it down but he continued to chase the others with it. When his father heard of the incident he punished him severely.[53]

War made its impact felt on one Norfolk holiday when the Sopers came across the guns of a German ship.[54] One day Donald and his father went to buy a newspaper and found on its front page a photo of the Kaiser in the uniform of the British regiment of which he had been a member. Suddenly the First World War became very real. The family quickly returned to London and Mr Soper was called up, but was considered medically unfit.[55]

What was the life of the Sopers like in 1914 when they moved to a large semi-detached house in Devonshire Road in Forest Hill? Mrs Soper had become the headmistress of Stillness Road Elementary School for Girls in Honor Oak, which stretched her organizing gifts to the full, yet she found time to produce a pageant to raise funds to help pay off a chapel property debt. On Sunday morning the Sopers sat together in the middle of the church, singing beautifully in harmony. Mr Soper continued his Sunday School and Band of Hope activities, the latter developing substantially under his inspiration. 'I thought of Mr Soper as a kind of Old Testament prophet,' Greta Reynolds, who knew him then, has commented, 'whatever he promised or planned he fulfilled.'[56]

Each month there was a magic lantern evening. Mr Reynolds, a member of the church, was a particular influence on Donald. He took children to Sunday School, helped many boys to read and also befriended Belgian refugees. Some years, shortly after Christmas, the Reynolds family held parties which the Sopers would attend and where their acting abilities in charades came to the fore. At the chapel itself there were concerts at which Donald would sing 'The Bold Gendarmes' with another boy of his age. 'The timing, the action and the humour,' Greta Reynolds remembers, 'were superb.'[57]

Donald's secure and stable childhood gave him a poise and assurance which he retained, though his sensitivity was always stronger than many noticed. This he learned to hide because small boys in the Edwardian era were not expected to cry. 'I had to be tough,' he observed. 'It was expected of me.'[58] Once someone dared him to jump off the roof of the station at Honor Oak Park, which he did, and laid himself out at home for about a week. Like many growing boys Donald was a member of a secret society, too, called the Panther Patrol, whose members promised not to divulge their secret code, even if tortured.[59] He read a lot and came to know well characters like Long John Silver and Black Dog in *Treasure Island*. Perhaps more importantly he had access to all eight volumes of the *Children's Encyclopaedia* which he often re-read.[60]

Being musical his parents arranged piano lessons for Donald but he aggravated his tutor because he played harmonies almost by instinct. He did, however, learn Mendelssohn and a little Chopin,[61] and later came to revere Bach, as he learned how to listen to the music attentively.[62] In 1913, when he was ten, he received a certificate for a piano solo in the South West London Musical Festival so some of his tutor's coaching at least came to fruition.

Donald's first romance, which involved his unrequited affection for his sister's girl-friend, occurred when he was about eleven. 'How I suffered! and how it lives and thrives in my memory,' he has recalled[63] and after that he fell in love frequently.[64] Perhaps more significant was his love of sport, particularly boxing. However, fighting his brother one night, he 'suddenly became aware that more had crept in than just fun', so took off his gloves for ever.[65]

Besides family life, Donald Soper was shaped by three other influences – St John's Church, Wandsworth; his school and an England still strong in Empire loyalties. St John's Church was a second home. Methodism in Wandsworth went back to John Wesley who on one visit was 'stoned by the rabble'. Ten years later, in 1758, when he preached in the house of Nathaniel Gilbert, among those converted were two slaves, who returned home with him and started the West Indies Mission. Around 1772 a small Methodist chapel was built in Wandsworth High Street, the first in or around London, where Wesley preached at least three times. Once he was presented with a chalice, the gift it is thought of Mrs Vazeille, a Wandsworth resident who later became Wesley's wife.

By 1861 the population of Wandsworth had increased and so had the Methodists who by 1864 had built a church on the site of the Fishmongers' Almshouses. By 1904, a year after Donald Soper's birth, yet another building and re-decorating scheme was underway.[66] Donald himself had been baptized by the Rev. Josiah Flew, the father of the eminent Methodist theologian and ecumenist, the Rev. Dr R. Newton Flew, and so became a Methodist through a local church which, symbolically at least, had roots deep in Methodism's heart. The church was in keeping with the area. Pew rents were still the custom and the communion table was behind the high and central pulpit. 'Wandsworth was a good address,' Frank Boysen, whom Donald took to Sunday School, in 1913, has written, 'and the congregation were dressed accordingly. Top hats were to be seen ... and one member was a well-known contributor to the *Boy's Own Paper*.[67]

'My first religious exercise,' Donald Soper has recalled, 'was attending Band of Hope lectures, accompanied by lantern slides, and sitting in the back row with a pea shooter ...'[68] Founded around 1850 the Band of Hope claimed two million adherents by 1891, attracting those like the Sopers who had a drink problem in their family and also figures like Philip Snowden, M.P., who made his first public appearance in October 1908 on a Band of Hope platform.[69] Donald, too, made his first speech at the Band of Hope, when he was thirteen. Young people especially were encouraged to be teetotallers and by 1913 100,000 had enrolled as total abstainers and 1,500 new societies registered due to the Young Abstainers' League.[70] Donald Soper was thus one of many captured by the fervour of this movement, encouraged, of course, by his father's views and by the son of Joseph Malins the founder of the International Order of Good Templars, who was his Sunday School teacher for a while.[71]

Teetotalism was only one aspect of St John's Puritanism. As a child Donald was taught that Christian commitment involved talking sparingly, as Wesley had enjoined, to young women and enjoying only folk dances. Fox-trots and the tango were definitely out of court. Gambling, too, was frowned upon. This Puritanism was strongest on Sunday, when the Soper family read only 'what were called religious books' and 'played what was called religious music'.[72] Indeed, the first poem Donald ever recited was from a Sunday School Hymn Book which began: 'With a shout of bold derision Goliath proudly came ...' the ethics of which made him uneasy, even as he recited it.[73]

Some hymns carried a supernatural message, however, and gave the sensitive young boy a sense of a world beyond time. As a Sunday School scholar – later he was also a Sunday School teacher – he sang with relish:

> I'm but a stranger here
> Heaven is my home:
> Earth is a desert drear
> Heaven is my home.[74]

Sometimes Donald won Sunday School Union competitions for singing and for religious knowledge, hardly surprising for someone so saturated with biblical knowledge. Some like G. W. Hawthorne rebelled against the Sunday rituals which ended when he cried himself to sleep to the sounds of 'The Old Rugged Cross', 'Abide with Me' or 'When the roll is called up yonder'.[75] Not so Donald Soper, who grew to love 'the sort of Sunday made up of regular excursions to church, interspersed with special meals (for which our family always *sang* grace) and hymns round the piano'.[76] Indeed, decades later he still felt 'the warmth and the reality' of those far-off Sundays.[77]

The morning service itself was Matins and the evening service a free form, when extempore prayer was supplemented 'by the magnificent and disciplined devotion of Charles Wesley's hymns'.[78] This weekly pattern of celebration on the Lord's Day was the norm: there was little, if any, celebration of the Christian Year. Rather, the religious world of Wandsworth Methodism was missions, special meetings, crusades and services, at one of which he heard Mark Guy Pearce speak, little realizing that this famous colleague of Hugh Price Hughes, the founder of the West London Mission, represented to him a Methodist presence in London it was his destiny later to develop and extend. In 1914, at one of these missions, according to a document signed by the minister of Honor Oak Methodist Church, Donald Soper gave 'his heart to the Lord and intended thereafter to abide by this undertaking'. No evidence survives, Donald once observed drily, to indicate any radical changes in his behaviour attributable to this event.[79]

Donald's early adolescence was most severely restricted by the First World War. For a while the First Battalion of the Grenadier Guards was deployed on Wimbledon Common and Donald carried one of the guns of a guardsman to Wimbledon station.[80] News about the war's progress was scant so people developed 'a siege mentality'.[81] Sometimes, of course, its reality would break in as one morning in 1915 when Donald heard the mutter of guns across the Channel. Later, in charge of a group at Laurie Grove Baths, New Cross, Donald witnessed one of two daylight raids on London as people clustered in doorways, both in terror and excitement.[82]

Donald was also caught up in the psychological environment of the war. An uncle used to sing 'Trumpeter, what are you sounding now?' and Donald thought what a splendid outlook the song encouraged.[83] Militarism was accepted almost uncritically, except for a few pacifists like Fenner Brockway and Bertrand Russell, who went to prison for their convictions. Near the war's end, when Donald saw barrage balloons overhead to intercept the Zeppelins sent over from Germany, it never occurred to him to doubt his country's righteousness. Indeed, when victory came, he was dressed up as a French *poilu* to sing the 'Marseillaise' in a Sunday School pageant.[84]

Besides militarism racism was also evident, even though the British Empire contained within it India, much of Africa and the Caribbean. Japan in particular was seen as threatening. 'I seem to remember,' Donald has commented, 'the almost delicious terror the words "the Yellow Peril" triggered off inside me . . . I knew practically nothing about the reason for the peril . . . but I was convinced it was going to be a world-wide, life-or-death struggle between yellow and white . . .'[85]

Donald was only fifteen in 1918 and a day boy at Aske's School, Hatcham, near New Cross, on a scholarship awarded by the Haberdashers' Company. The war poetry of Siegfried Sassoon and Wilfred Owen was not yet widely known but gradually he was becoming sensitized by the war. He took part in the first two minutes silence, when people were invited to think of the dead and of the misery and devastation, using the shock of corporate remembrance 'as the driving force of heart and mind so that it never happens again'.[86] In a radio interview he recalled an Armistice Day, too, when, as school captain, he had defended the son of a local Communist who had refused to stand still for the silence and walked round the playground. It was the start of his willingness to reach out to those who were different from him and respect them.[87]

While at Aske's Donald found his vocation, when at one breakfast his mother asked him what job he was going to do and his father had said, 'A minister, of course,' and he had agreed.[88] 'I suppose you started with great piety,' an interviewer once said to Donald, quickly getting the retort, 'I did nothing of the sort.'[89] Indeed, he was a very normal boy, with dreams and fantasies – of 'being a sort of super Hoot Gibson and Tom Mix, riding to school on a horse' and later 'a fantastically good' footballer – much like others.[90] His key decision, therefore, seems to have been made partly out of esteem for his father (he later thought this had a certain amount of sentimentality in it)[91] and also because, with his facility for talking and his love for the Church, he felt he could become a good minister.

At school Donald was captain of boxing, cricket, soccer and also enjoyed championship swimming. 'If you are fairly successful, you get more success,' he observed 'and I was a success at school.'[92] He realized he could do things if he was prepared to take them seriously enough. Hence he was assiduous but only in what interested him but for the rest he was lazy.[93]

His musical life blossomed at Aske's. A good tenor voice was developing and he sang duets with the junior master.[94] He also excelled at the scholastic level. He read much Shakespeare, partly to learn a new English word each day and because a master fired his enthusiasm,[95] and his love of Shakespeare, especially the sonnets, lasted. In 1918 he even appeared as Stephano in scenes from *The Tempest*.[96] Despite his success, however, he was fearful about the general conduct item in his school report,[97] but his worries proved groundless and one report noted not only his literary and sporting gifts, but also his organizing powers. The headmaster also felt Donald had influenced those under him for good.[98]

Two events, however, overshadowed Donald's time at Aske's. The first was his involvement in the Cadet Corps in 1918, which was instructed by a Grenadier Guardsman with only half of one hand and a broken gait.[99] 'I was,' he said later, 'a bayonet fighting instructor. I learned many forms of using the bayonet and the butt, and also unarmed attacks.'[100] He also wrote an essay on 'The Spirit of the Bayonet' which enabled him to pass the army gymnastic staff examination.[101] Once, away in Devon, and now a regimental sergeant-major, Donald had to teach men old enough to be his father how to stick bayonets in one another. Even here, however, he felt the call of the Church, so one Sunday morning in the sergeants' mess he left abruptly and ran several miles to worship because that was where he wanted to be.[102]

The second event occurred during a cricket match. One year the sun had baked the playing fields hard during a drought. Donald opened the bowling but the third ball kicked and it hit the batsman above the heart. 'He died on the pitch in front of me,' Donald recalled.[103] Combined with his Cadet Corps experience this event surely made him doubly sensitive to the violence of the twentieth century. It was not, of course, Donald's fault, and the batsman had a bad heart, but inevitably, as Donald said much later, it was 'traumatic to be responsible for killing someone'.[104] He never bowled fast again.

Once, at another cricket match, Donald heard the sound of 'Jesu, Joy of Man's Desiring' wafting over to him and the beauty of the melody and its lyrical charm captivated him.[105] Now, as he went to Cambridge, troubled both by the war and the death of the batsman, he carried with him a sense of moral obligation. Moreover, the person of Jesus had made an ineradicable impact on him. First off, when young, he had thought of Jesus as 'one who could help me to be a better child of God'.[106] At night he prayed for forgiveness for things wrongly done or neglected and had reflected, too, that Jesus never had anything to regret.[107] Now he needed Jesus more than ever. Despite his dislike of mission meetings, where the apocalyptic element in Christianity was foremost, Jesus was a hero to Donald because of His virtues, especially His manliness and His single-mindedness, which confronted him with a persistent challenge, perhaps because of his double- or even multiple-mindedness. He would look to Him now to overcome the 'many-sided jungle' inside him.[108]

He was overcome in his first term at St Catharine's College, Cambridge, however, by unexpected doubt, as well as by grief at the batsman's death and became very introverted. He was reading for the History Tripos and the optimism in 1921 about the future seemed too fragile considering the repeated wars, one of which had only recently ended and this, too, depressed him.[109]

A college friend loaned Donald J. B. Bury's *History of the Freedom of Thought* which dismayed him greatly. 'During the last 300 years reason has been slowly and steadily destroying Christian mythology and exposing the pretensions of supernatural revelation,'[110] Bury wrote, pointing out both inconsistencies in the Bible and what scientists had discovered about the world's origins. Donald found himself 'overnight an agnostic, if not an atheist', with 'horrid comfort in descrying the same processes' in colleagues.[111] His Sunday School class in Wesley Church, Christ's Pieces, had to be abandoned, though he played the piano for the hymns which he felt he could do 'in a strictly objective fashion'.[112]

Donald was also suffering from boils on his chin and neck, together with an internal displacement termed then a floating kidney, which prevented him from playing games. One night, unable to endure the pain, he took a razor blade and in the dark cut off part of his chin by mistake. He had a room out of college and this brought an inevitable loneliness, too, though he found the handicapped child of his landlady lovable and attractive.[113]

'Quite the most exciting and bewildering discovery I made,' he wrote subsequently, 'was a sudden change . . . to a life in which many decisions lay in my own hands . . .'[114] As far as his doubts were concerned, he was haunted by the words of the hymn 'To doubt would be disloyalty'.[115] Soon, of course, he realized he was growing up and when, after three months at university, he went to the Aske's School prize day he found 'the awe and sanctity' of his school days gone for ever.[116]

One sign of hope, however, pierced the gloom. By now Donald was an extremely good pianist – he later played jazz and became an addict of Fats Waller and Jelly Roll Morton and his Red Hot Peppers[117] – and at a freshers' concert he was a great success. The captain of boats invited him to tea the next day.[118] Donald had made his mark once more. In a year the situation looked very different. His prowess on the sports field was now apparent – he became a soccer ace,[119] captained the cricket team, and took up hockey, playing once or twice for the university.[120] He also became an active member of the Midnight Howlers, a college concert party where ale and smoking were abundant. 'The most popular turn was Soper on his . . . tin whistle: parodies of popular tunes with witty comments,' Walter Strachan, a contemporary, has written. 'He could play, and did, on any wind instrument.'[121] He even played duets with the jazz pianist Fred Elizalde. Had Donald abandoned his temperance beliefs in all this excitement? It seems not, as Dr F. S. Marston remembers, 'He was a keen advocate of alcoholic prohibition . . . when it was a vital issue across the Atlantic.'[122]

By autumn 1922 Donald had dealt with some of his doubts. 'The faith to which I returned,' he wrote later, 'was a pilgrimage of trust . . .'[123] There was a difference in his homecoming, however, for Christianity as a creed would always hereafter be less important to him than Christianity as a way of life. 'I found,' he observed, 'that there was a place for agnosticism as well as conviction in a measured faith' and that 'he that doeth the will shall know of the Gospel'.[124] Donald's parents resisted the inclination to fit him into their mould now, though his father insisted he gave weekly accounts of money spent and took direct action if these were not forthcoming.[125] Nevertheless they tolerated his intellectual difficulties, and also his pacifism and his emerging social conscience.[126]

In his second year Donald lived in on the 'B' staircase of St Catharine's College sharing it with 'Tar' Morrison, with whom he went on holiday to Italy for £30. Walter Strachan, a close neighbour, 'used to hear . . . Donald and partner indulging in a "rough house" – which seemed odd in an embryonic pastor, eager, however, to appear ordinary rather than a Wesleyan ordinand!' 'I certainly did not forsee the future committed pacifist or popular preacher on Tower Hill,' he adds. 'I could, however, sense the drive behind a frivolous exterior. He would be *someone*.'[127]

Donald's routine was daily study and lectures with afternoons given over to sport. The History Tripos, emphasizing politics, diplomacy and war, and later economic history, was in two parts, both of which he passed well, receiving a 2/2 for the first and a 2/1 for the second. Students like Donald covered the Counter-Reformation and the Council of Trent with the Dean of King's and when Donald appeared before the appropriate Methodist Committee for ordination he had just sat Part 2 of the Tripos. He was grilled on the Council of Trent by Dr Eric Waterhouse and was so fluent the other six candidates despaired of their own chances.[128]

Donald had another interest which absorbed his time. 'He was,' recalls the writer, Alan Ecclestone, 'a year ahead of me in St Catharine's and I remember him pretty well as an SCM enthusiast.'[129] There were two large groupings of Christians in the university, one the Cambridge Inter-Collegiate Christian Union, the other the Student Christian Movement, containing the more liberal Christians like Donald. Genuinely inter-denominational, it was prepared to consider any issue, and Donald was swept up in much of its activity, even chairing a joint council between CICCU and SCM.[130]

In 1922 Maude Royden visited Cambridge to conduct a brief campaign. She made a great impact on Donald because of her intellectual ability, drive and character. 'I heard the most powerful oratory I've ever heard in my life,' he recalled.[131] In 1924 there was a mission to the university itself. The most eminent missioner was William Temple, subsequently Archbishop of Canterbury, and he also impressed Donald. Through the SCM, too, and the preachers at Great St Mary's, Donald heard outstanding exponents of Christianity like G. K. Chesterton[132] and 'Woodbine Willie', the Rev. G. A. Studdert Kennedy, an electric speaker, with an immense capacity to arrest a meeting, who made Donald want to communicate with the same clarity and use of illustrations.[133]

A further influence was Dean Inge. When he spoke in Great St Mary's Donald sat in the front row to hear him and later read his articles, for he was impressed by the Dean's approach to theology.[134] Once Donald witnessed Dean Inge confront students who said there were no absolute morals. It was *absolutely* wrong to ill-treat a child and to mock the insane, Dean Inge argued and Donald never forgot the second absolute.[135] He also liked Inge's aphoristic way of speaking, using one of his comments – 'individual liberty is not necessarily a Christian virtue' – when he first spoke in the House of Lords.[136]

In April 1924 Donald Soper was a Methodist delegate to COPEC (Conference on Politics, Economics and Citizenship) in Birmingham, sponsored jointly by the Church of England and the Free Churches. Here he came across Dr Temple again who made one of his most memorable comments – that of all the world's religions Christianity was the most materialistic. One address was by Bishop Gore, another by J. H. Oldham, and at a public meeting on Christianity and international problems Studdert Kennedy was the speaker. 'Any delegate to COPEC,' Donald wrote later, 'who heard Studdert Kennedy describe the way in which he had, out of the stress of the war years, found his way to a new faith in Jesus would not assume lightly that the Church of 1935 stands where stood the Church of 1914.'[137] COPEC was thus for Donald a great occasion whose quality was reflected in the final Report. It had made him realize as never before that 'Goodwill was not a private, moral condition to be applied to a variety of public issues. It was . . . an attitude to one's neighbour and to one's neighbourhood and the second was not merely a corollary of the first.'[138]

In vacations open-air evangelistic campaigns were organized, partly through the SCM, with the support of E. S. Woods, the Vicar of Holy Trinity, whose goodness impressed Donald greatly. In Derby in 1924 Donald found a new skill, helped by his tin whistle when he, with three others, held a lunch-hour meeting for the workers of

Britannia Mills. Here he felt a certain sense of power 'and a deep sense of satisfaction that he had been able to say something of Jesus whom we were trying to follow'.[139] Later that lunchtime Donald 'unfledged and unknowing' went into the engine works and saw industrial life at first hand. 'I came out at the end emotionally a socialist,' he has explained. 'It was like a Billy Graham emotional set-up . . . From that moment I became politically involved.'[140] A year or so later Donald was again on a summer campaign, this time to St Helens in Lancashire and Marjorie Sykes, the Quaker author, was there too. Each student spoke about Christianity on a street corner. 'Donald Soper,' she remembers, 'was by far the best and most skilful of the speakers on the campaign.'[141]

By 1924 Donald had begun the process of becoming 'a Methodist parson' as he always termed it, though then he was more keen to find out what he could do for God rather than 'what the Lord could do for me'.[142] The thought of preparing sermons and taking services to qualify first as a local preacher in the Methodist Church and then offer himself for the ministry, a process which would take him two years, initially alarmed him. But Eric Baker, later Secretary of the Methodist Conference, guided him and, indeed, played the harmonium for his first service at Stow-cum-Quay when Donald chose elaborate hymns like 'Sometimes a Light Surprises' and the sermon, on the text 'What lack I yet?' was over in twelve minutes.[143] A farmer present at the service had only one remark: that Donald Soper had a good singing voice![144] But others felt differently. Indeed, such was the power of Donald's personality that even in the 1990s an old lady surprised him by recalling his first service in Cambridge and even recited the text![145]

'Only go into the ministry if you cannot keep out' a minister had counselled Donald. He could not, so by 1925 he was living at Cheshunt College and studying at Wesley House. He still kept his SCM friends, however. One of these, Alex Wood, had been his invigilator when he was taking his Cambridge entrance examination. A pacifist, Labour city councillor and scientist, in November 1923 he had spoken in the Guildhall against all war and showed Donald how a Christian could operate in society. His personality made an immediate impact on Donald.

When in 1926 the General Strike split Cambridge students, even those in the SCM, from top to bottom, Donald sided with the strikers and addressed a number of meetings in their support. With his

Wesley House friend, Joe Webb, he opened a centre for strikers in Romsey Town, at a Primitive Methodist Chapel in Sturton Street. Here they would gather, drink tea and listen to Joe Webb on cornet and piano and Donald on his penny whistle. In this centre, often surrounded by people sharp in their questioning, Donald discovered what he later called 'the fellowship of controversy'.[146] The strike had a dynamic effect on Donald's thinking as did the writings of R. H. Tawney, whose book *Religion and the Rise of Capitalism* was first published in 1926 and explained in particular the relationship between Protestantism and the growth of capitalism.[147] Donald's politics were passionate: 'most meetings were concerned with a crusade, speakers were speaking as if for revivals, the platform was not entirely unlike a penitent form, the penitent was required to believe, and having become converted, to go out and become an evangelist', he discovered.[148] Moreover, he came to believe the proclamation of the truth would lead to disciples being made and changes in social policies.

While at Wesley House, where Donald was reading philosophy of religion, he came under the spell of F. R. Tennant, the 'elusive don at Trinity College', as he has been dubbed.[149] Once a fellow student, Harold Moulton, attended one of Tennant's classes with Donald and took careful notes whereas Donald, chin in hand, listened attentively, for he was fascinated by philosophical theology, yet did not need to record a single word.[150] He read A. N. Whitehead, too, and was impressed by the fact that 'for him the Christian faith was integrated in the total philosophical framework'.[151]

The theological faculty Donald attended was largely Anglican until 1927, with Professor Bethune-Baker and Edward Hoskyns pre-eminent. Donald did not think his theological training influenced him greatly[152] but as he soaked up material and then reformulated it, can this be so? At Wesley House, for example, he encountered the Rev. Dr H. Maldwyn Hughes, who was his Principal. Though a dull lecturer, who disliked some of the habits of high-spirited students, who would cut a lecture if it coincided with a rugby match, Donald felt he was a good man. He took seriously Hughes' dictum that a preacher was never justified in telling the congregation for the good of its soul what was untrue.[153] In 1922 his book *The Kingdom of Heaven*[154] came out and in the mid-1920s, *What Is The Atonement?*[155] In 1927, the year after Donald had left Wesley House, Maldwyn Hughes' *Christian Foundations*,[156] an introduction to Christian doc-

trine, was published, the result of lectures he had delivered previously. It is inconceivable, therefore, that some of this learning did
not rub off on to his students.

Life was not always serious for Donald at Wesley House. At his
instigation, for example, two studies were merged into one, thereby
creating a room big enough for table tennis.[157] His friendship with
Joe Webb, of course, was crucial. It began when Donald found him
wandering round the court of Cheshunt College feeling lost.
'Whatcher cock!' Donald called out and from then on he and Joe
were inseparable. During this period, when Donald developed eye
trouble, Webb read texts to him.[158] The friendship begun in Cambridge lasted many years and was to involve Donald in a trip to South
Africa in 1937. Later Joe Webb was on several occasions a speaker at
Kingsway Hall though Donald and he did not see eye-to-eye on how
to end apartheid.

Another friendship was with Harold Roberts, Dr Maldwyn
Hughes' colleague, who taught Donald New Testament Greek. They
also went to Gilbert and Sullivan together and shared an interest in
philosophy. Donald appreciated the way in which Harold Roberts
presented the Gospel. He soon discovered, too, that Harold Roberts
had no 'side', always a plus for Donald.[159]

Once Donald went to London and returned, seemingly drunk. He
had difficulty in finding his college and his room, to which he was
led, keeping up the act in what a contemporary remembered as a
masterly performance until the door closed.[160] On another occasion
Donald took part in a mission in Essex. Eventually he went to its
leader and said: 'I'm sick of talking to Sunday School teachers. Is
there a night-club around?' One was found and during the evening
Donald sidled himself into a position near the pianist accompanying
the orchestra and tried the keyboard. Realizing Donald's capacities
the pianist asked him to take over so he could slip out for a drink.
Donald obliged, but after a while crashed both hands on the keys,
leapt up on the piano stool and in dead silence announced, 'For five
minutes I'm going to talk to you about Jesus Christ. Then we can get
on with the dance.'[161]

At this time Donald was still a smoker. He had originally promised
his father he would not smoke until he was twenty-one and promised
himself he would not smoke until a year later. 'Then,' he recalls, 'I
had a go at it.' His habit was short-lived. When the first Earl of
Birkenhead, the much criticized Secretary of State for India from

1924 to 1928, F. E. Smith, died in 1930, he left his cigars to Hannen Swaffer, the journalist, who gave three boxes to Donald who 'had a right royal time with them'.[162] By the end of it, however, he had had enough and his smoking career was over.

In Donald's second year at Wesley House he was elected Chair of the college on a 6/5 vote (Donald seldom won the allegiance of all). He encouraged the college to take part in retreat occasions, an early indication that, despite the high spirits, he had strong devotional leaning as he commended periods of quiet as 'a spiritual necessity'.[163] Even then Donald's intellectual honesty was evident, he knew what he believed and 'would not compromise in the slightest either because of the company he was in or any pressures from outside'.[164] Moreover, with his face often creased in an infectious grin and his eyes seldom leaving your face, he found out all he wanted to know almost by instinct. One other characteristic stood out sharply: he had few intimates, a trait which was to continue. His unceasing activity seemed to preclude continous relationships with any one person or group. There was also an essential shyness which cut him off from others and, like Michael Ramsey, almost his contemporary, he had no small talk.

Donald was away from Cambridge as his theological examinations drew near because of his eye trouble but took the last part of his Theological Tripos, Philosophy of Religion, and was awarded a First. Often during his two years he had given the impression of idleness. Yet his phenomenal quickness of mind and his power to both think and synthesize saw him through. 'Of course,' says Harold Roberts, 'he was an excellent examinee. He could arrange his material as it ought to be arranged, and it was a pleasure for an examiner to read what he had written. His handwriting was as lucid as his thought and there's no doubt he deserved the First.'[165]

Much later Donald reflected on his time at Cambridge. In an interview with the singer David Franklin he explained he had been free then to develop his mind and soul 'or whatever I did'. 'Wonderful years,' David Franklin prompted him. 'Oh yes,' Donald admitted gladly.[166]

Chapter 2

PARSON AND PARENT

ARTHUR KELSEY, FROM Oakley Place Wesleyan Methodist Church, just off the Old Kent Road, to which Donald was appointed by the Methodist Conference in 1926, noticed someone slip into a pew near him one Sunday morning. Soon his nostrils detected a fragrant perfume. Looking round he saw 'a most beautiful lady'.[1] Knowing Donald Soper had a lady friend he was not surprised, therefore, when later the unknown woman went up to Donald and he put his arms around her.

At Cambridge Donald had gone to a Christmas dance given by one of the rugby men who surrounded Marie Dean then. It was her elder sister Donald was anxious to meet, however.[2] Marie Dean's good looks stopped this plan instantly for Donald, too, was overcome by her beauty and arranged to meet her next day. To his astonishment she turned up in a gymslip, carrying a hockey stick.[3] She was not yet seventeen and Donald was in his early twenties and had to compete for Marie Dean's attention with rugby forwards and even with his own brother. 'You see,' she explained, 'at one time I found his brother far more attractive and I never could choose between them.'[4]

Marie Dean was born in November 1908, the fourth of eight children, five of them girls, to Arthur Dean, an electrical engineer in south London. Her mother was artistic and their house in Pollards Hill, Norbury, demonstrated her artistic flair as later Marie's homes also did. Arthur Dean found Methodists a peculiar people and the idea of her marrying a Methodist ordinand caused him some concern.[5] Marie had been privately educated by Roman Catholic nuns in Streatham. Catholics at Coventry Hall were instructed separately from others like Marie, nominally Church of England, but the Catholic atmosphere was all-pervasive and the nuns expected pupils, who came of their own free will, to accommodate themselves to it.

Marie did, responding to the chapel's beauty, even going on occasion to Benediction. She relished the education, too, and felt as a result of it one ought to be holy but 'not too pious'.[6]

The area round the Old Kent Road was a shock to Marie Dean for, like Donald, she had never seen the underside of London's life. But her visits to Donald's church and Scott Lidgett's Bermondsey Settlement began to prepare her for the future. Free Church worship, with its prayers, hymn-singing and preaching, was very different from her experience of liturgy as she found the Methodism into which Donald was pitchforked often comprised rallies where great preachers drew large numbers by the power of their personalities and messages.

If before Donald knew of the area only through the music hall song, now he learned its grim reality. As he walked down the Old Kent Road – 'optimistic and with less comprehension of the problems'[7] than he later gained – he passed in quick succession The World Turned Upside Down ('An exact description of the place after eleven o'clock on Saturday night'),[8] The Dun Cow, The Lord Nelson and The Thomas à Becket, built near a watering-place for pilgrims to Canterbury. On either side were rows of terraced houses in narrow streets. Immediately north was an area associated with Charlie Chaplin, and, beyond that, Pickwick and Quilp Street and Marshalsea Road, redolent of Dickens.

Donald's congregation was mainly working class, but some middle-class adherents came from further south to help 'the mission', who found it difficult to comprehend life in the back streets, with its unemployed and pubs where they sought solace. Despite the poverty – sometimes people would resort to the Bunhouse for treacle and bread only – there was much self-help. 'That was the best part about it,' one local resident has recalled. Those most destitute, however, went to Newington Lodge, the workhouse near by.[9] Not surprisingly the Communist Party was strong in the area, though the M.P., Dr Alfred Salter, was admired for his social involvement. He only lost his seat once, in 1923 – to Donald's immediate boss, the Rev. Roderick Kedward, who it was alleged, at Christmas gave away turkeys as a form of bribe, in 1922 distributing 1,600 and in 1923 3,268![10]

Donald soon responded to local needs and his breezy 'Whatcher' helped him make immediate contact.[11] So, too, did his visits to homes and his piano playing, as he came to know people whose recreation was attending funerals in a world largely bounded by hearses and crêpe. 'They spent so much time . . . at cemeteries and wakes, that the realities all around them were either ignored or distorted,'[12] he discovered. The contrast was stark between his lodgings in the home of a church member in Glengall Street in 'lower middle-class gentility not oppressed by too many problems and apparently fairly stable', and Rivet Street, where houses had no doors and some no furniture.[13] Once he visited a home where a man was attempting suicide. He found him in a room with two families, each huddled in a corner, the only furniture a soapbox and some rags on the floor.[14] The man was drunk, brandishing a razor, about to cut his throat. There were two children in the corner so Donald offered to shake hands with the man, who put his razor down. Immediately one child rushed out with it and the trouble was over.[15]

Another incident concerned two children whose mother had died and whose father was in prison. Donald rang the National Children's Home and talked to its General Secretary about the case. Did he recommend them? the official asked. If so, he would take them and when Donald said 'Yes' the children's immediate problems were solved. It was the start of Donald's long association with the National Children's Home.[16]

Oakley Place Methodist Church, the base for Donald's ministry, was well proportioned and imposing. Erected in 1874 its history had been chequered, sometimes full for weekday lectures and Sunday services, sometimes in decline, though by 1900 1,200 children gathered for events. In 1912, when a local preacher, Charles G. Ammon (later Lord Ammon) was secretary of the Oakley Place Brotherhood, lecturers had included Dr Salter and the M. P. Keir Hardie.[17] Donald discovered Ammon was a keen Labour activist and was a speaker in the 1927 May Day demonstration march in a south London park.[18] His daughter, Ada Ammon, was responsible for finding speakers for the Wesley Guild. Donald himself spoke at the November 1926 Guild meeting on 'Ignatius Loyola', an unusual topic for a young Methodist minister yet, as Arthur Kelsey observes, 'I almost feel that Soper and Ignatius Loyola could be blood brothers.'[19]

In discussions at Oakley Place Donald could be brash as during an argument about crossing oneself. 'It doesn't mean anything,' Donald commented rashly, 'I could cross myself' – and proceeded so to do.[20] He could, of course, uphold any viewpoint and also say to colleagues after a debate, 'You know where your argument fell down? You ought to say "so and so".[21] His first sermon, on 5 September 1926, was on 'The Kingdom of God is within you' and challenged the current view that it was something ethereal, descending on human beings from without. 'Donald maintained,' Arthur Kelsey recalls, 'that the Kingdom of God would emanate from the hearts and minds of those who were committed to Christ and thus spread outwards to the world.'[22]

Donald was also a pastor. Almost the first pastoral visit he made was to Mrs Kelsey, widowed in August 1926, to talk over her problems and leave £1.00, a great deal of money then, which, with two growing boys to feed, she greatly appreciated.[23] One Saturday evening, during the Magic Lantern Show, a drunken man broke into the schoolroom and demanded his children come home immediately. Donald took him outside, calmed him down and said his children would be brought home once the show had ended.[24]

The Charleston was all the rage in 1926 and Donald was not averse to demonstrating the step as he went down the aisle, so alive was he. At one party a small girl asked him to Charleston with her. He agreed, much to her delight, though his version was more dignified than the original. In those days, for 6d, you could be taught to tango at the Hammersmith Palais. When Donald's lesson was over his teacher said, 'Now, I've taught you something, what can you teach me?' Donald replied: 'The Gospel according to St Mark.'[25]

It was not the joyous exuberance and charm of Donald Soper's personality, or the fact he found his college learning 'very difficult to translate', which irritated people.[26] Rather, it was his liberal theology on issues like the Virgin Birth which annoyed more fundamentalist church members, who in his second year questioned whether he should be a minister at all. The Rev. Roderick Kedward heard of their reactions from Donald and decided to attend the meeting of leaders where Donald's future was to be discussed. It had hardly begun when in he walked, announced he would take the chair and dealt with the situation. 'He was my great friend,' Donald considered, 'and put up with my idiosyncrasies.'[27] A few members left, of course, because of the contretemps, but the church gained others instead. Those from afar no doubt wondered who was this handsome minister with blue-grey eyes, who allowed photos to be printed, which he signed, and which appeared on the bedroom walls of church members, yet there was nothing indiscreet in this behaviour.

Donald's gaiety and openness had one purpose only – to communicate with people in the inner city. Once the church needed repainting so Donald offered to do it, asking husbands of the wives who attended the women's meeting to assist. A number of complete strangers turned up,[28] one of whom he helped become caretaker in a Central Hall. A few men even joined the congregation when the job was done. On another occasion, in clerical collar and 'with great insouciance',[29] Donald pushed a coster's barrow up and then back down the Old Kent Road, having piled it high at the Central Hall, Bermondsey, with old clothes for those in need.

Some church members were uneasy about Donald's unconventionality. Christians were people able to speak about their faith, they felt. Donald, however, considered that George Burdet and others were a different type of Christian. George himself, Donald explained, was a man who followed Christ's command 'Inasmuch', for he knew George had cared for someone who was hungry and had taken him home.[30]

Donald was, of course, not only involved in local affairs. He retained his links with the Fellowship of the Kingdom which enabled ministers to meet together annually and responded to invitations to take special anniversaries. On occasions, too, he became involved with the law as when he attended court to support a member charged with 'what was rightly considered to be a number of disgraceful things'.[31] Donald also forged links with colleagues in the South London Mission. 'I am more than grateful,' he wrote later, 'for the way in which, in my first years as a Methodist minister, I was part of this all-round ministry.'[32] The mission included a number of chapels as well as Roderick Kedward's and also the Bermondsey Wesleyan Methodist Settlement, where the Rev. Dr John Scott Lidgett worked. Donald would take services here with an atmosphere and tradition far removed from the more liturgical services to which he was accustomed. He was active, too, in the organizational structures, at the September Quarterly Meeting in 1928 moving a motion attacking the Government for not acting on the growth of betting and pointing out 'the moral dangers from the wholesale facilities associated with the new Greyhound Racing Tracks'.[33]

Donald had preached his trial sermon before acceptance for training as a minister before Dr Lidgett and both men developed a healthy respect for one another. Technically Donald came under Dr Lidgett, who was Chairman of the District and, as a probationer minister, was expected to fulfil certain studies. Whilst not rejecting this discipline, Donald had other ideas, however, partly because of his response to the poverty around him. He was, remembers Kay

Fenn, one of his SCM friends then in London, so appalled at conditions that he burnt his sermons because they seemed irrelevant. He intended, he told her, to go to the London School of Economics, to discover how such poverty was created.[34] Here he had to argue his case for his Ph.D. with Harold Laski, who pointed out he knew next to nothing about economics. As Donald was about to leave the interview disappointed and dejected Laski said, 'Why not do something about the Gallican Church and Ultramontanism?' Donald agreed, knowing his knowledge of the period was good. It is difficult to know what Laski, then professor of political science at the LSE, and a Marxist in most respects, made of Donald's theme: 'Edmond Richer and the Revival of Gallicanism from 1600 to 1630'[35] for it dealt with the complex relations within the Roman Catholic Church and especially between those who believed in a strong, centralizing Church, focused in the Papacy (the Ultramontanists) and those, in France, who favoured a partial autonomy for a national Church. But when Donald submitted the thesis it was clear he could have become a scholar, so thorough had been his study of the inter-relations of Church and society.

The thesis gained Donald a doctorate (thereafter friends referred to him as 'Doctor') and pinpointed many underlying preoccupations of his ministry – the interaction of religion and politics; the role of Catholicism in history; the vexed question of the nation state in relation to international authority. Even in 1974 Donald was still drawing on his study, pointing out in relation to the establishment what could be learned from French history and observing a radical relationship between State and Church was needed. He hoped, he added, 'we shall learn from Gallicanism and from Ultramontanism, how dangerous are the attitudes of conflict when absolutes collide . . .'[36]

Donald paid a price for his doctorate, however. As a minister in training he had probationer examinations to pass. He came under Scott Lidgett for these, who 'scared him to death' till he found out how to handle him.[37] These he failed because he had insufficient time for study. 'Justice first, charity later,' Scott Lidgett said when Roderick Kedward explained why Donald had not passed and then proceeded to give him 'a wigging' stronger because Donald was truculent enough to answer back.

One other preoccupation consumed Donald Soper in 1927. It began almost casually. For some time he had felt his theological training had not prepared him for evangelism.[38] One day Will Thomas, who ran the men's meeting, came to Donald and said he went weekly to Tower Hill where Roman Catholics and evangelicals, among others, spoke about their beliefs and were often unintelligible. He longed for a reasoned Christian witness there. Donald was intrigued and agreed to go to Tower Hill to see for himself. So, very nervous, and clad in Oxford bags, one day in February 1927[39] Donald arrived at Tower Hill and found many meetings in full swing.[40] 'From an office window above Tower Hill I saw my minister leap on the raised stone platform and then vigorous clapping,' Reg Frost remembers.[41] He began to speak about faith in Jesus[42] and so began a consistent and controversial ministry for over sixty years.

To speak in the open air, wrote Richard Mudie-Smith, 'strong lungs and enthusiasm are not sufficient', though Donald had both in abundance. He had, too, the wooing note, 'the reasoning together, combined with persuasiveness and charm ...'[43] Mudie-Smith felt essential. Earlier Donald was challenged by Bernard Shaw's books, though not his plays, especially *Every Woman's Guide to Socialism*, and one Shaw comment had remained with Donald – that if people are not humble as they get older they do not realize how little they know.[44] It was good Donald realized this for at his first meeting he was asked about Marxism and floundered.

'At college I learnt something of Greek and the Early Fathers and Christian Evidences. But Marx might never have existed for all I was told about him,' Donald once observed.[45] Now, as he went back to Oakley Place and told the leader of the 1,000 strong women's meeting about his encounter, he determined to study Marx.[46] Accordingly he contacted Roderick Kedward, who suggested books to read about Communism, so by the following Wednesday Donald was able to hold an intelligent conversation about Marxism 'as the alternative answer to Christian argument'.[47] He now read Marx, Lenin and Trotsky with great deliberation and their writings made a deep impact. At Cambridge history had scarcely dealt adequately with economics. Now Donald had to face this issue head on, and decide if he, like Alan Ecclestone, should join the Communist Party.[48] 'Whether or not economics ... is the key to everything, from the basic struggle to survive to the superstructure of art and religion,' he concluded, 'it undoubtedly plays a dominant role in our lives. Goodwill, therefore, must take economic matters into the most serious account.'[49]

By October 1927 half of the 2,000 to 3,000 present were listening to Donald Soper.[50] He discovered he liked arguing and giving his opinion, too, as the immediacy of the Wednesday gathering, for decades 12.30 to 2.00 p.m., set his adrenalin going. In those days, often dressed in a bow tie and natty suit (his dress sense came from his mother), he lived life at the double and Tower Hill 12.30 became a time to which he more and more looked forward.

'Unless you're prepared always to keep an eye cocked on the entertainment value, then your crowd is going to disappear,' he told George Hunter,[51] who studied his technique, concluding he had strategies for crowd pleasing, including interesting subject matter, the provocation of controversy and a clever rhetorical style involving metaphor, hyperbole, litotes and irony. 'What,' asked a heckler once, 'is the shape of the soul?' Soper: 'Oblong! Next question?'[52]

The Communists sent their best troops to heckle Donald but his humour and logical argument overcame them. Jesuits and even Flat Earthers tried to confound him, too,[53] but Donald was nearly always on top. Some from his circle, like Theo Stuchbery, used to join Donald to give him moral support. George Dubock, too, like Harry Hobbs and Will Roberts, who left their offices, and a Quaker, Stanley Aldridge, also spent their lunch hours on Tower Hill, exhibiting a solidarity Donald much appreciated.

He was also grateful to Marie Dean herself. One Wednesday in 1929 Donald was questioned about marriage. Asked what he knew about it he admitted very little, but hoped to remedy the matter soon. Next week, with Marie present because later she and Donald were going to choose manse carpets,[54] he was presented with a silver teapot full of coins as a wedding present. 'The spokesman who handed it to me,' Doanld recorded, 'was a persistent heckler, and the good wishes that accompanied this present were voiced by a communist, a fervent agnostic,' as well as some who had hitherto showed little kindliness.[55]

One of forty-three, including Frederic Greeves and W. F. Flemington, ordained to the Wesleyan Methodist ministry in Plymouth, on 30 July 1929, Donald Soper married Marie Dean at Streatham Methodist Church on 3 August at 2 p.m., a daring thing to do, for newly ordained Methodist ministers usually waited five years to marry. At the wedding all the key men wore top hats and morning coats and the congregation sang 'The voice that breathed o'er Eden', and 'O Perfect Love'. During the reception it was announced that those wishing to drink alcohol should go to a certain room,[56] as though the Soper family was teetotal, Marie Dean's was not.

'My marriage to Marie Dean,' Donald has considered, 'was the best thing I ever did, and that silver teapot down the years has remained the symbol not only of the decency of an open-air crowd, but of the lasting happiness of a marriage rooted in the love of a wonderful and long-suffering wife.'[57] Later he was reprimanded for flouting Methodist arrangements. 'I promised not to do it again,' he recounted later, recalling the incident,[58] and he never did.

That autumn the Sopers moved to Islington Central Hall in Highbury, recently built for £44,000 to house two congregations which had merged.[59] Donald cleared the remaining £12,500 debt and his work became so well known nationally that by 1931 a *News Chronicle* reporter considered he was in a line of succession from General Booth.[60] Marie Soper, not yet twenty, had much still to learn about Donald when they moved into the two-up, two-down manse in Kinross Road, near Highbury Park, but when the Sopers left Islington in 1936 she was more accustomed to her whirlwind husband.

By 1933 the Soper family had grown to four with Ann born in April 1931, and Bridget in December, 1933. When Marie was expecting Ann the congregation kept asking Donald 'How's Marie?' Constance Willis, one of the many secretaries who assisted him over the decades, recalls: 'Nobody asks about me' he quipped in reply.[61]

Marie, as well as Donald, made an impact on the church, which she felt she did not handle well.[62] But with young children, and her husband's many responsibilities, the pressures on the lady all found so charming were immense, particularly as Donald was always moving on to his next task.

The effect of fatherhood on Donald was considerable and, as ever, he used this new experience to describe realities often hidden from view. In one of three books he wrote during his seven years at Islington[63] he tried to explain how the Bible itself could be interpreted as God playing 'hide and seek', as parents do with very young children. Just as they want to be found and give indication of where they are, so God inspires our search and rejoices when humans find Him, 'because our victory is His as well'.[64]

When first married the Sopers used to take scouts camping. Donald had been appointed both Group and Rover Scout leader of the 38th North London Group in 1929. Alfred Sleep, Donald's successor when he went to Kingsway Hall (and banished uniformed organizations because of possible military overtones in their style), remembers his great sense of fun. Once Donald joined the camp at Braunton Sands, near Ilfracombe. One evening as the scouts left worship local youngsters were on a bridge mocking them so Donald threatened to put them in the river straight away![65]

With London County Council approval and co-operation from local schools,[66] Donald also developed Children's Cinema, a ministry pioneered by the Rev. A. E. Binks in south London. From 1930 there were weekly film shows,[67] where children watched films which Donald and others judged 'not unsuitable'.[68] Most dangerous were those which glorified war[69] and disparaged working-class life, he felt, and those which depicted Asians and Africans in a demeaning way. Once a film was shut down because Donald thought 'it was going beyond the realm of decency'.[70] 'I was a bit of a prig,' he admitted subsequently.[71] Children came in their hundreds, not put off by the inclusion of prayers and hymns like 'O Jesus, I have promised', and 'Soldiers of Christ Arise', flashed on the screen for them to sing,[72] so respected was Donald, even when strict with them. Laurence Payne, later a Shakespearean actor, was entranced by films he saw after Sunday worship, which included *Don Quixote* with Chaliapin as the Don and George Robey as Sancho Panza.[73]

One hot afternoon in June 1931 Donald convened and presided over a meeting attended by 1,000 children who heard Leah Manning, a local Labour activist and later M.P., and the Rev. A. E. Binks. A Children's Cinematic Association was launched to organize cinema exhibitions.[74] By 1937 *The Times* reported on a gathering of 1,200 at Caxton Hall, under the auspices of the recently formed Cinema Christian Council, where Donald sponsored a resolution calling for films especially designed for young people.[75] 'The cinema,' Donald argued then, 'is the biggest single creative force in the world', which was why continually he went to Wardour Street to find films suitable for Islington's children, many without 'a comfortable fire at home to sit by'.[76]

Because of their deprivation every Christmas morning the Mission gave breakfast to about 500.[77] Donald suffered nightmares on Christmas Eve he would oversleep and not reach the church by 6.30 to organize the queue eager to reach the tables loaded with sandwiches, crackers, chocolate and Christmas stockings. 'I remember my dream teeming with visions of children running wild,' he has recalled, 'of a telephone waking me at 10 a.m. with the news that Islington Central Hall was in the hands of a raging mob singing the Red Flag to the tune of Christians Awake.'[78] No trouble did occur, however, and Donald went home to Christmas dinner happier because he had brought cheer to others.

Donald did not only watch films: he also watched Arsenal play, rejoicing especially at the goal which enabled them win the 1930 Cup Final.[79] With the help of George Irons, who conducted the choir, Donald also sponsored Saturday evening concerts, a feature of many Central Halls then. Surprisingly, despite competition from the cinema and a few remaining music halls, they were successful, though serious musical events were never as popular as variety evenings, where you could hear, at modest prices, 'Stainless Stephen', the violinists Bratza and Campoli, Gillie Potter, with Mabel Constanduros at the piano. Two big stars paid visits – Arthur Askey and Tommy Handley.[80] Arthur Askey took one look at the chandeliers and said playfully. 'You don't half keep your washing basins high here.' The old ladies, as they continued knitting, loved it.[81]

People were attracted to Donald because, as Marjorie Drake has explained, he managed to make goodness and religion 'sound interesting and sensible with a very humane approach . . .'[82] With hindsight Donald felt himself mistaken to think he knew 'the mind of the congregation',[83] but for the moment he set about creating a local church which would reflect the kingdom of God. Sometimes at evening worship Jack Hobbs, the famous cricketer, was there,[84] but mostly it comprised very local people, gradually drawn in through forty weekly events as the Central Hall became a focus for community activity.

Men still wore bowler hats to worship and Ernie Higgins, the organ-blower from a previous church, tended to sleep during Donald's sermons, as he strode up and down the platform making points.[85] Donald disliked this habit and wanted him removed, but another stalwart said this was impossible.[86] One Sunday a man walked in and interrupted worship. Donald indicated this was no time for a dispute, but would talk to the intruder later. The protestor was helped out and Donald's congregation was impressed by the aplomb with which he handled this potentially explosive situation.[87]

Donald was greatly assisted by the skill two deaconesses, Sisters Ethel and Margaret, brought to the pastoral tasks; they felt he was keenly interested in their work.[88] There was much to do for by 1931 converts from Tower Hill and Donald's Monday evenings at High-bury Corner, the headquarters, as he called it, of the North London Communists,[89] were much in evidence. Most Sundays there were 1,500 at worship, half of them men, and once 100 were turned away.[90] Of the sixty-six new members only four had been church members before. By 1932 another seventy had joined and 250 voluntary workers were now involved. In 1933 the congregation was swollen by another sixty and over 2,000 children attended the mission.

As at Oakley Place not all liked how Donald handled situations – especially how the manse was moved to Finchley – and those who disagreed with Donald's style and theology, left.[91] At one point Donald was even arraigned nationally before a spiritual court for publicly expressing disbelief in the Virgin Birth, but was acquitted, the committee of examination deciding a Methodist minister was not *required* to believe that doctrine.

At Islington Donald set up a 'Consulting Hour'[92] and also visited the TB patients in the Fever Hospital in Liverpool Road. There seemed no stopping him as a further ninety-five became church members in 1934.[93] The Rev. Dr S. W. Hughes, the successor to Dr John Clifford at Westbourne Park Baptist Church in 1915, came in 1934 on a second visit. Though a Baptist, he had grown up in a Bible class in Methodism, where he had learned about evangelism. Now deeply involved nationally with the Free Churches he was the one person in them Donald listened to and learned from, for mostly their leaders were ambivalent about one or other aspect of his ministry. 'It was my privilege,' he said when Dr Hughes died, 'to speak at a great Jubilee service in his honour at Walgrave; and I have preached with him, prayed with him, and swum with him. He has been called "a gay Puritan". He was certainly a living example of the "Nonconformist Conscience".'[94]

Donald, like Sam Hughes, was wedded to personal issues like temperance, in 1932 preaching the seventy-seventh Anniversary Sermon of the Band of Hope at his church and recalling his own Band of Hope days 'with gratitude'.[95] His conscience, however, made him concerned about unemployment. By 1930 he had begun writing to the papers. That year he attacked those who said if poor people did not work they could starve, dictating to Constance Willis one of many letters he subsequently despatched, which she delivered by hand.[96]

One year Donald visited the Welsh valleys to preach. His own job was secure enough. Suddenly he realized the economic insecurity of others. 'Whenever I think of unemployment . . .' he confessed later, 'I think of Gandiffailt. Ninety per cent of the men in that mining village, perched on the edge of a Welsh mountain, had been out of work for six years. Everything about it had the pallor of decay . . .'[97] He never forgot that visit. Accordingly, at the Mission a large hall was opened daily as a 'rest room' for unemployed people, with the junior minister in attendance, who called for Donald's help when necessary. Here there were games, magazines, books, and a canteen where tea and food could be bought cheaply. There 500 men enrolled – cutting each other's hair, mending each other's boots and patching clothes, though it was difficult to get worn clothes and boots for them.

By 1933 another centre had opened in St Clement's, Barnsbury, and the Mayor of Islington set up an unemployment committee on which Donald, among others, served.[98] Donald's centre was still active in 1936, with an average of 250 on the roll, by which time the Mission also provided a Poor Man's lawyer.[99] In May 1936 a new body, involving Islington Council, was created, with the Rev. William Paxton, nominated by Donald, to chair it and subsequently the Mayor came to open an exhibition of tables, stools and wirelesses, made by unemployed men from the Central Hall.[100]

Donald once invited Dick Sheppard, whom he had come to know earlier, to speak on unemployment at a public meeting. Sheppard was famous because of his broadcasts from St Martin-in-the-Fields and his books *The Human Parson* and *The Impatience of a Parson*. Donald especially admired the love and sympathy he generated,[101] as well as his candour and capacity for both friendship and leadership.[102] 'I was looking at that time not for a hero,' Donald has admitted, 'but a leader and I found in the question of peace and war Dick Sheppard filled the bill.'[103]

In February 1932, Dick Sheppard, Maude Royden and Herbert Gray met to consider the international scene where in China a conflict fomented by Japan and Russia was at its height. That January Maude Royden had suggested interposing an unarmed group between combatants and now, with Sheppard and Gray, she urged action. The result was a letter which appeared in the papers on 25 February 1932, calling for a Peace Army to interpose itself between the Japanese and the Chinese at Chopei, and appealing for volunteers. Over 300 volunteered in the first three days, including Muriel Lester, of

Kingsley Hall, Brigadier Frank Crozier, who had resigned his commission to avoid the Black and Tan atrocities in Dublin in 1920[104] and Donald himself. Some of these, including Donald, went to Tilbury to show their readiness for action but the soldiers of peace were not called on. Indeed, even governmental action was not needed, for soon the Foreign Secretary announced hostilities had ended.[105]

Later that year Dr Gray stated there were many more willing to 'die in the name of peace'[106] than in war. Some of these formed a procession that June and went to the West India Dock to protest against the steamship *Ben Alder* shortly to sail to Japan with armaments. Police barred their way and port officials refused to give the protestors entry permits, but from an open touring car at the dock entrance speakers, including Maude Royden, Muriel Lester and Donald, explained their objections to the arms shipment, as other Peace Army volunteers distributed leaflets among the gathering crowd.[107]

Donald was fully in accord with the non-violent outlook of the Peace Army and aware also of Gandhi's contribution to pacifist thought. Indeed, he had heard Gandhi speak at a meeting he addressed on his 1931 visit for the Round Table talks on Indian independence.[108] He persuaded Donald then, and subsequently, as the struggle for India's freedom intensified, 'that goodness can be a tremendous powerful force when it is resolute and consistent'.[109]

Besides Donald's involvement with Dick Sheppard and the 'War We Say No Movement', which led to the formation of the Peace Pledge Union (PPU), he also supported the Fellowship of Reconciliation (FOR), the Christian pacifist organization founded in Cambridge in November 1914,[110] speaking at its meetings, sometimes with Canon C. E. Raven, its theoretician. But Donald's primary interest lay within the Methodist Church itself. The Rev. Henry Carter, the secretary of the Temperance and Welfare Committee of the new Methodist Church (its several branches had united in 1932), had written a personal letter to the *Methodist Recorder* in 1933 declaring his pacifist convictions and seeking support. Carter's letter received much response, as had another to all Methodist ministers signed by him and thirty others.[111] By November, at Holy Communion in Kingsway Hall, members of the newly formed Methodist Peace Fellowship (MPF) made a covenant together 'to renounce war and all its ways and work, now and always', for war was contrary to the spirit, teaching and purpose of Jesus Christ.[112] By 1934 the group had started work, chaired by Henry Carter, with Donald and his Wesley House friend, the Rev. Eric Baker, as joint secretaries. The Islington Central Hall itself developed one of the largest branches, at one time over 300 strong. Concurrently there was a burgeoning of peace fellowships like the Christian Pacifist Crusade in Congregationalism, and the Church of Scotland Peace Fellowship, as the peace movement, fed by Dick Sheppard's work in particular, grew. In November 1934, for example, 2,700 attended a meeting in the Central Hall, Westminster, arranged by the Council of Christian Pacifist Groups, with 1,000 in another hall below. By Armistice time, 1935, a gathering was planned called 'Christ and Peace' at which Raven, Sheppard, Carter, George Lansbury, Gray, Ruth Fry (the Quaker social reformer), Alfred Salter and Donald all spoke. Interest was so great – Mussolini had recently invaded Abyssinia – that meetings were held simultaneously in three places, as over 5,000, many of them young people, wanted to attend.[113]

At Leicester, in January 1936, George Lansbury, no longer leader of the Labour Party, and Donald addressed 3,500 in the De Montfort Hall. 'Leicester has not known anything like it for years,' said one report.[114] In May Donald argued the pacifist case. There was, he said, an increasing conviction that peace was possible; and pacifism had begun to organize. People's fears that invasion would not result from Britain becoming pacifist needed assuaging, however. He could not, he admitted readily, give advice for specific situations, yet knew it was possible to work out responses to living 'pacifistically'.[115] The repercussions of non-violence, he declared – echoing Gandhi – 'must be those of spiritual force. The Cross has been and is the greatest weapon humanity has ever known; and there are many others such as forbearance, forgiveness, restitution, which have not had the opportunity of showing how keen is their edge . . .'[116]

Donald was active for peace locally and internationally (in 1935 he visited Canada and America through the international FOR network), speaking to meetings and attending the Islington Peace Conference in October 1935, where he moved a resolution calling on the British Government to convene a new Peace Conference through the League of Nations.[117] The year 1936 saw heightened activity in Islington, with Donald at gatherings with Reg Sorensen and Aldous Huxley's friend, Gerald Heard, and at a peace demonstration in Islington Town Hall, presided over by the Mayor.

He was clear, however, that for him peace was linked with the prospects for socialism and the Labour Party, which he had joined at Cambridge. Islington now politicized him irrevocably. Dick Sheppard and a few friends were present in Olympia on 7 June 1934, at a notorious Oswald Mosley meeting after he had left the Labour Party in 1932 and formed the British Union of Fascists, of which he had become leader. Donald himself, though not present at Olympia, had been in Ridley Road, Hackney, at another big demonstration, when Mosley's black shirts had clashed with opponents and the police, an experience which made him always wary of authoritarian styles of politics or religion. He stood, he was clear, for ethical socialism, a conviction he never shirked from making known. At one public meeting, for example, chaired by Joseph Rank, a great benefactor to the Central Hall, Donald looked across to him and said, 'I'm a Christian Socialist.' Rank replied: 'A Christian Socialist. Never heard of such a thing.'[118]

By 1932, when first listed in *Who's Who*, Donald Soper had become a household name in Methodism. He was invited to speak the length and breadth of Britain, becoming an itinerant preacher with power to draw hundreds to hear him. At the London level he often took part in London Mission Rallies, like one in March 1931 with Gipsy Smith and Ensor Walters. The following year he joined the All London Methodist campaign of evangelism, chaired by Dr J. E. Rattenbury, and spoke in Hyde Park on 24 May. He was there again in September, this time for a demonstration connected with Methodist Union, sharing the platform with Luke Wiseman and 'Gipsy' Smith.

From November 1929 he began visiting Wesley's Chapel, where he became a regular visitor. Here he talked about the obstacles to evangelism he saw preventing the good news of God's love from spreading.[119] Sometimes Donald spoke at large meetings like one in the Central Hall, Westminster, in 1933, immediately after the Rev. Douglas Thompson, later his first biographer. Thompson, recently returned from China, where he was a missionary, referred to the Christian international – 'Christ in all of us and all for Christ'. Donald picked up the phrase and for 'twenty minutes wove it into a dazzling picture of a world movement', a movement much stronger, if the challenge to discipleship were accepted, than the call of either Communism or fascism. Later, in the speaker's room, he caught up with Douglas Thompson. 'Thanks,' he said, 'I hadn't an idea of what line to take when I came in.'[120]

Donald's first contribution to the annual Methodist Conference occurred in 1932 when he spoke on the Church and the cinema. Thereafter he often spoke, on unemployment in 1933 and 1935, and in 1936 took Dick Sheppard's place at a big peace rally. In those heady years he believed a religious revival was imminent, but, as later, his tendency to make rash statements proved him not only incautious but wrong in his predictions. By 1935, however, Donald was in more sober mood at a meeting of the Christian Evidence Society, chaired by Winnington Ingram, the Bishop of London since 1901. Though the world *was* turning away from the alternatives to Christ it was not turning to Christ, he considered.[121]

In 1935 Donald had taken his evangelistic activity to the realm of broadcasting. 'I was privileged to broadcast a sermon from St Martin-in-the-Fields last summer,' he told the *Methodist Times*. 'Just before we began Dick Sheppard told me I should probably be speaking to more people than heard John Wesley in the whole of his life.'[122] In May 1935, the BBC broadcast a service from the Central Hall, Islington, itself and a second followed in 1936. Donald's broadcast talks, *Question Time on Tower Hill*, part of a series, the *Radio Times* described as memorable.

One topic above all radicalized Donald in the 1930s – the condition of British prisons. His chaplaincy at Holloway and Pentonville made a lasting impact on him because of meetings with governors, warders, voluntary visitors and contacts with the prisoners themselves. As Chaplain at Pentonville he was pastor to a young man soon to be hanged, which gave him an absolute conviction it was wrong.[123] The clatter of tin cups rattling across every doorway, the macabre silence at the time when the drop was assumed to take place, stayed with him and echoed across the decades.[124] The stench of Pentonville bowled Donald over as he saw what the solitariness of cell life did to prisoners.[125] 'I remember very well my first service and "welcome meeting",' he recalled. The setting – 'the bare walls and hard benches and locked door' – was grim, but the congregation seemed little affected by its surroundings as it began to sing 'Jesu, the very thought of Thee'. 'We are all post-graduates here,' said one wag, with 207 previous convictions.[126]

Donald used to visit cells and talk with prisoners as well as lead worship. Once a prisoner replied, 'What of it?' when he said, 'Good afternoon' and, as the two men talked, the chilling sensation came over Donald that had he been exposed to the same temptations he might have been in prison clothes, too.[127] He did, however, see the power of Christ change some prisoners, one prisoner after sixteen previous convictions.[128] Another made a small cross with his cobbler's knife from a piece of bone left over from dinner and a chunk of bakelite picked up in a prison shop, which he gave to Donald,[129] but such prisoners were the exception.

One episode haunted Donald: the afternoon he apprehended two burglars in his Islington office and let them off with a cautionary warning about prison life, for it raised the pacifist issue and Donald's response to violence. It raised, too, his own capacity for aggression, most noticeable in arguments at Highbury Corner and on Tower Hill. Once, for example, the friend of a doctor's son, who had joined the scouts, pushed Donald in fun and Donald knocked him down. Donald also liked to drive his car at speed (he regularly had a new one), and at times became reckless.

Islington Central Hall, 'that's where I made most of my mistakes, I suppose, and when I also grew up, I hope,' Donald reflected later.[130] Some doubtless found his autocratic streak hard to take when he would say, 'You do this' or 'You do that', on occasion delegating difficult decisions, yet with an organization of hundreds, which needed discipline and direction to maintain momentum, could he have done much else? On two things there was no disagreement: Donald's outstanding personality and his capacity to help others enjoy life despite the unemployment all around. At Alfred Sleep's twenty-first birthday party, for example, he sang a humorous song based on stories in the Bible which had many verses, accompanying himself at the piano.[131] It was a song he had learned in the Cambridge SCM, used at Oakley Place and now revived here.

The pressures on Marie Soper were considerable as Donald's ministry developed. It was as well, he felt, they had moved to Finchley, where there was less chance of burglaries and where his daughters could enjoy some protection. He did not expect his wife to be an unpaid curate and made sure a pattern was established whereby he had a home life in the suburbs and a public life in the inner city. 'You will never overcome the tensions between the ordained ministry and your marriage,' a minister recalls Donald telling ordinands one year. 'Donald Soper dealt with them by keeping the two worlds apart.'[132]

Each year, like many families of his background, the Sopers went on holiday in August, sometimes with the Westons, Donald repeating a childhood pattern. Bill Weston, a friend from Tower Hill, started playing tennis with Donald and found he was able to hold his own. Later their wives joined them, and the mixed doubles with Marie and Constance were played as competitively as Donald's and Bill's singles.

Donald needed Marie, he was certain. 'She is the catalyst for me emotionally and every other way,' he once admitted. 'It's always been like this.'[133] 'I let off steam at Tower Hill and come home as docile as a lamb.' 'You a lamb?' Marie Soper would query[134] in her slightly whimsical manner, yet knowing also she could at times be very firm indeed.

By 1931 Donald's Tower Hill ministry had some 500 'regulars', one of whom was James Callaghan. Dockers and manual workers made up most of the crowd as Donald's voice, which 'could bounce right across the river and back again', dominated the scene.[135] Lord Callaghan went to hear Donald 'because it was fun',[136] but also learnt about social problems, always in the context of his faith. 'He was a preacher, but it didn't sound like it.'[137] Not everyone agreed with Donald's pacifism, of course, but many respected his wisdom and fearlessness. What was it like, however, for Donald to stand on Tower Hill and be the butt of numerous comments and criticisms? 'In those early days,' he has commented, 'I spent a great deal of time arguing with a well-known personality on the Hill. His theme was scientific socialism and his message was cold and merciless . . .'[138] Hearing he was ill Donald visited him and found a very different person, grateful for the money he left to tide him over financial trouble.

Arguing with a young business man who had married and had a child, as a result of which his wife had lost her life, Donald's points about the fatherhood of God and life after death seemed cold to the grieving husband. He switched his approach, told the story of the Cross 'and as we sat together I saw his burden begin to lift', he has recalled.[139] One heckler came to see Donald in Islington, bearing no malice, whatever the relationship in the open air. He was unemployed, but wanted to go to a Labour College to learn the art of public speaking, with special reference to his atheist beliefs. Would the church help with fees? Donald found some money and the man, who could find nothing good in Jesus Christ, learned a lesson.[140] 'I come to Tower Hill as a Catholic goes to Mass,' said one regular who found a fellowship in Christ had sprung up there. Indeed, Donald conducted funerals for some, baptized others, and occasionally found himself invited to marry men who first brought their fiancées to hear him.[141]

In 1931 Donald had one of his most startling Tower Hill experiences when a large Communist-led demonstration against unemployment flooded his pitch and its leaders demanded he vacate his platform. When he refused he was pushed off and fell into the crowd. Once back on the wall, there was one more attempt to dislodge him, as Communist supporters seized his legs and the crowd swelled to between 5,000 and 6,000. Donald continued to speak, his voice still rising above the babel as police gathered near and further violence was prevented. It was this sort of courage – as when a man called 'Tiger Face' threatened and fully intended to knife Donald, but refrained because he knew Donald would not fight[142] – which made the 1931 demonstrators say, after listening to Donald, 'Why don't you come out of the Church – you ought to be on *our* side?'[143]

By 1936, when invited to Kingsway Hall, which meant superintending other churches also in the circuit, Donald, still only thirty-three, was mixing with leaders already his senior. There was one cloud in his sky, and it cast a long shadow. In 1934 his brother, Meredith Ross, married with his wife pregnant, and a master at King's School, Wimbledon, had died of diabetes, not long after a car accident. He was only twenty-seven. Once he and Donald had done a double act at the school concert in which Donald had demonstrated how (and how not) to sew on a button. Now all Donald had left was the memory of the only man to whom he was ever really close. 'The greatest sorrow of my life,' Donald called it later. 'So long ago; but it still seems as if it were yesterday.'[144]

During this period Donald sometimes met Lax of Poplar, who had started his ministry in London in the West London Mission with Hugh Price Hughes, one of the funniest speakers Donald had ever heard.[145] It was not, however, his humour he recalled most but his pastoral insight. Lax told Donald once of a lady he had visited, who just before dying said she wished she could hold Jesus's hand 'as I cross over the river'. Stretching out his hand Lax had said: 'This is the hand of Jesus.' The lady held his hand 'and crossed over'. Lax, Donald told the ordinands he was addressing, was a great pastor and lover of his Lord, humble and genuine. What he told the old lady was true. 'It is within the power of God to enable you, if need be, to say that.'[146]

As Donald moved to Kingsway Hall in 1936, with war looming, he could recall Lax's pastoral concern and his own political hopes. He had of necessity, too, to remember he himself had been tempered by suffering through the death of his only brother, whom he loved deeply and for whom life had been less than just.

Chapter 3

PEACE-MAKER AND
PACIFIST

ON 26 JUNE 1936, at a rally in Maumbury Rings, near Dorchester, organized by a local peace enthusiast and backed by the Mayor, between 8,000 and 10,000 people heard Laurence Housman introduce Vera Brittain, Dick Sheppard, George Lansbury and Donald Soper. 'Here my customary little speech in support of collective security would strike a discordant note,' Vera Brittain wrote later. 'Its basis was political, but the message of my fellow-speakers sprang from the love of God ...'[1] Donald himself had no trepidation as he roundly asserted that pacifism was practical politics. Indeed, unless the way of non-violence was chosen soon, a war might ensue whose front would extend everywhere.[2]

Earlier, in 1935, 7,000 men, who had responded to Dick Sheppard's call to renounce war, had met in the Albert Hall at another great gathering. A year later there were 100,000 and Donald was writing the Peace Pledge Union (PPU), set up by Dick Sheppard in 1936, now needed 100,000 women to sign the Peace Pledge, too.[3] In 1936 Donald was also refuting Duff Cooper's attack on Christian pacifists, a dispute triggered off by William Temple, who charged them with the Marcionite heresy, which saw the New Testament completely superseding the Old. 'The law of love is not applicable to nations consisting in large measure of unconverted ... citizens,' Temple, who considered justice the necessary condition for love's fulfilment, had argued, a view he later modified by affirming the primacy of love, whose task was 'to establish the principle of international justice'.[4] Donald Soper's riposte to such critics was simple. Jesus's life, which Christians must emulate, had involved a refusal to use any defensive measures, adding that 'the Church triumphed in that spirit, until it sold itself to the Holy Roman Empire ...'[5]

Donald had a busy 1936, for besides moving to Kingsway Hall, with Henry Carter he addressed the annual MPF meeting and chaired the Armistice-tide commemoration in November, when Lansbury, Sheppard, Stuart Morris and Eric Gill, the Roman Catholic sculptor, spoke. 'What is morally right can never be politically wrong,' Donald maintained, echoing Hugh Price Hughes in another context.[6] In November he attended a PPU rally in Glasgow, where a packed audience heard Keir Hardie's daughter speak along with Sheppard, Aldous Huxley, Crozier, Lansbury and Donald, who explained that in his experience people *expected* Christians to be pacifists.[7]

Donald, Siegfried Sassoon, Aldous Huxley and many others were sponsors of PPU, whose members now were asked to assent to a modified pledge which read: 'I renounce war and I will never support or sanction another.'[8] A further Albert Hall meeting was planned for 27 November[9] with Huxley, Donald, Lansbury among the speakers, Sheppard in the chair and Siegfried Sassoon reading war poems.[10] By 1937 Bertrand Russell, Vera Brittain, Charles Raven, George Macleod and Max Plowman, among others, were also sponsors, as the momentum for peace, under Dick Sheppard's dynamism, grew. Max Plowman, secretary of PPU then, like Donald, discovered Dick Sheppard's genius to weld together pacifists who had reached their convictions by many different routes. It was united, too, by *Peace News*, begun in late 1936 and by its second year selling 20,000 copies weekly,[11] as PPU mushroomed and an Executive began to meet.[12]

Donald himself was full of vigour and just back from South Africa, where there were many enquiries about pacifist movements in Britain.[13] But by December 1937 Dick Sheppard was dead. The sponsors met and arranged a memorial meeting in the Albert Hall to be chaired by Lansbury[14] at which Donald appealed for money to carry on Sheppard's vision. 'We may well be standing on the edge of a pacifist landslide,' he declared, 'and please God we'll be ready for it when it comes.'[15] The appeal raised nearly £5,000.

There was much work for Donald, now Vice-Chair of PPU, but halfway through 1938 he was ill for months when a routine appendicitis operation led to complications, leaving him with a permanent medical condition.[16] Back in action by 1939, in February, with Raven and Vera Brittain, he led 2,000 in a devotional meeting at Kingsway Hall for the Council of Christian Pacifist Groups and commented on Chamberlain's Munich actions approvingly.[17] His busy schedule that year also included a PPU meeting with the writer Ethel Mannin, an intercession service for the Free Church Federal Council, which packed Kingsway Hall,[18] and taking part in a 'No conscription' march from PPU HQ to Regent Street.[19] That October 150 pacifist civil servants met at Kingsway Hall, to create a fellowship across Britain,[20] as the church became a focus for peace work.

Donald explained his position in the *Daily Herald*, along with Conrad Noel, 'the Red Vicar of Thaxted'. 'I could not conscientiously refuse to fight,' he wrote, 'if I did not believe that this is God's world and that Jesus is the way.'[21] He would, he promised, support the community where he could help to save and succour life.[22] Above all, he would seek to lay the foundations of an economic commonwealth and 'some sort of federal union for Europe'.[23]

In 1939 Donald made an error of judgment. A group called The British Council for a Christian Settlement in Europe had sent him a statement about negotiating a peace, asking him to sign it if he shared its views. Donald agreed, but soon discovered supporters included one of Mosley's leading followers and Professor A. P. Laurie, formerly a member of The Link, an agency the Government itself had disbanded as a vehicle of enemy propaganda. Donald resigned instantly. Maude Royden, who had even addressed the Council, also resigned. 'Anything that has a Fascist or Marxist smell about it is not the Christian pacifism I prefer,' Donald told the *Birmingham Post*[24] as the resignations gained much press coverage.[25]

When war was declared on 3 September 1939, groups all over Britain met to affirm their opposition. At Kingsway Hall worship had barely begun when sirens rang out during the Lord's Prayer. A policeman in the front row said they should go to the basement and there Donald continued the service.[26] He felt a mixture of despair and resolution as war started but determined to speak out as before.[27] 'The Sermon on the Mount haunts the mind,' wrote Hensley Henson, 'though it does not, and cannot control the life.'[28] For Donald, and many conscientious objectors (COs) who now attended Kingsway Hall, that Sermon was the yardstick by which they continued to judge their lives, even when, like Donald, who was sent white feathers through the post, hurt by protestors.

By May 1940, when Germany invaded the Low Countries and France, Kingsway Hall was full. 'If those who now thronged the churches had thronged them during the last twenty years,' Donald commented, 'they would not now be meeting in such circumstances

. . .'[29] One of those helping the COs was Henry Carter who in 1940, with the assistance of the MPF, had set up the Christian Pacifist Forestry and Land Units, at its start only fifty strong but by April 1944 supporting 900. 'The units,' Huw Rees remembers, 'provided fellowship, security and opportunity to explore the implications of the pacifist position . . . The friendship between Henry Carter and Donald Soper led to Kingsway Hall becoming the base for the CPFLU office and Sunday evening became a meeting time for like-minded people.'[30]

Donald, too, counselled people like the entertainer Donald Swann,[31] attended tribunals and sent letters vouching for the character of COs he knew, in February 1943 writing to the West London Police Committee about the integrity of Stella St John, a member at Kingsway. His letter was unsuccessful and she was sent to Holloway Prison,[32] where Donald visited her, as he did Henry Rutland and Fred Jones who were in Wandsworth Prison.[33]

Donald seemed unaffected by the theological blasts against pacifism coming from Reinhold Niebuhr in America, who thought pacifist pressures had prevented Hitler being resisted in the 1930s.[34] Unlike many public figures he was not affected either, contrary to what Douglas Thompson has written, by the People's Convention for Peace, set up by disaffected Labour M.P.s and members of the Communist Party, which culminated in a Convention meeting in London in January 1941. Indeed, his name was not even listed among its 500 supporters.[35]

By spring 1941 such was the political atmosphere that the *Daily Worker* was suppressed[36] and the BBC, reacting to a pacifist broadcast given by the Congregational minister Leyton Richards, banned him, Raven, Macleod and Donald from broadcasting, and would not lift it even though William Temple and Nathaniel Micklem questioned the BBC's Governors about its wisdom.[37] Despite this setback, about which Donald had no complaints,[38] he continued preaching pacifism on Tower Hill and was treated well.[39] Once, however, after Dunkirk, Donald was unfair and proud when he made a heckler look foolish, who queried how Donald would feel if his only son had died at Dunkirk the week before. Donald was ashamed for a long time afterwards.[40]

At Hyde Park, where Donald spoke regularly from March 1942, though in the 1930s he had spoken there occasionally, his pacifism caused unremitting heckling and official reaction, as well. 'I once received a message, strangely enough from Sangster,' Donald remembered, 'who said he had been instructed to tell me that they would be loath to put me in prison.'[41] He was also informed notes were being taken of what he said in the open air.

Donald, now one of three distinguished Methodist ministers in central London – Dr Weatherhead had been at the City Temple since the autumn of 1936 and Dr Sangster at the Central Hall, Westminster, since the day war was declared – played a number of roles during the conflict. Willing to compromise, he conducted services, for example at RAF stations, choosing words carefully and not pressing 'the injunctions of the beatitudes',[42] and continued his peripatetic ministry visiting Sheffield, Swansea, Derby and Gwennap Pit in Cornwall. 'An undernourished people has thrust up these dictators,' he told a meeting in Glossop,[43] maintaining in Swindon only Christianity could end war and bring true peace.[44] Another compromise involved one of his daughters, now evacuated, who asked her father for 1/- for the Spitfire fund. It was insufferable, he felt, to make her suffer for pacifist principles so he gave the money, then asked her headmistress to 'direct my shilling as best she could to an RAF hospital fund'.[45]

In 1942 he was involved in a disagreement at the Methodist Conference about a proposed message to both General de Gaulle and Marshall Pétain, opposed by some, including Donald, who said if it endorsed present war policy it would divide the Conference. Moreover, Marshal Pétain could be defended with the same logic employed against him. Let Conference, therefore, say it was praying for the French people and remembered with gratitude France's glorious traditions of liberty. Cries of 'Vote, vote' were soon acted upon and a resolution sent to De Gaulle alone.[46]

Throughout the war Kingsway Hall hosted both MPF gatherings and annual Armistice-tide rallies, where leading pacifists like Charles Raven and Professor Macgregor spoke about their convictions and Donald himself warned of the tendency among them, desiring to end the war, to regard the evil being fought as 'less real than it was'.[47] By January 1944, MPF had affiliated to the National Peace Council and a series of lunch-time meetings was held at Kingsway Hall on the conditions of peace, involving Professor John Macmurray and G. D. H. Cole, the socialist writer, among others.[48] The following September Donald was on a bomb site in the City of London with William Temple, who was talking to business men about the post-war world.

'I remember Dr Temple saying,' he recalled, 'the prelude to all effective action towards peace and justice by the west was a humble penitence for the wars in which it has perverted the faith it professes.'[49]

Donald's other roles at Kingsway Hall were less public, though for a while the Sopers, their children and colleagues, lived in one of the shelters there. From autumn 1940 Kingsway Hall had become 'a rest and feeding centre' for those bombed out, often sent by the authorities, with Sister May in charge.[50] In addition, till December 1944, Kingsway Hall ran a breakfast canteen from 6.00 to 8.00 a.m. for those sleeping in the Tube and underground shelters, where, in one six-month period, 34,178 cups of tea and 26,232 breakfasts were served.[51] Donald himself was often at the till, alternating between taking the money and reading the daily newspapers, his constant preoccupation over many years. From 1942, at the request of the Ministry of Food, he also organized the distribution of two tons of surplus Covent Garden vegetables for hostels.[52]

Donald and his colleagues took services in the public shelters in Southampton Row, Donald often wearing his cassock. Even meeting those in acute distress did not check his pacifism and once, after a particularly bad blitz, he even preached on 'Love your enemies'.[53] One raid on the Theobalds Road area caused over 400 to flock to Kingsway Hall. Water and gas were off, but soon a tap was set up in the road, operated by Donald with a chain of runners maintaining it until normal services were restored.

At this time Donald influenced a number of people towards pacifism, though not everyone at Kingsway agreed with him. One was Len Barnett, who had come across Donald's work in the mid-1930s, another was Kenneth Lawton. A third was David Mason, in 1942 still at school. Soon, through a Kingsway member, he found himself in Trafalgar Square listening to speakers, Donald among them,[54] plead for the lifting of the blockade of Hitler's Europe to allow in relief supplies. The following Sunday he attended Kingsway Hall and stayed for several years, becoming a pacifist, a local preacher, a member of the Labour Party and a Methodist minister, too.

In July 1945, Henry Carter resigned as Chair of MPF and became Life President. Donald, elected his successor, took charge of the meeting and gave an address on the policy needed, which was then sent to members.[55] In October he chaired the eleventh anniversary gathering of PPU, listening yet again to Alex Wood.[56] The lecture hall at Kingsway was full for the first post-war rally that November when Donald suggested the MPF must win over Methodism to pacifism and witness within it against conscription and power politics.[57]

Donald was on a beach in Cornwall when he heard about the bombing of Hiroshima,[58] an event which dominated his life as his work for peace intensified. In March 1946, he chaired 'No Atomic War', a nationwide pacifist rally in the Central Hall, Westminster, with Raven and Wood among the speakers.[59] The world, he felt, was waiting for a Federation of communities, 'each with its own culture, religious emphasis, racial characteristics and common language'.[60] Justice itself had to be vindicated, he agreed, 'but if the guilt is exclusively presumed to be upon our enemies, the result will be vengeance, and the aftermath bitterness . . .'[61]

Changes were coming in Donald's peace work, however, though the National Peace Council and other groups continued to use Kingsway Hall for lectures and conferences. In November 1946, a closer union between the Fellowship of Reconciliation (FOR) and MPF was considered and effected and in 1947 Donald resigned as a sponsor of PPU, with which he had been dissatisfied for some time, after the April 1947 AGM agreed to work towards the abolition of the National Service Acts, a policy Donald and others argued was against the pledge members made on joining.[62] (He returned as a sponsor in 1967.)

During the war itself, when news reached Britain from Greece of lorry-loads of bodies collected each day, a group of FOR members – Raven, Soper, Wood, Vera Brittain, Muriel Lester and a by now frail Alfred Salter – went on a two-day fast and eventually a small amount of wheat was allowed into Greece, despite the Government's blockade.[63] Now Donald supported 'Save Europe Now', which under Victor Gollancz's direction was sending food parcels to Germany. By Lent 1947, Kingsway Hall had sent more than forty parcels of rationed food, each of 7lbs,[64] receiving letters of thanks in due course.[65]

Donald also agreed to be a candidate for the People's World Constituent Assembly elections in 1950[66] and allowed the No Conscription Council to have an office in Kingsway Hall, himself expressing his opposition to conscription that year during No Conscription Week,[67] as plans were made to re-introduce National Service because of growing tension between East and West. That was a key year in Donald Soper's life. That July, during discussions about peace and war, in the context of a decision to make the H-bomb, the Methodist Conference was set alight by a statement by Donald that he would rather see a world overrun by Communism than a third world war.[68] With the war in Korea then at its height, the Conference, chaired by Dr Sangster, its new President, was stunned into silence as reporters rushed to telephones to reach their editors with Soper's views.

The editor of *Picture Post*, sensing a story, immediately arranged for Robert Kee, the journalist, to take Donald to Middleton Murry's farm in Norfolk to thrash out the arguments. During the journey Donald had to put his leg up, the legacy of his phlebitis in 1938. 'I remember thinking, he won't last long,' Robert Kee reflected.[69] Middleton Murry, no longer editor of *Peace News*, had ceased to be a pacifist when the Nazi concentration camp atrocities were revealed. He therefore opposed Donald, accusing him of making a case solely in a Christian context, Donald retorting that his view was practical for everyone. The choice, he added, was not merely between spiritual deterioration and death, as Murry had stated. War itself had the same effect. Nor did he believe in the permanence of Communism. Moreover, a new climate had to be created to stop its onrush, for it would not be defeated by material means. The uproar Donald caused did not die down. Some alleged he was guilty of an hysterical outburst but Donald maintained he had said the same thing for years and his speech had taken much courage. Indeed, he was shaking at the knees when he spoke.[70] He received 450 letters, only seven disagreeing with him, but by August his chief circuit steward, Sir Malcolm Perks, had resigned. Donald was sorry to see him go, sorry, too, if it was thought West London Mission officials were implicated. Not all was loss, of course. Because of Donald's statement the press gave pacifists more coverage than since 1939, though national papers ignored growing demands for discussion of their alternatives to war.'[71]

On 6 August 1950, Donald spoke at a PPU meeting to 3,000 in Trafalgar Square, alluding to the controversy and his suggestion Moscow be bombarded with food and clothing. 'Not even the Iron Curtain,' he said, 'could prevent the Russian people seeing that there was a new spirit abroad in the world.'[72] The following year in May he was in Hyde Park, with Archbishop Fisher and the Bishop of London at a United Christian Rally to celebrate the Festival of Britain, proclaiming it was God's world in which Christians were to seek peace.[73] In June Henry Carter died and Donald became President of MPF. 'Out of his zeal and advocacy,' Donald said at his memorial service 'was born the Methodist Peace Fellowship. We all loved him.'[74] In July he took part in a Methodist Conference meeting on peace with the Rev. Edward Rogers and that autumn explained to London Methodists the changes he saw in peace work since he had shared platforms with Dick Sheppard. Instead of strong opposition to pacifist views ('in the earlier days I was regarded as a sort of moonbeam from a larger lunacy,' he once told peers),[75] non-pacifists were now almost overwhelmed by ethical questions raised by the atomic bomb and preparations for germ warfare.[76]

Donald visited America and Canada in 1951, where he talked to 5,000 young Methodists at Pardue University, outside Chicago, before going to the FOR office in Detroit to settle his itinerary. All the time he was on the move – with constant headaches during part of the trip – one minute preaching to André Trocmé and the international gathering he was attending, the next talking to congregations and ministers.[77] Later he flew to Vancouver and spoke in the Anglican Cathedral which was packed out.[78] Another meeting, with 1,800; a question and answer session; some broadcasting and interviews for papers; a final evening rally in the Auditorium with 2,000, and the brief Canadian excursion ended as he left for San Francisco and Australia.

In March 1954 a second American H-bomb exploded. Reports indicated there was to be a third, four times more powerful,[79] so Donald, now Methodist President, issued a statement saying 'whatever the cost and dangers such weapons should be entirely outlawed'.[80] What galvanized peace-makers finally, however, was the Government decision, announced on 5 April 1954, to manufacture a British H-bomb. Almost immediately Fenner Brockway sponsored and chaired a meeting in the House of Commons of some 200 where, on George Thomas's nomination, Donald was elected Chair of the H-Bomb National Campaign.[81] Its first objective was to collect signatures for a petition to Parliament, asking that a disarmament conference be convened and the United Nations be given greater power to deal with international disputes, as a way of backing Clement Attlee's speech on 5 April calling for a summit meeting of nuclear powers.[82] The campaign was to be launched in the Albert Hall on 30 April.[83] Earlier on Passion Sunday Donald spoke of his desperation. He had, he said, two small children (Judith had been born in October

1942, and Caroline in August 1946) and there were young people, too, for whose future he was concerned. 'Let me be like Jesus,' he prayed. 'Let me follow Him in spirit. When He goes to Jerusalem let me go with Him; and when He offers himself to me, too, give myself.' He appealed to the Kingsway congregation to sign the petition and 600 did.[84] Now, whenever possible, he opposed the manufacture of the H-bomb, starting immediately by participating in a ban-the-bomb poster parade at Piccadilly Circus, to last till the American test scheduled for 22 April had either taken place or been abandoned.[85] As he crossed Regent Street an American Air Force officer remarked, 'Gee, I wish I had the guts to do the same.'[86]

He kept up the pressure, leading a procession of witness through the West End after preaching to 1,700, his biggest congregation since 1939. Also in May he addressed 1,000 at Friends House and in August led a second anti-H-bomb rally. In September he spoke to a Labour for Peace gathering at the Party Conference at Scarborough[87] and for the PPU held a meeting outside the Sheffield Town Hall in October.[88] Despite eight months' work, however, the petition gathered under half a million signatures, not an insignificant achievement, but disappointing if judged by the Committee's fifteen million goal.[89]

At the final rally Donald shared the platform with Aneurin Bevan, Tony Benn and four rebel M.P.s – Sydney Silverman, Emrys Hughes, George Craddock and Victor Yates.[90] Just back from Moscow, he urged Britain to outdo the Russians in peace work.[91] Bevan, who made an impassioned speech, started by acknowledging his 'enormously increased' admiration for Donald now he had heard him speak.[92] In the New Year Anthony Greenwood, Silverman, Donald and Benn took the 357,000 signatures to Downing Street and asked Winston Churchill to call high-level talks.[93] Churchill's reply was brief. 'Her Majesty's Government have in fact invited the Governments of the United States, France, the Soviet Union and Canada to hold further meetings of the United Nations Disarmament Sub-committee on this important matter in London next month,' he wrote.[94] And there the matter ended.

Donald believed, after his Moscow visit in November 1954 at the Metropolitan's invitation, a move by Britain would evoke similar responses from others.[95] With Canon Raven (the party's leader), the Quaker Alec Horsley, Ebenezer Cunningham for the Congregational Church, the Rev. Dr A. C. Craig of the Church of Scotland and their own interpreter, they had visited cultural and theological centres and also met church leaders, for they aimed to discuss with the Russian Orthodox Church its participation in the World Council of Churches. Donald, like his colleagues, was impressed by Orthodox worship, the beauty of the singing and the fervour of the worshippers. He addressed some 2,000 at the main Baptist church in Moscow, who sang 'God be with you till we meet again', as the party left.[96] One evening at the ballet Donald asked his interpreter if it was better or worse after the Revolution, who replied 'There was no ballet before the Revolution.' 'Don't be ridiculous,' Donald retorted.[97]

Charles Raven was pessimistic about the trip, urging the International FOR to maintain friendliness and contact but 'insist that Christian pacifism and the fight for peace',[98] a slogan he found everywhere, were fundamentally incompatible. Donald, however, was more positive, feeling the Russian state was doing Christian work in its care for children, its refusal to permit exploitation based on wealth and in the provision of pensions.[99] At a Heathrow press conference he was unguarded. He had not discovered, he said, one Christian dissatisfied with the regime, though he conceded Russia needed a prophet for a religious revival.[100] Indeed, he could not accept that the Church was free to worship while others had the freedom of anti-religious propaganda.[101] Asked about the labour camps Donald responded, perhaps incautiously, by saying they were little different from 'any other prison'. Indeed, he was in favour of prisoners being usefully employed.[102]

Just as earlier Donald had tried to handle 'Red China' images positively, joining Emrys Hughes, Richard Crossman, Kingsley Martin and Compton Mackenzie[103] in a public meeting at Kingsway Hall in March 1953, and, as President, urged China's admission to the United Nations,[104] so now he determined to open up discussion of Russia's relationship with the West. When the Government announced that Mr Bulganin and Mr Krushchev would visit Britain in April 1956, Donald felt it would provide 'a welcome chance of overcoming evil with good; our evil as well as theirs'.[105] He now considered the possibilities of world peace nearer than before,[106] though recognized the Soviet leaders had hands stained with blood. The West's record was tarnished, too.[107] Britain should disarm unilaterally to show goodwill, he contended,[108] then wrote inviting the two Russians to worship at Kingsway Hall. There was no response.[109]

Donald continued to offer friendship to Russia throughout the

Cold War and was not averse to cautioning American leaders like General Eisenhower for some remarks, though in 1955 he responded positively to General Macarthur's exhortation to 'abolish war now'.[110] He often, however, commented of Britain's relationship with America, 'in many ways we are an occupied country'.[111] Krushchev, he considered, faced facts, 'and that is one of the highest forms of honesty. Of course he is a sinner and inconsistent and perhaps insensitive to many virtues. But these words of his are not empty.'[112] When later Mr Kosygin spoke to politicians at Westminster, Donald was there to hear him. 'We need to listen to Russian policies,' he urged afterwards, 'for their views for a settlement in Europe are more lively with hope and fraught with less danger than those which encourage a programme of German re-unification.'[113]

Donald's concern about the H-bomb did not diminish. In March 1955 (when Sir Richard Acland resigned as M.P. for Gravesend to fight a by-election on a No H-bomb ticket) in the *News Chronicle* Donald urged Britain to scrap all arms. *Peace News* reproduced his article in leaflet form and distributed it widely, Acland himself ordering thousands. In March Archbishop Garbett supported the development of the H-bomb. Donald sprang to the attack. 'He was dead wrong,' he told *Tribune* readers.[114] He was not alone, for Bishop Bell of Chichester and the Rev. Russell Shearer agreed with him.

Donald gave vigorous leadership to the MPF as well (its membership was still over 4,000), though realized his peace policies lacked widespread electoral support.[115] Disaster might follow from the recent nuclear explosion near Australia's coast, he considered,[116] yet another incident which helped spur him on. He had recently visited Poland and preached in Warsaw. In the 1960s he was to be taken to the Auschwitz Concentration Camp, now a museum, a visit which left permanent scars. The trip convinced him Poland was unique within the Communist world. 'The rejection of the evil elements in Stalinism began there earlier,' he observed, a view widely reported.[117]

By October Donald was speaking in Lewisham, after south London pacifists had campaigned for ten days, a spin-off from the anti-H-bomb gathering at Friends House in March. Along with Niemöller, Metropolitan Nikolai and Kagawa, he contributed to *Peace News* for Easter 1956. Peace-makers were brought to a halt later in 1956, however, by the Hungarian uprising and the invasion of Egypt by Britain, France and Israel when Colonel Nasser threatened to nationalize the Suez Canal. On 14 August there was a large meeting in Caxton Hall, chaired by Fenner Brockway, when Barbara Castle, A. J. P. Taylor[118] and Donald, who castigated the Government for disregarding the United Nations, spoke.[119] Some 1,000 marched with them to Downing Street to protest at the Government's illicit action.

Further protests followed, one in September after an evening service when numbers were swollen by mistake as Labour supporters joined it after theirs in Trafalgar Square,[120] and another in November, when, before 2,000, Donald advocated civil disobedience.[121] 'Donald made one of his most brilliant speeches,' Richard Clements reported, 'the argument unfolding like the themes of a Beethoven Symphony.'[122] Most who listened were sympathetic but a core of young Conservatives, there to defend the Eden government, were incensed and one, face red and arms flung, howled abuse at Donald and fled from the meeting in near apoplexy.

Donald's plea to Britain to 'March in protest' was reported in many national papers. He followed up his agitation with five sermons on peace, reproduced in the *British Weekly*. The world *can* live in peace he declared – if people really want it; if one great power takes the lead; if the Church believes her own Gospel. But ordinary people had first to follow the way of Christ, be obedient disciples, refusing to co-operate with violence, and collectively press for the abolition of weapons of destruction.[123] The only road to peace, he wrote in *Peace News* that Christmas, was 'one that begins at Bethlehem, leads on to Galilee, passes through Calvary, and reaches its journey's end in the Kingdom of Jesus, the Prince of Peace'.[124]

He planned more processions for spring 1957, sometimes with the Standing Joint Pacifist Committee, the final one in March a rally at Friends House with Donald, Niemöller, Kathleen Lonsdale and the M.P., Leslie Hale, his biggest meeting for a long while. He preached now on Christians and the nation state; imperialism; the United Nations; world government and the world family of God, commending Christianity as the religion of revolutionary change. March 1957 also saw Peter Lyon's Dove of Peace unveiled outside Kingsway Hall by two children, an event summed up by Steve Race, also a member of the congregation. In May Donald took his campaign to the FOR Council, urging concentration on the moral issues involved in the H-bomb. 'We are reconcilers,' he suggested, 'and reconciliation is not a scientific or political word, but a human and spiritual one.'[125]

In the late 1950s a number of other anti-nuclear groups were formed, some of which Donald supported enthusiastically. One which emerged, as a result of the concern of J. B. Priestley, Kingsley Martin, Canon John Collins, Bertrand Russell and many others, was the Campaign for Nuclear Disarmament (CND), formed in January 1957, and launched at the Central Hall, Westminster on 17 February, when thousands heard Priestley and A. J. P. Taylor speak, though there was scant press coverage. At the end of the meeting Canon Collins appealed for support for the Aldermaston March which another anti-nuclear group, the Direct Action Committee, was arranging that Easter.[126] This group, chaired by Michael Randle, involved a number of radicals like Pat Arrowsmith, April Carter and the Rev. Michael Scott, most of them pacifists, and six Quakers. Donald Soper, along with Martin Niemöller, Bertrand Russell, and several others, was a sponsor. He also became a member of the Executive of CND which included Michael Foot, Sir Richard Acland, the Priestleys, A. J. P. Taylor and Kingsley Martin. The way was thus set for a further development in Donald's work for peace.

Pat Arrowsmith organized the first Aldermaston March, *from* London to Aldermaston. On its second day Donald led the marchers part of the way. 'It was advocacy,' he later remarked.[127] Going through Hayes, despite the drenching rain, the entire Borough Council turned out to salute them. So, too, did large crowds, which Donald found very moving. With others he delivered to Downing Street a resolution signed by 3,000, urging Britain, Russia and America to stop testing, manufacturing and storing nuclear weapons. A similar resolution was delivered to the American and Russian Embassies.[128]

'This march,' Donald said in Maidenhead on 4 April, 'though small, is the beginning of something far larger than some people realize.'[129] However, a mass lobby of M.P.s that May drew only half the 20,000 expected, Donald himself leading a procession from St Martin-in-the-Fields to the Cenotaph, where he and others laid a wreath.[130] A further march was held in June, culminating in Trafalgar Square, the 6,000 addressed by Collins, Foot, Donald and representatives of the regional marches. A despatch rider took a letter to the Queen calling for nuclear weapons' testing and manufacture to end. Soon Donald was co-operating with the Direct Action Committee itself, which had staged a week's twenty-four-hour vigil at the gates of the Aldermaston Research Establishment and then for nine weeks that summer picketed it. Donald took part in the final demonstrations when Sir William Penney, its Director, refused to give an interview, sitting down in the car park outside the main gate with twenty-seven other pickets.[131]

On Easter Monday 1959, after joining the march at Turnham Green, Donald spoke in Trafalgar Square at the final Aldermaston rally and was in Trafalgar Square again that summer when 2,000 protested at the French Government's decision to test atomic weapons in the Sahara.[132] A press conference in September brought Donald, Benn, Levy and J. B. Priestley together to support anti-H-bomb candidates in the General Election and the following week Bertrand Russell, aged eighty-seven, spoke to 7,000 in Trafalgar Square at the end of Nuclear Disarmament Week. Donald was glad to follow Russell for he had never heard a better peroration, especially Russell's closing words about generous risks for the good of all and the need to think of human beings as one family.[133]

In the summer of 1960 Pat Arrowsmith and Donald Soper joined forces again when the Direct Action Committee tried to expose nuclear weapons manufacture in Bristol at the Siddeley Engines firm. A campaign was mounted to persuade workers to stage a token strike against making nuclear components.[134] At a lunch-hour meeting Donald, Pat Arrowsmith and the shop stewards' convenor spoke and 100 of the 500 who heard Donald at the factory gate prolonged their lunch hour by twenty minutes to make their point.[135] Afterwards Donald and others tried unsuccessfully to hand the management a petition but the gathering gained some local and national TV, radio and press publicity.[136]

The debate about nuclear weapons had been waged in Methodism with growing intensity since the Conference Declaration on Peace and War in 1957, where pacifist and non-pacifist views on nuclear weapons were explored in judicious paragraphs set beside each other.[137] This was the background of Donald Soper's initiatives then. 'A year ago,' he told the *Scotsman* in 1959, he had proposed 'a resolution and it was rejected. This year I proposed an amendment, which was a resolution for the unilateral abandonment of nuclear weapons, and, to the astonishment of many, this resolution won through.'[138]

The effect of his visit to Japan in 1957 at the invitation of the Japanese Christian Council, then celebrating one hundred years of Protestant missionary work, helped spur Donald on. He spoke in many Japanese cities, Kagawa himself translating for him at his first meeting. While in Japan Donald visited Hiroshima, a disturbing experience despite the absence of the emotions he expected, partly because there was only the museum, the memorial and one bombed building to recall the past.[139] A learned Japanese said to him that everywhere in Japan visitors walked on wood ash. 'I very quickly came to see,' Donald said later, 'what he meant. Every one of the great cities of Japan was razed to the ground by incendiary bombs. Two hundred and fifty thousand people were roasted to death in one incendiary raid. It would have been more merciless if they had lived in Hiroshima.'[140]

The curse of war he found seeped through conversation with every Japanese who did more than bow or drink tea, yet there was little penitence. But 50,000 Japanese students had demonstrated against H-bomb tests on Christmas Island and Japanese socialists believed the Labour Party would decide for unilateral action to end H-bomb manufacture 'and they are bitterly disappointed as I am that this was not done,' he concluded.[141]

As CND gathered strength – in 1960 40,000 attended the last day of the Aldermaston March[142] – Donald really did feel victory was in sight,[143] especially when the Labour Party Conference voted for unilateral nuclear disarmament. That autumn, too, the Christian group of CND was formed with Donald among the sponsors,[144] and by December 1960, when Bertrand Russell spoke at a press conference in Kingsway Hall,[145] a new phase of protest was clearly on the way.

For Donald 1961 was CND's peak, with 50,000 in Trafalgar Square that March. It was, of course, only 'part of the strategy of pacifism', as he explained in *Tribune*.[146] 'CND has won a battle. CND has not won the war.' Part of CND's success was to alter conditions on the battlefield. Now it must 'alter its tactics to meet new threats, and the new opportunities'.[147] Above all, CND needed an overall plan in which to regroup and redeploy its forces which, Donald concluded, 'should be total disarmament and the tactics will be unilateral'.[148] He urged campaigners not to shun orthodox political involvement and did not respond warmly therefore when Bertrand Russell and 4,000 activists sat down outside the Ministry of Defence, to protest at the Polaris missile base in Scotland.[149]

That summer and autumn he again plunged into activity, taking part in a rally in Trafalgar Square for PPU in July and Pacifist Fortnight Campaign in September. He argued again the case for involvement in Labour politics and not direct action along the

Committee of 100 model as Bertrand Russell and colleagues were developing it. However, by May 1961, he admitted the Labour Party was beyond CND after a speech by Hugh Gaitskell, which meant 'a longer stay in the wilderness'.[150] Political action was a continuously disappointing road, he knew, 'but there is no other route', he wrote in CND's magazine *Sanity*.[151]

By February 1963, within Methodism Donald was maintaining that non-pacifists were now the heretics, a view which annoyed many.[152] The 1957 Methodist declaration on war and peace, Quakers apart he said, was the only Christian statement officially to embrace the pacifist position 'as intrinsically involved in Christian discipleship'.[153] Pacifists were no longer a tolerated minority. To a crowded Methodist Conference meeting he spoke of Henry Carter's 'small stream' of pacifism which had 'now become a flowing river'.[154]

Earlier in April 1963 he had wondered if the Aldermaston March was worthwhile as Harold Wilson, now Labour Party leader, had pledged support for NATO. Donald felt it was, but political fruit must result. He had no time for the quarrels tearing CND apart and arguments about its officers. 'CND must grow up; or shut up,' he declared.[155] It must back Labour and argue the case for unilateralism within its ranks, a view shared by Labour's left wing. The Test Ban Treaty that year gave Donald some hope and the opportunity for Labour to set out a wider programme 'for international goodwill'.[156]

Donald's energy for peace was prodigious. He was as likely to turn up at a demonstration in Cardiff with Michael Foot and the M.P. for Merthyr Tydfil to oppose the presence of German troops on Welsh soil[157] as at a National Peace Council meeting on Berlin with Patrick Donovan of the *Observer*, Richard Crossman and Shirley Williams.[158] In addition in 1963, along with the secretary of the British Group of the Inter-Parliamentary Union and Field-Marshal Claude Auchinleck, Group Captain Leonard Cheshire, Lord Longford and Peter Ustinov, he was a sponsor of the National Council for the Registration of Volunteers for a World Police Force.[159] The idea gained considerable coverage in many national papers, but came to nothing.

Donald had a reflective approach to peace-making, too, in November 1961, with Canon Collins, leading a service in Trafalgar Square for 500 and urging 'repentance, prayer and dedication to the cause of peace'.[160] He was glad, too, to support Christian CND, addressing its Good Friday Procession of Penitence, Forgiveness and Reconciliation in March 1964, when it stopped at Kingsway Hall, and led a short service in Trafalgar Square at its close.[161]

In 1964, there was no Aldermaston March, though there was an Easter Monday march to Hyde Park. Indeed, that April Canon Collins had resigned as Chair of CND. Donald, of course, continued on his way and by May was again in Trafalgar Square speaking at the FOR's Golden Jubilee.[162] At the Methodist Conference he was re-elected President of MPF, and with the Revs Kenneth Greet, Gordon Rupp and others, answered questions on the theme 'Pacifism on trial'.[163] Charles Raven died in July, bringing an era to an end, for with his writings, and talks he had been both theoretician and practitioner in FOR and IFOR, since the 1930s. Donald took his place as President of FOR.

Though CND was languishing, and the Committee of 100 were out on a limb, at the international level new protests were gathering momentum, with the radical songs of Joan Baez, Pete Seeger and Bob Dylan and the award of the Nobel Peace Prize that year to Martin Luther King. Kingsway Hall itself continued to harbour peace activities, whether of the Fellowship Party, the Committee of 100, or the Christmas Fair of *Peace News*, now edited by Theodore Roszak. Donald might well have agreed with the Quaker Kenneth Boulding, however, who wrote that the peace movment, small and often sectarian, had not made 'much contribution to developing the institutions of peace, and it has not had much impact on the cause of world events'.[164] Indeed, in one candid moment earlier, Donald had admitted to Pauline Callard, a former Kingsway member, that the ownership of the atomic bomb had kept the peace.[165]

In the House of Lords Donald knew he could only make a witness there rather than converts for pacifism. Yet a political education had been achieved, despite massive Government counter-propaganda when CND was at its height. Governments thereafter would be unable to rely on public ignorance about the nuclear deterrent.[166] One place where Donald was appreciated, of course, was America and on one FOR tour the halls and temples were packed to hear him. At Boston University and in Phillips Brooks' pulpit at Trinity Episcopal Church it was standing room only and at Harvard Divinity School, where Donald lectured on the New Testament Basis of Peace-Making, there was great interest. Donald criss-crossed America on the same theme, from Atlanta to Kansas City, took in Washington

D.C., Evanston and Chicago, too, where 1,000 came to the Rockefeller Chapel. 'A biblical sense of justice and the never-ending battle to guarantee it defined every edge of the man,' wrote John Heidbrink, who organized Donald's tour. 'Peace and the pacifist witness were merely the outpouring of justice-telling.'[167]

The late 1960s were dominated by America's involvement in Vietnam. Donald's protest began with a letter to Harold Wilson, signed by M.P.s and many others, including Bertrand Russell and Benjamin Britten, requesting him to help end the war,[168] as Fenner Brockway set up the British Council for Peace in Vietnam. Donald thought Vietnam could become 'a second Korea'[169] and at the 1966 Methodist Conference sponsored a resolution asking the British Government to disassociate itself from American activities,[170] hoping his resolution would help stiffen radical Americans whom he knew sought support.[171] In February 1967, Donald was among 120 clergy, including Bishop Sansbury of the British Council of Churches, who witnessed for peace in Vietnam by marching from Kingsway Hall to St Paul's Cathedral and that autumn, after speaking at a meeting in Trafalgar Square, organized by the Overseas Vietnamese Buddhist Association, took a petition to Downing Street urging the cessation of bombing.[172]

In America in 1971 he found remorse for Vietnam amongst some, which even affected American troops. One American serviceman in Britain echoed this and gathered colleagues together at Speaker's Corner to make their protest known to the American Embassy nearby. Captain Carver was promptly court-martialled and Donald appeared in his defence, arguing that Speaker's Corner was 'the supreme place where the fellowship of controversy can be undertaken'.[173] By November 1972 President Nixon was withdrawing American troops from Vietnam but Donald, shocked by his policy of bombing Hanoi and Haiphong to bring its leaders to negotiate, on Christmas Day protested to the American Embassy.[174]

Donald compared American withdrawal from Vietnam and Northern Ireland, where British troops had gone in 1969, ostensibly to protect Catholic communities after increased tension and the fear the Civil Rights Movement had engendered among the Unionists. The consequences of withdrawing the troops were unknown, he knew, yet favoured this policy because their presence only seemed to postpone conditions for a settlement.[175] In 1972 he recommended possible re-drawing of boundaries[176] and by Christmas was supporting the proposed commemoration of the killings of 'Bloody Sunday' by the Derry Civil Rights Association. Support from Scottish, Welsh and English individuals and groups like trade unions, churches, would be welcomed, he stated in a letter to the *Methodist Recorder*.[177] Individuals and churches protested, and so did Irish Methodism, which held a special meeting of its President's Advisory Committee, its President saying Lord Soper's attitude appeared to condemn what the troops had done when a judicial enquiry was in train. 'I have been much concerned, and not a little distressed at the reaction to the letter I signed,' Donald confessed. He would not argue the case now, but wished to apologize if unwittingly he had made things more difficult.[178]

He had, of course, taken a firm position on Rhodesia and was shocked when Michael Ramsey, then Archbishop of Canterbury, had argued that Harold Wilson as Prime Minister should send troops to Salisbury to overcome Ian Smith's illegal rebellion. On the Mason Report *Violence in Southern Africa* he was equally uncompromising. If a just war was ever justified it could be fought in Southern Africa, he considered, yet could not agree with the Report's assumption that modern guerrilla fighting could be reconciled with the just war doctrine.[179] Jesus, though undoubtedly a resistance leader, gave 'no indication of the impractability of non-violent love'.[180] There were, he was convinced, non-violent means of support for apartheid victims and even evidence within the Dutch Reformed Church and the South African administration of change.

On the World Council of Churches' grants to the philanthropic work of liberation movements Donald was as trenchant, objecting strongly to money promised to groups which advocated violence, for such a policy could be counter-productive. The Council's task, he concluded, was not to 'pander to the heresy of "sanctified violence"', rather it was to declare, then implement, the good news of 'love which will overcome even this giant evil'.[181] Donald's views did not always win support, however, for church leaders like Dr Pauline Webb and the Rev. Colin Morris argued the option was not violence or non-violence but which form of violence would gain ascendancy, hoping the restricted violence of freedom fighters would force the settlers to do right, 'even if for the wrong reasons'.[182]

Throughout the 1970s Donald remained preoccupied with the gravity of the world situation. His arguments were always thrusting and often controversial – he was not in favour of interfering in

Cambodia, for example.[183] At the 1973 Methodist Conference he proposed a motion, with only one dissentient, condemning nuclear tests planned by France, and others recently carried out by China, urging Britain to put pressure on them to sign the United Nations Test Ban Treaty,[184] which was sent to the French Roman Catholic Council of Bishops and the French Protestant Federation, who had opposed the tests.[185] Donald was still sensitive to Northern Ireland's troubles, but felt the emergence of the Peace People was dangerous because, like CND, its moral fervour did not issue in a specific political view.[186] 'Withdraw the troops,' he therefore urged again, and public support 'for the IRA and its paramilitary Protestant opponents', upon which both depended, would be withdrawn.[187]

The year 1977, when Bruce Kent headed CND and its membership increased substantially,[188] was the fiftieth anniversary of Donald's open-air advocacy. In an interview he mentioned President Carter's arms deals with Arabs and Jews, despite once describing armaments as the merchandise of death. 'How cynical can you get?' he asked.[189] Donald was much exercised by the fact of nuclear proliferation and by the neutron bomb and feared if NATO adopted it, Russia would too. Surely, his interviewer argued, pacifism was unpatriotic in 1939's dangers? 'The last war,' Donald retorted, 'was won by a number of accidents and by the incredible stupidity of generals.' Hitler, he felt, on balance of evidence, had no intention of over-running Britain. 'And it was only after we'd gone in to defend the Jews, remember, that they were massacred. They were persecuted before that, but they weren't put into gas chambers by the million until after the war had started.'[190]

Opposed to the EEC, and a supporter of the United Nations 'for our health, despite its weaknesses',[191] he wrote in 1978 that CND had failed because it had run out of moral steam and the faithful had grown weary in well-doing. Moreover, CND saw violence only in one place; but war could not be treated as a separate issue. America could not even disarm immediately, for too many jobs were at stake in California. By Easter 1980, therefore, Donald was in despairing mood, for, like Solly Zuckerman and Lord Mountbatten, he felt an apocalyptic nightmare possible. He still wanted to help find an alternative outcome so supported yet another group, the World Disarmament Campaign, which Fenner Brockway and Philip Noel-Baker had just launched.

Because of his views Donald could not support some of the

activities of the women of Greenham Common, though he admired their courage, making a distinction between sitting down at the gates of Aldermaston and pulling down perimeter fences at the Cruise Missile base.[192] Moreover despite his convictions, as one writer commented, Donald Soper and George Macleod, too, were never able 'to push their denominations further than they would go'.[193]

Nevertheless, in 1981, in recognition of his endeavours, Donald Soper was awarded the World Methodist Peace Prize, following Sadie Patterson from Belfast in 1978, President Sadat and Abel Hendricks from South Africa. Donald had consistently risen above nationalism to embrace the good of all, the citation read, teaching that it was better to suffer wrong than impose it on others, both individually and between nations. 'You have taught us that the only way we can have peace is for all nations to establish good will among themselves,' the citation added, 'and for people to live on earth in co-operation and love as the saints live in the presence of God in heaven . . .'[194]

Chapter 4

POLITICIAN AND PEER

'A LITTLE WHILE AGO,' Donald Soper wrote in 1940, 'I had the privilege of meeting for the last time George Lansbury, a man who demonstrated fellowship wherever he went.'[1] They were on their way back from Dorchester and 'the whole train was changed by his complete friendliness'[2] he told the Kingsway Hall congregation, urging them to exhibit fellowship, too, for it was a key to implementing the ethical socialism he and Lansbury espoused.

Unlike the Nonconformists to whom he looked back – the Baptist John Clifford, the Methodist Hugh Price Hughes, or even the Congregationalist Sylvester Horne, liberals seeking to reform the system – Donald felt the Nonconformist conscience must 'pronounce upon the very social order in which nominally Christian communities were living.'[3] Yet, though expressing radical views, Donald was always at ease with the establishment, in one year attending a Buckingham Palace garden party[4] and baptizing an M.P.'s daughter in the House of Commons crypt chapel. He was mixing, too, with senior politicians like Isaac Foot at the thirty-fifth anniversary of the Bradford Methodist Mission,[5] and in Ilford with Chuter Ede, then Parliamentary Secretary to the Board of Education, as they helped young people plan for a new Christian social order.[6] His sympathies, however, lay with those setting up a Christian Socialist Group in Heckmondwike, to whom he sent greetings,[7] and the Poplar and Stepney Association against unemployment,[8] which he addressed in the Town Hall, with Tom Mann and Wal Hannington, (whom he first knew when Chaplain to Pentonville Prison), preaching plenty for all 'if only we share it'.[9]

In 1940 the Pope had laid down five peace points and soon these were expanded by senior church leaders,[10] who suggested five standards by which economic proposals should be judged. In 1941 further impetus was given by the Malvern Conference, where leading Anglicans considered social policy. The influence in 1942 of William Temple's book *Christianity and Social Order* (he was now Archbishop of Canterbury) and The Sword of the Spirit, backed by Cardinal Hinsley, led many, including Donald, to seek to educate public opinion about society's future shape.

In 1942 the Beveridge Report, *Report on Social Insurance and Allied Services*, was published, a factor, too, which heightened the perceptions of politicians and church leaders. What Donald needed now were audiences for his views and these he soon found as ecumenical gatherings emerged to explore what Britain's social contours might be after the war. Some 2,000 attended the Dome Mission in Brighton in March 1941, for example, to hear Donald defend the right of parsons to speak on economics, 'fundamentally a religious subject'.[11] In July, speaking about 'the new Christian order', he told his audience, amidst laughter, 'they would notice a slight tinge of "Red" in what he said'.[12] Echoing the nineteenth-century Anglican theologian and Christian Socialist, F.D. Maurice, Donald argued it was fallacious to claim brotherhood on earth unless people were assured 'that God was their father', adding 'if Middle Europe had been fed and clothed adequately from 1928 to 1938 there would have been no war'.[13]

He drove home only a few essential points, often pleading for fellowship – later he used the word solidarity – as he visited Dagenham, Southampton and Hitchin, where he addressed nearly 1,000 young people at the end of a Religion and Life Week involving The Sword of the Spirit also. 'I believe,' he declared, 'that we are living in an age when we are terribly clever, but not very good . . . we have lost the one thing necessary – the love and grace of God.'[14] In July he was in Hertford with Dorothy Sayers.[15] Visits to Stocksbridge, Exeter, Bradford (where 2,000 heard him in the Eastbrook Hall) and to Plymouth, before Lord and Lady Astor (the Mayor and Mayoress), followed. 'The tremendous truth being trumpeted abroad by the Archbishop of Canterbury,' he told one gathering, 'is that . . . it was the duty of the Church to lay down broad and unmistakable guidelines of justice and truth.'[16]

During the war Ellen Wilkinson, whose Methodist roots went back to childhood, spoke at Kingsway Hall at a London Mission Rally[17] and the Liberal Party itself held its Assembly there,[18] an indication of the church's link with politicians, even though Donald, who sometimes came across Labour politicians like Hugh Dalton and Sir Stafford Cripps, felt himself insignificant politically.[19] Unlike many, however, Donald had expected Labour to win the 1945 General Election because the returning soldiers would not want to revert to pre-war conditions.[20] He sought, therefore, to encourage Christian political involvement, at Kingsway maintaining links even through events like the 1947 Crèche sale of work, which was opened by Felicity Attlee, the Prime Minister's daughter.[21] Attlee himself he hardly knew, though he did once rescue him from hecklers in an East End meeting.[22] Nevertheless, on his death he wrote how Attlee had helped Labour to *govern*, the star in his crown being the star of India. It was, of course, Attlee's single-minded integrity which gripped Donald[23] and his capacity 'to handle such a diverse team', even though, as he observed, 'he did not light any fires'.[24]

In 1948 Lady Violet Bonham Carter and others wrote a letter to *The Times* warning of imminent danger because Russia refused to accept certain peace proposals. Donald, with seven M.P.s, argued that the proposals were unworkable and that Russia was justified in rejecting them, though it might have other motives, too. The United Nations itself needed fundamental changes, they concluded, without which collective security was impossible.[25] Such interventions, of course, often produced ambivalence. 'As a politician,' wrote one Labour activist, 'he would be a great leader, as a minister of religion, he is one . . .' Yet if Donald continued to mix politics with religion he would be just another 'also ran'.[26] Comments like these, however, left Donald unperturbed and when in 1948 he spoke in Coventry on 'Marx or Christ' not since the visits of 'Gipsy' Smith and Lax of Poplar had such crowds thronged a Methodist anniversary gathering.[27] Donald was, of course, aware of Labour Party defects. Nevertheless he defended Attlee's government, not because it was perfect, but because democratic socialism, 'heavily interpenetrated with Christian influence'[28] might produce social and personal benefits which Communists could only obtain by 'revolution, violence and totalitarianism'.[29]

In 1949, Donald addressed striking dockers on Tower Hill. The Gospel, he explained later that day, must be interpreted bearing their questions in mind, for 12,000 dockers did not strike without reason.[30] Two years later, on arrival in Australia, Donald was involved in another controversy. Speaking in the Domain, Sydney's Hyde Park, he commented on a referendum in which Australians were asked whether to give Government power to outlaw Communism and said he did not believe in using fear to fight Communists. 'He must be a brilliant fellow, if a conceited man to learn that lot in an hour,' commented the Prime Minister, Robert Menzies.[31] Papers across Australia and beyond reported Donald's observation and his tour, for good and ill, was radically affected by his indiscretion.

He made another misjudgement in the 1950s, stating in Ohio that socialism was 'imminent' in America, which would accept it if another word could be found for its concepts.[32] Information sent out by Reuters was picked up by British newspapers. Donald was again news in July, 1953, when he attacked a *Daily Mirror* poll on whether Princess Margaret could marry a divorced man, calling its proposal 'an unwarrantable and disgusting intrusion'.[33]

That autumn, as Methodist President, he preached at the pre-Labour Party Conference service, where Clement Attlee and James Griffiths read the lessons. It was nonsense, he told delegates, to tell the Church 'keep out of politics'.[34] Indeed, some things could only be done politically. But politicians always needed the inspiration the Church could give. Turning then to Communist influence in some trade unions he argued this was due to those who failed to attend union meetings and seek office.[35] An overflow in the church hall indicated Donald's power to attract crowds, evident again in August when 1,000 heard him debate with Tom Rowlandson, the Communist Party candidate for Wigan, on whether the 'hope for peace' was vested in Christianity or Communism.[36] Members of the Conservative Party, too, recognized Donald's oratorical gifts, its headquarters advising recruits to learn from him in Hyde Park, the better to equip themselves for the hustings.[37]

In 1953 Lord Samuel, the Liberal statesman and philosopher, made a speech about Britain's moral state, including a section on homosexuality. Donald promptly issued a statement calling for a Royal Commission.[38] Always he seemed able to highlight a contemporary issue, as when he became embroiled in a controversy over whether the Queen should go racing, because of its link with large-scale gambling, and the Duke of Edinburgh play polo on Sunday, because it involved others working. Suddenly these matters became the nation's talking point, the *Daily Sketch* reported, and the *Daily Herald* ran a series on the Queen, the Duke and the People, with contributions from Donald, A.J.P. Taylor and Anthony Greenwood.[39] Inevitably the controversy died down but now Donald was regarded as the voice of Methodism. The Royal Family itself obviously bore him few hard feelings for in January 1971, during the Week of Prayer for Christian Unity, Donald was invited to preach at Sandringham, the first Methodist minister to do so.

In 1954 Jack Lawson, now Lord Lawson, presided over a meeting for Methodist members of Parliament, when Donald spoke on the missionary task in the new age he knew had come.[40] By now he needed a more permanent outlet for his views, however, and this he found through Michael Foot, then editor of *Tribune*, the left-wing weekly founded in the 1930s by Cripps, Bevan, Laski, Ellen Wilkinson and others.[41] Foot wrote to Donald inviting him to expand his recently aired opinions on Moral Re-armament. 'We have not got a very big circulation,' he admitted, 'but we are read by many key workers in the Labour Party in every constituency in the country.'[42]

Donald agreed to write on Buchmanism and Socialism. 'A Christian spirit which is not directed and disciplined by the revolutionary Gospel of Jesus,' he suggested, 'must sooner or later degenerate into emotional dope, and worse still may issue in spiritual fascism . . .'[43] He resisted some contemporary movements, he said, notably MRA, because they seemed oblivious to the threat of illiteracy, hunger and the H-bomb, adding that nobody would have bothered to crucify Jesus because He went about promoting goodwill between pharisees, publicans and centurions. 'He was crucified because He preached a hard revolutionary and subversive Gospel.'[44] Without doubt MRA was full of sincere people, but Christians had to defend their faith from becoming 'a spineless organism without creed or programme'.[45] Rather they had to speak of a Jesus who saved people, not souls, in body, mind and spirit. 'Inspire the Labour Movement with this spirit,' he concluded, '. . . and I believe it will be invincible.'[46] MRA did not like this attack but Donald stood his ground.

He started his regular column – weekly, then fortnightly and later more occasional – in December 1954. Billed as a man of passionate beliefs, not worried by censures, Donald provided free copy, often written in terse, virile prose, as he tried to maintain the lively journalism George Orwell and others had brought to *Tribune*. It was difficult to sustain a weekly contribution, but says Richard Clements, Michael Foot's successor as editor, Donald's arguments were brilliant and he could marshal facts and find new angles on topics already covered whereas others ran out of arguments and ideas. Moreover, he knew how to tailor his 800 words to his audience.

Though he encouraged readers to take religion seriously, as Marx had because it was a fact of life, Donald was careful not to over-elaborate its metaphysics. Sometimes, of course, he dug his heels in, when determined to write on specific themes and then brooked no argument. But generally he co-operated, changing his subject if already covered recently.[47] Mostly he took topics like socialism as a creed, recent happenings in Government, the inadequacy of Tory political philosophy, the impact of science on human communities, racial problems in Africa, or the nuclear threat, and elaborated on them, his yardstick being how ethical socialists responded to these issues. Dominating all themes, however, was the rivalry of the USSR and the USA, from Eisenhower to Carter, Krushchev to Brezhnev.

Donald wrote about personal ethics, too – gambling, betting, drunken driving, smoking (which no socialist should indulge in) as well as on common ownership as the way to secure a livelihood for all. Sometimes he would comment on personalities like President Kennedy, whom he thought overrated, or Pope John XXIII, whom he commended for his common touch. Though not purveying religious convictions, he yet hoped readers would make a 'moral and intellectual pilgrimage to Bethlehem and Galilee and Jerusalem and Calvary so that they come to know Jesus whom I believe to be the saviour of the world, the elder brother who offers to lead us all back to the family table in our Father's house'.[48]

When the Labour whip was withdrawn from Aneurin Bevan in March 1955, because of his attitude to nuclear weapons and German rearmament, Donald was quick to argue that the Party needed Bevan, but also Attlee, Gaitskell and Acland – 'and thousands more'.[49] The welfare state, the most Christian thing to happen in his lifetime, had been accepted by the Tories, even by Churchill, so now in 1955 socialists had 'the harder and more positive task' of challenging people to become 'citizens of the New Jerusalem'.[50] Recently returned from a brief preaching trip to Sweden, he had found the social democratic tradition wilting, so warned that a Labour movement unable to help produce a morally as well as an economically more equitable society could not 'but degenerate'.[51] The task for people like him, therefore, now a General Election was called for May 1955, was to 'stimulate and preserve the morale' of those standing for Parliament.[52]

During the election, at which the Conservative Party under Anthony Eden was returned, Aneurin Bevan had remarked that

Conservatism and Christianity were mutually inconsistent. A furore developed but Donald promptly agreed with him, writing that Conservatives had 'no philosophy of life as is demanded by Christianity'. Indeed, their insistence on individual liberty was 'in direct contrast to the New Testament claim that we are members one of another'.[53] Moreover, while Conservatism co-operated with the grain of selfishness in human nature, Christianity drew on the potential goodness of people 'as an earnest of peace and goodwill'.[54] He was careful, of course, not to equate the Labour Party with Christianity. Nevertheless he saw the Labour movement as a scaffold on which Christians could build the part of the kingdom concerned with peace, justice and 'the bread and butter of life'.[55] He filled a waste-paper basket with letters expressing rage at this championing of Labour.[56]

Another conflict involved Lord Hailsham. 'Is Dr Soper consistent with Christianity?' ran a headline in the *Spectator* that July. Hailsham, who had written *The Case for Conservatism* in 1947, now took Donald to task, complaining about his arrogance towards those with whom he disagreed, arguing there were as many intelligent and sincere Conservative Christians as socialist ones. In Donald he found a depreciation, 'amounting at times to contempt', for private piety, and an identification of salvation with a political creed.[57] For Hailsham the inter-relationship of politics and religion was more complex and different. Indeed, after twenty years of observation he doubted if any parson who had 'invoked the political arena' (including William Temple) had advanced either his brand of politics or religion. He thought, in particular, that Donald Soper's attacks on the Royal Family – the background to which Donald had explained to Lord Hailsham privately – were unwise.[58] 'I leave to your own readers to judge,' he wrote in *Tribune*, answering Donald, 'Dr Soper's assertion, new to me, that Socialism is at heart "neither partisan nor political". As the Duke of Wellington observed in another connection, "Sir, if you can believe that, you can believe anything."'[59]

In *Tribune* Donald had argued 'that socialism is the political framework of the Gospel of Jesus'.[60] Hailsham, in criticizing him, especially his use of the Gospels, had taken liberties with the text of St Matthew, he explained, lifting out of context statements by Jesus about the kingdom of God – in the Sermon on the Mount itself, in a conversation of Jesus with His disciples and in an account of Jesus's arrest, thereby spiritualizing the Gospel. The sentence 'My kingdom is not of this world else my servants would fight,' he maintained, was a tremendous statement that God's kingdom could not be brought about by violence, 'for it is not that sort of Kingdom, and will be reached by the path of suffering love, which path He invited His disciples to take with Him'.[61] Further, he concluded, his opponent had picked out the wrong contrast in the Sermon on the Mount, which was not about those seeking security and material prosperity versus those seeking the other-worldly kingdom. Rather, Jesus was talking about one kingdom of righteousness and peace, of well-being and personal goodness – a kingdom which was both the 'spiritual experience of the love of God and a political expression of that love in justice and solidarity with others'.[62]

Donald remained adamant about Christian Socialism, despite the strictures of Lord Hailsham and others, some indeed in the Methodist tradition. He did admit Tories and socialists were sinners and knew also many Conservatives to be 'ardent Christians', as sincere as many socialists. That was not the point. 'It is,' he argued, 'the system they represent that counts.'[63] Indeed, even 'Crossbow capitalism' was doomed by 'the new gunpowder of the "planned society"'.[64] Yet perhaps Lord Hailsham was right to draw attention to Donald's tone and language, for elsewhere Donald wrote that whatever the eternal prospects of individual Tories they were thoroughly immoral when they thought and acted together in the political and economic field and 'should be consigned to perdition'.[65]

Donald's attitude to the Liberal Party was different, for he detected there a high degree of integrity and goodwill but no strategy, an aspect of politics always central in his thinking. Fundamentally Liberals were making a political protest, he recognized, but had no political philosophy. 'The fruit of true liberalism,' he contended therefore, 'will only grow on the socialist tree.'[66] Donald, therefore, threw himself energetically into the political community around *Tribune*, speaking for a decade at Labour Peace Fellowship meetings, in 1955 at the Margate Party Conference sharing the platform with Pastor Niemöller, Fenner Brockway and others, on German re-armament and colonialism.[67] In 1963 a statement on Labour's future foreign policy, supported by Donald, eight Labour M.P.s, Bertrand Russell, George Macleod and many others, was issued by the Labour Peace Fellowship, 6,000 copies printed and sent to every trade union head office and constituency Labour party. It warned against euphoria because of the Test Ban Treaty signed in August 1962, argued that Britain should become peace-maker between East and West and urged Labour to strengthen its support for both the Commonwealth and the United Nations.[68] That autumn at the Party Conference Frank Allaun introduced Donald Soper and Anthony Greenwood (on the eve of his election as Party Chairman), to speak on 'Make Labour the Peace Party!'

'Can left and right work together?' Donald had asked in 1956 on behalf of 'some average Labour supporters ... sick to death' of doctrinal quarrels.[69] He knew there had to be co-existence, unless ideas expressed in *Tribune* rallies with Aneurin Bevan, Michael Foot, Ian Mikardo and Jennie Lee,[70] and in the 'Victory for Socialism' pressure group, were to be disallowed. This group, which elected Donald President in 1960,[71] had been inaugurated formally on 6 March 1958, and was concerned with the propagation of socialism, especially the common ownership of the means of production to be implemented by Labour when in power. Donald would argue for this on platforms with Kingsley Martin, Sydney Silverman, Stephen Swingler[72] and others but continued to differ from them because he knew socialism needed a theological buttressing. So he wrote in 1958, anticipating an election, 'If the Labour Manifesto is good news; if it is a gospel for today, then it needs a prologue like the first chapter of St John's Gospel.'[73]

In 1959 the Labour Party issued a declaration on nuclear weapons. Donald admired the expertise with which both Hugh Gaitskell and Aneurin Bevan, now Shadow Foreign Secretary, recommended a policy compromise to heal party divisions in an election year, involving support both for a non-nuclear club and the British nuclear deterrent as a bargaining counter, but suggested that people's reactions outside the 'segregated world of Westminster'[74] meant the declaration's tactical merits were fatally offset by psychological faults which destroyed its usefulness.[75]

When the election finally came Donald's passion for socialism was unabated as he even argued 'the planned and to some extent regimented Soviet society produces, stimulates a vital energy that compares most favourably with the vaunted energies of the western world'.[76] He continued to support specific candidates, speaking for Ian Mikardo in Reading[77] and addressing two meetings for Arthur Henderson in the Midlands. With Herbert Morrison and Tom Williams he spoke in Hammersmith[78] and in Blackburn's Assembly Hall supported Barbara Castle. He spoke also for the Labour candidate in Devonport,[79] ending his election campaign on the eve of polling with the Labour candidate opposing the Prime Minister, Harold Macmillan, then addressing 600 elsewhere in Bromley.[80] More importantly Donald took part in a party political broadcast with Gaitskell and Bevan, where Tom Driberg questioned Labour leaders, Donald explaining why he was supporting Labour.[81] The broadcast was reported in many papers and Donald's election role much discussed, one columnist writing that 'dog-collar' politicians like Donald Soper, John Collins, Joseph McCulloch, Mervyn Stockwood and Trevor Huddleston, should be banned from TV.[82]

Inevitably, when Gaitskell lost so substantially to Harold Macmillan there were recriminations. The Rev. Oliver Sutton indeed suggested that, as the Labour candidates for Devonport and Hammersmith had been heavily defeated, Donald Soper's role in the election was less than creative. Barbara Castle thought the opposite. 'I was proud to have him on my platform,' she wrote. 'I know that his moving speech stirred men and women of conscience in my constituency to examine the issues carefully. The result? I increased my majority by nearly 500 per cent!'[83]

Donald had not been at the Labour Party Conference which Barbara Castle had chaired, but said in December she expressed the spirit of the Labour movement, though recognized the sound of the word 'nationalization' was a problem. He yielded to no one, of course, his conviction that socialism and disarmament belonged together and was equally clear, despite the election results, that non-socialists 'should get out of the way as quickly as possible'.[84] What Gaitskell said on a TV programme about the mixed economy was not socialism and even Aneurin Bevan had made contradictory statements. 'Which does he believe?' he queried, adding that if Hugh Gaitskell could not affirm socialism let Bevan take his place. 'Then we can get cracking.'[85]

The year 1960 was critical for Donald's crusade, for in January a meeting took place in Kingsway Hall to launch the Christian Socialist Movement (CSM), when 600 heard Father Groser, Tom Driberg, M.P., and Canon Stanley Evans speak, and saw Professor R. H. Tawney, now nearly eighty, grace the platform with his presence. Opening the proceedings, at the end of which Donald was interim-Chair, he asked all to stand while he prayed for Aneurin Bevan, then seriously ill in hospital.[86]

Donald had been captivated by Bevan, sometimes watching him in action when they went on delegations together.[87] 'I'm a Bevanite,' he told the Rev. Len Barnett,[88] his friend from the 1930s, though he had

77

to struggle to forgive him when he changed tack over the nuclear issue in 1957. In his opinion he culled more from the Old Testament than from Marx.[89] When Bevan caused a furore at the 1959 Labour Conference, saying he was unsure whether he was speaking 'as Father, Son and Holy Ghost', Donald suggested he vet his religious asides.[90] Later he encouraged Bevan to read the New Testament but he 'found it more confusing because he read it, than if he hadn't,' Donald observed.[91]

Now with Bevan ill, in fact dying, a great influence for good in the Labour Party was leaving the stage. By July Jennie Lee was telling Michael Foot about plans for her husband's memorial service. Though not a Christian believer, neither was he a 'cold-blooded rationalist', she wrote.[92] She therefore wanted a tribute which had no falseness and had asked both Donald Soper and Mervyn Stockwood to help.

At Waun Pound, high above Ebbw Vale in wild countryside, on a spot where Bevan had addressed many open-air meetings, one cold night just before dark Donald talked about Aneurin Bevan to a crowd of miners, steelworkers, M.P.s James Griffiths and James Callaghan, Michael Foot, Lord Brecon and prominent trade union leaders. Bevan had been cremated a few days earlier and Donald knew he must speak with tact and delicacy, particularly as many were asking why Bevan died so young. The event started with 'Guide me, O Thou Great Jehovah' and Donald responded strongly to the passion of the singing as he described Bevan's life as one dedicated to the well-being of his fellows, part of the true function of all religion,[93] and then said a prayer. 'I salute a man who was good in the essential sense of that word,' he continued, 'and whose goodness was no narrow piety, who was an architect of those things which in part we see, and which one day we shall see.'[94] The way to thank Aneurin Bevan, he added, was to seek to finish those things he had so faithfully begun.[95] 'The Red Flag', on Donald's suggestion, was sung, but people asked for 'Land of my Fathers', which was then sung in Welsh, after which many from the 5,000 crowd clustered around the makeshift platform to shake Jennie Lee's hand.[96] 'No-one else could have spoken as a socialist to colleagues, many of whom were not religious or agnostics, with such a command of appropriate language, sentiment and sympathy,' Michael Foot remembered later.[97]

Aneurin Bevan died when the CSM was but six months old. The amalgam of a number of Christian socialist groups, it came into being partly as a result of the publication on May Day 1959, of *Papers from the Lamb*,[98] a booklet produced by a group convened by Tom Driberg, who had felt a lack of guidance from theologians on several political matters. They included two M.P.s and a dozen parsons, including Donald, Mervyn Stockwood, John Collins, Father Groser, George Macleod, and Jack Putterill, Conrad Noel's successor at Thaxted, who had met every few weeks between 1956 and 1959 in an upstairs room of The Lamb, a pub near Driberg's Bloomsbury flat.[99]

Donald himself, of course, was in a Methodist tradition which included the Rev. S.E. Keeble, author of the first Wesleyan pamphlet on *Christianity and Socialism*, where like Donald he argued socialism needed the inspiration Christianity alone could give.[100] The Anglicans were also in a tradition, which included Charles Kingsley, F.D. Maurice and Tawney, himself influenced by both Bishop Gore and William Temple.[101] All had promoted an ethical socialism which in 1945 led to over 100 Labour MPs being members of the Parliamentary Socialist Christian Group.[102]

The new body's aims were similar to those advocated in *Papers from the Lamb* – common ownership of the world's major resources; a classless and just society; human and racial equality; unity of all Christian people; friendship between East and West; abolition of nuclear weapons, disarmament and world peace. The group, whose steering committee seemed to guarantee that 'these Christians will be uncompromisingly Socialist without being sectarian', as the *New Statesman* observed subsequently,[103] was also committed to study and to give and pray for its aims. It was, however, one thing to start a new group, supported by luminaries, quite another to develop it at the grass-roots. 'Ours is a struggling movement,' Donald wrote in 1962, 'and, if the infant is thriving, its development is undoubtedly slow.'[104] It was not surprising, he felt, that if Labour's aims were to be reached, as some leaders considered, by fiscal means, a movement advocating common ownership was 'not a spectacular success within the higher echelons of the Party'.[105]

Despite the difficulties CSM groups were set up across Britain. Donald, of course, helped form policy and guide CSM's Executive. Here, as elsewhere, he was a very efficient Chair, getting through business expeditiously, though committee members viewed him from their own perspectives. He ran meetings formally, from his desk, with his secretary by his side, taking notes as the Executive sat round the room in a semi-circle. 'Donald would be there when we arrived,' one member recalls. 'Donald would be there when we left. It felt very much as if it were his show.'[106] At one meeting, when the student revolt was discussed, a 'teach-in' was proposed to work out the movement's theology, for CSM was drastically out of touch with younger people. Donald responded negatively. He had, he said, 'worked all that out years ago'.[107] He did, however, listen to Tariq Ali and Daniel Cohn-Bendit and others one night in 1968, and, even though they hadn't 'baled their hay', he felt they had seen a genuine vision. 'This,' he suggested, 'is the revolutionary ferment of the 60s and we'd better join it.'[108]

One problem which faced Christian Socialists was disagreement over policy – not all were pacifists, for example. As far as Donald was concerned the role of Christian Socialists came to a head over the way Hugh Gaitskell was leading Labour. Already in 1960 he had written about Gaitskell's rigidity over what he termed 'theology',[109] though he recognized there was a real conflict of ideas within the Labour movement.[110] Labour's right wing was essentially divisive, he felt. The unilateralist, Clause Four socialist left provided the only conceivable platform enabling all finally to 'stand together'.[111] The right wing, of course, saw matters differently, using its Campaign for Democratic Socialists to defeat the unilateralists, supported by many leading people, including Earl Attlee. By 1961 it was accusing a militant minority of wanting to satisfy its own vanity and emotional needs rather than defeat the Tories. 'It points out that *Tribune* and Dr Donald Soper are keeping up their attack, which has been declared in Parliament, with Mr Anthony Greenwood and Mrs Barbara Castle pursuing their vendetta by contesting the leadership,' wrote one reporter.[112]

Over the previous year Donald had indeed kept up the pressure, saying to 400 in Scarborough Parish Church at a CSM meeting, which Anthony Greenwood chaired, there was something wrong with the socialist movement and with the Church.[113] Moreover, the attempted 'investiture' of Mr Gaitskell as the wise leader 'whose vocation is to save the movement from its unilateralist folly' was a development every democrat must resist 'tooth and nail'.[114] By November 1960, with CSM Any Questions? meeting near, Donald was telling *Tribune* readers he could vouch for almost 600 members who could not possibly regard Mr Gaitskell as leader. He should retire to the back benches 'at least for a time', he concluded.[115] When Hugh Gaitskell unexpectedly died Donald was in more generous mood, speaking of Gaitskell's 'courage, intellectual honesty, humility and sense of commitment'.[116] Strangely, for two people both deeply influenced by R.H. Tawney there was never a meeting of minds. 'I knew Gaitskell but slightly,' Donald admitted, 'but spoke from time to time on platforms with him . . .'[117]

Gaitskell's tragedy was Harold Wilson's opportunity. He set about bringing unity to the Party and promised a Labour Government would enhance Britain's prosperity by using the skills and expertise technology could bring. In February 1963, Donald had taken a memorial service at Kingsway Hall for Morgan Phillips, its former general secretary, with his family and most of the leading members of the Labour Party and the trades union world present, including Earl Attlee, Jim Griffiths, Lord Henderson, Denis Healey, Harold Wilson, Philip Noel-Baker and Vic Feather.[118] Now during the 1964 election campaign Donald spoke often, especially in Smethwick, where there was much racial prejudice,[119] and in Brierley Hill, for Peter Archer, where he talked about Labour's foundation principles.[120]

Earlier that year Harold Wilson and Anthony Greenwood had been guests of honour at the CSM meeting at Kingsway Hall. Donald had known Harold Wilson and his wife Mary as near neighbours in Hampstead Garden Suburb, where the Wilsons attended Hampstead Garden Suburb Free Church. Wilson regarded Donald as 'in a long and very great tradition of clergy who have played a part in what used to be called in Victorian times "the condition of England" question'.[121] Now, in autumn 1964, with Wilson victorious in the election, he invited Donald to lead the prayers (and Bishop Stockwood to preach the sermon) at a private ceremony in St Stephen's crypt chapel a day after the Queen's Speech, which some seventy Labour ministers attended.

Besides his involvement with national affairs Donald was also part of the London County Council (LCC), where he felt he was not very effective,[122] except when he chaired an approved school for five years.[123] 'I am penitent I did not achieve enough,' he told Illtyd Harrington, sometime Deputy Leader of the Greater London Council (GLC).[124] Appointed an alderman in 1958 for five years by the new Labour Council, (his maiden speech was on prostitution), Donald's involvement surprised many for he had no previous identification with the LCC. He accepted the Labour whip provided no matter of conscience was involved,[125] but found some were suspicious because of his pacifism, clerical vocation and left-wing views. However, Lady Serota has recollected, 'he was never expelled from the Labour group – we wouldn't have that'.[126]

With hindsight a clash with Sir Isaac Hayward, the Council's leader, was inevitable. Within a year an edict was given saying if members wrote to the press, or attacked policy decisions in public, the party whip would be withdrawn.[127] A standing order had to give *precise* authority, which patently this did not, Donald argued. 'I find it insufferable,' he concluded, 'and therefore, I publicly criticise, attack, repudiate, denounce, execrate and abominate it, and I hope that these words taken together will give an unambiguous impression of where *I* stand in the matter.'[128] He stood back to wait for results. There were few, except one Conservative Council member asked why the copy of *Tribune* containing the attack was missing from the Members' Reading Room. Labour members were now alerted to possible future encounters between Sir Isaac Hayward and Donald, but they learned to live together, 'two great individualists, and in their own way remarkable people, but bitterly opposed in terms of their belief', as Lady Serota has recalled.[129]

In 1960 Donald had two other clashes, one over civil defence, when he proposed his own amendment drawing attention to the inadequate provision made by the Government against nuclear attack, an amendment he won by 87 to 24. The second occurred when he accused the Labour group of projecting on to the public mind an unadventurous and uninspiring image of socialism, which led journalists to write about the state of local government. But the time Donald made most impact was when, with Conservative backing, he introduced a resolution expressing horror at the re-appearance of Nazi anti-Semitic activity and noting with confidence that Londoners would combat and reject 'this evil'.[130] 'It was,' commented Louis Bondy, a colleague, who had attended the Nuremberg trials as an observer, 'a very impressive speech.'[131]

Donald was not only the trenchant critic of County Hall. A member of the LCC Health Committee for two years, he was impressed by the range of its activities and the skills of his colleagues.[132] He was likewise impressed by the work of the Children's Committee, on which he served from 1959. 'He was,' says Lady Serota, its Chair, 'a valued member, especially on the relationship of voluntary and statutory organizations,' and always played an active part in policy discussions.[133] Once an employee was particularly difficult and Donald said he disliked him, but had to love him. 'And that just about sums up Donald,' Lady Serota added.

Others, too, appreciated Donald, however diffident he was himself about his contribution. 'He would never condone the attitude that said "We (on the LCC) have nothing to learn from the smaller authorities in London and elsewhere,"' Betty Vernon has written.[134] 'What happens when the twentieth Congress of Christianity takes place?' he quipped to Ellis Hillman, at the time of the twentieth Congress of the Communist Party.[135] Gladys Dimson, a member of the Children's Committee, felt 'Donald was a very interesting man,'[136] especially because he shared members' concerns and did not seek political office. For his part Donald liked being linked with those responsible for so many social and educational matters for it was here 'the battle for the Kingdom of God' was being fought.[137]

In 1964 the GLC was created, a move opposed earlier by the Labour majority on the LCC,[138] and Donald became an alderman on it. He was assiduous in his duties, attending eleven full Council meetings and the Housing Committee, but by April 1965 resigned for he was about to become a Life Peer, an appointment which disappointed Labour's grass-roots. Donald defended himself strongly arguing, 'If it is good enough for Fenner Brockway, it is good enough for any left winger,'[139] and explained the House of Lords would be 'yet another platform' for the propagation of his faith.[140]

In 1966 a second Labour Government was in office, now with a comfortable majority. Again Donald led worship, which ended with the singing of 'Jerusalem', and Bishop Stockwood preached.[141] Donald found a prayer for the occasion, which asked for a vision of a land of righteousness, plenty and peace, where excellence alone was honoured and there was love for all and ended with a request to God that people would be inspired to strengthen each other to make the vision a reality.[142] Harold Wilson concluded one of his Party Conference speeches with it, telling delegates, 'when the time comes, I would want this Government, this Movement, to be judged not only by the British nation but by history, by our success or failure in turning this prayer into a reality'.[143]

Donald continued to enjoy warm relations with Harold Wilson, someone with the most incisive mind he had ever met on subjects he had studied.[144] He welcomed Wilson to the CSM AGM in April 1967, when demonstrators, protesting at Labour's support for American involvement in Vietnam, were removed by police from the

Kingsway Hall entrance,[145] and to a social occasion before the 1971 AGM.[146] A more frivolous occasion was the much publicized breakfast he attended at the Connaught Rooms, hosted by David Frost, when the Prime Minister, the novelist Len Deighton, A.J. Ayer, the Bishop of Woolwich, newspaper chiefs Cecil King and David Astor, among others, engaged in animated conversation from 9.30 a.m. till nearly lunch-time.[147]

Donald was never a delegate to Party Conferences but either spoke at, or chaired, CSM's public meeting, as in 1962 when he introduced Tom Driberg, Stanley Evans, Tony Greenwood, and Leah Manning. Later he also welcomed Shirley Williams, the Bishop of Middleton (E.R. Wickham), Edward Short, Lord Beswick and Tony Banks. In 1980 Donald was still at this appointed task, chairing Tony Benn and Frank Field on 'Christian Socialism', though as President of CSM he was no longer active in its daily affairs.

For the 1970 election Donald wrote a pamphlet 'Why I Am Labour', printed and distributed by the Party itself. 'I have no use for those people who denigrate the Labour Party because in seventy years we haven't done what it took democracy 400 years to achieve,' he wrote.[148] In 1971 he also made a party political broadcast on Radios 1 and 2 at Christmas time where he explained how he linked his Christian faith with fellowship and community.[149] He supported the Labour candidate at the Sutton and Cheam by-election in February 1974, 'an old-fashioned Christian Socialist',[150] and that same month joined thousands of pensioners and trade unionists marching through London to demand a minimum pension, a protest organized by the TUC itself. Len Murray and Abe Moffat (the retired Scottish miners' leader) were there and Jack Jones, too, as well as Clive Dunn from *Dad's Army*. 'The vast majority of people realize that a society which tolerates poverty and in some ways exacerbates it, is not a civilized society,' Donald declared at the rally,[151] one of the few occasions he was involved in trade union activities, though in 1952 he spoke at the Durham Miners' Gala[152] and in the 1980s for the Northumberland Miners during the Miners' Strike.[153]

When the autumn 1974 election came Donald was in an apocalyptic mood but refused to be downed, continuing his *Tribune* articles and his role in the House of Lords, whose members he found possessed skills he had not suspected. Indeed, he later believed, if reformed and the hereditary principle abolished, it could become a useful second chamber, though its title would need changing and other groups, especially from the world of faith communities, would need to be admitted.[154]

Donald used to sweat before speaking, but even his maiden speech about the Trades Dispute Bill, on 25 May 1965, given without notes, impressed peers. He had been trawling through *Wesley's Journal*, he reported, and had found the following: 'I spent two or three hours in the House of Lords. What is a Lord but a sinner born to die?',[155] then explained how Methodists had 'a reputable and a splendid tradition in the story of the Trade Union Movement'.[156] Indeed, some of the Tolpuddle Martyrs were Methodist local preachers. Turning to current injustices he argued that disadvantages often made people act as they did. Could the Bill therefore 'once again establish . . . a way of emphasizing that we are members one of another . . .?'[157]

Donald Soper, who as Baron Soper of Kingsway spoke over 230 times, was extremely clear about his themes. He was never, of course, a member of the Front Bench team, but state of the nation topics became a prime concern, whether related to Sunday trade, the role of the media, attitudes to gambling, drink, sex or animals, or to education, the inner city or the economy. He was as keen to emphasize personal responsibility as Government policies, which either encouraged good behaviour or not. The criminal justice system also occupied his attention. When it came to community care Donald was always alert to the troubles of alcoholics and prisoners, whose cause he often championed. Problems of housing and homelessness, too, also concerned him and issues related to drug dependency and the role of the welfare state. He spoke, however, only on rare occasions on race relations. International affairs was another preoccupation of Donald's, especially southern Africa and the Third World, but when speaking of military questions he seldom flaunted his pacifist convictions.

Surprisingly he spoke little as a representative of the Free Churches so his religious utterances were either related to specific matters – the death of Lord Fisher, the assassination of the Methodist minister, the Rev. Robert Bradford, in Northern Ireland – or to new legal arrangements which he applauded – the Sharing of Church Buildings Act or the creation in 1972 of the United Reformed Church. On occasions Donald would ventilate his views on the Rev. Ian Paisley, with whom he profoundly disagreed, skilfully explaining to peers how he did not represent orthodox Protestant thought or outlook.

What impact did those speeches have? Certainly all enjoyed

listening to Donald's erudition, fluency and use of language,[158] and the Conservatives always filled their benches to hear him, for they liked a 'real man'.[159] No one regarded Donald as a politician, 'which he is to his bones', one friend has observed.[160] As a colleague he was redoubtable, too, willing, as Lady Stocks found out, 'to dig his trowel under some carefully hidden thing'[161] needing exposure and when she argued for voluntary castration as an alternative to prison for persistent and compulsive, but harmless, sex offenders, he supported her proposal.[162]

How did peers respond to Donald's views? 'Donald has always been listened to with great attention,' a former Bishop of Rochester has written, 'even when his pacifism has offended them . . . He can always be heard, is invariably courteous and has a good sense of humour – all qualities that commend him as a speaker.'[163] The Lords expected the bishops and Donald Soper to comment on social matters and international affairs. 'Donald has seldom failed them,' he adds.[164] Archbishop Michael Ramsey, too, regarded Donald Soper's role highly. Supposing Labour were to reform the second chamber, what future would there be for bishops there?, Richard Crossman once asked him. 'Well, the kind of cleric in a future House of Lords would be Donald Soper, the Methodist minister, selected on his merits as a life peer,' the Archbishop replied.[165]

Lord Carrington, for whom Donald was 'a sombre figure . . . dressed as he is in his black cassock', whose 'speeches are far from sombre',[166] admired most his moral courage, not only on Tower Hill and Speaker's Corner but also during the Second World War. His innate courtesy and his 'unusual, almost unique, talking without a note' he valued, too.[167] Moreover, despite his left-wing views, he had been a great example, and, even though feeling 'We are all very wicked' never showed it, exemplifying the part of Christianity which says, 'Forgive us our sins.'[168]

Mixing with personalities like Lord Montgomery, Baronesses Wootton, Summerskill and Gaitskell, who helped him greatly on his arrival there,[169] as well as hereditary peers, Donald also made an impact because he was a parson, for, says George Thomas (Viscount Tonypandy), the House of Lords still respects that vocation.[170] Few make a real dent in its outlook and traditions, but certainly Donald carved out a niche there, influencing some like Lord Bruce more than any other because he gave priority to conscience.[171] 'No one,' he has added, 'would dream of interrupting Donald. Would they dare?'[172]

Once or twice Donald put a motion down in his own name, one on material objectives and social well-being. He wanted peers to consider how the two could be reconciled and how effective participation in society could be developed, he said, calling on the Government 'to examine ways of evaluating the problem within a democratic society',[173] for compared with forty years ago, when there was idealism, community fervour, even in the Labour Party, had declined. Never had he found such cynicism. Yet if faith, hope and charity were lacking he did not think 'we have a very inviting future . . .'[174]

The debate thus opened, others like the Earl of Longford, Baroness Wootton and Viscount Samuel, along with Lord Ritchie Calder and Lord Platt, had their say, with Lord Sandford replying for the Opposition. Lord Donaldson, in particular, took Donald to task, finding his approach to practical affairs 'impeccably wise and generous'[175] but parting company with him over theory, especially that there ought to be a greater moral content in political decisions, as most evil in history flowed from 'other people's wrong moral judgements . . .'[176] For the Opposition Viscount Barrington, Donald's opponent in debates on abortion, was surprised that someone of cheerful and sanguine temperament,[177] who understood the wicked-ness of the world and was determined to stand up to it, appeared so gloomy. 'I can only say to him,' he continued, 'that I do not share his pessimism.'[178]

Donald never avoided revealing his Christian convictions, or lacing speeches with biblical allusions, or even admonishing peers like Lord Willis, who had an awesome regard for him, for misquoting Micah.[179] Thus in speaking about the Criminal Justice Bill he justified reforms in the prison service he sought with reference to the biblical injunction 'not to cause occasions for stumbling'[180] and in relation to Rhodesia and the Pearce Commission's Report urged peers, 'Be ye hearers of the word and yet doers also.'[181] 'I am at the moment seething with anger,' he said on 2 February 1972, as he objected to the behaviour of British troops in Northern Ireland.[182] The war in the Middle East, however, drew out only his despair, as he explained there was but one golden thread there and that lay in 'the hope of the Grace of God; the compassion of Allah and the righteousness of Jehovah'.[183]

When in 1977 *Tribune* was forty years old there was a rally in the Central Hall, Westminster. 'The whole left was there,' Tony Benn recalled. 'Ian Mikardo in the Chair, Neil Kinnock, Dick Clements,

Mark Saunders, Laurence Daly, Barbara Castle, Jack Jones, myself, Michael Foot, Fenner Brockway, who made a marvellous speech, Jimmy Reid, Donald Soper. A tremendous event.'[184] By April 1980, however, Donald was writing his last column for the weekly[185] to which he had contributed well over 500 pieces. No other columnist had lasted as long, generated so many letters or received such loyalty. For some, like Derek Willmott, he became a pundit. One of the first soldiers on the D-Day beaches he later became a barrister and law lecturer and Donald, first through his column and then in public meetings, continued his education, both spiritually and politically, once counselling him 'with great impartiality'.[186] 'I ended up a Quaker,' he has explained, 'and a member of the Quaker Socialist Society.'[187] Readers, like M.G. Maitland, saw Donald differently, of course, writing, 'Christianity, posing as socialism and preaching "moderation", "non-violence", "class harmony" and all other such humbug, has been a drag on the British Labour movement for generations. *Tribune* . . . would do well to dispense with the literary services of Lord Soper . . .'[188]

Donald aroused more opposition with *Christian Politics*, published in 1977, soon after he had chaired a press conference to re-launch the CSM itself, which had experienced a lean period. Bishop Colin Winter, then exiled from Namibia, reviewed it in the *Labour Weekly*[189] and fulminated against the title, for it reminded him of Afrikaner nationalist ideology. He attacked, too, the text, when he compared it with what Latin American liberation theologians were writing about politics which was rooted in people's struggles.[190] Donald was not, of course, writing for Latin America, but discussing law and order, violence, race, poverty, education and liberty as British issues and the role of compromise and theological vision in socialism. He could not, however, avoid what J.H. Oldham has called 'middle axioms', guidelines about actions for situations when Christian perspectives cannot be applied completely. Though against violence, Donald accepted that 'violence to the animal creation must in some measure be temporarily accepted, though closely scrutinised'.[191] On education he thought all children belonged to the kingdom of God and were therefore 'as entitled to the full requirements of the mind' as to adequate food, clothing and shelter for the body.[192] He accepted 'some use of force' was required to maintain law and order, but suggested a police force was not incompatible with non-violence.[193]

The auguries for his socialism were not promising, he confessed.

There was good news about the future, however, for hope and faith could be infused into a programme, especially if morality were part 'of the stuff with which creation is held together'. Once hope began to garrison the hearts and minds of people because God was creator, all things were possible to those who believed. 'And if this sounds like the end of a sermon,' he concluded with a flourish, 'let economists and politicians and parsons and people, say "Amen".'[194]

Chapter 5

POLEMICIST AND
PEDAGOGUE

IN 1936, FILLED 'with boundless energy and enthusiasm',[1] Donald
Soper set about renewing the Kingsway congregation which owed its
origin to Hugh Price Hughes and the nineteenth-century Forward
Movement in Wesleyan Methodism. After his first sermon on 13
September 1936, on Christ's authority, it was clear his preaching was
down to earth as he explained how Jesus was a brother who had come
to draw out what was in people's hearts 'from all eternity'.[2] Some
2,000 were present the following Tuesday to welcome the Sopers to
Kingsway Hall, including Katharine Price Hughes, the widow of the
founder of the West London Mission (WLM). The Methodist
President, the Rev. C. Ensor Walters, Hugh Price Hughes' successor
in 1902, in welcoming them linked Mrs Hughes with Josephine
Butler and Catherine Booth as servants of their generation.[3] As he
recounted the deeds, not only of her husband but his colleague, Mark
Guy Pearce, and of J. Ernest Rattenbury, Superintendent from 1907
to 1925, and Ira G. Goldhawk, whom Donald followed, he became
acutely aware of the Mission's history.[4]

A Superintendent should have courage, Ensor Walters continued,
the spirit of adventure, a passionate social enthusiasm and a belief in
the Cross of Christ, all of which Donald had, though he would also
shock some people. 'I want to be worthy of a great tradition,' Donald
responded,[5] adding, however, he did not hope to achieve most by
virtue, but through God. He cared little, either, about 'constitutions,
institutions and political nostrums',[6] though they would hear about
some in due time! Donald's friends were there that night from Tower
Hill and Islington. So, too, were Dick Sheppard, Sam Hughes, Luke
Wiseman and Sir Henry Lunn to hear the editor of the *British Weekly*
warn the congregation against making too many demands on Donald
and making his wife an unpaid minister.[7]

Donald's job was formidable, for the circuit went as far as Hammersmith and King's Cross and involved a great deal of social work including the Kingsway Crèche on the top floor of Wesley House (the large building adjoining Kingsway Hall), started in 1887 by Sister Katharine and Katharine Price Hughes' brother and then developed by Sister Hope. One Sister, Gertrude, who retired in 1947 after fifty-five years, linked Donald directly with Hugh Price Hughes himself, and was one of the most selfless people Donald ever met,[8] whose courage, especially in the blitz, was a tonic.[9]

Besides the Crèche, of which Donald was very proud, there was a Holiday Home for children at Barnet, a maternity hospital, a hostel for stranded girls and another for working girls – Emerson Bainbridge House, named after one of the Mission's many benefactors – a second-hand clothes depot and open-air work in Hyde Park, sustained by students from Richmond Theological College. There was a dramatic society, too, which one year presented Noël Coward's *Hay Fever* to raise crèche funds[10] and also popular Saturday night concerts, when artists like Suzette Tari, Flotsam and Jetsam and Bransby Williams, whose impersonations of Dickens' characters had first introduced Charlie Chaplin to literature,[11] brought new faces on the premises, though attendances at these were dwindling.

In addition, Allan Brown, one of several gifted organists the church employed, organized the music, which included Sunday worship and concerts by the Kingsway Choral Society, whose repertoire included *Hiawatha*, *Carmen* and *Faust*. Kingsway Hall was therefore full of interlocking groups, each with its own task, and a growing congregation, as converts came from Donald's Tower Hill and peace work and his broadcast talks, many of which, like *Christianity and Its Critics*, became books.[12]

'In 1922, though the high tornado of the Evangelical Revival had been dying away for at least half a century,' the poet Norman Nicholson wrote, 'there was still a following wind that blew ... Conversion, the changed life, "the heart strangely warmed", were still at the centre of Methodist theology,'[13] though for many something of a formality. Indeed, in his youth every five years there was a formal mission when Moody and Sankey choruses were sung. At Kingsway itself Gipsy Smith's 1923 mission produced hundreds of enquiries[14] and in 1937, during the Moody and Sankey Centenary, Luke Wiseman had lectured.[15]

Donald himself was aware of this broader evangelical tradition, as an analysis of hymns sung at Kingsway, from 1938 to 1968, demonstrates. Isaac Watts's 'When I survey the wondrous cross', and Charles Wesley's 'Jesu, Lover of my soul', and 'Love divine, all loves excelling', were sung over fifty times and 'What shall I do my God to love?' over a hundred. Such choices reveal a minister (Donald led worship most Sundays, except when away or ill) sensitive to the personal and pietistic aspect of faith, where God's grace becomes available through Christ's love streaming from the Cross. There was, however, a particular Methodist slant to the hymns, for Charles Wesley taught that the new creature in Christ should expect a progressive sanctification through the Holy Spirit.[16]

Other hymns, emphasizing the power of that Spirit – 'Come, Holy Ghost, our hearts inspire', 'Spirit divine, attend our prayers' – were, of course, also used, as were nineteenth-century ones by writers urging a deeper trust in God and a willingness to live as Christian disciples, 'At the name of Jesus' and 'Fill thou my life' being prominent. In addition, as Donald's sensitivity to liturgy grew – usually the Methodist form of Morning Prayer, when the Nunc Dimittis, Venite and Jubilate were regularly sung – Wesley's hymns on the Eucharist, like 'Jesus, we thus obey', became very familiar. Indeed, Donald often taught the congregation that 'Christianity is 99 per cent obedience.'[17]

Those who attended the popular women's meetings which existed before 1939, students from the London School of Economics near by (Donald started a weekly students' fellowship in 1937), young men who visited Pentonville regularly and Tower Hill converts, heard a similar message from Donald: Jesus cared for each person uniquely and *also* for social conditions. These talks, lectures and addresses, fed by his incredible memory, were as crystal clear, therefore, as the hymns.

'Donald Soper . . . came as a perfect answer to my needs,' Len Barnett, a young civil servant who attended a celebrity concert and stayed to become a church member, considered.[18] 'Sunday by Sunday, and Wednesday by Wednesday at Tower Hill . . . I was inspired, nourished, mentally stretched, as I listened to the impassioned and yet always flawlessly argued case for Christianity.'[19] It was, he discovered, Donald's insight into Jesus's life and teaching in particular, always related to the week's headlines, which fascinated the congregation, drawn by either the pacifist, socialist or sacramentalist strands in Donald's ministry, though seldom by all three.

Donald had one overriding purpose: to bring people to a decision. So, preaching on Mark 1:15 – 'The time is fulfilled, and the Kingdom of God is at hand: repent ye and believe in the Gospel' – he urged both self-examination and confession of all sins 'respectable or otherwise', asking those who repented to stay behind for Holy Communion.[20] From the start, therefore, he emphasized the Eucharist, an approach quite different from the main Central Hall tradition in Methodism, which attempted to persuade the 'outsider' to attend services on 'neutral ground, in a theatre or public hall'.[21] Indeed, though linked formally and financially with the London Mission, Donald kept himself somewhat distant, though always a welcome speaker at many Mission Anniversaries, despite the controversy he caused in 1945 by alleging the day of the Central Hall was over, 'if indeed it ever dawned'.[22] 'Heartiness is no alternative to reverence,' he stated categorically then, a view he never altered.[23]

Donald also wanted to interpret Christianity for half-believers, both within and beyond the Church. An early demythologizer, he was never entirely happy with some 1960s American theologians. When once asked by an American journalist, 'Dr Soper, do you believe that God is dead?' he replied, 'I didn't know He'd been ill,'[24] an indication he preserved a sense of God's transcendence when others lost it. Donald did, of course, believe Bultmann right to demythologize the cosmology of the early Church. It was important, however, as Bultmann also taught, to recognize all myth contained an ultimate core of truth. Demythologizing, therefore, was not banishing error but 're-shaping truth'.[25]

Following this approach Donald was flexible about the meaning of the phrase 'the resurrection of the body'. Because Jesus had conquered death Christians were 'sure of the God He made manifest, and, with God, are confident that all things are possible'.[26] On Easter Day 1949, he explained his view of the authenticity of the Resurrection more succinctly, arguing there was less reason to doubt it now because the biblical records, examined more critically than any other documents, had shown the writers so sure of the main facts they had not troubled to correlate the details. How would the Church have arisen if it were not for the Resurrection?, he asked. Indeed, Resurrection stories, like Mary in the garden, could not have been invented for they ran counter to all the human mind expected.[27]

Donald believed, too, in a life beyond space and time. Only so could he make sense of the world's injustices. 'You will meet your beloved in the beyond,' he wrote in one newspaper. 'I believe that those who are once loved can never finally lose the intimacy and fellowship that love inspires. Such a confidence begins with God . . .'[28] Three decades later Donald still felt the same. 'My father died a few days ago . . . I am glad I am not haunted or distressed about any speculation as to where he is or what he is doing. I am sure that he has gone to God, and that in that eternal realm all is well . . . He died with a strong and vibrant faith. He has gone to God, and there I will leave him.'[29]

During the pre-war period Donald was 'too busy',[30] even though he tried to discriminate between demands, a problem he never resolved during his time at Kingsway Hall. One minute he was at a medical missionary society exhibition, 'Conquest by Healing', which 4,000 attended, showing its opener, Emperor Haile Selassie (then in exile in Bath) around, explaining in French, 'We are not proud of our civilization but we do all honour Jesus Christ',[31] and all were gathered in a fellowship overstepping boundaries of class and race. The next he was taking his Boys' Club to Jimmie Butterworth's Clubland and speaking to a packed congregation of young people.[32]

In 1937 Donald found himself institutionalized when the Muswell Hill Methodist Church unveiled a stained-glass window, showing personalities from the New Testament, Church history and contemporary Christianity in action. Christians selected for these latter panels included Grenfell of Labrador, Baden-Powell, Albert Schweitzer and Donald himself addressing Tower Hill crowds, many of them dockers.[33] That May, shortly after Donald had celebrated ten years on Tower Hill at a meeting addressed by George Lansbury and Hugh Redwood, he commented that his voice, once baritone, was now tenor from answering over 20,000 questions as the WLM celebrated its fiftieth Anniversary with visits from the Salvation Army Band and Principal John Whale. The Mission also held a conference on its redemptive and social work at which Katharine Price Hughes launched the Guild of St Francis, named after the saint Donald said he had 'fallen in love' with because, in the spirit of his Master, he 'went about doing good'.[34]

By July, with Marie and his two daughters, he had sailed for South Africa. The Johannesburg *Star* commented that the Sopers were both pacifists who deplored the armaments race and its inevitable outcome 'unless friendliness and faith replace the present international suspicion'.[35] Their views were less well received when Donald spoke on

'The Christian answer to Communism and fascism', at a meeting of 2,000 in Durban's Town Hall.[36] As his preaching appointments in Pretoria, Cape Town and Johannesburg were solely in white churches, encounters with the black population were confined to noticing the poverty in which many lived[37] and watching Africans in rhythmic unity on their drums one Sunday afternoon in Johannesburg.[38] In the Kruger National Park they saw wild beasts which had learned to lose the fear of people because in the Park they never harmed them, he told one missionary rally on his return. If this was possible with wild animals, why be downhearted about the Gospel and its relation to the world?

Donald saw more clearly the preacher's job was to save people, he reported at the Jubilee celebrations that autumn as a galaxy of speakers, including Dr Scott Lidgett, Dr J.E. Rattenbury, Sir Josiah Stamp and others, took part. Hugh Price Hughes' Forward Movement looked back to John Wesley, he declared, who possessed a passion for souls, a spirit of audacity and a desire to help poor and troubled people, a characteristic also of Hughes.[39] Wesley's class meeting itself was the work of a supreme tactician and Methodists must rediscover its value in building Christian character. The celebration made him realize, too, he continued, the source of the Mission's power, especially when older Sisters described their work with spiritual fervour which gave 'an impression of Hugh Price Hughes as being goodness on fire'.[40] During the Jubilee Lady Sanders opened the Katharine Price Hughes Hostel in Doughty Street, the end result of sixteen years' work in a house in Drury Lane where the Sisters had protected and helped nearly 10,000 girls.[41] Some £8,000 was still needed to cover its costs but Donald was confident he could raise the money.[42]

W.H. Elliott, like Donald a popular radio parson, came to the fifty-first Anniversary in 1938, to hear of full congregations on Sunday evenings with 500 staying for the monthly after-service prayer meetings. More, too, stayed for Communion, including many of the eighty-seven new members. Now Donald planned to convert the Drury Lane house into a hostel for ex-prisoners. Always under pressure to raise funds, he raised more when concert and musical arrangements were re-organized. With Tower Hill men meeting on Wednesday nights and other new events, though the children's church Donald started remained stubbornly small, pastoral work had doubled, so assistants were sought to help him.

That year Canon Adderley asked Kingsway Hall to join in a Three Hour Service on Good Friday, which already involved Hampstead Garden Suburb Free Church and St Mary, Woolnoth, and so started a service which became the focus for Donald's teaching ministry. In July Donald led a procession of witness when over 1,000 went via Drury Lane and the Aldwych to Kingsway, where in Keeley Street hymns were sung, sometimes by onlookers, and where Donald spoke about Christianity as the only basis for righting wrongs.[43]

Donald, of course, chaired the diverse committees which sprang up, assiduously attending their meetings. He was, as he often said, 'the benevolent dictator of a modified democracy'.[44] Indeed, in later years at Kingsway one regular comment heard of Crèche Committee meetings was: 'If you miss the lift to the top floor, don't bother!' Donald's plans for development were brought to a sudden halt in 1938, however. At the end of July he had an operation for appendicitis at St Mary's, Paddington, which was successful, but took an unexpected turn when an embolism developed and a potential thrombosis had to be averted. Thereafter he had to be extra vigilant to keep his health stable.

Inactivity Donald found intolerable and often in his tour Diaries he would write the word 'bored' if he had half a day, or even a few hours, with nothing to do. Now he had inordinate free time and it irked him. Moreover, he was on his back and could only reflect as Britain became preoccupied with Chamberlain and the Munich crisis. He did not find it easy to hope as he contemplated the world from hospital bed and convalescent home, though remained convinced divine resources were available. When in December he returned to Kingsway it was a new Donald Soper who emerged to clamber, somewhat painfully, up the steps to preach, having left his two stout sticks in the vestry.[45] 'I found out during these six months, what I really most wanted to do,' he said later. 'It was to stand in the pulpit and conduct public worship . . . I don't pretend I'm pious, but that was heaven for me.'[46] Soon his adrenalin was flowing again as he ministered to the 400 at Kingsway Hall and the 1,000 in the circuit, and supervised a team of sixty taking services in lodging houses near by and crowded open-air services at King's Cross.[47] By the end of 1939 200 or more were meeting every Thursday (later Tuesday) for devotions in the Guild, too, the nerve centre for the church well into the 1970s.

In 1939 Luke Wiseman opened the Mission's first hostel for

discharged prisoners. During its first fifteen days no one came for help. Then a gangster sentenced to death in Utah appeared and the hostel was in business. In one year 288 stayed and jobs were found for 273. In addition, another 500 passed through and only eighteen of those with whom the Mission dealt returned to prison.[48] By now a club for young people in the Drury Lane area had started, at the request of the LCC, which attracted large numbers.[49] Many came in gangs, losing face if they took their caps off, a difficulty from the start. 'They were also armed with razors, hammers and batons, to keep their elders in order,' Donald commented. 'One night in their high spirits they actually demolished part of the premises downstairs. Another night, in a more warlike mood, they were arranged outside, armed with sticks, demanding the life of the Superintendent.'[50] Despite such hazards the twenty helpers kept some order as games were played and the jitterbug became the dancing craze.[51] Later more purposeful activities, including a dress-making class and a Red Cross unit, were formed.[52]

Donald was available for individuals, as in Islington, on Tuesday evenings – and later on Sundays after 4.30 p.m. – when he would listen to problems and, if asked, advise. 'What the heck is counselling?' he once wrote in his Diary, after attending a lecture in America, an indication that his advice was likely to be seasoned by his experience of life in war-time London. 'The amazing thing about Jesus,' he taught, was that 'when He had the whole world to win, He wasted time, as it were, in talking to Mary Magdalen, the woman at the well, Zacchaeus and Nicodemus, because Jesus knew that the whole meaning of life is personal, or it is nothing'.[53]

As far as Methodism was concerned Donald thought of it as an order within the wider Church 'able to take its place alongside the Dominican Order and the Society of Jesus and the Society of Friends'.[54] Yet he was deeply embedded in his church and when at the 1941 Anniversary Kingsway Hall was again full, he was never more at its heart than when he shared the platform with Dr Sangster and Dr Weatherhead.[55]

In 1942 Donald started yet another venture. For a while he had held three services each Sunday, partly to discuss the five points of the Malvern Conference. Now, on Passion Sunday, he invited the congregation to join him in Hyde Park, where they could indulge in 'mild heckling', though he hoped the meetings would not become 'a sort of Tower Hill on Sunday'.[56] By the end of April these gatherings were already 'a source of great encouragement and ... beneficial to the mission'.[57] They became weekly and soon Donald was to be found under the trees at the rear of the arena mounted on a stand fastened to the railings,[58] a successor to the layman Crook Palmer, who had spoken there over 400 times previously.

Three other events of note occurred that year – the Annual Meeting of the Christian Cinema and Religious Film Society, presided over by the Archbishop of Canterbury, and addressed by the film director, Michael Powell, and the celebration of the ninetieth birthday of Katharine Price Hughes, who reminded those present the original class meeting had started in a room in Greek Street, Soho, fifty-five years earlier.[59] The third event was Donald's discovery of the cassock's usefulness, especially when called out at night. Now after Sunday evening worship, though not immediately at Tower Hill, he donned his cassock and went down into the Holborn Tube shelters to meet those sheltering there.[60]

Summer, 1943, brought Donald himself another brush with death. The year had been positive till then. The Good Friday service had gone well, involving among others a German pastor in London and Dr Herbert Gray.[61] In May he had welcomed Jimmie Butterworth and the Clubland congregation to Kingsway for its twenty-first birthday because Clubland had been bombed. But that August, surfing on holiday in Cornwall, one leg gave out. 'I got an undertow among heavy waves and could not swim,' he explained. 'I was semi-conscious and fast going over when a cross wave picked me up and threw me on my feet. A girl life saver had bravely come out from the beach to help me and she assisted me in ...'[62] Once ashore Donald collapsed, was taken home by ambulance and only later able to thank his rescuer.

The congregation continued to develop, aided in 1944 by the appointment as organist of Fela Sowande from Nigeria, who had once played with Fats Waller, and who knew both Bach and Yoruba melodies.[63] Donald himself was taking up his temperance concern then, too, for drink was one reason young girls, who had left home, became pregnant, so there was need for the Band of Hope and its teaching.[64] By the time of the fifty-seventh Anniversary in May 1944 Donald indicated the discharged prisoners' hostel, now six years old, had interviewed 1,000 callers, had fifty residents and, was co-operating with the Discharged Prisoners' Aid Society. Katharine Price Hughes Hostel for girls aged 16 to 21, Sister Lottie reported, had served

3,000 meals a week; and another colleague, Sister Mary, had paid many visits, especially to St Luke's Home for the Dying. The Mission's clothing store was much used, too. The Easter services themselves were the largest since 1939 – Leslie Weatherhead was the preacher – when thirty-two new members were welcomed. A further sixty-two had stood on soapboxes in various places and spoken about their faith.

That autumn, near the time Arnhem was relieved, Donald startled many with press reports that he and colleagues proposed to build a 'Methodist cathedral' near Marble Arch, costing £20,000 or more.[65] With doors open to all, it hoped to make a contribution to Christian unity. It would provide a centre, too, for many interested in shaping the post-war world, indeed, could provide a focus for the nearly 2,000 who came to hear and heckle Donald at Speaker's Corner. Moreover, it would solve the problem of the inadequacy of the Kingsway site for over decades London's centre of gravity had moved westwards. Donald also hoped a Christian community could be focused on the proposed centre based on Iona Community lines, not a full community, however, but groups of people living and worshipping together for a week with resources pooled.[66] Not surprisingly the cathedral scheme never gained support but Donald's hope for a community emerged soon as the Order of Christian Witness (OCW).

Donald's ventures in the immediate post-war period expanded. The family itself had moved from Wildwood Road in Hampstead Garden Suburb, where it had lived intermittently during the war, to Radlett as Marie Soper began the task of bringing up what was in effect a second family. Donald had BBC talks to prepare, services and social work demands and itinerant preaching appointments, plus the open-air work, which in 1946 included speaking in Trafalgar Square during the Methodist Conference.[67]

In January the National Children's Home held its Christmas Festival at Kingsway Hall, attended by 'Uncle Mac' and the Zoo Man, David Seth-Smith. It was Donald's first contact with the broadcaster around whose personality *Children's Hour* had been built but by no means his last, for by July 1949, he had taken over John Williams' slot, contributing over the next period thirty-three items and prayers, including a reflection on rocks, in which he made a simple analogy between the rocks in New York he had seen on which the Manhattan skyscrapers were securely built and the rock which is Jesus Christ.[68]

Kingsway Hall was now making real progress at worship and during the week. Donald could not, of course, respond to requests without the help of the Sisters, and the Canadian Keith Woollard, for a time his assistant. Nor could he do without the financial and material help he received from Britain and abroad. Sometimes he would sit for hours signing letters, then tossing them to the floor in an almost frantic effort to make it possible to raise money to sustain the projects established. There was, too, the *Kingsway Messenger* to keep going, the church community centre to sustain, films for children in Soho and Holborn, and a junior church, as well as a new enterprise, The Hungerford, for destitute men, taken over from the Anglican Pacifist Fellowship, which, during the war, had run it under the arches near Charing Cross.

Soon transferred to Wincott Street in Lambeth, where the LCC leased the WLM a casual ward from an old hospital, over the year thousands slept there for one night and fifty men made The Hungerford their regular home. Some 300 to 400 came weekly to the clothing centre and one Sister visited Holloway Prison twice weekly, as colleagues cared for Pentonville's Nonconformist prisoners. Music and drama were not ignored either and there was even a sewing class to train young girls in needlework, which provided repairs to much worn garments.[69] A Poor Man's Law Centre was also opened on the premises, running weekly for two years before transferring to Lincoln's Inn Fields.[70]

In 1947, with the help of the Methodist Missionary Society, the Sopers paid a month-long visit to Ceylon, where Donald presented his convictions to Asian audiences in a Buddhist setting. Travelling there via Cairo and the Pyramids, Karachi and Bombay, they found a new sense of national oneness and a desire for colonialism to end. On arrival they were met by a Methodist colleague, the Rev. Dennis Lansdown, who organized their tour and has recalled that right away 'Donald Soper was a larger than life character',[71] at the opening reception playing both 'Crimond' and jazz on the piano. It greatly helped, of course, that he was an avid supporter of the Labour Party, then in government under Attlee.

Donald's first activity was to give an ordination charge when as usual he spoke extempore, astounding everybody, who soon found themselves enchanted and amazed at him. Thereafter he was plunged into early morning Bible classes in the YMCA in Colombo, to which once 300 came. It ceased after a while, however, for Donald was living in a bungalow surrounded by roads, with rickshaw pullers sleeping on its verandah, whose coughing from the effects of their deadly job made sleep difficult.

The numerous question and answer sessions were filled to over-flowing. 'Christianity goes further than Communism,' he told one meeting, 'since it holds a belief in a classless society of people where we are brothers within the fatherhood of God',[72] a process which involved 'a levelling up rather than a levelling down'.[73] Donald's range of topics was vast – the way to interpret Scripture, capitalism and socialism, world government, the contribution of Aldous Huxley and Gandhi to thought, as well as how to understand the significance of Jesus, the relation between the faiths and ethical issues. 'There is,' he declared, 'great impudence in any who is a Christian telling Buddhists, Muslims or Hindus what they ought to believe,'[74] adding that as a Christian he had learned one thing 'and that is the virtue of intellectual courtesy'.[75]

One Sunday an open-air forum was arranged on the Galle Face Green, the fashionable sea front parade, and some said 5,000 turned up.[76] On a platform, with his back to sea and setting sun, Donald faced the crowds and answered written questions, speaking especially about love and non-violence, suggesting that love, which was both self-identification with others, and an attitude of utter tenderness, could achieve more than the violence many espoused and drew attention to Albert Schweitzer's philosophy, maintaining he was 'one of the greatest people alive'.[77] Elsewhere Donald met 2,000 university students who heard him present Christianity as the fountainhead of justice and goodness, an idea, it appeared, entirely new to them.[78] Once, at Trinity College, Kandy, a young man fired a volley of questions at Donald from the far corner of the packed meeting about Christianity's responsibility for global capitalism, the oppression of workers, imperialism and its support for evil states and monarchies. There was a pin-drop silence as he concluded. 'Young man I fully agree with you,' Donald quickly responded. 'Look me up whenever you are in Britain and I'll take you as one of my local preachers.'[79]

Donald was fascinated by Asia. His curiosity was aroused by his meeting with Buddhists and the different sights and sounds – the mixture of palm trees and cockroaches, the elephant working on road repairs, fireflies and mason wasps and even the occasional jackal. For him the highlight was the trip to Kandy through emerald paddy fields, where women were thinning the rice, singing dirges as they worked. He went to the Temple of the Tooth and was shown a tooth of the Buddha by a Buddhist abbot, who made a great impression on Donald who felt he was 'a saintly human being, whose goodness was as recognizable as the colour of his robe'.[80]

'There's a social revolution going on in Ceylon,' Donald wrote in his Diary for 16 September. 'And we're not part of it – bad show!' By October, such was the interest he had generated, he was writing 'If only this is all followed up.' But was it? Were any of his tours to Australia, New Zealand, Nigeria, Canada and America followed up, or was he merely casting bread on the waters? Certainly it was clear he had made an impact on the leaders of both Tamil and Singhalese communities as he talked with them over evening meals, but Dennis Landsdown admitted later there was nothing tangible to report from Donald's four weeks of hard work and that its effect had been elusive.[81]

One thing had emerged for Donald himself: a greater sense of his role as teacher, as he spoke about the Bible's authority and inspiration, the relation of the two testaments and how Jesus revealed God's true nature. Throughout the tour, too, Donald was sensitive to its multi-faith setting. 'I remember saying in a broadcast talk fifteen years ago,' he replied to one questioner, 'that the Old Testament in Ceylon should include a great many of the sayings of Buddha, and that of the Old Testament for India ... a great many of the Upanishads ...' ideas which horrified fundamentalists who were continuously battling with Donald.[82]

Donald's view of biblical inspiration involved an acceptance that an intimate relation between Bible, Church and believer was necessary. Moreover, Scripture readers needed an awareness that it contained different approaches and 'the Word' contained within all the words.[83] Indeed, the Bible was only one path to Jesus, the supreme way being through the Church itself.[84] 'The Bible is not enough,' he argued subsequently. It was a most incomparable library yet the most intolerable of masters.[85] He had taken great care, therefore, to ensure his children only read the Bible when ready and equipped to understand it.[86]

Whilst in Ceylon Donald tried to explain the complexities of Bible study – the multiple translations, themselves biased; the different approaches of Mark, Luke and Matthew. At one point he tried to interpret a passage in John, 'In my father's house are many mansions', a sentence of Scripture he was often quoting. Drawing on William

Temple's *Readings in St John's Gospel*, which had an immense influence on him, he explained carefully the way caravans passed Jesus's village into the desert and the role of the dragoman, the servant who went ahead towards evening, to look for an inn. What Jesus meant by the phrase quoted he said was that 'along the road of life there are many stopping places ... If we believe in Christ, He goes ahead so that He can prepare a place for us, so that where He is, there we may be also.'[87]

Donald returned to such themes frequently. 'The last chapter of St John – this is the Word of God,' he declared at Hyde Park.[88] 'But the second chapter of the Book of Samuel or Leviticus?'[89] For him the Book of Revelation was 'more trouble than it's worth', and 'the Song of Songs is a pagan love story'.[90] 'I do not believe the Bible,' he said on another occasion. 'I believe passages in the Bible.'[91] The most dangerous piece of nonsense therefore was to assert 'the Bible says', for it 'says what you want it to if you look up the appropriate text'.[92] Prophecy was dangerous, too, and though he did not deny there was fulfilment of prophecy, in reality it was 'much more spiritual insight than mechanical foresight'.[93]

Donald's insistence on the Spirit and teaching of Jesus, of course, presumed he knew what it was. Yet students of Scripture often disagreed and so did the Church itself, however much biblical scholars – and Donald had been taught form criticism – found a consensus. 'All that can be understood and gathered from this Book is summed up, consummated in Jesus Christ, who we find in Bethlehem, in Galilee, in Jerusalem, on the Cross, by the empty tomb and then among His friends again,' he had written in 1937.[94] Donald's awareness of the Spirit at work can be understood more clearly perhaps by considering his comment about Bertrand Russell, who had recently explained why he was not a Christian. 'He makes criticism of many things in the life of Jesus that appear in the Bible,' Donald explained. 'By whose standards did Russell make those criticisms? He made them by the standard of the Jesus who already lived in his heart. What other standard is there?'[95]

Donald seems, therefore, in his pneumatology to see a thread – Bible–Church–Believer – through which the Spirit works, yet nowhere explains systematically how they inter-relate and by what authority a particular view is acceptable and another not. When it comes to deciding what the Spirit and teaching of Jesus are then Donald takes the classic Protestant position that personal conviction takes precedence over any other authority. As he said in Ceylon, if this opened the way to mistakes, error, misjudgement, then so be it.[96]

Before Donald could return to England there was a tour of Australia to complete without his wife, who had gone back to London. Large crowds came to some rallies and services, especially those on Christianity and Communism, but not always. Once he had a fierce argument with Buddhists; another time he felt 'a strong smell of mothballs',[97] about Methodism. He did not feel either that the Methodist Church could provide a Christian Socialism that had within it the 'great qualities of the evangelical revival'.[98] Nor did he come across one trade unionist in any church he visited. The service from Alan Walker's congregation, when Donald talked on Christianity and Communism, was broadcast, but Donald found politics in Australia 'almost as cryptic as in Ceylon'.[99]

Tired after his visit there and some two weeks into the tour he needed a rest from preaching. Fortunately there was time for listening to Bach and Schumann and 'dreaming of home',[100] and one night he went to bed early with 'a wad of thrillers'.[101] He also indulged his passion for cricket, listening on the radio to Bradman getting his one hundreth test century. The tour was partly difficult, of course, because letters from home were long in arriving. 'Still no word from Marie,' he wrote, 'I can stand most things but this gets me down.'[102] On 8 November he was able to phone her and this helped.[103] By December, however, the nerves of his leg were troublesome and he had had enough. His final cryptic comment in his Diary conveyed his sentiments precisely: 'December 5th, 1947. Home – and not a moment too soon.'[104]

Once in London again he was soon back on the treadmill he had created, as he played out his many roles. Though he had few funerals to perform there was the normal diet of any parson and weddings and baptisms at which to officiate, though not frequently. Before the war Donald had married mainly people from lower middle-class backgrounds, but now the marriage registers contained the names of what Donald called a 'far more cosmopolitan crowd':[105] a chef, an actor and actress, social workers, an art lecturer, a scientific research officer, a writer, and two men later peers.[106]

The congregation itself was exposed to a greater variety of visitors, too, Marjory Fry speaking on the death penalty,[107] and Bishop Bell, the friend of Bonhoeffer, coming to the 1950 May Anniversary.[108] At one moment Father Beaumont was talking about the Twentieth

Century Folk Mass[109] and at another Harry Corbett and Sooty were visiting the Crèche.[110] Preachers from abroad helped, too, like Alan Walker and Joe Webb and when Donald was often away during his Presidential year Dr Eric Baker and the Rev. Edward Rogers, among others, held the fort. Not long after Donald had returned from his three-months tour Katharine Price Hughes died aged ninety-four. She was the last major link with Hugh Price Hughes and the church had now to shape a new history, if it was to survive in the 1950s.

Kingsway Hall, of course, continued to provide a haven for many diverse groups. In September 1950, for example, district allotment societies met to demand more ground from the LCC.[111] Each year the congregation would sing carols out of doors, too, a tradition which had started on the steps of St Martin-in-the-Fields[112] and then migrated to Trafalgar Square when in 1948 Donald led a choir of 400 from the plinth of Nelson's Column, an idea he pioneered with two American Quakers.[113] By 1953 5,000 were singing carols by the Christmas Tree sent by the Norwegians, now an annual gift.[114] On Christmas Day 1952 there was a great celebration in Kingsway Hall, too, with paper hats, the full traditional dinner, games and competitions, a mock pantomime and a Christmas cake made by the Sisters. The celebration culminated in the film *Oh Mr Porter*. 'It was,' wrote one reporter, 'a perfect Christmas day.'[115]

How did the congregation keep up with all the activities? Partly attending each January the internal mission, usually conducted by Donald. In 1951 he gave four evening addresses, talking about penitence and the need to look back in confession, then to look at Jesus and compare the disciples' response with the Lord's.[116] Secondly, he talked about deliverance from the burden of the past. This implied forgiveness. 'In many cases God takes away the scars,' he taught. 'But His forgiveness costs God something, although it is His free gift to us.'[117] On the third evening Donald's theme was thankfulness and the need to express gratitude in worship and praise, for it contained a cleansing power. Thus prepared, the members of Kingsway attended a service of Holy Communion 'to consummate all that we had thought and experienced',[118] as one member put it.

Donald, too, needed a balance in his life for he lived for Kingsway Hall. Sometimes, if he arrived back late, he would sleep there to be ready early next morning for another day's hard work. Seemingly inexhaustible in 1950, by the autumn of 1955 he had to cut engagements outside London and was suffering from insomnia. Next year he was advised to get away from London and, as a compromise, accepted an invitation to Poland![119] It was perhaps on his 1951 Australian tour that his health first began to crack when on his mission to help the nation-wide Crusade for Christ he was beset by headaches. Though he spoke to 2,000 in Sydney's Hyde Park on consecutive Sundays, to 1,500 on the Yarra River Bank in Melbourne and to another 2,000 outside Brisbane Town Hall, all was not well. Part of the trouble was the controversy about his views on the referendum to outlaw Communism, but also he came up against the conservative nature of the Australian churches. Donald, of course, was in his element speaking on wharves, in iron foundries, railway works, meat factories (a visit to one abattoir turned him into a vegetarian almost overnight) but overall, he felt the tour was unsuccessful. Unusually for him he became introspective and the tendency to melancholy he usually managed to suppress began to obtrude.

The year 1952 saw the twenty-fifth anniversary of Donald's Tower Hill work. He did not believe the church was much nearer 'the secret of getting to the outsider'[120] than when he began, he told an OCW training weekend that February. Yet Donald himself had found a way to reach the secular world, even though he did not know 'what I was talking about', before his late 1940s tours.[121] Like the social work, open-air speaking rooted Donald in reality. 'I would sooner speak on a hundred Tower Hills,' he once told Olive Delves, the cook at Kingsway, 'than get a fractious child to bed.'[122] He was not afraid even when violence erupted as in January 1948, when Communist Party members tried to grab his stand because refused a room at Kingsway for a meeting.[123] Donald could now speak ad lib on almost any topic, but had also learned he needed to speak from a position well above the crowd. 'Take a laugh against yourself as it comes,' he advised, 'and never hit back below the belt. Always be the sportsman, or you'll not have the sympathy of your hearers.'[124]

Did the heckling worry Donald? Not when it was true heckling, for he knew without it his meetings lacked dynamism. Indeed, he once observed he would much rather be heckled than thanked and owed almost everything to Tower Hill and its people.[125] In a moment of candour, too, he admitted he was not always fair. 'Had I been more poised and not at times so "het up",' he confessed, 'I would have answered better.'[126] Sometimes, of course, Donald's opponents changed tack, one of the most persevering, 'who in his mildest moments called me a perishin' liar', offered lozenges after sessions[127] and another, impressed by Donald's patience, stopped heckling because he felt guilty about it.[128] Sometimes, too, Donald was out of his depth, though he seldom admitted this in case he lost control, as with a passing remark about the Monroe Doctrine in America. 'Who are you?' Donald asked a challenger and was taken aback when he replied: 'I'm just a Federal Judge of the USA.'[129]

At Tower Hill and more especially at Hyde Park, since the departure of the dockers made questioning at Tower Hill more sedate, Donald developed a clear technique with hecklers. Words like 'fathead', 'scoundrel', 'silly man', 'rascal', tripped from his lips and phrases like 'You haven't listened to a word I've said', or 'You've got it wrong as usual'. Injunctions to 'ask yourself', 'be sensible', 'I'm sure you will agree with me', were ways he devised to encourage support and win the crowd to his side. He admitted, of course, he was only a 'would-be Christian', which was usually enough, though at Hyde Park in particular there were some who questioned fiercely both his life-style and his politics.

Donald's open-air work was essentially pre-evangelistic and apologetic, though there were converts, too. Indeed, requests to baptize, marry and bury members of the Tower Hill and Hyde Park crowds continued after the war as before. Essentially Donald tried to demonstrate how Christianity touched all life. Moreover, when a heckler needled Donald about the hypocrites in the Church Donald knew that heckler was revealing part of the cultural script of a whole community. He had, therefore, to learn about its attitudes, beliefs and assumptions to present a Christianity which made sense.[130]

There were three clear ingredients to Donald's Gospel advocacy. One was to define clearly what he was talking about. Another was the use of definition as a premise for argument, a third the argument from division, either saying one or other of two contradictory possibilities was true, or untrue, or offering several alternatives, refuting each except the one to be commended.[131] Donald admitted much of his argumentation resembled scholastic deduction, though he was inductive rather than deductive in his thinking. Refutation was important in open-air arguments, too, and exposing an opponent's views by reference to truths already accepted. It was also important to expose linguistic fallacies in opponents.[132] Donald warned, however, against using only the sharpness of the mind. Rather, open-air work should show people genuine love and the exercise of goodwill.[133]

Donald's remarks in November 1968, the weekend Edward Heath

sacked Enoch Powell from the Shadow Cabinet for a speech many considered incited racial animosity, showed his skill. He began by discussing Powell's message, alleging he did not care 'a fig' for the blacks he was repudiating.[134] There was a problem, he conceded, but Powell's solution was fatuous. Jesus's kingdom of God, which implied a multi-racial society, was more fulfilling than either Powell's alternative, or the current situation. No pure 'English' population existed as he assumed.

Where matters of housing were concerned, more people emigrated from Britain than to it, so the housing shortage was caused by the capitalist system. Moreover, there was but one Commonwealth, which had asked its members to fight wars and currently blacks were making contributions to Britain's economy. There was no 'immigrant problem', only English hypocrisy and selfishness to which Enoch Powell appealed, though condemned by Christian faith. Let's have a model of life based on God's kingdom, he concluded, and unlearn the hostility between the races and use the Labour Party to bring it about.[135]

The development of this argument, was, of course, punctuated with interruptions, expostulations and disagreements, which Donald handled deftly and sometimes lightly, for discussion of racism was potentially volcanic. Now with wit and frivolity he prepared his audience to look at it not only pragmatically but theologically.

Questioner: What would you do to cure it?
Soper: What would I do to cure what?
Questioner: Powellism.
Soper: Our friend is asking, 'How do you deal with sin?'
(Laughter) That, of course, is the ultimate question; I'm very glad you asked about it. (Chuckles) It's up my alley if I may say so. (Convulsive laughter) It's not so easy; let's start there. I've been at it for some years, and there's still a fair amount of it going round. Mind you, it's my stock in trade, so I don't want to exhaust it before I retire.[136]

Sometimes Donald tackled large theological themes, as in 1976 at Speaker's Corner, when he discussed the after-life. There is no proof of anything, he alleged, admitting, of course, he could not conceive of eternity or imagine what it might be like, though great music like

Mozart's had a timeless quality. So, too, did love. Death itself was perhaps a passage from one existence to another. Developing this he pointed out that even scientific discovery did not begin with knowledge: it began with faith.[137]

As well as Donald's impact on the general public there were other more intimate influences. Professor Gordon Rupp, for example, used to hear him on Tower Hill and was encouraged thereby to go into the Methodist ministry;[138] and David Lange was turned into a Christian Socialist in the 1960s by his membership at Kingsway Hall. Donald himself was deeply affected, too, by Paul Winter, whose family had died in Auschwitz, whom he met in rags and misery in Hyde Park. Broken by suffering 'he kept himself alive',[139] Donald explained, by examining the 'Trial of Jesus', then writing a book, with a preface by Donald, himself influenced by its thesis about who killed Jesus and why.

What always saved Donald was his irrepressible cockney humour. One Sunday at Speaker's Corner a heckler interrupted Donald in full flow. 'Never mind the politics, Soper – what matters is, is your name in the Lamb's Book of Life?' Donald affected a look of injured pride. 'In it – it's on the cover,' he responded.[140] On another occasion a Communist shouted: 'When we get in power, we'll put you down a mine.' 'I suppose,' Donald said coolly, 'there are places down a mine where one can preach.' A wag in the crowd shouted out: 'Yes – he'll start an underground movement.'[141]

By 1969 there were reports that Donald, now in his sixties and suffering from arthritis, was losing out to hecklers but a reporter found him as lively as ever, using all his old tricks.[142] His open-air Golden Jubilee was in 1977, an achievement surpassed by none. 'I think one would honour him if he had done it for ten years and then found himself too busy,' Harold Wilson observed in the early 1970s. 'But he must be honoured all the more because he has kept it up for nearly half a century ...'[143] Basically, topics had not changed but some new ones had emerged, often reflecting newspaper headlines. 'When I began there were no questions, for instance, on birth control, abortion or homosexuality,'[144] Donald commented. 'One thing that has been beaten into my experience,' he added, 'is that the overarching reason for the decline, both in Church and Christianity generally, is that most people do not believe it.'[145] In such a situation there was only one thing to do: 'slog it out'.[146]

And that Donald proceeded to do, whether the audience was large or small, the weather wet or fine, now haranguing the crowd on the subject of the saints – 'If you want to know about God look at those who are most like him'[147] – then asserting 'the love of God demanded planned parenthood'.[148] 'I intend to go to Holy Communion tonight to get some of the strength to carry out what I profess. I advise the same to you,'[149] he counselled on one occasion, adjuring the crowd on another that 'hating sinners is bad; hating sin is good'.[150]

'I'll be here next week,' he rounded off each excursion in Hyde Park and with that he would be gone, aided by a loyal band of helpers without whom none of his open-air work would have been possible over the years.

Chapter 6

PASTOR, PREACHER AND PRESIDENT

'SOMETIME BEFORE WILL SANGSTER became ill,' Leslie Weatherhead wrote in the late 1960s, 'I wondered whether it might have been a good thing for him, Donald Soper and me to stump the country and try to bring revival, leaving behind our private successes. If we could have made a team, we are so different, we might have done better than Billy Graham.'[1] It was an idea to capture the imagination of thousands, representing as the three ministers did the intellectual, political, emotional and evangelical strands in Methodist preaching. As it was they appeared together only occasionally, at Kingsway Hall, on Wesley Day in the Central Hall, Westminster and sometimes at Methodist Conference meetings, though they used to meet regularly, ideally once a month for a couple of hours, to share ideas.[2]

Donald was intellectually most in tune with Dr Weatherhead. 'To understand him,' the Rev. Brian Duckworth observes, 'you have to understand Weatherhead and the very liberal form in which Methodism received the critical biblical tradition.'[3] Donald learned much personally from Leslie Weatherhead, particularly how Christian faith could be lived and different aspects of it balanced as, like him, he 'sat loose to some of the doctrines'.[4] One of Leslie Weatherhead's books, *The Transforming Friendship*,[5] seems especially to have shaped some of Donald's thinking, for both he and Dr Weatherhead aimed to show how Jesus's friendship made God accessible and personally related to each individual. He also learned from him the importance of the 'new' psychology and the need for the common touch in preaching.[6]

Like Dr Sangster Donald was an evangelical preacher who offered Christ. Even if he perceived the biblical narratives differently, he yet had a similar passion for holiness. Donald, however, believed discipleship was also social and integral, rather than peripheral, to faith and action. For Donald, indeed, as for John Wesley, there was 'no holiness except social holiness'.[7] He was also a preacher who thought hard about the secular age and its doubts, paradoxes and ambiguities,[8] which he felt helped preachers back to the spirit of the Sermon on the Mount, the meaning of the Crucifixion and the relevance of the 'Pentecostal experiments in Communism'.[9]

Sometimes Donald started sermons with humour, as in Trinidad, where he described himself as a Methodist 'who had seen better days'[10] – he had just ceased to be President of the Methodist Conference – and on other occasions he linked his opening to a contemporary issue, as in his sermon on Prayer and the Geneva Conference.[11] Preachers naturally now needed sophistication, for every competence shown by politicians and economists required of them a new relationship between advocacy of the love of God and its mediation to the secular world.[12]

Donald often preached thematically, of course, as on the Seven Deadly Sins, or took phrases like 'in thought and word and deed' and built reflections around them. Yet more were based on expounding a hymn by St Francis Xavier or G.K. Chesterton. Perhaps the most original series took as a theme the hymn 'It's hard to work for God'. Some thought there was insufficient Gospel preaching as he reacted to Faber's words about the difficulties of taking God's part in the world; not losing heart; seeing God in larger terms than people often do, as he explained how impossible it was make the case for Christian justice if a disciple's purview 'was limited to this world'.[13] Yet in this series of sermons Donald was trying to help worshippers understand the importance of perseverance and how to cultivate it, for he knew how hard it was to maintain Christian hope.

Donald seldom wrote his sermons down. Indeed, when in 1960 he gave a series of lectures at Yale Divinity School he had no script, though his lecture stand had blank pages on it as though he was reading from a prepared text.[14] He seemed able to recall incidents and personalities from the past at will and also to use his flowing style, sometimes too flowing, to be sure, to exemplify Phillips Brooks' remark that preaching is truth mediated through personality. He did, however, admit that, though he could be eloquent in spots, he never had the opportunity – 'or perhaps I have been too lazy'[15] – to devote much time to 'the cultivation of a particular twenty minute oration on Sunday',[16] relying instead on 'a certain facility of speech'. 'I confess,' he added, 'I have sometimes stood up in pulpits unprepared.'[17]

As a preacher Donald seldom expounded biblical passages in their historical and linguistic background, though his expositions of the Lord's Prayer, the Sermon on the Mount and a passage from Romans, given to local preachers in training in 1944, indicate that he could. Rather, he returned repeatedly to over-arching themes – the significance of the birth and death of Jesus, the search for the kingdom and the need to be nourished by the Eucharist as the Church, the body of Christ, sought the pentecostal experience of sharing and fellowship, which he saw as the norm for Christian living.

Donald's impact through preaching was considerable because he drew on personal experience and tried to emulate the clarity he learned from Professor Joad of *The Brains Trust*, who insisted on using words intelligibly, advice Donald took seriously, particularly Joad's ability to put truths simply, even if at times it mean they had to be over-simplified.[18] Rachel Newton, then teaching deprived children on the outskirts of Liverpool, heard Donald's ninetieth birthday sermon on faith, hope and love, which also impressed Tony Benn, and it made her want to return to Kirkby and re-double her efforts. 'If Donald could have that effect on me when he was ninety,' she observed, 'what effect must he have had on people earlier in his life?'[19] One of them, Kathleen Richardson, the first woman President of the Methodist Conference, was certainly affected deeply by his sermons in the 1960s and they were part of the process which led her to seek ordination.[20]

Donald often spoke graphically, as in 1940 he urged the congregation to: 'Ask God tonight that you may go with Jesus Christ on Palm Sunday, that you may go with Jesus Christ on Good Friday; that you may share in the triumph of Easter Sunday.'[21] Similarly striking was his description of prayer: 'The thing which binds us together when we pray is that we try to see the footmarks of Jesus Christ. And as we see those footmarks, and as we try to put our own feet in those marks, then we can pray.'[22] He had, too, a common-sense approach to Christianity, not confusing his listeners with difficult questions of metaphysics, which he eschewed, though he preached occasionally on the doctrine of the Trinity, but demonstrating how practical Jesus's Gospel was. So he would suggest that 'Jesus takes us to the lilies, to the harvest, to the housewife, to the epileptic, to the shepherd and shows us God at work.'[23]

Disciples should not be surprised at how much they had to learn he once intimated. He wrote:

> It does not necessarily follow that a work of Stravinsky has no musical merit, because on first hearing it, or even after hearing it many times, you can't grasp its meaning, or its counterpoint bewilders and irritates you. I am not for a moment suggesting you haven't tried to understand the Gospel; but to enjoy Stravinsky demands a special equipment in musical appreciation; catch his spirit and you will see the significance of his strange harmonies. So with Christianity: before its words can become intelligible to the mind its spirit must be captured by the heart.[24]

The core of Donald's preaching was, of course, a desire to encourage disciples to act in society. Moreover, if there were doctrines they found difficult perhaps fewer might as easily suffice. Christians may 'have to go many days through desert country,' he explained, but should not worry provided they had their iron rations with them, 'rations of belief – a belief in God, a confidence in Jesus, and a knowledge of His Cross'.[25]

Donald was also aware there was an art in sermon construction as he indicated to his local preachers in 1944. First there was the formal sermon, pictorial, expositional and biblical, where a preacher took an individual text and expounded the passage, traced it historically, then pointed the moral and showed its contemporary application. An alternative sermon would be the reflective, personal or mystical one, based on a passage like 'He restoreth my soul.' There was yet a third type, he considered, which could be hortatory or declamatory, in which a topical problem was presented and its solution suggested.

A good sermon for Donald dealt with one subject only, perhaps the text 'He restoreth my soul', where a preacher could use the old-fashioned evangelical method, taking the words in order, or make the experience of the Psalmist, the disciple and the preacher the three ingredients. Break the ice in the introduction by briefly stating the sermon's task, he advised, then analyse the theme and end with a conclusion and application, which should contain an appeal. Use different types of illustration, preferably topical, he added – a picture, metaphor, allegory or image; give personal experience, too, and use scientific or historical data, including illustrations from nature.

He was as concerned about delivery as vocabulary and quotations, which should be brief. Use words which convey exact, especially pictorial, meaning, he counselled, employing humour if possible. It was dangerous to consider Christianity as a way of thinking: rather, it must relate to concrete situations and preachers should present Jesus as the model of the point being made, though drawing also on Church history, doctrine and the Old and New Testaments.[26]

Donald was naturally capable of a sophisticated analysis of a text as he showed in the 1944 class, basing his exposition of the Sermon on the Mount on form criticism, as he explained what might be the original source passed on in oral tradition. Here, making use of a knowledge of Aramaic and Greek to find cross-references to other parts of the Bible, especially the Psalms, he was at pains to point out a comparison with Genesis as he looked at the structure the writer of Matthew employed. The Sermon on the Mount, he taught, should be interpreted as a holiness and kingdom passage, for which disciples must strive, though he did not indicate whether the kingdom was now or in the future.[27]

Like Tolstoy Donald Soper regarded the Sermon on the Mount's injunctions as realizable and they reproached the churches for weakening Jesus's demands, especially on peace questions. For both the key sentence was 'do not resist one who is evil' – the demand of powerlessness. Yet Donald had affinities, too, with the theologian Leonard Ragaz, for whom the sermon was a counsel for the oppressed, and 'the unheard message of world revolution through God . . .'[28] The key question, however, remained unresolved. Was the Sermon on the Mount applicable only to Jesus's followers? One commentator wrote:

> Even if the Sermon on the Mount does not place in our hearts a political, juridically derivable conception of acting by which states and people can be governed, we may not infer from this a revocation of its claim. Thus, as Jesus himself, in his life and death, set a universally valid example, the Christian community is called to place itself under the word of its Lord, to shape the realm of the church in accordance with the Sermon on the Mount, and to realize an exemplary existence that will shine into the world like the light into the darkness.[29]

Donald, of course, knew that discipleship was difficult and that people shrink from some Gospel exhortations, once observing:

The trouble is that though we are glad to go to the wedding feast with Him, to sit at His feet on the Mount, to share in the wonder of His transfiguration and even join with Him in proclaiming that the Kingdom of Heaven is at hand, the day comes when He says, 'We go to Jerusalem,' and then we forsake Him . . .[30]

For Donald, therefore, all preaching focused on the Cross. Even though Christians could not carry Christ's Cross, they could and must catch something of that spirit of self-denial in Jesus 'who emptied Himself of all but love'. Because of this he attached much importance to the Good Friday Three Hours Service for over forty years and explored meditatively the depths of each remark from the Cross.

Donald always preached that the forgiveness offered by Jesus, who displayed in His death 'those qualities which He advertised so completely in His life',[31] was God's love taking away the power and destructiveness of sin,[32] which gave a hope and confidence to be found nowhere else. But he also taught that 'forgiveness is the preparedness to take upon ourselves the role of reconciliation',[33] where the person who had done evil was treated as a brother or sister who could become more worthy. Was the Kingsway congregation in such a mood of forgiveness? he enquired. Or even determined to forgive? If so, Jesus's first words from the Cross, 'Father, forgive,' enabled human beings, by God's grace, to act and be 'God-like'.[34]

Donald's other great preaching theme – the kingdom – seemed to possess him always. 'We cannot,' he wrote, 'hope to establish the Kingdom of God until its principles and plans have been declared by Christian preachers.'[35] The Church must expect the traditional Christian metaphysic to decay further.[36] 'Preach the Kingdom of God,' he advised, undaunted, 'and discover the power and the grace of that Kingdom in Eucharistic worship,' iron rations which would prove sufficient for the times.[37] What did Donald mean by the kingdom? The world itself had an innate moral order which would only blossom when its roots were set in God's kingdom, the key elements of which were peace, purity, honesty and unselfishness, he taught. 'As we link ourselves . . . with them,' he concluded, 'life becomes intelligible and worthwhile. This is the great justification for the Christian ethic . . .'[38]

With his carefully worked out message Donald became a familiar figure within Methodism and in many Anglican cathedrals like

Canterbury and Chester, for he was guaranteed to make a success of the 'great occasion', like the centenary service of St Paul's, Stoney-croft, in Liverpool. From Sheffield to Bristol, Walsall to South-ampton, he took his message, tailored to the occasion, which he would also deliver abroad, particularly in America and Canada, once lecturing with Paul Tillich at Berkeley.

What then was Donald's Christology? If Studdert Kennedy empha-sized the suffering Jesus and Dick Sheppard the Jesus of good fellowship, Donald emphasized Jesus's full humanity, the man of peace, who cared for and healed people and showed God as Father, a human being out to revolutionize the world by his convictions. There was, as a consequence, little in Donald of the Jesus of Paul, or the writers of Colossians and Ephesians or Revelation, for he rooted himself firmly in the Gospels, especially the Gospel of St John. Indeed he seemed more gripped by the everyday than the mystical. Nevertheless, Donald was clear Jesus was not a first among equals and was content to say in the phrase consecrated by the Church 'the only begotten son of God' if used 'domestically', as a theological interpretation, but if in the open air would say that Jesus was 'the perfect photograph of God'.[39]

Not everyone liked either Donald's style or sermon content, the Anglican preacher Cleverley Ford for one. He considered,

> The feeling is produced of being in contact with a man after the stamp of one of the Hebrew eighth-century prophets. There is no artificiality about his speaking, no protrusion of sermon outlines or making the matter conform to a self-chosen style. He speaks straight, not with symbols, opening his mouth because he has something to say.[40]

Nevertheless he had doubts about his theology. He explained:

> We are left with the impression that man could make this world a better place by bringing in the Kingdom of God if only he would follow Christ, especially in His life of sacrifice. But has not God done anything for us sinful men except to provide a supreme example of the sacrificial life? Is this good news? Is this all that can be preached to modern man?[41]

Stewart Denyer first heard Donald Soper speak at the old Spurgeon's Tabernacle when the daring and courage with which he spoke about the Gospel's social implications thrilled him. Then, however, Donald had not been attracted by the vigour and colour of the Catholic faith as he had,[42] partly the legacy of his family background.[43] What turned Donald into a Eucharistic Christian was his encounter with the Rev. J. Ernest Rattenbury, one of the original members of the Methodist Sacramental Fellowship (MSF) founded in 1935, who had written two books, *The Eucharistic Doctrines of John and Charles Wesley* and *The Evangelical Doctrines of Charles Wesley's Hymns*, where he argued the Wesley brothers had combined in theory and practice the frequent celebration of Holy Communion, which they saw partly as a converting ordinance. MSF members had been shaped by this outlook and Donald found them 'appropriate company'[44] for discussing the Eucharistic truths to which Dr Rattenbury had alerted him.

In its early years the fellowship passed through troubled waters, as *Joyful News* attacked it and some leading members became Roman Catholics,[45] but by the late 1930s its relation to Methodism was clarified when Dr Rattenbury, now MSF's President, had defended it in the 1938 Methodist Conference and agreed to modifications in its aims. The war years and their immediate aftermath produced an inevitable slowing down yet the fellowship survived.[46] By 1949 London members were meeting at Kingsway Hall,[47] and Donald, now a member, wrote in its magazine about Holy Communion and the Order of Christian Witness to explain the link he had made between evangelism and the Eucharist, probably the first time this had been made so explicit since the eighteenth century.[48] He knew nothing which presented Christianity in word and deed to compare in clarity, precision and economy, he said. As a surprised campaigner once remarked – 'It's all there in fifteen minutes,'[49] adding that in one campaign 6,000 people had taken part in nine great Communion services.[50]

In 1950 Dr Rattenbury retired as President and Donald took over. Admitting the group was better understood in Roman Catholic and Anglican circles he urged members to make the Fellowship's work more widely known within Methodism,[51] at the 1951 annual MSF Conference stating it stood for the purification of worship, which was often slovenly and careless, without form or structure. Once a quarter at least, he considered, Communion, with sermon, should be the main service and at circuit rallies it could also be celebrated. Flirtation with fundamentalism, and a false individualism going by the name of evangelism, should be avoided.[52] Churches themselves should be beautiful as an aid to worship, he added.[53]

Donald became President of the Methodist Conference in 1953, a watershed year for him as Dr Scott Lidgett had recently died at a great age and so had Dr Henry Bett, a pacifist colleague, who in the 1940s had publicly urged him not to work so hard. Every President brings to the post a particular approach. A number, W.E. Sangster, Colin Morris, John Vincent, were really themselves 'writ large'. One, Gordon Rupp, had a team with him. Donald, likely to be more controversial than most, proposed to link the Eucharist and an open-air event as the focus for his Presidency. He wanted, he said, to strengthen and affirm the meaning and importance of the sacrifice and self-oblation of the Church, and to demonstrate the marriage of work and worship which lay at the heart of the incarnation.[54]

When Donald was inducted at the Birmingham Conference (for the first time the opening service, the Order of Morning Prayer, was televised), there were protests from those who had not appreciated Methodist worship was as much liturgical as free. There were few protests, however, as Donald celebrated the Eucharist across Britain. Indeed, as he told MSF members in a letter written between changing trains, there had been very large crowds, nearly everyone had come to the Lord's Table and he himself had been gratified and humbled by the evidence of the evangelical power which he had found 'within the disciplined framework of this historic means of grace',[55] adding that he needed their prayers because the celebration of Holy Communion almost daily was a serious spiritual problem for the celebrant. By March he was in thankful mood for still there were large attendances and he was discovering 'the doors through which we ought to go are ajar'.[56]

Donald's understanding of worship was deepened immediately after the Presidency during his visit to Russia, where he encountered for the first time the Russian Orthodox Church, whose strength he found lay in 'the beauty, reverence, awe and mystery of the Divine Liturgy'.[57] 'I shall never forget,' he commented later, 'the rapt attention of the worshippers, the unmistakable sense of power, and, most of all, the pervasive feeling that something was happening to those who were gathered before the Lord's table.'[58] One Russian priest confided in Donald that sometimes he had to say 'twenty "Our Fathers" in a row before the materialist barrier breaks down and the way is open for Jesus to come in'.[59] On holiday in Russia in the 1960s

Donald celebrated a Eucharist in an upper room in a hotel in Leningrad, which brought his Eastern Europe experiences to a climax in one symbolic act. He wrote later:

> We were able to make use of a ledge by a window as the Holy Table and as I lifted up the cup and looked out across the city of Leningrad, I remembered the words of Jesus – 'and if I be lifted up I will draw all men unto me'. I felt with a new significance the tremendous challenge of these words, especially in a country officially pledged to the elimination of Christianity.[60]

Donald had become President halfway through the Year of Advance of the world Methodist community, as British Methodists responded to its summons. In January 1953, Dr Sangster had caught the media's attention when he had listed things he considered 'a religious revival might do for Britain, including a reduction in the divorce rate and an increase in the output of work'.[61] Donald had then responded saying it was of little use to hope for a revival of religion until the mass of people had been given the opportunity to grasp what 'religion is and is not'. Now, in his address to the Methodist Conference as President, he explored the topic further.

If Methodism had any doubts about his underlying motivation (he had been elected President by a small majority), these may well have been cast aside during his explanation of the context in which Christian faith had to be offered, after he had reassured doubters he would seek to represent the whole Church.[62] Revival, he reminded them, had not come, especially among the urban artisan masses, despite many efforts. In fact there was a ravine stretching between Church and world. There was large-scale doubt, too, about the supremacy of the Christian faith in a society which encouraged scientific methods at every level. Indeed, many came to church not necessarily for moral or theological but for aesthetic reasons. Others hesitated to respond when they compared the non-violence of the Hindu Gandhi with the power politics of 'so-called Christian statesmen'; or the tolerance and charity of Buddhists with the persecuting zeal of Christian sects. It was useless, moreover, he continued, to deride the material goods Communism aimed to provide, for great benefits had been bought. Two other facts checked Christian impact – the feeling people had that Christian ethics had more to do with

Governments than with God; and the sexual changes wrought by the pill. Rather than turn away from these events he suggested Christians must seek a prophetic way through them, which could not be done if they continued to back armaments against development.

Jesus Christ still claimed his allegiance, he testified. Indeed 'for all the goodness and greatness of the other world religions ... it is ... by the standards of Jesus that their goodness and greatness are measured ... it is Christianity or chaos'.[63] Warning them against over-spiritualizing, he recognized the true welfare state was 'utterly dependent on the Gospel of Jesus Christ, alike for its direction and its spirit'.[64] The answer to the secular state, therefore, 'with its terrific power',[65] was the kingdom of God. Indeed, he was convinced secular society could be outmatched by the Divine Society, for it commanded 'illimitable resources'.[66] 'I believe it is my responsibility to lead,' he said a week later. 'I ask you to follow me. I will not lead you astray, partly because of your prayers, but mainly because I myself have seen the way. It is not the only road, but it is the royal road . . .'[67]

Donald had thus launched his Presidency, laced with his characteristic humour, as, taking extracts from Keats' 'On first looking into Chapman's Homer', he made a wry comparison with certain lines and the Conference Agendas.[68] He had, he told delegates also, bought his Presidential suit: within a week his house had been burgled and the suit stolen. (Laughter) 'I have looked carefully round the conference.' (Loud laughter)[69] Doubtless Donald's friend from South Africa, Dr Joe Webb, who was present, was reminded by Donald's skilful handling of this large assembly of the actor he had seen emerging in Cambridge, especially in the matter of timing. More seriously Donald linked this high peak of his ministry with his mother, who was present, and his father, who was too crippled to be there, acknowledging his debt to them and to Marie Soper.[70]

During the Birmingham conference Donald had held one big open-air gathering, his adrenalin flowing freely, when he addressed 800 in Birmingham's Bull Ring, covering topics like the infallibility of the Church, birth control, the Virgin Birth, pacifism and Communism. By August, adrenalin still flowing, he was out on the campaign trail, taking part in an OCW mission in Oldham, which included addressing large numbers at lunch-time open-air meetings outside two firms.[71] By September he was in Exeter, where there was a crowd of 2,000 to hear him, with the same number attending a question and answer session the next night. He visited a steam laundry and the fire brigade during the campaign and answered questions put by 300 prisoners in Exeter City Prison.[72]

'Wesley believed that if you love God and if you cast yourself in faith on Jesus Christ,' he said in a broadcast in September, 'you can have the conviction inside you that what you are doing is right.' He added, 'You will still have to meet your sorrows, but they will not break you. You will still have your moments of doubt. But you can still have that inner conviction that all things work together for good to them that love God.'[73] That September Donald paid a visit to Watford, the local paper describing how nearly 1,000 stood by the pond in Watford High Street and 'while cars drove past noisily said the Lord's Prayer . . .'[74] It also reported his 'Soperisms', perhaps the first time Donald's pithy and aphoristic comments had been so called.

By Christmas the *Evening Standard* was giving inches of column on Donald's Presidency. In newspaper libraries he had graduated to the large size cutting envelopes, it reported, still columns behind the Archbishop of Canterbury, who rated eleven envelopes, but soon due for a box to himself.[75] The interview it conducted with Donald allowed him to express his views and reveal his humanity – his colleagueship at Kingsway Hall with Fela Sowande ('off duty we used to have some Memphis style duets,' he admitted)[76] and his love of philosophy, detective stories and popular films. 'Is he just a Big 'Ead?' the columist asked, or even a meddlesome crank? No: he wants to make people think, 'to persuade them . . . not bully them,' Donald summed himself up.[77]

That autumn he met thousands, 11,000 alone in the Liverpool district in the open air, in halls and churches, including nearly 1,000 at the Gladstone Docks, more at the Pier Head. It was the same turn-out in Wigan, Southport and St Helens. 'I have tried,' he summed up at half-time, 'to bring before the Methodist people the truth that that the Christian life is a marriage of work and worship, a blend of controversy and communion.'[78] He had, of course, tried to keep his Kingsway Hall commitments but was able to be there only every other Sunday. He did manage to lead the internal mission, however, because he set such a high priority on it, but a colleague took his place as Chair of all the social work projects.

By the end of January he was in Plymouth, competing with biting cold and Plymouth Argyle as he stood in brown overcoat and scarf but no hat on a small platform on one of the city's few remaining bomb sites. Further visits, despite snow and sleet, did not daunt Donald or prevent him from preaching on an open-air site on the Moor at Sheffield after a question and answer session with 300 university students in March, or holding a small open-air meeting in Truro on a tour of Cornwall in April, when the British Legion refused to attend the service because of his pacifist views. During this tour, such was his stamina he was able to attend twenty functions in five days.

Back in the north of England by May, he led a long procession of witness to a spacious bomb site in Hull where, against a backdrop of war-scarred buildings, he addressed hundreds in the cold night air from the back of a lorry, a pattern repeated in Doncaster and Barnsley, where the celebration of Holy Communion and other events surpassed all expectations. His vitality seemed unflagging. His great stores of exact knowledge on a wide variety of subjects were always at the call of his ready wit; and with great good humour and urbanity, not in all cases shared by his questioners, he dealt 'with inquiries varying from the H-bomb to vegetarianism'.[79] In Llandudno in June, 1,500, many of whom had waited two hours, filled the bandstand area to hear him as the sturdy and cassocked figure, sea behind him and hills and mountains in front, addressed the crowds like a latter-day Wesley.[80]

One major controversy of Donald's Presidency involved a dispute about the Greater London Crusade launched by Billy Graham. Speaking to lay people in London he had warned against the use of 'totalitarian methods' in presenting the claims of the Gospel. Some passages in Dr Graham's latest book he considered were 'intellectual rubbish' and 'emotional escapism'. A revival of biblical literalism was a short cut which would not contribute to the kingdom of God.[81] Unusually, the *Methodist Recorder* rebuked him for his antagonism to Billy Graham in a paragraph headed 'Evangelism and Tolerance'.[82] That April in the Castle Grounds in Barnstaple fundamentalists attacked him with phrases like 'Blasphemy' and 'Child of the Devil'.[83] It was the same during his thirty-hour trip to Belfast when Ian Paisley stood under a banner saying 'Dr Soper denies the Virgin Birth of Christ', as he conducted his first open-air meeting in the city.[84] For the remainder of his time as President, and indeed in the ensuing years, the issue of Dr Graham and the need to link personal and social convictions in evangelism would follow him wherever he went.

He had many detractors, of course, for his remarks about evangelism. Yet he had his defenders, too. 'No greater modern evangelist lives today than Dr Soper,' wrote Dr J.E. Rattenbury, now a very old man.[85] 'He preaches the full Gospel and individual conversion, as well as a new Christian social order.' Charles Wood, who was not a Methodist, also wrote in Donald's defence. 'What is expected of a President?' he asked. 'Must he be a saint, have no ideas of his own, and just hold services in a church which are not too disturbing to his hearers? If so, you have elected the wrong man.'[86]

Throughout the Presidential year Donald Soper played several roles besides those of controversialist and sacramentalist, as he switched almost effortlessly from one to the other. One of these was pastoral care as he tried to do something about the plight of ministers' widows. At the focus of his concern was his sense that because Jesus had washed the disciples' feet, so must his followers, as he said in his Presidential sermon.[87] Jesus had also said that the quality of that service must spring from love. Love was goodwill on fire; love was expendability; love was that quality whereby Christians persistently sought other people's good. It was this quality he always tried to bring into his pastoral work, exemplified by a strange story concerning a friend he had known in the 1920s. Years later during a sermon Donald suddenly became convinced he must contact his friend and immediately after the service therefore drove across London to his house. His wife opened the door and told Donald that suddenly that morning he had been taken ill and died – at the very time Donald was preaching.

Donald was seldom as intuitive as that but was always more than a rationalist or a socialist politician. 'Have you ever had a parishioner come to you and say, "Look, I've just had this amazing experience"?' Shaun Joynson once asked him. When Donald admitted that he had he was asked how he counselled them. Donald responded by saying it was necessary to 'respect the experience, not to cast doubts upon it'.[88] For himself, he had to admit such occurrences were rare, though his wife had experienced visions of his younger brother 'standing at the end of the bed one night',[89] whereas he had none. Yet he knew the world was a far more mysterious place than many allowed and people's perceptions more complex than sometimes even they were willing to admit.

To those who saw only the public figure it was often a surprise to discover how much time each day Donald gave up to people like the minister whose son was killed in a cycling accident, with whom he shared his own grief over his brother's death. Often such interviews were at short notice or with no notice at all and much later, sometimes when they had forgotten their troubles, Donald would ask discreetly 'whether they are safe at the other side'.[90] A measure of this commitment can be seen in miniature in the story of an alcoholic who had remained dry for eighteen months and then began drinking again. In utter despair, the keener because he had been sober for so long, he now felt in an abyss from which he would never recover. 'But he will; *I know he will*,' Donald told his congregation. 'All the same, I know how he felt. I have, and I am sure most of us have, known that kind of despair, when the bottom seems to be knocked out of your world. You set your store on certain things. For a long time they seem to work, and then they fail . . .'[91]

In his sermons Donald often recounted incidents which made it clear he had a pastoral side. He was feeling sad, he said, during one sermon, as just before the service he had been told a friend of his, whom he had known at Wesley House, and whom he had seen two weeks before, had died. 'He was frail and weak,' he indicated, 'and in great physical distress, but he had great spiritual peace.'[92] Though not in theological agreement with him Donald conveyed by this story his capacity to accept people with qualities different from his. 'Donald Soper has been able to be inclusive about those with whom he disagrees,'[93] Dr Pauline Webb has observed, a facet of his personality which has made it easier for people to seek him out when in need, whether in the Labour Party, at Hyde Park or in church. Lady Stocks, for example, as she grew to know, 'even to love him',[94] through their work together saw Donald 'gently and tactfully'[95] come to the aid of colleagues in distress, one example among hundreds of Donald's pastoral care which must remain hidden.

Donald regarded his pastoral role as much for his own benefit as for those he helped.[96] Most people, he discovered, needed a listener for they knew what they wanted, but it helped if a pastor could imagine a problem creatively. If Donald could be 'either the dustbin or the chalice into which they put their troubles',[97] then pastoral activities became real, he found, as he brought his horse sense[98] rather than trained counselling skills to bear on problems. Some, like long-standing legal ones, were less tractable, of course, and minds warped by something which they repeated over and over again. Sometimes confession helped, too, but not in the formal sense. During one of

Donald's one-to-one sessions a revolver was produced, which its owner had been tempted to use. A practical pastoral response was needed so Donald agreed to hand it over to the police, who eventually agreed to receive it.[99]

In discussions of intimate problems Donald discovered the importance of both confidence and discretion. Once, too, he had to lay down the conditions on which his silence would be observed. But over the years a certain realism set in as he realized pastoral activities often failed if the pastor sought them 'as events which have come to a terminus'.[100] Indeed, sometimes he had to say he was unable to help any more and asked the person in trouble to leave and only return much later.[101] He found baptisms, weddings and funerals were an opportunity for the Gospel, especially if he could talk to people beforehand and never hesitated to raise the sexual side of marriage when preparing couples. Like many Methodist ministers, provided he was sure of the bona fides of those entering a second marriage, he was prepared to marry them.

Sometimes Donald was asked to handle more public occasions like the funeral of Lord Underhill, when the Front Bench of the Labour Party in the House of Lords was present among the mourners, or the memorial service for Sir Hugh Foot (Lord Caradon) in the Central Hall, Westminster. At another time, in St Mary-le-Strand, he preached at a Taxi Drivers' Service, to mark 333 years of London's licensed taxi service and had an opportunity to be a pastor in an inter-faith context, for membership of the Licensed Taxi Drivers' Association, who had organized the service, was 50 per cent Jewish.[102]

Perhaps his most delicate pastoral situation occurred when Tony Hancock died. A memorial service for the comedian was held in St Martin-in-the-Fields and his mother, whom Donald knew, invited him to speak at it. He later wrote:

> The occasion was a very moving one. I had known Tony Hancock a little, admired his professional skill enormously, and I felt as we sang Bunyan's hymn 'Who would true valour see' that there was ample justification for gathering his friends together to remember one who, with many struggles and much failure, has brought pleasure to millions and who was making a genuine pilgrimage to a country of which as yet he knew so little.[103]

'Love, as Christ taught it, makes other men's sorrow *our* sorrow, their joy *our* joy,' Donald had once written. 'We are responsible to God for ourselves – and for one another.'[104] In the service for Tony Hancock he exemplified his eloquent sentiments.

Sometimes Donald affected the lives of others through his writing. Jack House was one who, when only fifteen, heard Donald speak in Bristol and read his book *Practical Christianity Today*, a gathering together of thirty Broadcast Talks, the five related to Christmas later issued as *Singing Towards Bethlehem*. But recently 'converted', and finding himself in a narrow, fundamentalist Christian community, he came to appreciate that discipleship meant following Jesus in the world rather than withdrawing into the Church,[105] an insight which led him to embrace CND, Greenpeace and the Labour Party, and to make links with the Iona Community and the Franciscans.[106]

Donald's travels also sensitized him to the pastoral needs of individuals and communities. Visiting Bute Town, the dock area of Cardiff, before he went to sleep one night he 'cudgelled my brains' about what ought to be the Christian attitude to those who were often 'the flotsam and jetsam of greedy and ruthless individuals'.[107] Again, in Colombo, he walked its streets and was shocked at the sight of the rickshaw coolies dragging people around the city in the humid sun.[108] Love in action meant a change in the structures of society, too, Donald knew, if the broken people in Bute Town and Colombo were to be helped.

Once, perhaps surprisingly, he contributed to a book called *Pieces of Hate*, along with Mary Whitehouse, A.L. Rowse, Ann Leslie and others. Donald's contribution was on ecclesiastical fascism. He detested fascists, and fascism, he confessed, in whatever form it emerged. Was his hatred justified? He had an uncomfortable feeling that it was not as ingenuous or as pure as he would like to think. Was he, he wondered, a hater of totalitarianism because in his less guarded moments he was 'attracted to it'?[109] 'Am I,' he asked himself 'actuated by false modesty and a sneaking wish for superiority?'[110] when opposed to pride in others. Whatever the psychological jungle in which his thoughts dwelt he intended to go on hating fascism, he concluded. 'I may have acquired this bête noir by a somewhat more dubious mental transaction than I confessed but I believe that it is theologically and practically a "good buy" and can therefore be of real value in the quest for the good life in which all hatred will be unnecessary ...'[111] But will it? If Donald the pastor knew from personal encounters about the ambiguities and paradoxes of life, including his own, can love ever transcend the finitude of all experience in dealing with their conflicts, angers and fears?

As a minister he had to learn to forgive others and his own fallibility. He had to learn, too, to be diligent and discreet, which involved both openness and distance, two threads running throughout his life. The way to get close to Donald Soper the parson, therefore, was to listen attentively to his ordination addresses, where he urged intellectual honesty and the need to find more than one place from which to speak one's mind as he had.[112] How do you preach, he went on, when you are tired or suffering? The answer was to be found in disciplined, objective worship. Be obedient, too, he urged, and remember Holy Communion was a converting ordinance. He felt, he added, the most exhausting part of a minister's life was the continual drain on energy which people's troubles caused. 'It comforts me,' he went on, 'when I realize what a poor fish I am to think that I must love people a little because I listen to them better than I did.'[113]

He believed, he said, that if ministers really put themselves alongside people they would love them, especially if they saw their calling and message against an eternal background.[114] Love for the Church could be a strong scaffold, too, in the ups and downs of ministry.[115] However, there was no easy method to reach those outside the Church, but a genuine personal care was needed for those within earshot. He was satisfied that love did conquer all and if they showed persistence, the supreme mark of faithfulness, because others were brothers and sisters in Christ, they would find a great reward.[116]

What each minister did with loneliness was important, he reckoned. Indeed, the calibre of ministry would largely depend on the character of the minister's inward, spiritual life.[117] How will you cope with the silences in your spiritual life, he queried,[118] again making it clear that for him Christianity was obedience, not only the obedience which came gladly, 'but that obedience which is dark and dangerous'.[119] 'Look away from yourself,' he advised finally, to let God 'finish in you every work to which He has called you'.[120]

The devotional strand which Donald revealed in his ordination addresses emerged again in 1956. Hitherto he had created books from his journeys and broadcasts. *All His Grace* was different for it was an extended meditation on Jesus which could lead Christians to a modern imitation of Christ. To any at the 1980 ordination service, conducted by Harry Morton, a minister Donald deeply influenced, when he said on occasions he had carried a rosary 'though I do not accept many of the beliefs that go with it',[121] *All His Grace* was not surprising. But for those who did not see Donald Soper's activities rooted firmly in his encounter with God his book, still in 1994 in use at Wesley House, Cambridge, was puzzling.

For Donald the rosary was an emblem of remembrance, helping to bring him back to things temporarily lost.[122] Similarly, his reflections on the eight facets in the diamond which was Christ's life had deepened his awareness of God's grace. 'I remember Martin Luther's insistence on the primacy of that "moral union" that Jesus enjoyed with the Father,' he wrote in his introduction, as he explained his book related primarily to 'the moral approach to the Cross of Jesus',[123] for it was the goodness of Christ which challenged Donald's sinfulness, acted decisively in human history and made all things new.[124] Watching Jesus going to his death, his mind set on fulfilling his vocation, taught Donald 'the marvellous economy' of his character.[125] Moreover, Jesus had serenity, peace and an integration Donald knew he lacked, often refusing to centre his actions on the known will of God, which had bedevilled his mind and plagued him 'so often with fears and anxieties'.[126]

Jesus's courage as He concentrated on God's will for Him, seized Donald, too, especially the quiet heroism from the Cross 'of a man ruling His spirit with iron discipline'.[127] He was indeed, Donald considered, 'the great statesman of courage',[128] with a bravery disciplined and canalized until it became the perfect instrument of power.[129]

Donald's response to Jesus's honesty was related to his respect for truthfulness. Like '*logos* for St John, truthfulness for Him was active power',[130] he maintained. By contrast Donald felt he was more academic and passive, wanting to 'bolster it with diplomacy'. Yet when he had 'resisted the temptation to deceive'[131] the result had been remarkable. Donald quoted the words of the German hymn-writer 'O Jesus Christ, grow Thou in me, And all things else recede',[132] when he considered meekness, the third facet of the diamond, the litmus test for which was the capacity to distinguish between 'amour propre' and 'righteous indignation'. Compared with Jesus, able to denounce enemies and condemn sins because indifferent to personal prestige, Donald knew he dare not ascribe righteous indignation to himself 'because of the self-interest that stains my motives'.[133] There was, too, he continued, a kind of nakedness belonging to meekness and cross-bearing to which he responded, partly because on the Cross Jesus had emptied Himself of all but love and called him, too, to empty himself of pride and violence so he could wield the Cross as he carried it.[134]

Hopefulness, one of Donald's continual themes, he saw in Jesus as persistent cheerfulness and buoyancy of spirit,[135] which made His handling of His friends' perfidy a positive challenge to them.[136] So Donald hoped God would take his own disappointments and turn them to occasions of new achievement. 'If He knew the medical answer to cancer and kept silent about it, His intellectual perfection is being maintained at the expense of his moral goodness,' Donald observed of Jesus's knowledge.[137] Also if 'sinlessness' meant Jesus met every simple temptation with an immediate moral response, or the complete absence of moral imperfection, he had no conception of what it meant.[138] Yet he wanted to preserve the idea of Jesus as sinless, because He achieved the topmost peak of moral quality,[139] from the Cross itself exhibiting positive, rather than negative, emphases, so great was the expulsive power of that love.[140]

Donald was also anxious to preserve Christ's humanity as he considered Jesus's faith, so depicted Him as a man limited by the same frontiers of the mind as those around Him. Moreover, some elements in Jesus's faith, like struggle, were the same as Donald's.[141] Indeed, for Donald faith in God was hard to come by and harder to keep, as the arguments *against* theistic belief seemed almost as persuasive as those *for* it. However, in the struggle to believe, Donald found a truth beyond doubt through his discipleship, as Jesus's words 'Seek and ye shall find; ask and you shall receive, knock and it shall be opened to you', became apposite.[142]

Love was the crown of all, a total activity of the personality in the service of others, which shone from the Cross,[143] a love rooted in will rather than feelings, which had simplified and clarified his thinking, he indicated.[144] Sometimes he felt 'little or no zest for the life of Christian love',[145] and at others almost cynical because of its ineffectiveness 'in this wicked world'.[146] Then he had realized his response must be what he saw perfectly in Jesus: 'the performance of goodwill, the persistent intention to seek the good of others'.[147]

As his extended meditation ended he suggested a way out of human ambiguity and double-mindedness because Christians were 'partakers of Christ's goodness'.[148] Indeed, was there any point in thinking upon Jesus's goodness, if they were but 'watchers of a splendid, remote and inaccessible Everest of moral attainment'?[149] Fortunately that goodness was available now, he concluded, to influence those who both saw and appropriated it, especially through the Eucharist and when he had taken his 'fears and sins and half-visions' there in that Sacrament he had found Jesus Christ had come alive.[150]

Chapter 7

PRESSURE GROUP PATRON

DONALD SOPER WAS ONE OF many caught up in the development of pressure groups after 1945. Indeed, he fitted the phenomenon as though born to work with such groups. There was, of course, little new about pressure group activity, either to achieve specific goals, like the abolition of slavery, or to pressurize Parliament on occasions, as the advocates of temperance did. What had changed was the legal position within which pressure groups operated and the political atmosphere in which they were set. Methods of achieving goals had changed, though the campaigning and leafletting, the public meetings and the arguing, the use of dramatic events, like the time suffragettes chained themselves to railings, remained constant. But with the growth of the power of the press and especially the rise of television, it was easier to publicize an issue.

The hanging of Derek Bentley in the 1950s – his father used to go to Hyde Park to ask Donald to do something about it – brought him into the heart of the debate about abolishing the death penalty.[1] He took part, for example, in a large public meeting in St Pancras Town Hall in 1953[2] on the subject and when President of the Methodist Conference that autumn authorized a personal statement when the Royal Commission on capital punishment was issued, urging Britain to 'abolish hanging'.[3]

'The death penalty,' he told a TV audience when on a panel with Dr Cockin, the Bishop of Bristol, who thought it justified in certain circumstances, 'is disgraceful and unclear.' It was neither reformative 'nor especially deterrent'.[4] When he spoke like this his memories went back to when he had sat in the condemned cell with three men. One, living with his mistress and drinking heavily, had come in to the kitchen, found the meal not ready, taken a knife and killed her 'while little children came crying to their mother', he told the Kingsway congregation.[5] Donald went to see him and they talked for hours. Naturally he did not condone the wrongdoing, but found 'there was something of dignity, beauty and goodness about that man',[6] as he spoke of 'the love he really bore to that woman and his infinite sorrow'.

Another man, overcome by the sharp end of life, felt no one cared for him so Donald tried to reassure him that he was a child of God.[7] Clearly, as here, Donald's opposition to hanging was on theological grounds as society said some crimes put people 'outside that love which Jesus Christ would have us bear'. For Donald, however, there had to be 'a door at least ajar'.[8] 'When my father forgave me many a time when I was a boy,' he added, 'I noticed – I could not avoid noticing – that that forgiveness in no way impaired the rigorousness of the penalty.'[9]

Donald timed what he said to coincide with an Albert Hall gathering on 24 May 1956, when he would be in Warsaw. The meeting was crucial, for Sydney Silverman's Bill to abolish hanging had received two decisive votes in the House of Commons, but its fate was still uncertain.[10] A great deal of work had been undertaken to reach this state of affairs – a petition to the Home Secretary from the Howard League for Penal Reform for an end to hanging, signed by a hundred people in public life including E.M. Forster, Peggy Ashcroft and Donald himself,[11] followed by the creation of the National Campaign for the Abolition of Capital Punishment. Led by Arthur Koestler, Victor Gollancz, Gerald Gardiner and others, whose Committee of Honour included Harold Wilson, Henry Moore and Donald, it aimed to campaign in ways the Howard League could not.[12] In addition, people like Ludovic Kennedy and Donald wrote letters to the press.[13]

By autumn, however, the Silverman Bill had fallen. Donald issued a statement many papers printed, which read: 'If the Government fails to honour the clear and repeated intention of the House of Commons to end capital punishment it will provoke a constitutional as well as a moral crisis. The government is in danger of betraying its most sacred obligations.'[14] He continued to speak out over the next period, in 1957 exhibiting concern over the hanging of a Kenyan during the Mau Mau Emergency[15] and disagreeing forcibly with the Archbishop of Canterbury, Dr Fisher, who said there was no immorality in the death penalty.[16] Three years later he pleaded for the life of Francis Forsyth, who had been involved in a murder in

Hounslow[17] and in 1964 joined in the campaign to save William Dobby, a retired miner who had shot his mistress, from hanging.[18] The battle concluded in 1965 when a reforming Home Secretary, Roy Jenkins, steered a Bill abolishing capital punishment through Parliament.

One other big issue emerged in the 1950s – the rise of apartheid in South Africa, as western governments themselves began a process of decolonization. In America, too, blacks began to demand civil rights while Britain became more clearly a multi-cultural society. Donald himself had become sensitive to black and white issues during his 1937 South African tour, of course, and through his contacts with Labour Party and missionary groups. To an open-air crowd in Huntingdon he made his view clear: 'Until we give black people equal rights, we shall be beating the air . . .'[19] Fenner Brockway, too, saw this clearly and in 1954 helped the Movement for Colonial Freedom (later Liberation) to emerge, the amalgamation of three other groups. Among its initial sponsors were eight M.P.s, Canons Collins and Raven, Dame Sybil Thorndike and Donald.[20]

Donald was further sensitized when he visited British Guiana in September 1954, meeting its Governor, Forbes Burnham, and Mrs Jagan, both of whom impressed him, but found living in Georgetown like 'sitting on a powder keg',[21] because a state of emergency was in operation. Once back he urged the Labour Party to meet Forbes Burnham, a non-Marxist nationalist leader, advice which attracted the anger of Cheddi Jagan, the other leader, whose paper *Thunder* accused Donald of interfering in British Guiana's affairs.[22]

At the end of 1954 Donald heard from Canon Collins that the message he had signed to Trevor Huddleston, along with Violet Bonham Carter, Peter Ustinov, Dorothy Sayers, Vaughan Williams and others, had 'done a lot to help him and those who were with him'.[23] By 1955 he was asking urgently what could be done about apartheid.[24] Perhaps Britain should propose that a country with apartheid was not morally fit to be in the Commonwealth, he suggested, but Britain would have to put its own house in order in Rhodesia, too.[25]

In 1956 Trevor Huddleston was at the centre of such controversy that his order, the Community of the Resurrection, withdrew him from Sophiatown. Back in Britain he held meetings continuously to explain what was happening to blacks in South Africa. Donald was present at some of these, thus learning about the situation at first hand.[26] Concurrently he was reading *Naught for Your Comfort* for review.[27] 'It was,' he wrote later, 'one of the most uncomfortable documents I have ever read.'[28] The same kind of race problems that South Africa had, he observed, may be Britain's 'if the influx of West Indians continues at its present intensity'.[29] He urged readers of *Tribune*, therefore, when the South African Prime Minister, Mr Strijdom, visited Britain, to encourage the United Kingdom to look at itself, where there were ominous signs of an attitude 'almost as unregenerate as anything in Alabama or Johannesburg'.[30]

Donald now became more and more involved in anti-apartheid work. Some £10,000 was sought for the Treason Trial which began in South Africa in 1957 and Donald was one among many – James Callaghan, Gerald Gardiner, David Sheppard included – who appealed for funds.[31] He felt the moral blindness in Pretoria and that the perversion of the community was similar in London, Bristol, New Orleans and Savannah, in the days of the slave trade.[32] Nevertheless, if the moral factor predominated, he felt South Africa would be Christian after apartheid, though if the economic factor predominated, then she would become Communist.[33]

At the end of the year 123 world leaders called for an international protest, linked to Human Rights Day on 10 December. Mrs Roosevelt headed a prestigious committee backed by Alan Paton, Earl Russell, Martin Niemöller and Pablo Casals, along with Tom Mboya, Carl Jung, Eric Fromm, Martin Buber and Donald Soper and others.[34] The following year the Movement for Colonial Freedom held a rally in Trafalgar Square, and Donald spoke, along with M.P.s with Fenner Brockway in charge, saying he still felt a true community of peace and justice was within reach 'if we seek it'.[35]

Nyasaland exploded in 1958 and Guy Clutton Brock at Cold Comfort Farm, whom Donald 'almost revered',[36] found himself in conflict with the authorities. At the root of the black struggle Donald felt was the African response to Christ's teaching, through missionaries, the race-less Islamic priest and the Moscow-trained Communist agitator and therefore only a politics embedded in a socialist philosophy stood any chance of African co-operation.[37] He was more gloomy that May, however, when he felt the future lay either with the Pan-Africanism of Nkruma and Touré or a continent given over to Communism.[38]

May, too, saw Donald giving his name to a new group, Defence and Aid, set up to help all those in the Treason Trial now under way.[39] As July approached Trevor Huddleston and Julius Nyerere launched the Anti-Apartheid Movement with a campaign to boycott South African goods in spring 1960, when South African exports to Britain were highest,[40] and the intention of encouraging companies to dis-invest.

Donald himself was greatly impressed by Chief Albert Luthuli, President of the African National Congress, who in 1960 called for 'an orderly burning of passes', and when there was a suspension of them felt it was a tremendous victory as was the boycott, which he hoped would continue because a new force had arisen in the shape of 'a world-wide moral conscience',[41] which could overthrow the South African Government. He did, however, feel there were objections to it, but such a desperate moral cancer as apartheid needed a desperate remedy. It would not, he knew, bring South Africa to economic disaster – paradoxically he would feel it harder to support a boycott if it carried with it the threat of starvation – and realized, too, with characteristic honesty, that logically 'we should be boycotting some-one or some Government on some issue every day'.[42] By June he felt the Johannesburg Stock Market was 'sitting up and taking notice',[43] a step in the right direction which had to be intensified.

In March 1961 2,000 marched in silence to Trafalgar Square from Marble Arch remembering the dead in Sharpeville and Langa a year before, where Donald, introduced by Barbara Castle, spoke along with Anthony Greenwood, M.P., and others.[44] There was another protest meeting there in May when Donald and Canon Collins were among the speakers.[45] By the end of the year South Africa had left the Commonwealth. Donald approved, but drew attention to outrages elsewhere in Pakistan, Australia and Canada.[46]

Now at home a great controversy arose over immigration laws. So the Movement for Colonial Freedom lobbied and Donald, Fenner Brockway, Dr David Pitt and others spoke at a meeting in St Pancras Town Hall on 10 November, which was severely interrupted when a significant number of the audience, who were fascists, put in operation their plan to cause maximum disruption. As bedlam broke out, wild anger replaced composure and tempers were lost 'every second'.[47] The Government, Donald considered, should have intro-duced a Bill making racial discrimination a criminal offence, as Fenner Brockway had long advocated, instead of introducing a Bill which would further stimulate racial hatred.[48]

The early 1960s were a time when Donald became very sensitive to the situation in America, stimulated no doubt by his visits there. Once he spoke in a big church in Harlem where he found the singing 'Let us break bread together on our knees' at the Communion service 'very moving', for it had 'tremendous emotional colour to it'.[49] His reading of *The Negro Revolt* also filled his mind as he was exposed to all strands in the black struggle, including the Black Muslims. 'Whatever future awaits the Negro,' he concluded, 'awaits America.'[50]

Donald was unable to leave his South African concern for long, even though he knew the fight against racism affected so many other countries as well. He wondered now if South Africa was near insurrection. Luthuli had spiritual calibre and maturity but not all were like him: indeed, criticism was now growing about Luthuli's policies as Nelson Mandela and Walter Sisulu and other ANC leaders were sentenced to Robben Island for life and the effects of the Sharpeville massacre continued to reverberate across the world. Donald knew apartheid to be ultimately self-defeating, of course, but it was not clear now what remedies to propose.[51]

He kept his eye on what was happening in Africa continually. In fact, apart from articles on Russia and America, he wrote more in *Tribune* on Africa's revolutions than on any other topic. He also made sure he spoke out about racial discrimination in Britain, so took part in a march and public meeting against it in November, along with artists and M.P.s, but only 500 attended to support Fenner Brockway and his Racial Discrimination and Incitement Bill.[52] Donald had been made aware of discrimination at the grass-roots now, for he was responsible for the Notting Hill Team Ministry which made him even more supportive of Fenner Brockway's campaign as the Movement for Colonial Freedom went ahead over the next few months both to obtain support for his proposed Bill and to get Parliament to scrap the Immigration and Public Order Act.[53]

Martin Luther King was now an international figure because of his leadership of the American Civil Rights Movement. Donald knew him to be a man of deep conviction and undaunted courage, but felt as a leader he lacked 'clear-cut political objectives'. He was, therefore, 'an inspirer rather than a leader', typical of an American radicalism which had yet to find an ideology. He hoped it would quickly, for 'the shadow of Malcolm X and his ideology is sinister and apparently lengthening'.[54]

The revolution in Africa – 'the wind of change' of which Harold Macmillan had spoken when addressing the Cape Town Parliament in 1960 – now affected Rhodesia. Donald was glad his own missionary society had condemned its UDI, but would not support armed intervention.[55] He felt his humanist and left-wing friends were 'woefully ignorant about badness' and this had led them, the Movement for Colonial Freedom included, to advocate military action. For his part Donald felt sanctions designed to reform would only achieve their objective if 'completely freed from the threat of armed force'.[56] Nevertheless, the Rhodesian tyranny had to be overthrown, especially to stop 'the spread of apartheid' northwards.[57]

Donald now paid another visit to America and felt, certainly in Carolina, blacks had made some progress, despite a white backlash and the growth in Black Muslim support.[58] But the Southern African scene looked as bleak as ever, with Harold Wilson's Government having said it would not use force. No one now knew what to do but Donald felt it better to refrain from taking a wrong course, uncomfortable as the situation certainly was.[59]

The year 1967 brought the death of Chief Albert Luthuli and the growing power of Martin Luther King, now protesting against American involvement in Vietnam, exemplifying to Donald the holistic philosophy of General Smuts.[60] There was no question about the rightness of his vision, nor of Stokely Carmichael's conviction that America needed a fundamental change, but neither he 'with the wrong programme of action, nor Martin Luther King, with no appropriate strategy yet to reach his goal',[61] had found a way through.

Eight months later Martin Luther King was dead. Donald spoke at a memorial meeting for him at Kingsway Hall which the Movement for Colonial Freedom called.[62] A week after he had been shot in Memphis he commented generously on the dead leader. 'Of the death of Pericles, Thucydides wrote: "His sepulchre is in all the earth." So said Nehru at the funeral pyre of Gandhi. So it is with the assassination of Martin Luther King.'[63] 'At the foot of the cross on Good Friday,' Donald consoled his *Tribune* readers, 'the way of Jesus, of Gandhi, of Martin Luther King, may look like defeat, but Good Friday is not the end of the Christian Year, only its beginning. The end is Easter morning when even death is swallowed up in victory . . .'[64]

The same year Donald was taken aback by the racism Enoch Powell's speeches revealed.[65] More protests, therefore, were called for, so he backed an anti-racist rally which started outside the Marx Memorial House in Clerkenwell Green and went to Downing Street where Lord Brockway and Stan Newens, M.P., handed in a letter against racialism.[66] Donald was protesting again in November, with twenty-four Methodist theological students from Bristol, outside Rhodesia House in the Strand, as he took part in an all-night vigil to urge that no independence be given to Rhodesia before majority rule.[67]

In 1969 the World Council of Churches held a consultation in London on white racism out of which the Programme to Combat Racism was set up in Geneva. As noted earlier this led to a breach between Donald, the absolute pacifist, and colleagues. He did not, of course, stop protesting about apartheid, and was soon involved in campaigning against the Springboks' tour of Britain.[68] He also backed the British Council of Churches' proposal to stop selling arms to South Africa,[69] leading a Standing Joint Pacifist Committee delegation to the Foreign Secretary on the issue.[70] With Trevor Huddleston, George Macleod, Archbishop Roberts and others in March 1970 he was reminding people it was now ten years since the Sharpeville massacres.[71]

His concern for race relations never flagged, even if by the mid-1970s his energy was somewhat depleted. On a visit to Vienna in 1977, for example, he managed to get into a meeting of businessmen to hear Mr Vorster, the South African leader, lecture them, and in 1980 was again in Trafalgar Square, this time to open the Finale of the multi-cultural ethnic arts festival 'London Entertains' of which he, Cardinal Hume and Trevor Huddleston were the initial sponsors.

Donald's other great campaigning issue was drink and gambling. 'Let me confess to you that I find a certain excitement in the prospects of gambling and, were I not prohibited by my faith and my background,' he once admitted, 'I should probably most likely get a sort of fetid and hectic excitement out of it.'[72] But because it was hostile to 'the Kingdom which Jesus sought',[73] it was a no-go area for Christians. Accordingly he condemned both a Methodist choirmaster who won the pools and was asked to leave his post, subsequently committing suicide, and J. Arthur Rank, who, if it were true as alleged, enjoyed playing gin rummy and taking small sums from those he defeated.[74]

Gambling became news in 1956 as Parliament considered the laws relating to betting shops. Perhaps surprisingly Donald took the view when he addressed the Churches' Council on Gambling that it should not oppose the legalizing of betting shops then being proposed in the

Betting and Lotteries Bill and thereby implementing the recommendations on off-the-course betting and gaming made by the Royal Commission, which had reported in 1951. He did not like existing legislation which denied the same opportunity to working people as others, despite his view that gambling had supplanted drinking as 'our greatest social problem',[75] so supported legislation which brought all equally under the same law.[76] John Gordon, in the *Sunday Express*, took Donald to task for alleging police were open to bribes to help people get round the current law. 'I suggest that the Commissioner of Police should ask Dr Soper to produce his evidence,' he commented. 'That would establish whether he really knows something or is just talking through his clerical hat. As I suspect he is.'[77]

Donald lacked neither courage nor verve in carrying on his educational task. 'Legislation of organized gambling in Britain is wrong,' he stated categorically before members of a Cardiff gaming club as a participant in a BBC Wales programme *Lion's Den*.[78] He did, however, welcome the Home Secretary's intention to regulate casinos in the Queen's Speech of November 1967, but hoped they could be finished off 'and good riddance'.[79] When it came to the Lotteries (Greater London Council) Bill he opposed it tooth and nail and acted as a teller, though admitted he spoke as a churchman who had 'sinned in the matter of bazaars'. Supported by the Bishops of London and Portsmouth he won the debate on the Bill in the House of Lords and his amendment was carried 76/60.

Donald never repudiated his other *bête noir* topic, drink, nor his Band of Hope links. Indeed, various of its groups met at Kingsway Hall regularly until the end of the 1960s, when due to the partial collapse of its ceiling it was no longer possible for the large annual Band of Hope demonstrations to be held there. He was in one Labour Party mainstream, too, for Keir Hardie, Lord Ammon, Sir Stafford Cripps and George Thomas were teetotal. Indeed, in 1940 Donald addressed the annual temperance meeting at the Labour Conference in Bournemouth along with the M.P. Margaret Bondfield.[80] In this movement, which aimed to exercise the maximum pressure on both brewers and Parliament, he found himself moving with M.P.s Cyril Black and Frank Medlicott, who shared few of his other convictions. So strongly did he feel, partly as a result of his work with alcoholics, that with Sir Cyril Black and others he signed a letter to Harold Wilson expressing concern at the Monopolies Commission Proposal, which, if adopted, would encourage alcohol consumption. A demonstration through London to back up the letter, however, drew only 400 to it.[81]

At the Methodist Conference in 1949 Donald and the Rev. J. Brazier Green had tried to submit a motion on temperance, inviting members individually to accept the total abstinence pledge, but this astringent proposal was not acceptable in a tradition where the question was left to individual conscience.[82] In the same year he preached to the Good Templars, a harbinger of 1968, when he gave the Joseph Malins Memorial Lecture and became President of the Grand Lodge of England as well as being guest preacher at the Centenary Service in Canterbury Cathedral. 'Temperance belongs to the Kingdom of God,' he said in his lecture, 'and alcohol shuts people out of the Kingdom of God.'[83] He did, however, think alcohol was part of a complex of social evils and only as reformers dealt with these would they make progress.[84]

Donald's views on alcohol were helpful to groups like the United Kingdom Temperance Alliance but again, as with the issue of gambling, Donald was only called in on specific occasions. Yet his freelance role was valuable for he could argue for total abstinence from an independent position, as he did on BBC radio with John Arlott and Mary Stocks in the 1950s, or co-operate with the National United Temperance Council to oppose the application by the LCC for a modification to the rule banning alcohol at dances at the Lyceum Theatre (they lost). Once he even made his witness when he declined his sweet in a Welsh TV studio because on sniffing the trifle he detected sherry in it.[85]

Inwardly, however, Donald felt he was losing a battle – 'teetotalism is now almost a naughty word in suburban vestries'[86] – and when Lord Mackintosh (as he became) introduced Premium Bonds he felt he had to mourn the death of the Nonconformist conscience itself. 'I wish that this conscience had been more broadly based upon the full scale social gospel,'[87] he confessed but erosion was evident everywhere, in class meeting and party meeting alike. He at any rate would continue pressurizing. So in the House of Lords he looked for opportunities to ask the needling question on alcoholism as well as imparting statistical and other information about the situation in Britain and elsewhere, for alcoholism, he warned in 1971, was on the increase.[88]

He considered there were two things he had to do: to educate and to help those stricken by alcoholism, so when the Teachers' Advisory Council on Alcohol and Drug Education was set up he was there at the start to support its campaign. Vigilance was always necessary so he opposed the extension of licences to late night clubs because drivers might cause accidents on their way home.[89] However, he seemed finally to have become a little more flexible. He admitted:

> It almost blisters my teetotal tongue to say it, but I think there is a reasonable case for the intake of alcohol – I would not accept this, but I think it is reasonable to deploy this argument – when it is part of a civilized accompaniment to eating and pleasure-seeking; indeed if I were pressed I might say that when the earthly paradise does arrive light wines might ecclesiastically be permitted.[90]

The 1970s brought Donald Soper two further pressure group commitments, besides his work for the League Against Cruel Sports, whose President he had become in 1967: Shelter, the campaigning group for the homeless as it was to become, and the Euthanasia Society. Donald's role in Shelter was clear and concise – to chair it and bring stability when its life had been turbulent after a change of staff. Donald, 'a figure of overwhelming rectitude and stability all could trust, whose judgment was firm and sound',[91] was not to be involved in detailed weekly work, so when in 1974 approached by Douglas Tilbe, the Director of the British Churches' Housing Trust, one of six groups which had set up Shelter in November 1966, he had readily agreed to help. At quarterly Board meetings with his incisive mind he was able easily to separate various elements in a situation once briefed, but after some four years of chairing these meetings it was clear he must make way for his successor, so Lord Pitt took his place and Donald and Shelter parted amicably.

He did, however, speak on housing in the House of Lords, a topic he had first grappled with when the WLM had run an old people's home (Goodliffe House in Sydenham) before handing it over to the local authority.[92] Briefed by the Joint Charities Group – Char, Shack, CPAG and Shelter (which played a minor role at that point) – in 1973 he asked if the Government was satisfied with what was being done to house homeless people.[93] He next spoke in June 1975, having urged the Government via a speech at the Methodist Conference to give local housing authorities legislative authority to care for homeless families.[94]

Tony Crosland, the minister involved, had pledged legislation at the start of the new Wilson Government the previous year, but nothing concrete had resulted. Donald tried to tease out what in fact had happened to the Government's 'wide-ranging review', announced in June 1974.[95] No one seemed responsible for seeing all different groups were housed, he observed.[96] Indeed, of the 369 local authorities outside London, 120 had not implemented the Circular of February 1974, which had said local authorities had a duty to house the homeless. Shelter, he added, wanted a housing inspectorate established.[97]

In 1976, in a debate on the Address that autumn, he referred back to his question of eighteen months ago, noting there was no mention of homelessness in the Queen's Speech, yet now 50,000 were homeless. There could be no more delay.[98] By 1977, as Peter Shore succeeded Tony Crosland, a further issue developed – that of homeless young people. A private member's Bill was accordingly introduced and pressure again applied on the Government not to withdraw its commitments. However, the M.P. Stephen Ross agreed to introduce the Bill, so the focus moved, but not before the Bishop of London had asked a question about the August 1976 Government Working Group on Homeless Young People. It was not good enough to put the responsibility for such people in local housing departments, Donald argued in the ensuing debate in March 1977. What was needed, too, was a marriage of local and community and voluntary bodies to tackle the issue.[99]

Donald Soper's involvement with the Voluntary Euthanasia Society (Exit) did not begin until September 1977, when he agreed to become a Prominent Supporter. His interest in the subject, however, started much earlier, as the impact of questions in Hyde Park made him think about it.[100] He looked back, too, to a boyhood hero, Captain Oates. 'He committed suicide,' he told one reporter, 'but I believe he carried the accolade of his Lord.'[101] 'To kill myself is never a sin and can be the peak of unselfish goodness,' he added later, a view recognized partially in the 1961 Act, which removed suicide from the criminal code.[102]

The modern movement for euthanasia had begun in 1935, when the Voluntary Euthanasia Legislation Society was formed, but it was not until 1969 that a Bill, broader than one which had been introduced into the House of Lords in 1936 and defeated, was again brought before peers by Lord Raglan, which provided for the painless inducement of death in patients suffering from irredeemable conditions. But this, too, was defeated. Donald had spoken then, in favour of euthanasia, but not the Bill, maintaining the decision for or against death should not be left to doctors.[103] What was sacrosanct in human beings was that they were alive 'in a self-conscious sense',[104] but what if this had gone? he asked. It seemed Christians clung to life as much as others, despite the promise of heaven. Not so his father, he told peers, who was much concerned at the interference of doctors who seemed to be delaying his departure for heaven. 'I think he had come to feel that somehow the Lord had mislaid his file,' Donald explained.[105] Surely, he reasoned, it was presumptuous to talk as if the ending of life was extinction: it was the gateway to eternity,[106] a relevant fact without which Christian faith became absurd. As for himself, he felt if he reached a 'sub-terminal or terminal condition', he hoped he would have 'the courage and the intelligence to opt to give my life, and if I did, I believe that I have the right to ask the medical profession to stand back and let me die'.[107] He would not ask doctors to kill him, he concluded, but they should not keep him going as a mechanism. The current Bill did not give people the human right he believed was 'part of our Divine freedom and, when exercised, can be for our good,' he added.[108]

Donald had come to this conclusion some years earlier. 'I think there comes a time when we should let old people go to God instead of keeping them in hospital,' he told the *Observer* in June 1960, and when the Bishop of Derby had raised the temperature of the debate about modern drugs and very sick patients in 1962 Donald had responded in the *News of the World* by adding, 'I am quite certain that the doctor should withhold life-prolonging drugs if a patient is really dying.'[109]

Earlier Leslie Weatherhead and Dr Major, the editor of the *Modern Churchman*, had also addressed the topic of voluntary euthanasia and in 1950 the Dean of St Paul's, Dr W.R. Matthews, had spoken to the Annual Euthanasia Society meeting about it, arguing that sometimes the idea of the sacredness of the personality had to be modified by the all-sufficient principle of *agape*.[110] Human beings should use their 'reason, conscience and freedom of choice when we are faced with evils that have a remedy,' he had continued, maintaining his view of providence made him give earnest consideration to the proposal to legalize voluntary euthanasia,[111] an opinion which opened floodgates of protest. Now seemingly Donald Soper was the only prominent church leader to support some form of euthanasia publicly, though the 1974 Methodist Conference considered a statement by its Division of Social Responsibility about the role of medicine in alleviating acute pain and the withholding of drugs,[112] both actions which could lead to death, though could not be described as euthanasia.

The topic, of course, would not leave legislators alone as people lived longer, and yet were only half living, and in 1976 Baroness Wootton introduced the Incurable Patients Bill, a Bill Donald felt he could support, though he wanted some re-wording. Once again he maintained death had to be seen in the context of eternity. He believed, moreover, that something like the proposals envisaged in the Bill would sooner or later become inevitable. However, despite attracting much support, the Bill was not passed. The whole question blew up again in 1980. Donald was addressing 200 at a conference on euthanasia at Oxford. Exit proposed to publish a booklet called *A Guide to Self-Deliverance*, which included guidance on methods of painless suicide and an appendix listing lethal overdoses. The legal opinion was that the society could be prosecuted under the Suicide Act of 1961 for aiding and abetting and an internal conflict emerged about the decision not to go ahead and publish. As a Prominent Supporter Donald had to decide about the booklet, already available in Scotland because of its different legal system. 'I am against it being published,' he declared. 'Providing what is in fact a suicide kit is like handing a bread knife to a child. It is fat-headedness.'[113]

The upshot of the debate was that Donald resigned as a formal supporter of the Voluntary Euthanasia Society, but by 1985 he had become a Vice-President, 'a great help to us because people say we are humanist and atheist,' says John Oliver, one of its officers.[114] 'As I understand it,' Donald wrote in 1989, 'the purpose of life is to love God and enjoy Him for ever. I believe that voluntary euthanasia can be a means to that end.'[115]

Donald Soper's pressure group activities, at times perhaps too variegated, stemmed from his over-riding sense of the need to act to express God's love for the world, including animals. So when *Tower Hill 12.30* was re-published in 1963 one of its new chapters was called 'Animals and the Kingdom of God'.[116] When the Sopers had lived at Radlett they had a black dog, and in Hampstead Garden Suburb at one point two cats were known to follow Donald on a short walk to its Free Church and back again, but it was not this concrete contact with animals which stirred his conscience. Rather it was his revulsion from any form of violence.[117] He had, of course, become a vegetarian (though he was not always strict here) after his first Australian tour. But the roots of his sensitivity went further back, to Ernest Hemingway's writings on bullfighting, which had a profound effect on his approach 'and depreciation of Hemingway'.[118]

His *Tribune* articles tried to look at animals in a theological context as he reflected on their presence in nativity paintings where Christmas was recognized 'as good news for all living creatures'.[119] Moreover, perhaps people could be brought to repentance through recognizing the suffering brought down on the animal world.[120] He was, he added, angry at the thought of how monkeys, passing through Heathrow for experimentation purposes, were treated. 'For their sakes,' therefore, and 'because their salvation waits inexorably on ours, we must make our pilgrimage to Bethlehem. A Happy Christmas,' he therefore ended, 'to you – and a Happy Christmas to the dog.'[121]

By January he was writing he had made the highly unpopular decision to prevent his children going to the circus, while admitting his own childhood joy at seeing the horses, elephants, dogs, sea-lions, monkeys and lions in the arena. He could now see, he wrote, the circus was the product of cruelty and that animals suffered as did human beings, if not in the same way. 'I shall take our children to see *Lady and the Tramp* instead,' he told his readers, 'he's a bit horrific, but thank God for Walt Disney.'[122]

Next Christmas he reflected on the anomaly of children who delighted to think that all creatures were 'the friend of the baby Jesus and are welcome at His cradle',[123] seemingly unconcerned that their Christmas dinners were responsible for wholesale slaughter of these 'friends of Jesus'.[124] He had to admit two things, however, that Jesus was neither a vegetarian nor teetotaller, though He might be both now.[125] More significantly he confessed he accepted the necessity sometimes of imposing 'a certain amount of pain on animals',[126] if it were the only way to make certain discoveries. Indeed, in Ceylon even a Buddhist he had met had put poisonous snakes in a corked-up bottle and thrown it into the jungle.

Whatever the rights and wrongs of certain aspects of vivisection he was clear blood sports were wrong in principle and practice, so supported Sir Frederick Messer's attempt to ban stag-hunting.[127] He was nauseated, he told *Tribune* readers, by the blooding of little children at fox-hunting, too. He therefore supported animal welfare societies and in 1961 was glad to appear as a speaker along with Lord Dowding and Marcus Lipton, M.P., at a conference organized in connection with the World Day for Animals.[128]

With this background Donald was well prepared for his work with the League Against Cruel Sports, a pressure group whose ancestry went back to 1925, when he succeeded Lord Listowel as President after addressing its AGM in 1967, chairing his first one in 1968. One of Donald's initial activities for the League was in 1968 in the debate on the Conservation of Seals Bill, which he told peers he welcomed, arguing again if animals were treated better, human beings might learn how to behave more satisfactorily to one other.[129] He was active again for the League in 1972, in the second reading of the Hare Coursing (Abolition) No. 2 Bill, introduced by Baroness Bacon, where he was a teller, arguing it was against any principle that emerged from Christian faith. The motion, however, was lost.[130]

He spoke again about hare coursing in 1978 to support Lord Houghton, now Chair of the League, who asked what conclusion the Government had reached on the Select Committee Report on it. By now the League had sustained a campaign to save the otter, which had led to Parliament making it illegal from 1 January 1978, to take or kill one. Yet on hare coursing, despite the support of Harold Wilson, who made a surprise visit to the League's 1976 AGM, there was no breakthrough.

At the end of the 1970s Donald provided a photo opportunity for over fifty journalists who came to the League's press conference to hear the results of a poll which had considered the public's attitude to the continued support blood sports received, even from members of the Royal Family, at which Donald appeared with Calamity, a vixen rescued from Ashford Valley Hunt after its mother had been killed. Donald called attention to the continued fox-hunting activities of Prince Charles and Princess Anne which were a matter for general concern, he felt, and suggested the Government should follow the examples of Germany and Canada, where fox-hunting was now illegal.[131]

By the start of the 1980s Donald had been with the League for fifteen years, some of them tumultuous. Each AGM he had learned how to handle the various groups, from far right to far left, so the pressure group had been kept on course, despite occasions when internal dissension had broken out affecting the whole organization. Indeed, he had given the League credibility which it 'could not have had without him, or someone like him . . .', James Barrington, the League's executive secretary, has considered.[132]

Donald's pressure group work was done as he sustained other commitments, so could only be undertaken at salient points. 'He was curiously disengaged,' one observer of his Shelter work remembers.[133] Yet this was often the very quality which helped groups and also suited his temperament. Undergirding all his work was his concern for the individual, of course, particularly civil and human rights for those in political trouble and for Jews still in distress.

In 1959 Donald was supporting an appeal for 3,000 Greek political prisoners[134] and in 1960 took part in a march of 1,000 from Marble Arch to Trafalgar Square, organized by Spaniards in London against the official visit of the Spanish Foreign Minister, headed by three M.P.s, James Griffiths, F. Elwyn Jones and Robert Edwards, who had fought in the Spanish Civil War.[135] In his speech Donald said he was prepared 'to forgive former fascists who had now repented', but not those who thought their iniquities were forgotten.[136] 'I raise my voice in dissent at this fascist intrusion,' he added of Señor Castellan's visit.[137] The year 1961 saw Donald, Professor Ayer, C. Day Lewis and colleagues writing to President Kennedy for two men in prison for un-American activities, a letter organized by the Union of Democratic Control.[138] Even the train robbers gained his attention when he signed an appeal for the reduction of their sentences, along with Canon Collins, Eric Lubbock, Arnold Wesker and others.[139]

When the campaign for International Human Rights Year began in 1967 Donald was at its opening and one of a number of panel members, including Marghanita Laski and Quintin Hogg.[140] Four years later he was concerned with the human rights of Pauline Jones, a young woman aged twenty-three, given a twenty-one month sentence for abducting a baby in Harlow, Essex, which Donald found 'barbaric, antediluvian and immoral'. 'The whole system of government under which we suffer,' he commented 'and the whole system of law has almost entirely been created by men. But they are out of their depth when dealing with cases such as that of Pauline Jones.'[141]

He never let up, one moment pleading for the life of Allende's adviser in Chile, Jaime Barrios, demanding he be set free and presented physically before qualified witnesses; the next photographed in Hyde Park with Mrs Betty Ambatielos, the wife of one of thirty-four leading Communists arrested in Greece, whose release was being demanded by the League for Democracy in Greece, of which Donald was President. Because both Greece and Britain had Christian backgrounds Britain should exert pressure on the Greek Government to encourage it to alter its ways, he argued in the House of Lords.[142]

Once Donald was part of an ecumenical delegation to the Soviet Embassy to seek information about those in jail in the USSR for their religious convictions, a visit made to mark the beginning of Prisoner of Conscience Year.[143] The group was asked to return in a week but the arguments employed – churches ought to concern themselves with Northern Ireland and unemployment in Britain for which they surely had prior responsibility – did not augur well for the reply.

'We can never repay the debt we owe, or indeed extirpate the crime we have committed in condemning this magnificent race of Jews for nearly 2,000 years in our official testimonies in the Christian Church for the greatest of all crimes – that of deicide,' Donald admitted to peers in a debate on the Middle East War in 1973.[144] His sensitivity to this issue was the source of all his work on behalf of the Jewish community from the 1950s, deepened by specific contacts like going to a synagogue one Friday night in Moscow and his Auschwitz visit. By 1959 he was signing a letter, along with Earl Russell, Lord Boothby, Tony Benn and Philip Toynbee, drawing attention to the plight of Romanian Jews[145] and in 1960 devoted a late night TV programme to new waves of anti-Semitism he detected, exemplified by slogans, swastikas and telephone calls.[146] He also took part, along with 75,000 others, in a silent march to the German Embassy, with Bishop Stockwood, M.P.s Barnett Janner and Anthony Greenwood, where a letter expressing concern about the resurgence of Nazism in Germany was handed in.[147] Pathe that year decided to make a film about anti-Semitism in Germany and Donald took part in that.[148]

Soon he was writing in the *Jewish Chronicle* about books which explored early Jewish/Christian links, including Paul Winter's *The Trial of Jesus*. His article drew a considerable response. 'Christians and Jews should be encouraged by the mutual advantages that flow from this kind of historical detection,' he reflected.[149] Donald's friendship with the Jewish community was severely strained in 1961, however, when he said the trial of Eichmann was 'a mistake'.[150] He should, of course, be tried and punished, but not killed, he observed, even suggesting world Jewry might be prepared to forgive him 'and shame the rest of us'.[151]

The plight of Soviet Jews also preoccupied him, and with others he wrote to *The Times* about it.[152] Much later he spoke in Chelsea Town Hall with a former Israeli Attorney General and two Jews from Leningrad about two people there under threat of death,[153] three months later chairing a meeting in a north London synagogue to plan a boycott of the Red Army Tour shortly starting at the Odeon. By now events in the Middle East had taken centre stage with the first of a number of Arab/Israeli conflicts. Donald was convinced Israel should be supported 'in principle', because the Arabs wanted to annihilate her,[154] but it was wrong to go to war 'even for the salvation of Israel', not a view likely to win him Jewish friends.[155]

The 1970s was a decade in which Donald was more and more involved in Jewish affairs, joining the British Committee of Concern for Jews in Arab Countries,[156] seeking and succeeding in having the defamatory definition of the word 'Jew' removed from Cassell's dictionaries,[157] and joining the Chief Rabbi and other Jewish leaders in Trafalgar Square to speak to 1,500 about the plight of Jews wanting to leave Russia for Israel.[158] Subsequently he became patron of an all-party Parliamentary Committee for the release of Soviet Jewry and by 1973 was also a patron of two more, one concerned with Arab,[159] the second with Soviet, Jewry.[160] He also went on a delegation to the Syrian Embassy to ask for Israeli POWs to be treated according to the Geneva Convention, but its doors remained firmly shut.[161]

All this activity led to Donald being highly acceptable in the Jewish community, so he was invited to a number of domestic Jewish occasions, like the fortieth Anniversary of the North Western Reform Synagogue in Golders Green, where he was on a panel with Rabbi Lionel Blue and others to look at religion forty years on[162] and in 1976 to open an exhibition in Brussels, where he mixed with 1,000 delegates from thirty countries, including Golda Meir herself, who had gathered to consider the plight of Soviet Jews.[163]

In 1975 the United Nations vote on Zionism took place, which branded it as 'a form of racism and racial discrimination'. The World Council of Churches itself appealed to the United Nations to reconsider and rescind its resolution. Donald, too, deplored the resolution. 'It is a misconception of Zionism as a national aspiration of Judaism,' he considered. 'It is a setback for the credibility of the United

Nations.'[164] Donald was careful, however, despite the complicated pressure group work in which he was involved, to keep his options open on a solution of the Arab/Israeli conflict itself. He agreed accordingly to speak at a gathering called by the Association of World Federalists to consider a supra-national world political state, set up in the Israeli-occupied territories, to be known as Zion. The national secretary of the Baha'i World Faith, the editor of *New Humanity* and Trevor Huddleston (then Bishop of Stepney) also spoke. It was a dream which envisaged Jerusalem having extra-territorial status – where the world state of Zion would have its headquarters, the three monotheistic religions there to be responsible for the control of the holy places.[165] The idea obviously stayed with him for in 1978 he wrote in *Tribune* suggesting a way to break the Arab/Israeli deadlock was to make Jerusalem a supra-national 'free city'. The *Jewish Chronicle* reporter, who acknowledged Donald had shown his sympathy for Israel's security fears, was not impressed. 'What exactly he meant by it, I don't know. I guess that neither Begin nor Sadat would want to know.'[166]

In 1980 Lord Carrington, then Foreign Secretary, said he did not think the PLO 'as such is a terrorist organization'. The Jewish community was in uproar. The Board of Deputies of British Jewry organized a massive protest in Trafalgar Square to say 'No' to what the PLO was doing. The police said the crowd numbered 15,000 – others put it at 40,000. On the plinth this time were Lord Shinwell, then in his nineties, Topol, Greville Janner and Donald Soper. 'You are right,' he told the gathering, 'You should be supported and that's why I am here.'[167]

Despite his support for Israel Donald knew he had to tread warily, or he would be considered Zionist, or at least lacking balance, when the Palestinian tragedy was considered. Yet he evidently did not support Israeli military activities, keeping himself involved only at certain points in the Israel/Palestinian dispute, when it related to human rights, the golden thread which held together his disparate pressure group activity, which he undoubtedly saw at the centre of his Christian ministry. For if the Church was not *seen* to be engaging itself with questions of human rights, how could it ever be treated as relevant?

Chapter 8

PUBLICIST AND PANELLIST

'OF COURSE, HE'S EVERY JOURNALIST'S dream to interview,' a reporter in a South Wales paper wrote in October 1981. 'The man talks in quotes.' Moreover, from 10 June 1934, when Dick Sheppard invited Donald Soper to broadcast, it was clear, as the Rev. R.B. Shapland indicated in the *Methodist Recorder* in 1935, Donald had a microphone in his nursery.

If Donald himself felt diffident he was soon reassured by the Rev. F.A. Iremonger, who told him how pleased they were with his broadcast address from St Martin's.[1] Soon it was William Temple's wife herself who was speaking enthusiastically about his broadcast series *Question Time on Tower Hill*,[2] as the BBC used Donald more frequently. 'We shall, at some future date . . . be introducing our new television programmes,' wrote Iremonger in 1936, explaining to Donald he was convening Dick Sheppard, the Dean of Liverpool and himself, to talk over the implications.[3] Later he was consulted again, this time by Iremonger's successor, Dr Welch, along with Eric Fenn, Geoffrey Dearmer and others, to consider Sunday broadcasting in wartime.[4]

The national papers did not really 'discover' Donald Soper until the controversy over Communism and a possible third world war in 1950, though before then he was often invited to talk or write about his open-air experiences from which his books and broadcasts flowed and which, as the *Eastern Daily Express* acknowledged, had made him 'a familiar name to people everywhere'.[5] By the mid-50s the media were intrigued, annoyed, even alarmed, by this parson who seemed to have created the 'sound bite' long before the phrase was invented.

As Donald began broadcasting, of course, he had to learn how to give talks and adapt worship for radio. 'I am quite certain it is impossible to say that war is the result of capitalism,'[6] Iremonger observed after he had read one script and one of his successors commented, 'Is it quite fair to slap down the Marxists as you run past them?'[7] By 1938, however, it was already clear that religious broadcasting owed a 'great debt to your husband', as F.A. Iremonger wrote to Marie Soper when radio work was cancelled due to his illness.[8] Television, too, claimed him but not until New Year's Eve, 1947, when he presented the first religious TV *Epilogue* from Alexandra Palace.

Before 1939 Fleet Street saw Donald more as the parson with the popular touch than the controversialist. The magazine *John Bull* even wanted to give him something for his courage in admitting on radio where the Church was wrong, in answering so tolerantly and with such understanding, his many critics – 'yes, and for his guts in speaking on Tower Hill, once a week, and arguing a hostile crowd into friendliness'.[9]

In 1937 the Archbishop of Canterbury broadcast an appeal for a return to religion. Donald was invited by the *Daily Herald* to respond. He used the opportunity to explain that the Church's task was to declare the Christian form of social life.[10] The Kingdom of Heaven, he asserted, was a 'non-violent communism', and only 'a non-violent Church will persuade the world that it means what it says'.[11] He realized, of course, this was a hard and dangerous thing to say, but did not doubt its truth as he ended by pleading for one of the great historic churches to call for a 'new co-operative commonwealth'.[12] That April a number of papers covered Donald Soper's ten years on Tower Hill, the *Evening Standard* and *Reynolds News* among them, and by 1938 the *Sunday People* was asking Donald to open its series 'If you had only one sermon to preach'. 'We must show the Christ-like character, while hitting as hard as we can above the belt,' he wrote, urging Christians to show concern for the needy, willingness to establish justice besides bringing comfort and healing.[13]

In 1938 at the Methodist Conference there was a debate about women's ordination, following a report suggesting they should offer as candidates if financial guarantees were forthcoming. Donald was soon on his feet suggesting that to admit women to the ministry might 'stop the rot' in Methodism,[14] a phrase which was picked up by the leader writers and made a headline in several papers.[15] The following year Donald did two things for the BBC – *After Tea on Sunday*, a programme for children involving some of his brother's Sunday School class, which ended with a short devotional contribu-

tion from Donald, and three talks, *Will Christianity Work?* Donald
told his listening audience,

> In previous broadcasts, I have been concerned with the reason-
> ableness of the Christian faith and I have tried to justify my
> confidence that Christianity does say and mean peace and
> happiness in the Kingdom of God on earth. The consideration
> in *these* talks is a practical one. Can this reasonable Christian
> teaching be carried into effect?[16]

He was not asking people to renounce 'manly qualities' in asking
them to renounce war, he said, for they could be exercised in the
spheres of reconciliation and Christian apologetic, 'not to destroy but
to create, not to subdue others but to win them'.[17] Then he rehearsed
his familiar themes – the Christian revolution, the world as one
family, the primacy of love, the necessity for faith, which by God's
grace enabled people to change the world.[18]

'It was always obvious what he was going to say,' wrote the Rev.
Edwin Robertson, who found Donald a good broadcaster, easy to
produce, 'but he had a way of saying it that made it sound fresh.'[19]
Indeed, the attractiveness of Donald's voice, coarsened though it
became through continual open-air work, and his gift for using
contemporary secular images to make his point, captured many, so
that soon his broadcasts produced considerable correspondence,
which the BBC asked him to answer.

Because of the war-time broadcasting ban Donald's voice was
seldom heard except at Tower Hill or Hyde Park, though now and
again he made headlines in local papers when a visiting preacher or
speaker, one of which spoke of 'Soper bubbles'. 'I should hesitate to
speak about Russia,' he said at a youth conference in Essex. 'You see
we are all buddies now . . . It is a shame when you have to look at
your morning paper to see who to hate.'[20]

In July 1945 the BBC started the Light Programme with the
intention of appealing to millions and Donald was invited to make his
contribution. After discussions with the religious broadcasting staff
two series emerged, *Talking with You* and *The People's Service*, to
which some three million listened. The first tried to bring together a
Christian with something to say and a listener in the mood to respond
to someone who would talk *with* him in an intimate way for five
minutes. *The People's Service* was geared to a mass audience and did

not assume listeners were familiar with either Christian language or ideas but tried to help them find in their everyday experience an underlying religious reality.

'Talking about Christianity without saying anything about sin is rather like discussing gardening and not mentioning weeds,' Donald started one of his talks,[21] immediately evoking the listener's response. 'Do you remember Noël Coward's production at the London Coliseum, *One Damn Thing After Another?*' he began a second. 'I believe it was a very good show but as a definition of life I've often felt that I wanted to quarrel with it. My trouble is "Too Many Damn Things all at once"' – this by way of introducing the question of Christian priorities.[22]

He wished he could have answered all the listeners' questions but there had been too many, he said at the end of a second series. He would reply by letter, but meanwhile he would explain about true prayer, 'the power to change you, not to change God – to change your lives and circumstances by changing your desire and motives, so that you come to want what God wants for you'.[23] He could not, he continued, prove God was wanting to hear prayer – only *he* was sure God was – so why not try it out? 'Jesus prayed the perfect prayer,' he suggested as he invited his hearers to think about it 'just before Good Friday and Easter: "If it be possible let this cup (i.e. the suffering and shame of the Cross) pass from me, nevertheless Thy will be done."' 'God didn't,' he concluded, 'answer that prayer by letting Jesus off, but by enabling Him to go through with it. I wish you'd say a prayer like that tonight – I know it will be answered.'[24] Then, in a phrase so often on his lips and in letters, he ended with 'God bless you', and left the microphone for others to use.

In 1947 and again in 1948, 1951 and 1952, Donald was asked to take *Lift Up Your Hearts*, a series he had first contributed to in 1940. Once again he used homely illustrations, recollecting how he once saw a man rescued from drowning off the Devon coast as he protested he did not know he was drifting near rocks and using this as an illustration of the relation of Jesus Christ to humanity.[25] There was about himself as others, he admitted, a fatal flaw invariably present in his best thoughts and intentions, which God alone could deal with.[26] But we could help in this task. One day, he told listeners, he had found a fourpenny packet of seeds in his mackintosh pocket as he left for work and sprinkled some in the front garden. 'It couldn't have taken more than a minute,' he narrated, 'and I didn't give them another thought until yesterday when lo and behold there were my seeds already above the ground. You and I have time now,' he concluded, 'to do something like that with ourselves.'[27] The German philosopher Lotze was right, he continued, when he maintained 'reality is richer than thought', for 'there's much more to life than things you can touch and handle'.[28] Donald could not know all the answers, he had to confess, but he was now satisfied to know only some, 'the vital ones' in his view. Indeed, there was no such thing as a final and complete knowledge, though human beings did at least have a picture of themselves as God intended them to be.[29]

The 1950s saw the rise of his television appearances, both on the BBC, and in 1955 on ITV, which Donald initially opposed because of its commercial nature, though where he subsequently appeared, for example, on Ulster TV with Rabbi Levy on the subject of the Ten Commandments, and in London Weekend's programme *The Hot Seat* in 1970. He made the transition from radio to TV with consummate ease, though it needed somewhat different skills. He was obviously televisual and his capacity to think on his feet, as well as his commanding intellect, gave him a head start. There were many letters, Grace Wyndham Goldie told him after the Lime Grove Press Conference she had produced, when Andrew Shonfield, Francis Williams, among others, questioned him on subjects as varied as violent crime, gambling and leisure.[30]

Throughout the 1950s Donald was in steady demand on the BBC, one moment having a discussion with Max Robertson on football pools,[31] the next with Leslie Weatherhead on matters of faith and doubt.[32] Contributions to the late night *Epilogues*, to a series from Bristol called *Christian Forum*, and interviews on the current affairs programmes *Panorama*[33] and *Tonight*,[34] followed. When Vernon Sproxton launched *Late Night Final* instead of *The Epilogue* it was to Donald Soper he turned to help start it, who then became a frequent contributor to the series.

Panorama on 7 May 1956 included an eight-minute discussion between Donald and Malcolm Muggeridge on whether church leaders should make public statements on political issues. Malcolm Muggeridge felt this could be dangerous, which Donald readily admitted, adding 'if it's not dangerous' there was something wrong with a parson's ministry.[35] Jesus, he agreed, had not identified with Jewish nationalism, but he had entered the city of Jerusalem as Messiah. Surely, Muggeridge retorted, Jesus's kingdom was 'not of this world'.

The kingdom, Donald replied, could not be built up like the Roman Empire. Malcolm Muggeridge countered by arguing surely there was something beyond the earthly struggle. In reply Donald said parsons who drew a clear distinction between the secular and the sacred, were not fulfilling their ministry, which was to present the kingdom of God as a way of life on earth, representing the love of God and living according to God's laws. Muggeridge drew attention to St Francis of Assisi, but Donald was ready with his answer: after all St Francis had been the plenipotentiary of the Crusaders to Saladin.

Malcolm Muggeridge then wanted to know what happened if a parson was identified with a particular party. Donald was clear you identified yourself with a cause, not a party, which you ought to remain free to criticize. What about St Paul and the issue of slavery then, was the riposte. Clearly St Paul was acting as a Roman and a child of his time in his attitude to women, Donald answered. He would have preferred St Paul to have transcended his time and, indeed, his conviction that the powers that be are ordained of God was 'one of the most vicious things represented at the Reformation'.

Muggeridge was now clear that Donald's view would have 'destroyed Christendom'. But, retorted Donald, 'there might have been Christianity'. 'Do you really think that a priest can fulfil a dual role in life?' Muggeridge queried and can he speak up as a citizen, without detracting from his priestly functions and keeping alive before us the idea of 'something beyond this world'? 'I remain, I'm afraid, even after this discussion, sceptical on this point.'[36]

Sceptical, too, was Quintin Hogg, when he and Donald confronted one another again, this time in 1967 in a Radio 4 programme on religion and politics chaired by Robin Day, a subject Donald frequently explored on TV, sometimes on a specific point, sometimes more generally. Whether the topic was being a patriot,[37] or the Cambridge Union debate in 1981 on nuclear disarmament, with Vladimir Bukovsky, Bruce Kent, John Nott and Giles Kavanagh,[38] there was seldom a year went by without Donald appearing on the media.

As far as radio was concerned he was even more popular, commenting on subjects as varied as death on the roads, outer space research, vandalism, A.I.D., blood sports and euthanasia, the proposed national lottery, MRA, school religion and marriage, and even on one occasion the use of Valentine cards! People, too, he was asked about, ranging from Frank Sheed and Maisie Ward, the Roman

Catholic apologists whom he had known at Hyde Park, to Bertrand Russell, and Michael Ramsey when he retired. Sometimes he would appear with other personalities, like the authors of *Jesus Christ Superstar*, with whom subsequently he had a discussion about their interpretation of Jesus,[39] or on *Wogan* with Jeffrey Archer.[40]

The types of radio programmes which he learned to handle as a professional were as varied as his comments – chat shows, question and answer programmes, panels and discussions soon becoming his forte. So, too, did interviews, which he liked best, appearances on *Woman's Hour*, and as guest celebrity elsewhere. In addition, of course, he kept up a regular flow of contributions to religious programmes, like *Silver Lining*, where the pastor in him was most in evidence and, latterly, *Pause for Thought*.

During a visit to Exeter University, where he was debating with Anne Scott James and Leon Brittain on the Divorce Bill then going through Parliament, Donald was confronted by Rhys Williams about his media appearances. 'Why do you appear on such appalling programmes as *The Simon Dee Show*?' he asked. 'Don't you find it demeaning appearing on such rubbishy programmes?' 'How do you know I've appeared on *The Simon Dee Show*?' Donald replied. 'I've seen you. I've watched you at it,' said Rhys Williams. 'Don't you find it demeaning watching such rubbishy programmes?' Donald swiftly retorted.[41]

Through trial and error Donald learned to respond at different levels according to a programme's needs, style, outlook and type of audience. Obviously what was needed for *The World This Weekend* was different from his contribution to *What's the Idea?* where he was confronted by distinguished interlocutors on Total Abstinence and he himself confronted members of the Lord's Day Observance Society. Different again were the contributions to the BBC Overseas African and Asian service.

One of Donald's most widely reported TV encounters occurred in April 1963, on the satire programme *That Was The Week That Was* when a controversy had blown up around the Peace Movement nicknamed by the press 'Spies for Peace'. Donald and a number of Aldermaston Marchers were invited to the late night show, which made David Frost a household name, to be confronted by Bernard Levin, whose job was to ensure a lively piece of television occurred each week. Accordingly he charged CND members with being hopelessly split and with keeping the company of treasonable people.

As leader of the group Donald made the opening reply, but thereafter the item degenerated into a free for all, a fracas into which Donald was not drawn. 'He sat quiet and still while the battle of words went on until he judged the right moment had come,' said one report. 'Then, suddenly, he spoke; quickly and calmly, yet his voice cut through the hubbub and everyone fell silent to listen to him.'[42] The item was then brought to a swift end with a chord from the band.

Throughout these years Donald remained a potential news story for Fleet Street, the more so after his Presidency than before. During this period, too, he was continually writing articles for the *British Weekly* and the *Methodist Recorder* where he could explain his convictions more deeply than elsewhere. For the latter especially he often contributed a series of four, or was the subject of interviews, sometimes as a result of his activities, which were accompanied on many occasions by photos. His pacifist work, however, was not featured much during one period, though the *Methodist Times* gave him substantial coverage until its demise. For the rest of the papers, as with his TV and radio work, he tailored his message to a few salient areas in order to address the secular world.

In 1955 he wrote in the *News Chronicle* about 'goodwill', which had to become 'the dominant motive of millions'.[43] Governments could only respond in that manner if the public conscience encouraged them, though there would always be inevitable compromises, he continued, and the job of idealists was to provide clear-cut political expressions of goodwill which could act as models for propaganda and education.[44]

The following January Donald's observation in *Tribune* about a growing hostility in Britain to America was picked up by several regional papers. So was his comment 'Every parson should stop smoking' in response to the 1962 College of Physicians' Report on Smoking and Health. One enterprising local paper took a straw poll to find out how many intended to respond to Donald's dictum. Few said they would.[45] Much more coverage, however, was obtained when Donald said he disapproved of Lord Rank's attitude to Bingo at the time he was treasurer of the Christian Citizenship Department of the Methodist Church.[46] The *Evening News* wrote in March 1964,

We have been analysing what the world would be like from a study of items publicly disapproved of by Donald Soper in the past year or so. It would be without nuclear weapons (fair enough) trading stamps, TV advertisements, meat dishes, *Z-cars*, landlords, Mr Bernard Levin, tobacco, bingo, alcohol or Beatles.[47]

Donald was obviously newsworthy but was he effective? Did he not create a deep ambivalence in people as they responded to now this, now that, view which he held? Did such a style enable him to pursue his overall goal of preaching Christ in a secular world? Geoffrey Palmer, of the YMCA, who heard Donald speak in Durham just after the war, whose oratory he thought on a par with Churchill's among others, has probably made the most accurate comment: 'Everybody likes something about Donald Soper but nobody likes everything about him.'[48] So even the *Humanist* reported benignly an account of his and Professor A.J. Ayer's talks to the World Parliamentary Association, though added, 'Soper's plea that the brotherhood of man entailed the fatherhood of God was more than the Vice-President of the British Humanist Association could bear, but he demolished it gently.'[49]

For his part, Donald knew he took risks by becoming so involved with the media, always looking for an angle to a story and making a headline out of an aside, or a comment peripheral to an argument. 'I'm glad there weren't tape recorders in my early years,' he once commented,[50] for it was only latterly he learned a greater discretion both in what he said and how he said it. Despite the hazards, however, the rewards were greater, as in 1964 when Donald addressed the Modern Churchmen's Union in Oxford. 'If it is becoming increasingly difficult to present Christianity in dogmatic, formal fashion which will be relevant,' he said, 'I think it is also true to say there is an unparalleled opportunity for the presentation of the moral case.'[51] Science understood superficially had conveyed the idea that the main body of doctrine ought to be jettisoned, an indication perhaps that the battle between science and religion was concluded. Nothing could be more foolish, yet he knew the symbolic forms of Christianity had to be modified 'so that the essential Gospel could shine forth'.[52] This was hardly newsworthy stuff but his speech was reported in *The Times*, the *Daily Telegraph* and the *Scotsman* and in regional papers like the *Sheffield Telegraph*, an indication yet again, as Geoffrey Palmer has observed, that Donald can say things 'which people can digest'.[53]

Donald's capacity to reach a wide audience was never more in evidence than in his contributions to *Any Questions?* A member of the panel for over twenty years, he started when Freddie Grisewood was Question-Master but also made appearances under the chairmanship of David Jacobs and on occasions Anthony Howard and John Simpson. During his nearly fifty appearances he sat alongside some of the most distinguished and lively personalities in politics, the arts, commerce and industry. On his first panel, from Southampton in February 1953, he shared the platform with Jennie Lee, Ted Leather (the Conservative M.P. for North Somerset), A.G. Street and on his last in 1987, from Taunton, with Michael Spicer, M.P., John Pardoe and Mary Goldring. In between he sparred with people as diverse as Mary Stocks, Violet Bonham Carter, Ralph Wightman, Enoch Powell, Margaret Thatcher, Edwina Currie, Shirley Williams, Peregrine Worsthorne and Marghanita Laski.

'As Chairman,' Donald has commented, 'Freddie Grisewood was extremely knowledgeable and well versed – he knew everybody so to speak. He was also very avuncular, creating a sense of intimacy that nobody since has captured.'[54] Later the mood changed somewhat and there was a sharper edge to it. 'I can't imagine that this *Any Questions?* has got any terrors for him,' Freddie Grisewood said introducing Donald to his first audience. And it did not seem to have, unlike Donald's appearance on *Desert Island Discs* in 1966, when he seemed less sure of himself.

'I'm not going to make any apology for bringing in theology,' Donald said right away. 'We're living in a world which is not our creation but is God's world, and anything that brings us back, however rudely and tragically [a questioner had asked about the East Coast Flood disaster which had occurred that winter] to the fact . . . is a good thing.'[55] Yes, he said in answer to a question about England being worse off if its churches were closed for a year, Christians could do with 'a bit of persecution – it would do us a power of good. If it happened we'd have a revival of religion in the open air like Wesley and Booth.'

Some panel members were terrified by the obligatory funny question. Donald's first question of this kind was 'If unmarried who would the team post a Valentine card to?' 'If I hadn't collected one by now I should have given it up as a bad job,' he responded amid much laughter. Then he added: 'Seriously . . . Nehru.' 'What was the motive of *Tribune* attacks, especially towards trade union leaders and the Labour Party?' asked another questioner. Jennie Lee, intimately associated with the weekly, stoutly maintained it was 'just healthy discussion'. For his part, Donald, not yet a regular contributor, drew attention to what he detected underlay the question: a departure from the high ideals and principles which once animated the Labour Party. 'I for one,' he declared, 'would like to see a great deal more Christianity in socialism, otherwise I am quite sure it will fall apart ... What is needed is to bring socialists together in not a new programme, but a new spirit,' a view which won him a round of applause. Jennie Lee rebuked Donald strongly. After all, she said, Keir Hardie was spirited in the paper he once ran. 'There was nothing wrong with the Labour Movement.'[56]

Donald was not often beaten in argument over the ensuing years, but he was often contradicted, once by Freddie Grisewood himself about a remark on Wagner, which Donald withdrew when his view was challenged.[57] He was, of course, not averse to interacting strongly with some team members. 'What is discretion for?' asked a questioner in 1961, referring to the phrase 'the age of discretion'. Donald responded,

There is no word like discretion in the catalogue of Christian virtues. I think courage, enterprise, pertinacity, goodwill – they are – or at least they ought to be – Christian virtues. As in revolutions – and this will probably draw Lord Boothby – I think that discretion is a thoroughly disagreeable thing to attain and it's mainly a capitalistic experience.[58]

The remark drew much laughter. The following year Donald Soper and Lady Violet Bonham Carter got into an exploration of Lib/Lab pacts. He did not believe in temporary pacts to get rid of the present Government, he said, nor did he believe in any permanent alignment between radicals 'who are not committed to socialism as a general principle'. For her part, Lady Violet thought it dangerous not to have an alternative government ready to take office. Indeed, she was in favour of a re-alignment 'but to coalesce with Labour at the moment would be like trying to coalesce with a rainbow or with a handful of confetti. I respectfully disagree with Dr Donald Soper when he says the Labour Party is fundamentally socialist.' 'That's what it ought to be,' Donald retorted, who was soon taking exception to Lady Violet's reference to the Labour Party as an ancient monument. 'We don't want a re-alignment of the Left,' he went on, 'we want the re-conversion of the Left.'[59]

Donald was often surprising in his responses. In the same programme he told the audience, when asked why the Devil was always depicted as a man, that the idea of the Devil was 'a very necessary prop to any serious thinking',[60] a view he re-iterated in 1964 in the BBC TV programme *Meeting Point*, to which he was a frequent contributor, when Malcolm Muggeridge and a group considered evil as presented in William Golding's *Lord of the Flies*. His humour, as usual, was not far from the surface. A question was asked about the team's attitude to frozen foods and Donald revealed that he was not sure if his food had been frozen or not. It was just put on the plate and he ate it![61]

In 1964 Donald appeared in the 600th edition of *Any Questions?* which came from Hampshire. 'Which of the seven deadly sins would you fall for?' he was asked. He started to list them but stumbled after the fifth and ran out of time. In a later programme panellists were asked which of the seven deadly sins they had committed, 'or even deadlier ones'. Donald had committed most of them, he confessed, and had a sense of penitence about it. There were too many, he considered, listing them all, then added another for good measure – violence![62]

No theme frightened Donald so when a question was asked about the Queen's visit to Germany in 1965 he used the occasion to maintain Britain itself was not guiltless. 'I should very much object,' he went on, 'if this question were assumed to carry with it the assumption that if only the Germans would behave better, then the world would be a happy place.'[63] 'In one sense,' he continued, 'we are to blame, not perhaps so much as the Germans, but I think there's a real need for penitence all the way round, and that understanding must be built on humility and not the sense that we've been in the right and the Germans are the scoundrels and it's about time they repented.'[64]

Controversy was always not far off with Donald on the panel like his clash with David Howell, M.P., over whether people abused national assistance and who was entitled to it.[65] But the most clear-cut argument occurred in 1970 between Margaret Thatcher and Donald over the projected South African cricket tour. Donald explained he had previously demonstrated peacefully against the Springboks at Twickenham because South Africa had brought politics into sport. He would do the same over the planned cricket tour, for he wanted to be able to look South Africa's future – and the whole of Africa depended on South Africa's future – in the face. Mrs Thatcher took the opposite view – she hoped the tour would go ahead. Britain would not stop the Bolshoi Ballet coming, she argued. Indeed, South Africa could learn much from 'the amicable way we conduct our affairs here.'[66] It would be a tragedy if it was put off because a minority of demonstrators stopped the majority of people watching cricket. Donald reminded Mrs Thatcher that it was only because minorities had the chance of turning themselves into majorities that true democracy had a chance of survival. Mrs Thatcher replied firmly, both to Donald and Kenneth Allsop, another panellist, who sided with Donald's position of peaceful opposition to the tour: a minority could turn itself into a majority at election time in a democratic country.

Later in the argument Donald maintained that a standard had to be set and stuck by. This was a matter of absolute principle. Well, said Mrs Thatcher, in that case no one should be allowed in Britain from Russia while the Jews there were treated as they were. Donald had to concede her point, but said he believed consistency was a virtue 'where you can find it', yet there was no such thing as total consistency. At least Russia in principle was committed to equality, whereas in South Africa the professed policy was inequality. So, Mrs Thatcher added as a rejoinder, 'theory matters more than practice'.[67]

At one point in the 1970s the panel was asked what animal it would like to be if not a human being. 'Not a fox,' Donald said quickly, remembering the earlier discussion in the programme on blood sports. His first choice clearly would be a shark from the standpoint of efficiency, his second a porpoise, for its intelligence.[68] 'Fancy pacifist Lord Soper wanting to be a shark. I can't get over it,' said one of the listeners who wrote in to *Any Answers?*

Christmas (and Easter, too) were, of course, times when Donald was often a panellist and here he was able to be the preacher more easily, though he once found himself in a somewhat un-Christmas-like banter with Terry Wogan.[69] One Christmas, this time Jimmy Young was a panellist, the team was asked about its favourite Christmas carols. Donald named 'Once in Royal David's City', recalling one verse in particular, where Jesus was pictured as knowing smiles and tears, so unlike the Luther carol 'The little Lord Jesus no crying he makes'. 'That's far nearer the truth,' he declared. He would be singing the carol frequently that Christmas – 'and believing it, too'.[70]

Over the years Donald learned a technique, of course, involving quick interventions and one line responses to other panellists. In 1979 he was embroiled in a substantial argument with Lord Robens, who thought Donald 'years out of date' on economic theory, which led to discussion about how to interpret the Sermon on the Mount. The argument was at full tilt when David Jacobs intervened, as Donald declared he believed in 'original sin; but not total depravity'. 'I'm going to stop here,' he said, 'knowing Donald of old he'll throw back something.'[71]

Often the ripostes from other members to Donald were most lively, as when Enoch Powell expressed his sorrow that Donald had not experienced the joy of hunting.[72] Or John Pardoe's comment, in what was Donald's last *Any Questions?* appearance, that it was quite amazing 'what you drag theology into, my Lord'.[73] The questions now were perhaps more serious from the beginning – can God address the world through men and women?; how can there be more individual freedom yet secrets still retained?; AIDS and homosexuality; privatization. He still retained a certain confidence the world was not getting worse, he said, and 'had a lively hope', for unless hope was kept alive the human race did not have much else to rely on.[74]

'I have complete faith that we live in a spiritual universe,' he said on another occasion;[75] yet somehow when he made statements like this it did not irk people. Perhaps the secret of his success was in his presentation of himself as ambiguous and compromised like those in the audience, as when he admitted his favourite TV film cartoon was *Tom and Jerry*, who were both violent and lethal, but very funny. Moreover, he confessed 'as a sin', he was addicted to watching boxing.[76]

'As for the audience,' John Mortimer once observed of *Any Questions?*, 'they ask questions to be entertained, not to discover the secrets of the universe.'[77] Donald therefore always had to tread warily, but this combination of deftness of touch, articulateness in explanation, plus humour, enabled him to use a further platform to make known his message. Impossible to quantify, it no doubt was another part of the scaffolding which held together the theological and political edifice he was building.

There was a prophetic side to Donald and now and again this burst through even the most unexpected of media presentations. On 6 January 1968 Donald appeared on a late night BBC TV programme *At the Eleventh Hour*. 'Your confession' was the theme. He did not believe the Church had a monopoly of stated truth about everything, he declared, nor that it was indispensable as hitherto known. So many lived without the Church and there were so many propositions and practices linked to the Church with no contemporary relevance. Despite this he did believe the truth of Christianity, 'and therefore this effervescing word must be expressed in new wine put into new bottles'.[78]

From time to time someone had to say 'uncomfortable words', Donald explained later when a furore developed over his words. He was merely trying to break through to young people who had written the Church off. Hence his statement which used the word church in the sense in which the secular world understood it. A very different Donald appeared on Thames TV in a Good Friday meditation at the end of the 1970s. Here was a young man, a revolutionary, he explained, who was tried, then killed brutally for confronting the powers of his generation. But Jesus was a revolutionary without a sword who asked forgiveness for the very soldiers 'who had driven nails into His body'.[79] Three sorts of people watched Jesus die – the centurion, the religious leaders, those who passed by. Of course, religion could go bad, yet human beings were religious animals and made for God. At the heart of Jesus's death was a mystery, he continued – the mystery of suffering which can be powerful as in the Cross itself, though it was also about doing good and forgetting oneself. Sometimes he sat at the foot of the Cross to hear what Jesus said, he reflected; and sometimes he stood, to be counted among the revolutionaries seeking to receive the power and persistence to seek Christ's kingdom. In the end, however, he had to kneel 'with all other sinners', for at the Cross was 'the grace and power that makes penitent', calling him to a different life. If he stayed there, on Easter Day he would be able to rise with Jesus 'to proclaim with joy that He is risen'.[80]

The shots of Donald were stark and simple, backed up by pictures of Mother Teresa, the Salvation Army and of Christ on the Cross. There was little assumption that the viewer knew much of the background of the Crucifixion, nor was the language other than straightforward. Though in fact Donald quoted both St Augustine and Luther, he made no reference to this. Rather, he did his best to make his narrative contemporary. Earlier, he had done the same in 1957, in the *About Religion* series, when Tower Hill was transferred to TV and transmitted initially live from the large stage of the Hackney and Wood Green Empires.[81] As ever, Donald was felt to be controversial and his producer was told by a senior person in ITV in charge of programmes that some questions asked about pacifism and socialism one Sunday were not allowed, so tight was the TV Act about certain parameters which commercial TV had been allowed.[82]

Donald also appeared in one of ABC's first regular series called *Living Your Life*, which ran from 1957 to 1964 in various formats. One of the most lively in the early 1960s was the time Tower Hill was reproduced in the Gladstone Dock with Liverpool dockers.[83] There were more serious occasions, too, like the ABC programme on worship in 1962 in the series *Four Freedoms*, with Michael Ramsey, Anthony Bloom and Martin Niemöller, and an exploration of Christian Agnosticism with Tom Driberg, Joseph McCulloch and Katharine Whitehorn in 1961. Most controversial of all was the discussion between Donald, Canon Kenneth Woolcombe and Father Michael Hollings, the latter two from Oxford chaplaincies, on the role of Mary in Christianity.[84]

'We think of her affectionately because she was Jesus's mother,' Donald wrote in the *TV Guide*, speaking from a Protestant perspective, 'but we do not revere her.'[85] Yet Mary had the 'important advantage' of showing 'another side of God ... God's fatherhood of mankind is only part of the story'. Indeed, in his view Nonconformity was impoverished by 'the lack of the sense of the motherhood of God'.[86]

Just as certain aspects of the radio and TV media wanted material from Donald which covered in depth his outlook and attitudes, so, too, did Fleet Street. *The Times*, for example, not only reported his comments on a wide variety of topics, including speeches in the House of Lords, but now and again solicited special articles. So in 1969 he was invited to write on Anglican/Methodist unity[87] and in 1982 on disarmament, to coincide with the special session of the United Nations on the theme.[88] It also reported his views on organ transplants, his warning to TV producers to restore the balance between permissiveness and violence in their programmes, his comment on Enoch Powell's attitude to the churches' declaration on world poverty, and his support for a Christmas appeal for Biafra. (He had earlier chaired the first meeting of the British/Biafra Association.)

The *Daily Worker* (later *Morning Star*) also gave Donald considerable coverage. Naturally it emphasized his attitude to the Cold War and his concern for peace and social righteousness, rather than his religious ideas, in 1950 telling its readers about the speech on Communism or a third world war, which brought him such notoriety. Often he made the paper's front page as when he supported 'Young communist league member Paul Garland's right to remain a scout', being against 'all witch-hunting'.[89] When he answered questions for over an hour on his return from Russia the paper gave his replies much coverage, including his comment that 'every Christian should wholeheartedly support a very great deal of what in fact Russia is doing'.[90] It did report the founding of the Christian Socialist Movement, but seldom relayed either Donald's philosophical objections to Marxism or his conviction that his socialism stemmed from his understanding of Christianity, though latterly in writing about Pascal and Dostoevsky he was able to hint at the relation of science, politics, economics and faith.[91]

Wherever he was Donald felt the need to be an advocate for Christ. If publicity helped, in a publicity-conscious age, he would go on the *Wogan* show and make his point, be interviewed on Pete Murray's or Jimmy Young's shows or discuss morality with Brian Redhead. He would give numerous broadcasts, too, for good causes like Crisis at Christmas, which was powerful enough to make Lincoln's 'official atheist', Roger Minshull, give up what he was doing and work voluntarily thereafter for the organization.[92]

He would, too, use his oratorical skills whenever asked to debate at the Oxford and Cambridge Unions, as well as at London University, Durham and Exeter. His visits to the Oxford Union ranged from the occasion in 1955 when he debated with Oleg Kerensky 'This House refuses to be frightened by the Communist bogey' ('he had not met the same people that Mr Kerensky's friends had met,' commented *Cherwell*, 'there all was sweetness and crèches, freedom of religion and production through joy'),[93] to a debate on 9 February 1983, which attracted the world's press, and was also covered by ITN: 'That this House will in no circumstances fight for Queen and Country', a motion which this time was defeated 187/416, though there were 200 abstentions. Here Donald was ranged with Helen John from Greenham Common and Tariq Ali and against Douglas Hogg, M.P., Lords Home and Beloff. Lord Home admitted that the original King and Country debate had not of itself encouraged Hitler, but taken in conjunction with the PPU questionnaire, it had created the impression that Britain was going pacifist. 'It certainly caused Baldwin to delay re-arming for about two years.'[94] 'The world desperately needs a new dynamic,' argued Donald, for it now had a do-it-yourself kit for its own destruction.[95] 'But his gentle idealism, as the opposition were quick to point out, sounded slightly out of place in the cut and thrust of the debating chamber,' wrote the *Oxford Mail*.[96]

The subjects Donald was asked to speak about give a clear picture of how the university saw him – 'The Country suffering from a lack of national pride', set against Dr A.L. Rowse (29 November 1958), to the thesis that 'Christianity has more to give the world than science ever can'. Peter Jay though, writing in *Isis*, was not taken with Donald Soper. For him he was 'dogmatic, patronizing, Marxist ... in fact possessed',[97] an indication some remained unmoved by his brand of oratory. Once he was pitted against Michael Heseltine, now M.P. for Henley. It was the seventy-fifth anniversary of the founding of the Labour Party and the debate veered between Donald's conviction that socialism would triumph because 'the alternatives are manifestly ineffective'[98] and Heseltine's argument that it was not realistic to believe that groups such as miners or railway workers would 'put the interests of the community before their own'.[99] The motion was defeated 378 to 265.

Donald's statement about Communism and a third world war led the Cambridge Union to invite him to debate the motion, which was defeated, with Selwyn Lloyd, M.P., in the spring of 1951. He was back in the Cambridge Union in a year, to debate 'If you want peace, prepare for war', a motion which was defeated 339 to 109, perhaps because most arguments were so weak and the voting took place after Donald's speech. In 1981, he was arguing many of the points he made in 1951 in a debate on nuclear disarmament to yet another generation of undergraduates, a debate which was covered by *Newsnight*.[100] But the debate which stood out above all others in Donald's Cambridge Union appearances took place on 11 May 1954 when Sir Oswald Mosley came out of retirement to debate the motion: 'This House welcomes the attempt by the Union Movement of Great Britain to advocate by legal means a complete change in the system of Government'. The evening itself was hot but before the Union's doors were open undergraduates were already queueing, with police keeping a wary eye on Mosley's supporters, who were also outside the Union building. The doors were shut before the debate started so not everyone who wanted to heard it. 'If the intention had been to debate the perils of authoritarianism within our society, Sir Oswald Mosley was precisely the wrong man to invite,' said the *Cambridge Review*. 'The Union, or rather Mr Attlee, disposed of him years ago in this same chamber. This time a Methodist minister was summoned to do service for the opposition . . .'[101]

Mosley himself took nearly an hour dealing with the motion, including his response to comments made from the floor about some of his allegations. Remnants of his debating skill occasionally broke through 'to illuminate the poverty of his brief,' wrote one reporter, 'but the House discovered little of even the avowed intentions of his party'.[102] By contrast with Sir Oswald, Donald was brief. 'Well,' said Donald as he began, 'Sir Oswald is here with his guards with brains like biscuit weevils.'[103] He tore through the verbal inexactitudes on which Sir Oswald's case had rested and poured scorn on his plans for the world. He denounced, too, 'pestiferous notions' on which his view of human beings rested, its fruits and the violence inherent in it. Against Sir Oswald's view Donald set his conception of a Christian and a socialist world. Now and again avuncular, he spoke rapidly and without oratorical effects, which enabled him to gain the warm sympathy of the house and the support of most present. Privately, as he recalled later, he had felt sorry for Sir Oswald because during the Second World War while imprisoned he had not received proper treatment for a blood clot and he knew what that experience was like in his own life.[104]

'I regret I have never met Donald Soper face to face and can only testify to his influence through rallies, books, radio talks and television appearances,' wrote the Mayor of Warrington in 1993.[105] He is typical of many who responded to Donald, without his ever knowing it, over the years. Colin Adams is another who felt inspired by Donald's 'clarity of thought and compassionate attitudes,' as it was expressed on *Any Questions?* 'Donald Soper was in the room,' wrote Roger Minshull. 'He was just chatting to me – and it put me on the spot.'[106] Many thousands felt the same as they encountered Donald through well over 500 TV and radio broadcasts, to say nothing of local radio interviews when he visited a town, but not all took either to his style or his utterances. Taking him to task for his view that prisoners in the main should not spend more than a few years in prison but find healing in society not outside it, Edward Pearce in the *Daily Telegraph*, in a series called 'Latter Day Saints', complained that 'when he involves the vocabulary of historic religion, rattles its sacred relics to us, and generally adopts for his political speeches the tone of a thirteenth century Pope pronouncing anathema upon Cathars and Bogomils, the tolerance of the unjust is unreasonably tried'.[107]

Maybe the journalist who wrote those words missed what a reporter in the *Staffordshire Evening Sentinel* found in Donald's TV programme with Liverpool dockers – that he 'was able to laugh at himself'.[108] Perhaps, too, he had never come across a side of Donald which revealed that he had reflected on some of those statements over the years which had caused such a furore, statements like his one about Methodism dying, which came as he reflected on the Nottingham Methodist Conference of 1972 and which was picked up by the national and regional press.[109] 'Time and time again I have regretted comments I have made,' he told Shirley Davenport. 'If I had been able to write them down first and pray about them, I may have put them another way.'[110] Nevertheless, it was Donald's willingness to chance his arm and be vulnerable if necessary which made people notice him. 'I cannot think of any Christian leader who has been so used by the media, especially radio,' Neville Ward observed of Donald's communication skills.[111] 'If you could bottle the essence of his television success,' commented one regional paper, 'politicians would pay dearly and fight for it.'[112]

Actors, too, came to study Donald's technique for a film on their craft made in 1967 for American broadcasting, which was nominated for an EMI award. It included a two-minute clip of Donald on Tower Hill, showing how to hold an audience.[113] Canadian TV featured Donald in a series with Pierre Berton, which also included Malcolm X and Jean Shrimpton. Reuters Television also used clips of Donald in Anti-H-Bomb Marches, a Trafalgar Square demonstration to remember Sharpeville, the row at the Movement for Colonial Freedom meeting in 1961, the Peace for Vietnam Rally in Trafalgar Square in 1965, as well as Donald's warning at Hyde Park about racial violence in February 1967.

Most surprisingly there was a clip of the former President of Katanga, Moise Tshombe, attending worship at Kingsway Hall in 1964, clearly indicating that in his media work Donald Soper exemplified John Wesley's saying that the world was his parish.

Chapter 9

PIONEER AND
PHILANTHROPIST

IN HIS FIRST PERIOD AT Kingsway Hall Donald Soper mixed with
Dr Townley Lord from Bloomsbury Baptist Church, Dr Colin
Roberts, the leader of the Christian Commando Campaigns, and
forged links in Australia with the Rev. Alan Walker, but subsequently
contacts changed substantially, as did the entrance hall itself, where
John Hutchinson, a member for many years, painted Christ reproving
Peter.[1] Radical Anglican priests like Stanley Evans and Paul Oestreicher came to address meetings or hold services; so, too, did
Austen Williams from St Martin's. Kingsway Hall itself had excellent
acoustics and was used by EMI and Decca to record Maria Callas,
Gigli, Joan Sutherland, conducted perhaps by Sir Thomas Beecham
or Sir Adrian Boult[2] and the money from its hire used to fund the
ever-growing social work.

Each year there was a money-raising Christmas Fair and in
January, as well as the internal mission, a Stewards' Party. Every
month there was a fund-raising social, too, and Rescue sales for those
in great need went on for three days. Lettings (which latterly
diminished) provided more cash, for the appetite of the West London
Mission for work was gargantuan and the budget large. Drama, too,
was not ignored: one year Tennessee Williams' *The Glass Menagerie*
would be produced, another Christopher Fry's *The Boy with the Cart*.
Once Britten's *Noye's Flood* was presented with Donald Soper as
God, who was overheard to say: 'They told me to shut up. And I'm
God.'[3]

'There are probably more seekers than saints,' Donald commented
of his congregation in the late 1950s, which included working-class
people from the neighbourhood[4] (though attempts to reach these
were not very successful), and M.P.s like Arthur Henderson, who
was one of the Circuit stewards. Representatives of Africa and Asia

were also present, and on Sunday evening, according to Derek Walker, one of many talented people Donald attracted to Kingsway, 'the scarves of a dozen London colleges' were visible.[5]

Sunday worship started with Communion in the crowded Little Chapel at 10.00 a.m. Often at 11.00 there would be 400 for Morning Prayer and at night 800 to 1,000, with men in the majority, though membership itself was around 580. Sometimes visitors from abroad like Kenneth Kaunda from Zambia would worship at Kingsway; or distinguished Methodists, like Dorothea Price Hughes, Hugh Price Hughes's daughter, who died only in 1964. Donald's sermon series, like that on the Seven Deadly Sins, advertised on Tube hoardings, were especially successful, the church being packed for the address on lust!

Besides the activities of the Community Centre, Luncheon Club, Guild and Youth Work (which deaconesses were responsible for), each quarter the magazine *Kingsway* was produced and 10,000 copies distributed. Even Sean O'Casey, the Irish playwright, was a subscriber. 'Enclosed a tiny spark for the West London Mission fire,' he wrote to Frank McCarthy, one of Donald's key workers, who had known O'Casey for twenty years. In fact he got a very generous cheque.[6] Donald reported in *Kingsway* on his world-wide work and in it, too, were published his sermons, taken down verbatim by people like Sheila Townson, the warden of Katharine Price Hughes Hostel, who also made copious recordings of occasions in Hyde Park and Tower Hill. One of his reports told of his Caribbean visit in 1954, from which emerged Antigua Parties, for which tickets were sold to raise money to build homes there,[7] two of which were built by 1960.[8]

Donald also raised money from statutory and voluntary sectors for the social work. 'He squeezed the LCC till the pips squeaked,' Denys Orchard, one of his Circuit stewards, remembers, approaching the task as if managing director of GEC, though he did not always raise enough.[9] He always signed thank you and appeal letters personally, sometimes by the hundred,[10] but often only sketched out replies, leaving a competent secretary to write the text. In addition, he donated royalties from his books to the Mission's work.

Once Donald learned staff from a project were eating pub lunches. Summoning them to his office, he dressed them down, arguing it was not right for them to be seen frequently there. Similarly when he discovered Circuit stewards were drinking sherry at a wedding party he accused them of being inebriated, which they were not. 'I know I'm extreme about teetotalism,' he later admitted.

Donald's attitude to his employees – at one point numbering over 300 – was firm. If there was a whiff of impropriety, as with one organist, who was sacked on the spot, he could be very tough indeed. On Wednesday mornings the chief project staff met with Donald to enable him to keep his finger on the pulse. He chaired all Executive meetings, whereas at other similar London Mission meetings they were chaired by the District Chairman. Thus he controlled the whole enterprise, the mixture charted by what he wanted to do, which others accepted because they had 'a high regard for the immense wisdom of Donald Soper'.[11]

He was in control of Sunday, too, when normally there were printed service sheets of hymns and prayers. 'Dr Soper wrote a time in red for each section of the service,' Tony Bradshaw recalls, 'and kept to time within minutes. No notes, no sense of hurry or padding out to detract from the act of contemplation and worship.'[12] Indeed, Donald was so time-conscious he kept his watch in a certain way the more easily to see its face. It was the same at Hyde Park, to which he was driven for years by Stella St John, where he would arrive early and wait in the car a short distance away.

Naturally with so many groups and personalities involved it was difficult to please everyone. 'I have given up trying to please you all the time,' Donald Soper declared,[13] his wife adding, in the eyes of some 'Whatever he does, he does it wrong.'[14] Perhaps the most sensitive moments occurred immediately after one of Donald's controversial statements. Donald himself would be out of harm's way in his office, whereas staff on the premises would be approached and blamed for what Donald had said.[15] Despite these frictions, however, and Donald's essential shyness which often inhibited intimate contact, he was able to generate great loyalty, Muriel Place, for example, only retiring in 1962, after forty-four years at Kingsway,[16] Jessie Michener, too, who ran the Enquiry Office, joined the clerical staff in 1915 and stayed for forty-three years.[17] Secretaries as well, like Miss Key and Margaret Antill (later Marshall), worked with Donald many years apiece and managed in part at least to keep him in order. Deaconesses, also, like Sisters Lottie, Kathleen and Marjorie, brought consecration to the work which Donald spoke of when praising Sister Lottie's personal ministry, oversight of the philanthropic and social work, ability to find the right people for jobs and help for 'desperately needy people'.[18] With the assistant ministers, who came mainly for short periods, there was less intimacy, though during David Smith's time a re-evaluation of Kingsway's work was undertaken. In fact Donald was always better when acting as a pioneer than with close colleagues, perhaps because of his imperative need to act on those things which consumed him.

The social work, which developed substantially after 1945, kept Donald rooted in reality as he chaired the Relief Fund from which Christmas gifts were given and the Holiday Fund Committee.[19] What impressed Sister Marjorie Watson most about her six years at Kingsway was his readiness to change, especially in relation to the social work and the hostels. 'If one piece of work had served its purpose,' she has recalled, 'it was abandoned and something new took its place.'[20] There was another factor at work, too, the availability of people to help. 'We find many difficulties in staffing the dozen or so sides of our social work which lie behind the mission,' Donald said in 1957 at his twenty-first anniversary celebrations. 'The flow of social workers available to us during the war, because of our pacifist position, somehow seems to have dried up.'[21]

Donald presided over an organization which included a much used clothing store and a daily crèche, attended by fifty. The Hungerford, run during the war under the arches at Charing Cross as a centre for vagrants by the Anglican Pacifist Fellowship had been taken over by the WLM. Alfred Hartley and Sydenham Houses catered for old people, Kingsway House for mothers and babies, Katharine Price Hughes Hostel for girls in need of care, and Fellowship and Emerson Bainbridge Houses for students. There was, too, Kingsway Youth Club, run for many years by Donald's long-standing friend, Bill Weston, which Donald visited only a few times, for he trusted his colleague. 'Everything going all right, Bill?' he would ask casually. 'Yes.'[22] Thus satisfied, Donald would proceed to his next task. The hostels and the Crèche itself each had collages in them given by Marie Soper, who made them with meticulous care as her contribution to her husband's work, a husband she and her family saw infrequently so much did he live for the West London Mission and its outreach.

Donald's involvement with a project was sometimes immense, as with The Hungerford, finding it a new home, with Lambeth Council's help, and raising money and appointing staff, including two Kingsway members, Denys Orchard[23] and Stella St John.[24] As with Gertrude

Owen Hostel, Donald chaired meetings whenever possible and, if abroad, ensured others took his place. Numbers and quality of staff fluctuated but Donald persisted, even when in 1957 a new matron had to be dismissed. By now both men and women were given support but in 1960 the hostel was closed for renovations, later re-opening as St Luke's and St Mary's Hostel for the care and rehabilitation of alcohol abusers who are homeless and rootless, with Norman Ingram-Smith, (later head of St Martin-in-the-Fields Social Work Department) in charge.[25] 'The chair of the LCC Health Committee said some very kind things about our recent experiment with alcoholics at St Luke's House,' Donald Soper reported in 1962,[26] which pleased him for St Luke's was a pioneer project, one of the first in London, for people in such acute distress, backed up soon by two 'follow on' houses to provide sustained support.

Donald was similarly committed to the Crèche. 'My one clear memory,' Rachel Squire, M.P., has recollected of the years 1955–9, when she attended it, 'is a visit by Father Christmas. I did not, of course, realize that it was actually Lord Soper as I still believed in Santa Claus.'[27] Her mother, like many others, went to work and so needed a place for her child from 8.00 till 6.00 p.m. Here Rachel Squire and the other children in the Crèche, which served as a training nursery for students resident on the Mission's fifth floor, received meals, medical care, and played on the roof garden, where there were toys, sandpits (disliked by Donald), a paddling pool and prams.

Other employees included Beatrice Holmes, not untypical of others, who ran Grove House in Clapham for young girls who were pregnant. Originally its Assistant Warden, she became Warden in an emergency and stayed for twelve years, growing used to Donald's ticking off with a curt 'Don't do it again',[28] and his few words and looks, which conveyed his meaning.[29] He was firm, too, about the need for boundaries, urging her not to remain involved with girls who had left. Like others Miss Holmes was in awe of Donald, partly due to the way she saw him handle Staff Meetings, as the project leaders discussed their work.

Miss Holmes never knew Donald miss a House Committee. He was a good employer with no fuss. 'A nice hat you've got on,' he would comment. 'And a nice face under it.'[30] And with that he was gone. He was particularly supportive when things went wrong. Once there was much feeling against a member of staff. When Donald came to sort things out he treated all in the conflict the same so no one was up in arms, even though the situation did involve medical advice and the departure of a colleague. On another occasion Donald met one of the 500 residents who passed through Grove House over its lifetime. With a cheery hello he asked, 'When do you expect your baby, my love?'[31]

The 1959 summer edition of *Kingsway* indicated the scope of the activities over which Donald Soper presided. During the previous year over 100,000 had attended worship and over 100 open-air meetings had been held, it reported, involving some 140,000. Some 68,000 beds had been occupied in WLM Homes and Hostels and there had been nearly 1,500 'Relief' applicants interviewed at Kingsway. Daily fifty children had attended the Crèche and there had been over 100 visits to Pentonville and Holloway, with sixty prisoners helped, as well as 150 visits to hospitals. In addition, 789,000 lunches had been served at the Kingsway Lunch Club.[32] When he looked back, however, Donald had to admit the statistics were disappointing,[33] for most young people involved left the care of the WLM more or less as they entered it. Moreover, even if the mission had achieved an '8 per cent success rate', that figure was often a temporary judgment,[34] though when he compared photographs of 1920s and 1960s Crèche children, a great improvement in their physical condition was evident.

At a National Children's Home Conference meeting in 1961 Donald described his role on a licensing committee for the release of young people, some with terrible records, from an approved school. Running through most stories was 'an evil thread of deprivation' through inadequate housing.[35] When he worked with Sheila Townson, the warden of Katharine Price Hughes Hostel for over twenty years, he found the same was true for those on probation or in trouble with the law. This work, started in Doughty Street to help prostitutes in the West End, and subsequently moved to Highbury Grove, Islington, involved Donald, after the 1948 Children and Young Persons' Act, in intricate negotiations with the Home Office and deeper engagement with the Probation Service. Residents could stay up to two years and were regularly visited by their probation officers and sometimes there were even weddings from the home, Donald himself taking two or three.

Sheila Townson could see clearly how to adapt Katharine Price Hughes Hostel to changing circumstances so at the start of the 1970s it was closed and re-built, opening shortly after, with a broader age range, and for both young men and women, with Sheila as Warden again. 'I am concerned that the whole prison system is irredeemable,' Donald told peers in 1967, as he commended yet again Katharine Price Hughes Hostel and asserted he could 'testify to the remedial processes that flow from this end of punishment, which is reformative'.[36]

Donald was always concerned to offer hope to those in trouble, a point he made in a debate on the welfare of illegitimate children (there were only illegitimate parents in his view) inaugurated in 1967 by Lady Summerskill. Short-term accommodation was needed, he suggested, like Hopedene, the WLM hostel for unmarried mothers and their babies, who could stay for up to two years and where often both hope and penitence emerged and a new sense of responsibility.[37] Moreover, society needed to pay heed to the way 'imperfect human beings endeavour to deal with those who, in their judgment – and quite rightly so in many cases – are even more imperfect,'[38] he indicated and observed elsewhere he had once chaired a day's seminar on alcoholism and listened 'with a horrid fascination to a description of these particular symptoms and discovered that I had most of them myself – and I am a teetotaller'.[39]

Donald had two other major commitments at this period, the Order of Christian Witness (OCW) and the Notting Hill Team Ministry. It was Donald Chesworth, an LCC colleague, who had alerted him to the problems of North Kensington, though these had become high profile in 1958 and 1959 through race riots there and elsewhere in Britain and the murder by white youths in Kensal New Town on Whit Sunday, 1959, of Kelso Cochrane, a young West Indian carpenter.[40] There was landlord intimidation, too, and it was this Donald Soper, and his two LCC colleagues, Donald Chesworth and Mrs Olive Wilson, decided to investigate. He was appalled that West Indians were exploiting their own people, he remarked in Hyde Park that May. Such was the over-crowding and poor housing conditions the Government must act. The Kensington Borough Council could help, too, by referring extortionate rent demands to the Rent Tribunal[41] he suggested in letters to *The Times*[42] and the *Kensington Post and News*, which gained a speedy response from the Council leader, who said he *would* act if he received accurate information.[43]

Donald chose the 1959 Methodist Conference to make one of his pungent speeches. 'He had,' remembers Kenneth Greet, 'a remarkable way of timing his interventions which was uncanny. They had a great effect, and were sometimes controversial.'[44] The Bristol Conference was no exception. During a debate on London Mission Affairs he called attention to racial tension in North Kensington, where it seemed the Church had been totally inadequate. Methodism, he argued, which previously had initiated ventures of evangelism, should now be prepared to start in the secular field to deal with Notting Hill's problems.[45] He urged the Conference therefore to help and by the end of the debate, aided by the sympathetic handling of the issue by his friend Dr Eric Baker, President that year, had the co-operation of the key figures in power, with access to money and people if a plan emerged. Shortly after his return to his office a proposal for a group ministry in Notting Hill from David Mason, now a Methodist minister in the Potteries, arrived on his desk. Donald responded immediately with a phone call saying the proposal was what he had in mind and when could he begin?[46]

The scheme, which envisaged three ministers running a community-based church in North Kensington, started in 1960, when David and Ann Mason moved into the area as Lancaster Road Methodist Church came directly under the West London Mission. Two other ministers and their wives joined the team later, one, Norwyn Denny, with experience of work in Jamaica, the other, Geoffrey Ainger, with experience of the East Harlem Protestant Parish in New York.[47] Donald was Superintendent from 1960 to 1967 and always available for consultation when things were difficult, either on personal or political matters, supporting the scheme, which was not without its critics, and providing money. 'Without him the experiment would not have got off the ground,' says David Mason. 'I think it illustrates ... that when other prominent church leaders agreed intellectually but lacked the courage and the will to act, Donald Soper made good this deficiency.'[48]

Sometimes he would visit the area and in 1962 preached a series of sermons on social questions. By then membership had virtually doubled, youth clubs had been set up and a multi-racial church with strong community links established.[49] As at Kingsway Hall the Eucharist was their focus, as Notting Hill Methodists allowed their premises to be used for social and artistic purposes. 'One of the things we have discovered in the group ministry in Notting Hill for which I am responsible,' Donald commented in 1965, 'is that community care must cover the whole of human life.'[50] Slowly now the groups expanded, as clergy from other traditions joined it, and indeed more lay ministries were developed. 'I believe,' wrote Donald Soper as the Notting Hill group separated from the WLM in 1967, 'that it has set a new pattern for the kind of ministry needed ... particularly in such multi-racial areas.'[51]

Donald had backed the Notting Hill ministry partly through his zeal for evangelism. 'I am,' he wrote in 1994, 'by profession an evangelist,'[52] a vocation even evident in the war-time as he discussed with eight people just back from Hyde Park whether they, like him, could speak in the open air and if so, how? He also raised the matter in church meetings and by the summer of 1942 eight men and women, some local preachers, visited Dorking for a week, invited by local Methodists. 'We went with great uncertainty,' Jean Shackleton later recounted, 'and like a flock of baby sparrows round their parent,'[53] but soon all were speaking to soldiers and civilians from three strategic spots in the High Street.

So began the Kingsway Preachers, who next year visited Cornwall. In 1944 it was Barnstaple's turn and this time a family of Salvationists from Regent Hall was also involved. In the spring of 1945 Donald wrote to 372 ministers and 110 circuits in Greater London, inviting them to consider 'Preaching from the pew', explaining Kingsway Hall itself now had seventy-five open-air speakers. On the day some 500 came, who agreed to set up machinery to develop what Donald had begun,[54] under the title The London Christian Campaigners, 140 of whom that year visited Salisbury, where the market place was their focus for two days, as from noon till well after dusk open-air speaking was maintained.[55] Donald concluded most meetings but he expected speakers to be well prepared, too, and insisted their addresses were written out three times to get them right.[56]

Denys Orchard, on his first campaign, met a positive reception at Salisbury but wondered if the campaign was successful. He felt that only when the Order of Christian Witness, as it became the following year, when many of Salisbury's features were repeated in Plymouth and twice the number involved, had been sown in unattractive virgin soil, and the best seed faced opposition, would they know 'what a true campaign harvest really is'.[57] It was a perceptive comment, for as campaign succeeded campaign, both at Easter-time and in August, whilst it was clear campaigners were deeply affected, some becoming parsons, it became extremely difficult to quantify the effect of the week (or weekend) on the local churches, towns and neighbourhoods visited. Of course, there were individual successes, like the family whose baby Donald Soper baptized on one campaign, which kept links with one campaigner for years, but, once the OCW teams had left, any development depended totally on the local churches.

There was no doubt, however, about the enthusiasm a week-long visit generated, nor the calibre of the people Donald Soper was attracting, as OCW mushroomed. One of the Plymouth team in 1946, for example, included a teacher of classics, an engineer, a university student, a dispenser, a prospective missionary and a policewoman. Campaigners also included people from Africa, the Caribbean, Germany, Australia and Canada. One service, held in a ruined church, drew 2,000 and the combination of open-air gatherings – outside cinemas, on the Hoe itself, on bomb sites – with great public meetings called 'Question-Time' or 'Hecklers' Hour', made the campaign the talk of the town. Even though 2,000 gathered for Communion as the climax to the week, however, there were no mass conversions. Rather there was a readiness to hear, a sympathy and surprise that the campaigners had paid to go, given up a week's holiday and were willing to rough it in church halls.[58]

That November OCW, whose style was caught by the three words – Communication, Community and Communion – was formally inaugurated at Kingsway Hall at a Eucharist.[59] Membership, which was ecumenical, was open to those who believed each Christian had a responsibility to witness to Christian faith by life and works; was willing to do this with others, and prepare and be available for one week-long campaign in August.[60] In 1947, some 300 campaigners, many in their twenties, descended on Huddersfield and lived in school halls in seven 'families', led by a commandant responsible for contacts in the area designated. On the Sunday 120 services were undertaken with Donald himself preaching in the parish church. Each day started with prayer and a briefing led by Donald and for the first time there were visits to factories and to three prisoner of war camps, where the reception varied. Some also visited pubs, while others went to women's groups or spoke in the open air. At the opening meeting in Huddersfield Town Hall the Mayor pointed out that even Gracie Fields, who had recently sung there, had not drawn so many[61] and on the last night, when Donald visited nine rallies the timing had to be stop-watched.[62]

Cannock Chase 1948, another big campaign, involved over 300 in an area of 100 square miles, which was divided into thirty 'families' on the Huddersfield model. The ten campaigns, operating side by side, were co-ordinated each morning by Donald at the general assembly. 'Donald Soper could have led a Crusade,' June Strick, a member of Kingsway Hall, once observed. Now in OCW he had a modern form of it, but this time the crusade was against a secular society, whose paganism continued to trouble and vex him.

Many of the commandants later held responsible positions in church life like Kingsley Turner (Chairman of District), Roy Trevivian from the City Temple (the BBC), and David Mason. Pauline Callard, too, one of the Kingsway Preachers, subsequently became Principal of Southlands College. For her OCW was contrary to her family upbringing, but the 1953 Exeter campaign broke her shackles, introduced her to teamwork and Christian fellowship at a deep level. John Stacey, and his brother David, also became involved in OCW, the former first at Cannock Chase. Though persuaded to take evangelism seriously by OCW, he found one over-riding problem existed: young campaigners were always trying to imitate Donald, 'without his ability or opportunity or persona'.[63] Nevertheless, at Cannock Chase visits to factories, canteens, clubs, pubs, youth clubs and dances, and open-air work, (Donald spoke to 500 on Pelsall Common) did have a lasting effect on the area.[64]

Though most in OCW, according to Frank Kelly, 'were never Soper satellites, nor even in orbit around him',[65] campaigns were not the same in Donald's absence,[66] for his experience of reaching non-Christians was unique, though he admitted in 1952 the Church was not much nearer the secret of reaching them than when he began.[67] Yet by 1953 OCW and its forebears had nearly twenty campaigns behind them, including two in Germany. One unexpected development occurred at this time after a campaign in Cardiff and Barry, which had caused a revival in the churches' belief in mission in the community.[68] Already OCW had one long-term project on a housing estate in Honor Oak, south London. Now Alfred and Phoebe Willetts, with their children, set up a second project in Cardiff's Tiger Bay area after two OCW missions in Bute Town. They were two of the many Donald influenced, and at one point he had to visit Phoebe in prison during her six months' sentence for sitting down with others outside the entrance to an atomic research establishment.[69] Another radical working with Donald was Dr John Vincent, who went on

Donald Soper's parents.

Donald and Marie Soper, wedding day, 3rd August 1929.

The Sopers with Ann, left, and Bridget, on holiday 1936.

onald, left, aged 14, with his sister Millicent and brother
Meredith.

Mr and Mrs Soper Senior's Golden Wedding,
1st August 1950.

The Rev Donald Soper coming out of the Methodist
Conference, early 1930s.

Dr Soper addressing a crowd in Trafalgar Square, c.19

Three Methodist preachers: Drs Sangster, Weatherhead
and Soper, early 1950s.

Donald Soper's largest open-air meeting, Galle Face,
Columbo, Ceylon, 1947.

Soper and an Order of Christian Witness team, Risca Valley, South Wales, 1949.

Dr Soper in Russia, 1956. To his left: Canon C E Raven, leader of the delegation.

rd Soper at the Centenary of Fernhead Road Methodist Church, London, 1985.

Dr Soper's 90th birthday Eucharist, Hinde Street Methodist Church, 31st January 1993. To his right the Rev Doreen Hare, Methodist University Chaplain.

Tower Hill, December 1934.

Hyde Park, July 1994.

With Mary and Harold Wilson at a Christian Socialist gathering, Kingsway Hall, March 1971.

In the hot seat, Tyne Tees, early 1960s.

Lord Soper with George Thomas, the Speaker of the House of Commons, and Methodist MPs and Lords during the Presidency of the Rev Norwyn Denny, 1993.

Dr Soper at launch of Fellowship, Freedom and Equality, with (left) Dr David Ormrod (editor) and other Tawney lecturers Dr Pauline Webb, Father Kenneth Leech and the Rev Cedric Mayson, London School of Economics 1990.

Donald Soper and Tony Benn at County Hall, London, at the launch of *Facing the Future as Christians and Socialists*, 1985.

At the Dorchester Peace Rally, 20th June 1936. *From left to right:* Robert Gray (organiser), Dick Sheppard, Florence, wife of Thomas Hardy, George Lansbury, Vera Brittain, Donald Soper and Laurence Housman.

Dr Soper with Trevor Huddleston, C.R., and Father Rayne his Superior, at a meeting in the Central Hall, Westminste April 1956.

Dr Soper debating pacifism with John Middleton Murry, 1950.

Lord Soper, President of the League Against Cruel Sports with Eric Heffer MP, 1968.

Lord Soper with Mr T E Chester Barratt, playing 'Annie Laurie' at the National Children's Home Caring '72 meeting.

Still campaigning for nuclear disarmament. Outside County Hall, London, 1984 with two representatives from the Battersea Peace Pagoda, The Very Rev Edward Carpenter, Illtyd Harrington, Ian McKellen and Bruce Kent.

Leading a Fellowship of Reconciliation delegation to Downing Street with a statement about the Gulf War.

Outside the refurbished St Luke's Centre, with a donor from British Telecom, 1990.

Lord and Lady Soper outside Parliament, 1965.

On holiday with Lady Soper and some of the family, Po Joke, Cornwall, August 1973.

Hon DD, Cambridge, with some of the family, 1988.

Lord and Lady Soper with their family, Diamond Wedding, House of Lords 1989.

OCW campaigns for ten years. During one at Pontypool in August 1961, four nightly meetings were held in the Town Hall on trade unionism, nuclear politics, the crisis in the family and sex and at the final Communion service many dedicated themselves to Christ who had come to this decision through the 'situational' appeal for discipleship made each night.[70]

The style of evangelism Donald used at Pontypool was typical of the concreteness of his approach, a way of communicating Christ which taught Harry Morton, at one time secretary of OCW, all he knew about the subject. Others, too, like Jim Bates, subsequently Chaplain at Southlands College, learned much about doing theology in the world[71] and some Donald influenced went on to found the Methodist Renewal Group in the 1960s. Yet more were given 'a magic start to adulthood', like Anne Ord, who spoke at the huge opening rally of the Rhondda Valley campaign in 1957.[72] Clifford Sharp, too, found himself speaking to large numbers, in his case addressing 2,000 men in the RAF[73] and once Yvonne Griffiths, on house-to-house visiting, had to rescue a woman about to gas herself because of her husband's tragic death some months earlier.[74]

Jan and Kathie Wills, however, represented another strand in OCW, which they had known since the 1953 Isle of Man campaign, for though on the receiving end of a campaign in Burslem they later developed a community development approach for the inner city. Donald Soper was for them, therefore, a catalyst who let them grow away from him to find their own vocation.[75] Most startling of all perhaps was the quiet and somewhat timid woman who became a local preacher, a Greenham Common protestor and a speaker in the universities of America, where she went to jail and became entangled in legal actions which involved the American Foreign Affairs Department.[76]

David Hatton, another of OCW's secretaries, found Donald had a humility as when he stayed with his family, potted their baby and offered to clean their shoes.[77] Others like those who manned open-air sites in Highbury, Lincoln's Inn Fields and Shepherd's Bush[78] found Donald helped them discover a new courage as they flung themselves into the movement. Herein perhaps was a defect for, unlike the Iona Community, OCW had no firm organization and when some early enthusiasts left, there was a lack of strategy and continuity.

'No great Order has ever developed in the Christian Church which has not been founded on a common prayer life,' John Vincent had warned from America, where he was studying. 'From the early months of Dr George Macleod's Iona Community, the basis of common life in Christ has been in a devotional discipline. Has OCW been falling behind in this?'[79] Certain training events were provided, of course, and Donald himself reckoned he learned how to run the WLM itself as a result of his OCW experiences. It was also in touch with the best exponents of mission available, Ernest Southcott in Halton, Ted Wickham in the Sheffield Industrial Mission and George Macleod himself, and conversant, too, with the best writers on mission, from the Abbé Michonneau's *Revolution in a City Parish*, to Major Fred Brown's *Secular Evangelism*. But though over fifty campaigns had been held since 1946, some large, some small, did OCW members have a rule of life which bound them together?

Some grew restless and by 1967 it was clear a candid assessment was necessary, as it was admitted 'for some years we have been in decline'.[80] There was uncertainty, too, about the place of OCW in the life of the Church. Birmingham, 1960, had been the last big campaign, though the Burslem and Bury Campaigns in 1962 and 1963 involving Dr Marjorie Lonsdale, headmistress of Trinity, Southport, had 120 campaigners.[81] Mostly, however, OCW found itself working more intimately with the local congregations in their ongoing work, inevitably in the 1960s taking place amid secularism as the debate about *Honest to God* raged. Yet did this new approach not necessarily mean OCW lost contact with the outsider?[82] Perhaps those OCW groups which continued after a campaign was over, or which sprang up in a local context, some of them abroad after hearing Donald speak of OCW's work, were the only ones equipped to stay the course and develop what was in essence a form of pre-evangelism by Donald and the teams.[83]

Donald's personality, the focus point for OCW campaigns, allowed him no let up ever, though he did admit by 1970, when he was sixty-seven, he was working at 75 per cent of his former pace! Throughout the 1960s and the 1970s he kept up his heavy schedule, admitting in 1964 he took on too much, which meant he had 'little time for active leisure, home life or the cultivation of the arts'.[84] He was still in demand as a preacher at Anniversary services in the Missions of the big cities and at special occasions from Cornwall to Northumberland, for his presence ensured a large congregation and local media interest. Secular groups, too, like the League of Friends of Poole Hospital,[85] invited him to speak, which almost always ensured a press story related to his visit.

Donald's open-air work kept him in the public eye, too, as in 1979 when a young police constable alleged Donald was obstructing the environs of Tower Hill and asked him to leave, or be arrested.[86] Many wondered how Donald managed so much but he was, of course, highly disciplined and organized, on long train journeys reading the latest large book. At Kingsway itself he would be in his office by 9 a.m., do *The Times* crossword, see people, make the necessary phone calls before letters, then go to the House of Lords or elsewhere, seldom preparing formal speeches, sermons or lectures. Now a London institution, with his Hyde Park forays listed in West End hotels, he was as likely to turn up in Westminster Abbey to preach at the National Children's Home Centenary Year service[87] as to be on a home-grown *Any Questions?* panel in Harpenden, organized by Ann Bird, an OCW contact, with Eric Morecambe, Marjorie Proops and others, to raise money for cancer research.[88] His message was still the same, however, as he told Joan Bakewell in a dialogue at St Mary-le-Bow: the kingdom of God would come because there was a power which operated through human obedience.

Donald was seldom far from Methodism's centre either, whether intervening at Methodist Conferences, or hosting with George Thomas the Annual Presidential Dinner for Methodist members of Parliament during Bill Gowland's Presidency, a minister with whom he had much in common. Sometimes he would go out of his way to make pastoral visits, like those to Miss Key, his secretary for twenty years, just before she died, or to his mentor Dr J.E. Rattenbury on his birthdays. In this period, too, he extended his trips abroad, as he and his wife took groups of twenty or thirty to Russia, Egypt, Turkey and Israel. Donald, of course, also went on tours alone, taking a week's mission in Nigeria in 1963, and speaking at the opening services of the United Church of Zambia in 1965, afterwards touring the country. He took a short mission in Nashville, Tennessee, visited New Orleans to address a Methodist Congress on Evangelism and in 1968, after being part of a crowd of 25,000 at Pope Paul VI's Easter audience, subsequently had a private meeting with him.[89]

Donald continued to be controversial and was still restlessly testing new ground like a prospector. Once when he was asked to reflect on 1965 he shared his 'fantasies' which included banning Bible study for a year; moving to group ministries and compelling every minister to read Bonhoeffer and shun Tillich. 'I must,' he added, 'search my own heart to see where I have drawn back from that reasonable service to which I am called.'[90] His suggestions caused considerable uproar.[91]

'The WLM has been a pioneer church in days past – we have blazed many a trail over the years,' he asserted in 1970. 'I hope that we in the mission may be pioneers again, leading the way into the sort of institutional Christianity which is both apostolic and suitable to the conditions that face us all in the years to come.'[92] His sentence came at a time of crisis in the Mission for one Sunday evening in January 1969, when Donald had but recently returned to work after an illness, a section of Kingsway Hall's ceiling collapsed.[93] As worship had ended before 7.30 nobody was hurt, but it was a portent, and the congregation never worshipped regularly there again.

The cost of repairs threw the debate about the future of the WLM into the melting pot. Already in 1965, when £100,000 was needed to restore the Central Hall, Westminster, at the Methodist Conference that year Donald had proposed the sale of Kingsway Hall and a joint ministry in Westminster,[94] a proposal not supported by a Methodist Committee which reported to the 1966 Conference.[95] Already a debate had been stimulated about Kingsway's future, suggesting changes, for others were now pioneering, travel costs were affecting numbers and the local population and day-time workers were largely unattended to.[96]

There was another strand in the dynamic, also: Donald's love for the Church of England. Though he had a high regard for the Roman Catholic Church – the supreme historical realization of Christianity[97] with 'more saints per square mile than every other church',[98] as he once explained in an article in *Punch* – he could not become a Roman Catholic because of its doctrine of Papal Infallibility and unresolved theological questions about 'the person and dignity of Mary'.[99] But with the Church of England it was different, especially for Methodists. In 1956 he had said he wanted to see the Methodist Church become a Methodist society within the Church of England[100] and now, with formal talks between the two churches in progress, he hoped for positive results from such conversations. Accordingly he built a friendship with Holy Trinity, Kingsway, the two churches manning a soup kitchen in Christian Aid Week and joining in other activities. He remained hopeful that at the national level Anglicans and Methodists would unite, even when it became clear there was insufficient support for the unity scheme being proposed, and argued the timetable for this new Church had not been lengthened 'but may indeed have been strengthened', by its rejection.[101] (In fact, the Church of England turned down the Anglican/Methodist proposals for a second time in 1972.)

Donald decided, therefore, to see if Holy Trinity, Kingsway, could become a shared church, an idea received with hostility by some in both congregations, if not by their clergy. He had two objectives, the first being 'the *appearance* of *unity*', and the second 'dignity and beauty in worship'.[102] Progress was slow but by September 1969, shared Sunday evening worship began at Holy Trinity, Kingsway.[103] In 1970 the Area Pastoral Committee of the London Diocese heard the Bishop of London explain that Donald Soper was seeking alternative accommodation in the area once Kingsway Hall was sold. (He was negotiating with the property developer Harry Hyams at the time, but in 1971 negotiations were called off.)[104] Discussions with Holy Trinity had now broken down as its Parochial Church Council was unwilling to make arrangements involving guarantees for a long period and the Methodists were unprepared to use their money for improvements without them.[105]

Donald's proposal, therefore, foundered though the Pastoral Committee believed Holy Trinity, Kingsway, could have been adapted for shared use without difficulty and, indeed, supported the proposal. It was not so forthcoming, however, about Donald's attempt in 1971 to share St Mary-le-Strand, and after taking advice took no further action on any proposal, partly because by now joint services were well established at Holy Trinity.[106] Indeed, these services, which continued under the Rev. John Arrowsmith, including con-celebrated Communion,[107] lasted for some years, though the venture never worked well, even though Donald explained the Methodists did not view the scheme as a take-over.[108]

At this time Donald also made a highly personal attempt to break the impasse between Anglicans and Methodists. In 1946 he had been willing to offer himself for ordination 'with any who will join me, by the Archbishop of Canterbury and by the Moderator of the Free Churches',[109] because he wanted 'corporate credentials',[110] for a re-united Church, not because his ordination was invalid or insufficient, though he accepted it was irregular, if some particular period in Church history were judged the norm, a test affecting 'nearly

187

everybody else's ordination'.[111] Now he responded to an initiative by the Rev. Harold Goodwin, an Anglican priest and journalist, then attached to St Giles-in-the-Fields, who approached Donald because he believed the ordination to Anglican orders of a well-known Methodist minister would break the deadlock in Anglican/Methodist relations. Donald said he was willing to be 're-ordained for new functions',[112] a phrase sufficient to encourage Goodwin to approach the Rt Rev. Robert Stopford, then Bishop of London. 'Implicit in the plans,' writes the Rev. G. Thompson Brake, 'was that Soper would be ordained deacon and priest almost simultaneously, so that he could immediately exercise a full ministry in association with the incumbent of a London church.'[113] The Bishop replied that it seemed to him that Donald Soper was trying to 'jump the gun',[114] and the matter rested there, to be revived again in 1981, provided it was clear for what function Donald was being ordained, but again Anglican authorities did not warm to Donald's openness.[115]

With the collapse of negotiations to sell Kingsway Hall and the failure to link with the Church of England it was not surprising there was an air of depression around. Numbers had now declined rapidly, so in effect the mission was kept going by money received from lettings rather than by the giving of the congregation or the support of other institutions, though Donald could still attract big money for projects. Partly the decline was due to the joint services with Holy Trinity, as Sister Marjorie Lewis, one of the early OCW campaigners, found when she returned to Kingsway Hall to take over from Sister Kathleen Lee, who had left in 1973 after ten years there. But it was also due to the style of the operation, for the 1970s public was more inclined to be sceptical about charismatic leaders, though but for Donald's reputation Kingsway Hall might have declined earlier. Partly, too, Donald was a victim of his own success, for from 1960 he had fingers in so many pies he seldom had time to plan for the future.

'To live on the frontier all the time means you haven't got time to stand back and think,'[116] Jeffrey Harris has observed and maybe Donald Soper can be faulted here. But if you considered there was need for a united Anglican/Methodist church in Kingsway, did Donald really lack a strategy? Certainly the Rev. Harry Morton felt that, like Samson, Donald had brought down the Temple when they discussed their common experiences on a BBC programme chaired by Dr Colin Morris.[117] Yet Austen Williams, at St Martin's, took a different view, whilst conceding none had an adequate city centre theology, and that Christians in the central London desert were not adequately supported by their denominations.[118]

With no Anglican/Methodist church now possible in Kingsway, in July 1971, Donald started discussions with Hinde Street Methodist Church, until the 1950s part of the same circuit, indicating when Kingsway Hall eventually closed he would retire. Hinde Street was alive with university undergraduates and graduates, the result after 1945 of focusing Methodist student work there, a policy Donald himself had encouraged then. Now in 1972 an application to the Methodist Conference for the amalgamation of the two circuits was accepted and negotiations between them began which were pro-tracted, partly because Donald's decisions had to be re-run in a more democratic way between the appropriate bodies of the two congrega-tions. Some fought the merger until the last constitutional moment, but Donald remained loyal and unswerving in his decision, chairing many meetings dealing with the merger, but always left for home at 7.00 p.m. even if they were not finished.

The main elements in the agreement involved the redevelopment of the Hinde Street site to accommodate the WLM offices, from where the social work would be run, the closure of the Crèche, and the encouragement of Kingsway members to worship at Hinde Street in due course. There was still the problem of the sale of the building to ensure the future of the social work of the WLM, but this was resolved in 1977, when the freehold of the Kingsway complex was sold to British Land, a property company wishing to develop the site for office accommodation. The deal, similar to others in Manchester, Bradford and Bristol, as an era in Methodist work in city centres came to an end, brought in well over two million pounds to the WLM, which was then invested. Camden Council, however, decided to designate the area for housing development only, so the Kingsway congregation continued its life in Wesley House, the six storey block they retained under the lease-back arrangement, and the lecture hall, now a chapel,[119] knowing their building's future was still unresolved. Sadly a subsequent agreement with British Land by a charity wishing to use the complex, in which case it was hoped a Methodist congregation could stay on in Kingsway and the Hall itself become a multi-racial arts centre for London, fell through at the last moment when British Land sold Kingsway Hall and Wesley House to the Women's Committee of the Greater London Council.

Donald, of course, continued working despite the changes, at one moment supporting local people who came together to protest at GLC plans for the future of Covent Garden,[120] and at others travelling across Britain for preaching appointments. His weekly pattern varied little – three services on Sunday, Hyde Park and interviews afterwards; administration and writing for *Tribune* on Monday; the Guild on Tuesday, which continued to meet till the end, where people like Olive Delves, the cook at Kingsway for over thirty years, felt they received from Donald an academic education as he gave a resumé of a Shakespeare play, or *The Brothers Karamazov*.[121] On Wednesday there was Tower Hill and on Friday sometimes time off for golf. Through the week, too, there was attendance at the House of Lords and social work committees to chair, which, to the annoyance of some, always met at 5.00 p.m.

In 1963 Donald had turned up for a cup of tea with Sister Kathleen Lee, just starting at the mission, looking miserable. It was his sixtieth birthday she discovered and he was dejected. Now, as he contemplated relinquishing his Superintendency, even if, as he said, he was only 're-treading', the thought of giving up his office, stark and shabby as it was, with only John Wesley's bust for relief, was difficult. He would miss, too, the bedroom next door, where he had so often slept, especially during the war, and the thought made him more consistently depressed than in 1963, when he realised he was sixty.

He would also miss the fellowship which he so prized, and the eucharistic worship, whose centrality he had come to appreciate, and the sense of wonder, a phrase he had picked up from Aldous Huxley, it generated.[122] It was this aspect of worship fact which formed the core of his sermon on 30 July 1978, when over 1,000 people, Michael Foot, George Thomas and London Church leaders among them, went to Kingsway Hall for a thanksgiving service for his ministry, an occasion which made him very apprehensive, recalling perhaps his emotions a month earlier when the entire Methodist Conference had stood up as he approached the tribune to declare he had been content to be one of Wesley's travelling preachers and that this had brought him joy, though he had failed 'all too often'.[123]

'Don't make it too painful,' he therefore urged Michael Foot before the service,[124] which was to contain four hymns epitomizing the theological strands in Donald Soper's life – 'How Shall I Sing that Majesty', about the greatness of God; 'Jesu, Thou Joy of Loving Hearts', the Bernard of Clairvaux hymn about the living bread which is Christ; 'Behold the Mountain of the Lord', with its projection of a time when the kingdom had become glorious on earth; and finally, Charles Wesley's 'Love Divine, All Loves Excelling', epitomizing Donald's great stress on the love which can change all.

When Donald preached he linked his address with the hymns, the first 'great poetry',[125] written by someone who was Pascal's contemporary. He wanted to testify to the world of wonder and awe, he said, to the humility which comes from remembering that 'where reason fails with all its powers, there faith remains and love adores'.[126] For those who pretended the only way into truth was 'by the doorways of rationality', he would say he had found an enrichment of the spirit through faith. He believed, too, in the Jesus the second hymn spoke about and the liberating and enfranchising knowledge that came when he lived in His spirit and teaching. The saints gave adequate testimony to that, some of whom had sustained Kingsway Hall itself.

The third hymn he declared brought him much satisfaction. He had once listened to a charismatic preacher in America, who lifted his arms and hands to heaven, and said, 'We don't want pie in the sky. What we want is ham where we am.'[127] 'That's Christianity,' Donald reiterated, and the golden thread which held together the three ways of approach to which he had testified was the truth that God is love. 'Love is not a sentiment,' he explained, 'though it includes it, it is not a feeling, though it is enriched by it, love is an activity – it is something you do. It is goodwill on fire . . .'[128] It involved caring for people you did not like, some of whom, as in the WLM hostel, could 'curse you as quickly as they thank you'.[129] It included, too, tenderness. How he wished he had that 'abiding love of Christ in which it seems He encompassed the whole world',[130] a message proclaimed in the greatest hymn in the Methodist Hymn Book, 'When I survey the wondrous cross',[131] he concluded.

Though the days were dark he had ultimate confidence the kingdom of God would come, and hoped all present could say 'those great words – the city of God remaineth'. And with that, after it had been sung as the recessional by the City of London Choir, one of the many groups, mainly social, of which he was either President or Patron, the service was over and Donald Soper's forty-two years at Kingsway Hall ended. Afterwards he saw Denys Orchard, the Circuit steward who had watched him mellow over the years and who had found the buyer for Kingsway Hall. 'Denys,' he said, 'I just want to say "Thank you". Goodbye.'[132]

Chapter 10

PHILOSOPHER AND PURITAN

'THE SAME CROWDS WHO FOUND in Wesley's preaching the road to salvation are today much more conditioned to look to other pathways to assurance. Marxism is one of them, Fascism is another, science is a third,' Donald wrote in 1979,[1] showing his sensitivity to the responses twentieth-century people had made, as he endeavoured to preach Christ in the context of a scientific revolution which had led to philosophical questioning about the nature of faith itself.

From F.R. Tennant at Cambridge he had learned to argue and analyse. He had also introduced him to Kant and Plato, who Donald considered 'knew as Jesus did if you persist in doing what is wrong you gradually destroy your capacity to do what is right'.[2] Kant, Donald found, had been persuaded there was a God because of the human capacity for awe and wonder.[3]

F.R. Tennant was a philosophical theologian who was convinced that the intellectual status of theology must be tested by seeing how it stood in the light of psychology and the methods and limitations of science. For him theology was about ethical theism. 'God, men and the world constitute a chord,' he wrote, 'and none of its three notes has the ring of truth without the accompaniment of the other two.'[4] His approach influenced Donald's thinking substantially. He took to heart Tennant's warning not to overlook, or reject, something which was true in an enthusiasm to get rid of errors,[5] and also his conviction that the Church's task was to make explicit the implicit – the working out of the general principles of God's purpose and their application to contemporary needs.[6]

Tennant helped Donald employ legitimate inference in argument; to use words in their right context and couch problems philosophically.[7] He persuaded him, also, of the value of inductive rather than deductive processes of reasoning, where a conclusion was postponed and made dependent on the evidence.[8] Donald learnt other points, too, which stood him in good stead – if you cannot solve a problem, it is still helpful to state the problem precisely;[9] revealed religion presupposed natural religion;[10] and that theology has no practical value unless it is 'anthropic' through and through.[11] Above all he came to believe that, though there were many 'dis-teleological factors' in the world, nevertheless 'the environment is hopeful'.[12]

Such ideas recurred continually in Donald's speeches. He was equally alert to the revolution in thought scientists had created. But they were also recognizing, he noticed, much had to be taken on trust.[13] Indeed, both religion and science dealt with 'what defies analysis if you try to describe it'.[14] Indeed, 'matter and spirit are the obverse of the same coin,' he once observed, but people would continue to say religion and science were in inveterate opposition until this was realized.[15] Moreover, the best scientists were saying that belief was 'an essential part of all true knowledge'.[16] Indeed, Spinoza, Eddington and Einstein had all been religious.[17]

What then was Donald Soper's belief? Essentially it was a trust in the power of reason to discover truth by enquiry, dedication and testing. For him the world was basically a reasonable place,[18] and 'the most reasonable' people were 'probably religious'.[19] Christianity itself, argued and thought out, was even a protection against psychosis.[20] If it were fantasy, of course, something else had to take its place, but evidence pointed otherwise.[21] Nothing seemed ever to shake Donald's conviction about the 'reasonable universe in which we seek peace and justice',[22] yet he recognized there had been a flight from reason, as remarkable a phenomenon as the flight into outer space. 'I hate it,' he commented.[23]

Donald did not retain beliefs he could no longer defend and there were, he admitted, many questions he could not answer and problems he could not solve. But he felt he had enough answers to be going on with, and so could endure the gaps in his knowledge.[24] He was, therefore, philosophically a mixture of empiricism and existentialism. Jean-Paul Sartre, he informed his Tower Hill listeners in 1986, had a frame of reference by which he lived and died. Donald could have been speaking for himself, for he argued there must be a point of reference from which 'to have a view in the first place'.[25]

As he studied philosophy Donald learned from the logical positivists, too. 'As a satisfactory theory of knowledge it seems to me to be open to the gravest of objections,' he wrote. 'At the same time I am grateful to the linguistic philosophers for their emphasis upon a problem ignored by the majority of standard philosophers. Words are the only precise means of communication we have, and there is a danger of assuming that familiarity gives them explicability.'[26] 'Linguistically speaking,' he explained, 'it is significant to say that Jesus was a man, whereas it is insignificant to say that Jesus was divine.'[27] For Donald, therefore, the persistent and unavoidable question was whether what Christians professed was consistent with the reality they experienced.[28] In this probing, however, Donald remained sure that whatever modifications were made both in language and in the Christian view itself, Jesus remained 'the way, the truth and the life'.[29]

This assumption of Donald's, of course, was built on a reality which was multi-faceted, yet he had confidence in this approach, for he realized a scientist who 'knew his stuff' would agree that metaphysical fantasy was 'the prelude to metaphysical knowledge'.[30] First, a picture was built up and its worth evaluated, which itself assumed that knowledge could be gained. Always, too, there had to be a willingness to correct a picture if further evidence was forthcoming.[31] 'A great deal of music and poetry and art are much truer than those things which you can get in philosophical textbooks by way of rational thinking,' he considered.[32] Indeed, only art was not destroyed by time.[33] They, therefore, formed part of his picture of reality, for God was known in a universe He had created, 'as the poet is revealed in the sonnet which he has composed'.[34]

How could he discover faith, for neither the philosophers nor the scientists could help him here, whatever their wisdom and knowledge? Donald looked at the universe and found evidence of purpose. 'It looks forward,' he explained, 'it moves; it evolves.'[35] Most importantly, 'there is a bias towards inbuilt Good. Everyone of us knows it, and everyone of us responds to it to some extent.'[36] A doctor who looks for a cure of cancer must believe it is a good world and he can find a cure, he argued elsewhere, or he would not continue his research.[37] Indeed, this innate goodness was the basic requirement of law. If not, it would be impossible to have a police force, law courts or any social justice. 'Now,' he concluded, 'when I speak of God, I speak of the bringing together of these elements, and . . . say that . . . "God" must be the word to describe that combination of Intelligence and Purpose and Good.'[38]

Naturally Donald thought of God as personal, at least as personal as those able to think about Him. Otherwise, the part would be greater than the whole, 'the painting would be superior to the artist'.[39] Some assumed God was not a Person, but Donald wanted to maintain belief in a God who brought together Intelligence, Purpose, Good – all found 'supremely in Jesus Christ'.[40] There was a further reason for belief, he also considered, even though nature did not give irrefutable evidence of God's love,[41] and there was no proof available to satisfy the honest mind of the supremacy of Christianity.[42] This lay in the fact that unless there were a God, surely no one would want to find Him?[43]

Donald, of course, only won his faith through a continual struggle to believe. 'I have doubts myself, and I hope to continue with them,' he admitted in 1958, 'for they have a kind of vitality about them, and I would not barter them for secure acquiescence which by-passes the truth.'[44] He felt, moreover, that the arguments *against* theistic belief were almost as persuasive as those *for* it. 'Purely from the static and academic standpoint' he felt compelled to describe himself 'as an agnostic,' he declared, 'because the evidence that comes to me from various fields of human experience does not ... add up to any coherent pattern . . .'[45]

This facet of his personality made Donald very sensitive to the difficulties people found in believing, so he was always open to the contributions of humanists and agnostics. Indeed, when in the 1950s Mrs Margaret Knight, in her BBC Reith Lectures *Morals without Religion*, opened a Pandora's box of protest and received unprecedented vilification both from Church and press, Donald defended her right to criticize religion. Some theologians, he wrote, seem to act as though courtesy and controversy are mutually exclusive terms.[46] Christians would do themselves much harm, he admonished, if they assumed that Christianity was a 'hot house plant that needs to be protected against the weather'.[47] However, he did consider her talks consisted mainly of undigested moral philosophy, 'bristling with mistakes'.[48] Had she read any contemporary theology, by Charles Raven or Jacques Maritain or A.E. Taylor[49] (his Gifford Lectures *The Faith of a Moralist* had earlier helped Donald understand morality was the key to healthy religion), he wondered.[50] Indeed, religion was not an argument but an announcement, the offer or power by which to follow the truth as scientists, among others, revealed it.[51]

Donald's second attempt to relate to the agnostic and atheist community – 'most teachers in schools and most lecturers in universities are today agnostics,' he believed – occurred in the pages of *Tribune*.[52] Dr Julian Huxley announced that in a hundred years it would be impossible for intelligent people to believe in God. Donald was stung, alleging there was more 'arrogance than erudition'[53] in Huxley's atheism, as his claim that the 'public knowledge' of the laboratories was infallible, whereas the 'private knowledge of the oratory' was illusory.[54] Dr Huxley replied in kind, maintaining that for years he had been searching not for '*the* Truth', (for he believed there was no such thing) but for more and better truth always with a sense of wonder at the back of his mind.[55]

Donald was convinced that the doubt of which the agnostic and atheist tradition was the bearer had percolated to the public which gave any who listened to a presentation of the Gospel a sense that what they heard was dubious, if not fictitious.[56] The forms and symbol of Christianity must be changed and simplified, therefore, so that the essential Gospel could shine forth.[57] Accordingly he welcomed the turmoil the publication of *Honest to God* brought in the 1960s. Only the naive would assume it was breaking entirely new ground he concluded, though it was useful for discussion. Indeed, the first three chapters expressed ideas with which he had grappled at Cambridge.[58] Of another book which 'took off' – *God Is No More* – Donald also wrote positively, particularly because of its unique flavour. What the writers had to say about forgiveness in marriage he found especially insightful.[59] But the Death of God controversy, which grew out of American explorations in the 1960s, he was less keen on. The controversies which developed over these books (and the subsequent one associated with David Jenkins, then Bishop of Durham) did not discourage Donald, of course, for he believed doubt was 'the midwife of truth'.[60] Moreover, any future Christianity would depend utterly on a reduction of doctrines and credal statements by eliminating 'those which can be shown to be outworn and untrue' and putting into the agnostic 'basket' those which were 'speculative and optional'.[61]

How did Donald deal with the philosophical problems belief in God presented? Certainly he found little use for the traditional arguments from St Thomas Aquinas onwards for the existence of God. Nevertheless, he felt the evidence of what was left allowed room for the theistic interpretation of life and 'in many respects encourages it'.[62] He found compelling, too, the fact that human beings seemed to have minds which wanted to believe in goodness. Again it

did seem to him possible there was in history an increasing predomi-
nance of mental and moral qualities. Yet the facts of life only posed a
question, rather than provided an answer.[63] The answer came in
responding to the overall teaching of Jesus, with an emphasis on the
adventure of discipleship, which reason did not contradict, but
neither fully justified, for like the argument from nature 'the claims
of Jesus are not self-evident to the alerted mind'.[64] What surely *was*
compelling was the story of the saints who had found the claims of
Jesus to be true and the story of the survival of the Church amid all
its vicissitudes and wrong turnings.[65] Moreover, as far as Donald was
concerned, there had to be commitment. He himself, he wrote once,
had to take the 'various thoughts and facts, the evidence for and
against the Christian faith', and do something about them, not waiting
either for a heart that was pure or a mind that was free from doubt.[66]

Despite his own confidence Donald felt the whole world was
unlikely to subscribe to the Christian faith. Indeed in Europe he
detected an inexorable decline in belief. Moreover, was not the ethic
of Jesus a pipe dream from which realism demanded a withdrawal to
more practical activities? The questions came to him with a certain
poignancy, as well as urgency, he admitted, as he was accused by left-
wing students of letting them down with his pacifist doctrine which
they spurned. 'We've listened to your so-called Christian ethic and
look where it's got us,'[67] one expostulated in 1970, a response Donald
wanted to query, related as it was to a closed-system, which ran
counter to theistic belief and also to scientists who were constantly
making discoveries which fundamentally altered both the balance of
power and the course of events. Why, therefore, Donald asked, could
there not be 'undiscovered and untried spiritual agencies'[68] which
could fundamentally alter the course of events, too? For him certainly
'obedience to an impossible ethic today makes that same ethic possible
tomorrow'.[69]

What use did Donald have for theology as he interacted with the
world of doubt and unbelief? Of one thing he *was* certain: theology
generally should be 'a sort of scaffolding' through which 'we do our
thinking', rather than a substitute for it.[70] He was clear, too, that the
traditional presentation of pure theology in the Protestant Church
had broken down as was beginning to happen in the Roman Catholic
and the Eastern Orthodox Churches.[71] Yet even those who had felt
compelled to reject the historic metaphysical framework of dogma
because of its assumption of intellectual sufficiency, still found

themselves looking for an equally precise and exhaustive alternative statement. 'What we must learn,' he advised, 'is that we must not only reject the dogma but also reject the frame of mind within which it has been set.'[72]

Accordingly, he tried to interpret the Incarnation itself anew. The fact that Jesus was humbly born and not miraculously set down on the earth, that the revelation of God's love was not made in some metaphysical demonstration of Divine Power, but in Christ's perfect obedience, who was fully human and tempted as human beings were, constituted the basic data which for Donald were enshrined in the Christmas message. They were truths which had to be distinguished rigorously from all other devotional, mystical, imaginative and poetic interpretations which had quite properly gathered round them.[73]

'If anybody could convert me to religious faith it would be Donald Soper,' Richard Clements, the long-time editor of *Tribune* once observed, 'for he has understood the argument of those who could not believe.'[74] Yet despite many hours of presenting Christianity in a highly sophisticated way with people like Michael Foot, Donald often failed to convince those who doubted. The intellectual objections were too strong, the witness of the churches too incredible, the world, with all its suffering and pain, too puzzling a place for belief.

For all his philosophical ingenuity and theological explorations Donald was not able to find a new approach to the problem of suffering either. He had to agree with what he once heard William Temple say: finally, there is no intellectual answer to the problem of pain. Eventually a believer had to come to the foot of the Cross 'and there you can be personally satisfied, although you cannot be overwhelmingly satisfied in your mental processes'.[75] Nevertheless, Donald found it convincing that some of the greatest people had believed in God's love despite their suffering. Yet he realized that without his belief in eternity it was impossible to reconcile God's love 'with the fact of suffering . . .'[76] even though he knew people created much of it themselves. Surprisingly for a rationalist like Donald he was much taken with C.S. Lewis's philosophy of pain, which considered that earlier there had been a 'war in heaven' and the contingent world experienced now was carrying forward problems and exhibiting characteristics from that pre-temporal time. 'Now, that may sound strange and bizarre to modern minds,' he admitted, 'but I think there is a great deal in it.'[77]

Because evidence for belief in God's love came to him in so many ways Donald never jettisoned his faith because at one point he was still perplexed.[78] Nor could he believe there would ever be Utopia on earth, even when all unnecessary suffering and brutality were abolished. Indeed, he could never be completely happy until he met his brother again.[79] 'There is,' he maintained, 'a residue of suffering which is the very heart of God's purpose, and therefore cannot be evil in origin. It is rather part of the raw material out of which God intends to grow our souls.'[80]

Perhaps here he was intimating he believed in an ongoing struggle without which human life had little meaning. Indeed, Councillor Arthur Downes, one of Donald's followers, has indicated he may have been influenced by Hegel, in seeing the necessity for a clash of ideas in life's dialectic.[81] Certainly it is impossible to understand Donald without exploring Marxism's impact on him. Yet even in the 1930s he was sensitive to Communist errors, both at the intellectual and practical level. Moreover, the forcible overthrow of the existing order, if necessary by terror and mass violence, was incompatible with the Gospel because of Donald's pacifism, though he knew violence was not unknown in Christianity itself.[82] Nor could he accept that a Christian should first stress economic liberty and argue that political liberty mattered little. Nevertheless, as long as churches considered it a prime duty to 'make holy war against the Marxist infidel' they would not appreciate 'how much the infidel had learned from Jesus'.[83]

John Macmurray was an influence on Donald here, with his stress on Christianity's discovery that human life was in essence personal, where love and forgiveness were the clue to history. Moreover Macmurray's conviction that inherent in the Hebrew mind was the effort to achieve a universal family which became fully explicit in Jesus[84] became one of Donald's core convictions, too. 'It is not without significance that John Macmurray calls Jesus the first Dialectical Materialist,' he observed in the 1950s, adding that for him the material was the indispensable midwife of the spiritual.[85]

Yet if Macmurray was right to point out that Christianity and morals 'must be founded on personal terms and not academic and rational ones',[86] there was also the Marxist truth that the environment mattered.[87] Accordingly, Donald argued for a Christian environment which went alongside a Christian ethic and destiny, without which he knew they would wither away. Capitalism, socialism and fascism were not varying systems, therefore, which a Christian could choose or not, provided they were operated with compassion, altruism or equality. Rather, such systems had inbuilt characteristics which had to be susceptible of Christian moral judgment. 'Original sin and original goodness,' he concluded, 'belong as much to systems as they do to individuals within those systems. It is high time that organized Christianity took the task of thinking about what is the Christian economic system . . .'[88]

This was vital, for if there was more economic justice, he was convinced that at least ninety per cent of quarrels would be amenable to argument, and resolved without terror or warfare.[89] Of the Marxist argument *per se* Donald admitted there was truth in it, but 'still more error in what it denies'.[90] Everything came *through* matter, he thought, but that was different from arguing that everything comes *out* of matter.[91] Communism itself, of course, was a religion, perhaps the most closely articulated religion ever, and had much success in the early days of the Russian Revolution. Christians should recognize this and see it as a vindication of the human soul rather than a justification of the Communist position.[92] Nevertheless dialectical materialism had not worn well and Lenin had propounded theories of revolution which were now 'almost pathetically out of date'.[93] Nor had religion withered away as Marx had claimed it would.[94]

It could be argued that the Communist revolution had been based on necessity rather than hate, Donald considered, yet he was equally sure it was unable to distinguish between human beings and their institutions, so winsome qualities were lacking in Marxist propaganda and their invective was not only acrimonious but rancid. 'Even the great Lenin,' he judged, 'was incapable of appreciating the truth of the Christian claim that man is always better than his actions, or the still greater truth that humility and revolution can go together.'[95]

On Tower Hill and at Highbury Corner Donald had often come across Marxist fervour in the speeches of Tom Mann and Wal Hannington, as they proclaimed the certainty of revolution and 'all things working together for the good Marxist'.[96] Yet the Magnificat put the Communist Manifesto in the shade[97] and the Little Red Book of Mao Tse Tung was the dullest document it had been his misfortune to read.[98] Much of it was incompatible with Christianity Donald readily accepted, but added in a trenchant Soperism, 'a great many things Christians say are incompatible with what Jesus said'.[99]

What then was Donald Soper's political analysis? 'What Jesus says is that the overthrow of the systems of this world with their incredible wars, and class struggles and insoluble social problems, must be as absolute as anything canvassed by Marxist–Leninist philosophy,' he wrote in 1965. 'The difference is in the methods rather than the objectives of the revolution, and if this offends anyone who reads these words, the end of the second chapter of Acts which describes the Communist experiment of the very earliest Christians under the guidance of Pentecostal grace should help to convince them that this is true.'[100] His politics, therefore, were rooted in his theology, though he was always ready to admit R.H. Tawney's influence on him[101] and accepted his analysis of 'the way in which the heresy of the irrelevancy of the Gospel to the establishment of an earthly Kingdom developed . . .'[102] and that the rise of capitalism in the West 'destroyed the vision splendid, desiccated the universal realm and replaced Christian morals by utilitarian ethics'.[103] Moreover, by its fatalistic and cynical acceptance that human beings were selfish creatures, whose very selfishness became the raw material of the economic and industrial structures of capitalism, 'it pushed the Kingdom of God out of this world into the next'.[104]

It was, Donald admitted, a melancholy fact that since COPEC Christians had moved away from the theme of the kingdom. 'Those were the days,' he confessed, 'when I first came to understand and to accept the meaning of words like "pacifism" and "socialism" and "world government". Now I am told that "pacifism" is a diversionary word, we have outgrown the basic ideas of "socialism" and that "world government" is a sentimental over-simplification.'[105] What replaced such objectives? 'Confrontation', 'participation' and 'dialogue'. 'Now I am all for confrontation,' he wrote, 'and I believe in participation and I am not averse to dialogue, but, my word, they add up to a pretty poor diet for a soul who is hungry for the Kingdom of God.' For him, therefore, Jesus's teaching was still that Christians should 'seek, and offer the power to find, a world-wide, non-violent, loving Commonwealth . . .'[106]

He was clear, too, about his priorities. 'The Kingdom of God will not come when we have thought out some new scheme,' he said in 1944, 'or made some new arrangements; it will only come when we have made up our hearts and minds that we will follow Jesus to Jerusalem, to the courtyard, and to the Cross.'[107] By 1970, however, he was admitting there were signs that political philosophy itself was disappearing. Even more dangerous was the decline in religious belief, for when it died there was no foundation for politics.[108] Here clearly was an opportunity for the churches to proclaim the kingdom of God, the search for which was 'the only sufficient objective for any political party'.[109]

For Donald, therefore, as he informed readers of the *Morning Star*, Clause Four of the Labour Party 'creed' was the modern translation of the eternal truth that the roots of brotherhood and sisterhood lay in the fatherhood and motherhood of God.[110] He told Norman St John Stevas,

> For me Clause Four expresses, within the framework of a contemporary situation, what I believe to be the ultimate principle that emerges from our Lord's teaching, that this world ought to be considered as a home ... and that everyone has an inalienable right to food, clothing and shelter, whether they be good, bad or indifferent.[111]

Donald, it is clear, was in a social tradition which embraced Booth, Manning, Gore and Temple, rather than the Fabian Society or the followers of William Morris, though he seemed to be linked with strands in these movements, too. Certainly he disliked the block vote system of the Labour Party, nor did he think that, unaided by grace, Labour leaders could realize their dreams. Indeed, he came to believe that the apocalyptic element in Christian thinking – 'that we are at least within shouting and shooting distance of the end of the age' – was the only true and appropriate concept.[112] Faith, therefore, which could encourage others to believe non-violence and social care was appropriate now, was 'the only answer approved of God, sanctified at the Cross and verified in the Resurrection morning'.[113]

Was Donald Soper a perfectionist seeking a Utopia which was unreal, for what he wanted, he conceded in the 1960s, seemed further away than ever. Was he perhaps unconsciously exemplifying the holiness strand in the Methodist tradition as written about by Scott Lidgett, Sangster and Newton Flew and expanding Wesley's doctrine of perfect love, seeking to apply it to contemporary national and international conflicts and issues? Certainly he saw Christianity not only as justification but sanctification, which enabled Christians to outshine others, even in 1934 urging them to unite, as he proclaimed 'You have only your lives to lose and God's world to save.'[114] By 1953 he was anticipating 'a new culture of perfection in the Christian Church ... not on the broad plains ... of all the world but on the more personal and private realms where ... we shape our own lives'.[115] He was naturally aware that perfection was a horizon rather than a destination, yet wanted to keep his eyes fixed on it steadfastly for it was God's will, affecting worship and conduct alike.[116]

The sense of compromise he detected as necessary in public affairs had invaded the more personal realm so many found their private piety infected. Yet, for him at any rate, it was not true that personal ethics had to be content with an approximation to goodness as was the case in economic and national affairs. Rather, he wanted to see a revival of perfectionism as the ideal in matters of sexual purity, total abstinence, day by day truthfulness, the honouring of domestic promises and in financial scrupulousness.[117] 'We are living in a day when saints are rather in short supply,' he said later. 'We could do very much better with a lot more good people ... in a world where there are so many clever ones.'[118] 'How can a Christian be a saint?' asked someone at Hyde Park. 'By following more closely in the steps of Jesus,' Donald replied and cited Charles Wesley, judging by his hymns, when asked if there were any Protestant saints.[119]

It was when he was urging non-violent activity that Donald was most perfectionist. An attitude of 'harmless (and often suffering) goodwill to others' was the criterion of judgment by which he faced problems and challenges, for he was convinced it was the secret of the tranquillity which characterized a Christian's life.[120] It had come to embrace his attitude to war, hanging and the capitalist system itself 'which brutally ignored human personality and rode roughshod over human values'.[121]

Steeped in the thinking of pacifist leaders like Raven, Cadoux and Macgregor, and persuaded that the early Church was pacifist from his studies of books like Heering's *The Fall of Christianity*[122] among others, Donald seemed rock-like in his attitude but admitted he often had doubts 'about this tremendous venture of non-resisting love in a violent world',[123] at the same time as he was strengthened at the foot of the Cross, where he found his faith in Christ confirmed.[124] His doubts came because of his exploration of 'the most neglected problem in Christian ethics', the question of compromise.[125] He tried, therefore, to wrestle with the unity and comprehensiveness of the ethical principles laid down by Christ, ('and indeed lived out and died out by Him') and the 'diversity and particularity of the human conditions' under which the principles had to be expressed.[126] In justice, economics and supremely in war, was it possible to live as

Jesus had taught? Always there had to be adjustments at the moment when principles were applied to cases. Even in the life of Jesus, he maintained (accepting for the first part of His ministry the indirect protection of Roman soldiers; withdrawing temporarily from possible clashes with both Rome and Jewish authorities), there were compromises in order to reach His ultimate goal.[127]

There had to be priorities, too, he argued, an idea he had first heard from Aneurin Bevan. 'For long stretches of his life the Christian is called upon to buy time,' he considered, 'even at the expense of being silent about some evils and becoming involved in others.'[128] One compromise Donald accepted was the need for a police force, even the use of tear-gas and water cannon.[129] He drew the line, of course, at weapons which killed. For him the distinction seemed to be the difference between the use of violence and the use of force. But could non-violent resistance itself be a form of coercion? Mulford Sibley has asked, in reviewing Niebuhr's *Moral Man and Immoral Society*. The New Testament itself spoke of the constraining power of love. Was this coercive? If so, in what way did it differ from the coercion of sit-in demonstrations? Or did it differ? For Niebuhr, Sibley continued, all social cohesion relied ultimately on force. But what is force? Perhaps Christians needed to think more about their use of terms.[130]

Niebuhr, whom Donald once met, and found most impressive, accepted that pacifism expressed a genuine impulse to take the law of Christ seriously and not be overcome by other political strategies. Yet he felt such perfectionism only helpful when the standard of perfect love was applied to individuals, for the world only achieved a precarious justice by the use of power. For him grace was, therefore, pardon rather than power, a view Donald rejected.[131] Indeed, he set his face against power politics. The way of uncompromising love was the way Christ himself took 'overcoming evil by good, winning the victory over the enemy by winning the enemy . . .'[132] So it must work in the long run. Indeed, 'by the grace of God we do possess His power to overcome the wars and hatreds and evils from which we suffer,' he suggested.[133] Niebuhr's attack on those who 'imagine that the egoism of individuals is being progressively checked by the development of rationality or the growth of a religiously inspired goodwill',[134] was not therefore the final arbiter in deciding how to act. Indeed, Donald took a different view of how God's grace affects history as he came to wish he had been 'less brash and more sympathetic as a would-be reconciler'.[135]

For Donald Soper a certain type of person was needed to carry out the revolution he sought. 'Has it ever struck you that what we need is a Puritan Revival?' he asked in 1947.[136] Christianity was narrow-minded in the sense that its mind was set on the 'narrow way', which Jesus had said lead to life. Christians had to go into moral training as diligently as footballers trained, or parents made sacrifices for their children. Indeed, most of the excellencies in the British character came from the Puritans, people who, as children of God, were called not only to be as good as their neighbours, but live at higher levels and set an example.[137] Often Donald surprised his agnostic or liberal colleagues and friends by this, to them, unsuspected aspect of his personality, as he declared 'I am sure family life depends for its recovery on a new Puritanism',[138] and, commenting on the Profumo affair in 1963, argued it was impossible to separate personal and public morality. 'I want at the risk of being dubbed narrow-minded or Puritanical,' he wrote, 'to put in a plea for the supreme importance of private morality as the only sure foundation for any satisfactory state of affairs.'[139]

To be such an uncompromising Puritan in the permissive society, while winning the allegiance of so many, was remarkable, as Trevor Huddleston has observed: 'It can only be due to something far deeper than charm; it belongs to "charisma" itself.'[140] Donald, of course, did not come over as a kill-joy, for there was nothing in him of the Puritan spirit which stood against people enjoying themselves.[141] Nor was he a strict sabbatarian – indeed, the first day of the week was a commemoration of the Resurrection and therefore a day of worship and gladness and not 'a day of mere legal prohibition and abstention from work'.[142] He knew, too, the Nonconformist Sunday was over and Christians had to come to terms with secular ministry.[143] Nevertheless, something of his family background lingered on in him. 'I'm prepared to condemn some of Picasso's works,' he stated categorically,[144] and did not respond positively to the 1950s drama of realism. Nor was he enthusiastic about The Beatles, though he did like Cilla Black. 'If this is western society,' he said of them, 'then with all their faults give me the Soviets . . . At least in Russia life is related to political beliefs.'[145]

Perhaps surprisingly when the debate about the publication of

D.H. Lawrence's *Lady Chatterley's Lover* occurred Donald supported the Bishop of Woolwich's right to be a witness, as Donald was, too, in the trial to which the publishers were subjected under the pornography laws, over against the Archbishop of Canterbury, who thought John Robinson's 'evidence for the defence a mistake'.[146] He did not agree with those who regarded *Lady Chatterley's Lover* with 'a holy communion look', but did think it an excellent piece of literature and a sincere attempt to present one side of married life.[147]

Earlier he had responded to Dr Geoffrey Fisher's suggestion that adultery should be made a criminal offence. It was not workable Donald explained. 'At the same time I doubt whether the public realizes the extent to which adultery has become general.'[148] Donald's views were reported in many papers, including his comment that 'it may be that certain forms of adultery involving a breach of trust might be made criminal offences to the advantage of the community'.[149] In 1976 he found a clear-cut case for condemnation with the proposed film on the sex life of Jesus, which was halted after protests. 'This is first class evidence of what has been feared for long years,' he wrote, 'that there is a very real decadence in the world today.'[150]

When it came to homosexuality Donald was extremely sensitive. He did not like the way footballers embraced on the pitch after their own side had scored a goal, but was not as rigid as might have been expected. In 1967, during the second reading of Lord Arran's Sexual Offences Bill (No. 2), he claimed to support the Bill on behalf of Britain's Free Churches, one of the few occasions he made such a claim. He believed, he said, the measures outlined in the Bill represented 'a necessary change in the laws' and 'a proper attitude to some aspects of homosexuality'. 'It does not draw the distinction which I believe to be a necessary one,' he went on, 'between sin, lesbian practices, adultery . . .' adding that though some consenting behaviour between adults was 'sinful in many respects',[151] this was not necessarily always so. Moreover, the Bill could help remove much tension and fear from many 'good and decent homosexuals'.[152]

On the question of pornography Donald was adamant. In the 1960s there was much debate about its nature. C.H. Rolph edited a book, *Does Pornography Matter?* to which Donald contributed, along with Lord Birkett, Sir Herbert Read and Geoffrey Gorer among others. It was, he argued, a mark of the progress of secularism that the question was asked at all. For the Christian pornography certainly mattered because all were made in God's image. Pornography – 'sex out of all context except that of sensational enjoyment' – was not in accord with the way of the kingdom,[153] though he conceded in previous centuries Christians had been over-censorious about the sins of the flesh.[154]

Without doubt pornography was sinful and those involved in it needed God's forgiveness for thwarting God's purpose and corrupting society. In his experience, he indicated, nothing had eroded the good life more quickly as the persistent reduction of experience to the levels of 'physical pleasure and immediate satisfaction'.[155] He had seen this in the work of the West London Mission, particularly among adolescents, especially girls who had turned initially to prostitution for excitement. The only way forward was to produce an environment free of pornography by the community removing its stumbling blocks, for such they were.[156]

'Are you still anti-pornography?' Lord Longford asked Donald in 1993, who through illness had only attended the first meeting of the Longford Committee on pornography. He replied he was as resolute as ever, because he was committed to 'a sacramental view of sex'.[157] The Report itself, which he had read assiduously, led to a measured response from him when it was debated in the House of Lords. 'I stand up and talk about pornography,' he explained, 'but I should not be prepared to do it unless I was also prepared . . . to talk . . . a great many other evils which I think are undoubtedly greater than pornography.'[158] He ventured one criticism, too, of the section on homosexuality. He respected many homosexuals though he did not pretend to understand them and added: 'In certain places in the Report I feel we owe an apology to them.'[159]

The Puritan and the Philosopher, the moralist and the modernist, thus co-existed in a tension in one personality. There was yet a third strand which related to that part of his mind which made him always an explorer on a pilgrimage, both intellectual and spiritual. A member of Christian MENSA, he sought to use his outstanding intellect to the full as he probed both philosophical and human possibilities.

He only met Arthur Koestler once – not the sort of man 'I would want to go on summer holidays with' – yet he had to admit in *Darkness at Noon* he had written a sombre and a dynamic account of totalitarianism.[160] In his major work *The Act of Creation* he had explored the meaning and significance of humour and this aspect of Koestler's genius appealed to Donald. If a sense of beauty, music, and poetry belonged to God's realm 'so does a sense of humour'.[161] 'It can even sweeten sorrow,' he considered. But Donald never stayed in one place long, as his interest in now this, now that, aspect of life intrigued him and drove him on. He was not, however, very mystical, though he was certainly aware of dimensions other than the rational as when in 1948 he maintained to a gathering of spiritualists in the Albert Hall that 'it was in the discovery of the spirit world that our material world would find the solution to its problems'.[162] In 1954 he spoke again in the Albert Hall, at the Spiritualist Service of Reunion on Remembrance Sunday and subsequently agreed to become a Vice-President of the Churches' Fellowship for Psychical and Spiritual Studies.

Donald appreciated most St John's Gospel and learned much from William Temple's interpretation of it. 'With St John I am at home,' William Temple once said;[163] so was Donald Soper. He learned not only about St John from Temple. He learned, too, the need for both an ecclesiastical staff and a political sceptre because Christianity, as Tertullian and Origen had shown, was materialist through and through.[164] 'Church and state must co-exist in some sort of fellowship,' he argued in the House of Lords magazine.[165] It was a theme he had lived with since the time of his doctorate and his encounter with the period after the Council of Trent from 1575 onwards – with Madame de Saint Beuve and the Ursulines, Berulle and the Oratory and the way they had demonstrated the power which traditional religion could have. Edmond Richer, the subject of his study, who had opposed the Ultramontanists, arguing for Scripture, tradition and reason to provide a commonwealth governed by a divinely appointed aristocracy of bishops, thereby refuting papal absolutism, seemed to Donald more easily to harmonize with Pauline theology and 'the Christian spirit of fellowship'.[166]

Without doubt Donald's interventions on topics like abortion and legislation to regularize it, involving both philosophical questions about when a human being was conceived and the right of the State to draft laws on such a medical matter, and arguments on many a street corner about social questions, all stemmed from his conviction, borne in on him by his thesis and tested by time, that the Church and the society were inter-penetrative. Both had functions and without both being done well society lost its savour.

How then did Donald nourish his spirit so he could make pertinent comments and give sound advice? Latterly he turned to the Roman

Catholic theologian, Hans Kung, and his study of the Western mind from Pascal to Neitzsche, Freud to Karl Popper. He also appreciated his writings because he was concerned philosophically to build a world where it was possible for people to say yes to reality instead of to nihilism; yes to God as an alternative to atheism and, more specifically, yes to the Christian God, in response to a rational apologetic which Donald relished.[167] He also warmed to Dostoevsky's writings – his insight in *Crime and Punishment* into the part environment plays in the beginning of redemption[168] or what goes on in the human mind, as in *The Idiot*.[169] Most of all he responded to *The Brothers Karamazov*, which he read in French, where Dostoevsky showed how the official Church has betrayed the Gospel in the interests of power.[170] But the figure above all who was a soul friend for Donald Soper was Blaise Pascal, a personality who combined scientific gifts with a theological quest. His insistence that 'the heart has its reasons that reason itself cannot comprehend', appealed to Donald the first time he read the *Pensées*. 'How strengthened and consolidated has been the impact of that aphorism as the years and the vicissitudes of a ministerial calling have gone by,' he once reflected.[171]

Donald also appreciated Pascal's pure mind and his linking of heavenly wisdom with logical thinking. 'He offers to the aged,' Donald wrote as he considered ageing, 'a wager infinitely worth making. Believe in the life of heaven beyond death. If it comes off you win. If you lose it won't matter – because you won't know that you have lost!'[172] It was this paradoxical quality in Pascal which drew Donald continuously, though latterly he also savoured the thoughts of Montaigne. 'If the compassion of God is so great that He instructs us to our benefit, even when He hides Himself,' wrote Pascal near the end of his *Pensées*, 'what light ought we not to expect from Him when He reveals Himself?'[173] Here clearly was a thinker with an aphoristic style, whose wisdom reached the depths of Donald's personality as few others did, particularly his understanding that doubt was inseparable from belief.

What did Donald envisage for the future? Though largely untouched by the world of psychoanalysis, he did know, from both his personal experience and from Alexis Carrel's *Man the Unknown*, there were 'possibilities, physical, mental and spiritual', within human beings.[174] He knew, too, not only from scientists but from books like *Recovery* by Starr Daily, that remarkable physical healings had occurred. 'Here is ample evidence to discredit the assertion that we live in a "closed universe", of which the scientist is the true expositor,' he said in a foreword to *Recovery*, (one of the many forewords he wrote) 'and everything is governed by so-called scientific law.'[175]

He explained his view of creation most clearly when he considered the relationship of plants, animals and human beings. 'I believe the whole creation is soul-like,' he said in 1976, 'from the amoeba to the fully determined saint.'[176] 'I would prefer to believe that the soul is sleeping in the stone,' he elaborated later, 'dreaming in the animal and possibly awake in man. I don't believe we have souls. I think we are all in the process of being souls – the whole creation is animate in that sense.'[177] 'We still have a long way to go before we can appreciate that the will of God flows through the whole, or there is an element of goodness which is intrinsic to a world which is infinitely more complex and more difficult to understand,' he concluded in 1993.[178] He looked forward, therefore, to a 'pragmatic' Church which could respond as cells of Christians created new life on the New Testament model.[179] Worship, prayer, Holy Communion and personal piety, were imperative in this Church, 'the gateway to the Green Pastures of God's presence', a phrase from his mother, who had died in 1967, he remembered from one of her addresses.[180]

A nineteenth-century philosopher Donald regarded highly once said: 'The ultimate freedom is the freedom to be good.'[181] Donald Soper's passion was to plead for the cultivation of goodness and his philosophical insights and his Puritanism were called into the service of that great task. It was imperative he knew to see that Christ could help us to do this *because* of a divine self-emptying and not despite it. Good and evil, reward and punishment, responsibility and effort, became meaningless, he considered, without this view. 'What seems to me to be the Christian message most needed ... is that by the Grace of God we do possess His power to overcome the wars and hatreds and evils from which we suffer,' he considered. 'We are partners with Him in true omnipotence; that is the fact of the Gospel – the good news which I would like you all to hear and to believe.'[182] To enter that spiritual universe which penetrated this material one we needed the help of the Holy Spirit – God active in every one and uniquely in Jesus, enabling human beings to solve their questions and dilemmas.[183]

'We are all potential philosophers. No one is ultimately satisfied with only facts,' he once asserted.[184] For him the great fact was Jesus Christ and, like all seekers of the historical Jesus, from Renan through

Albert Schweitzer to Conrad Noel, Donald Soper, by focusing on the Gospels rather than the Epistles, also rooted himself in what he conceived to be fact, albeit refracted through early tradition. Building up a picture of Jesus for himself and taking large themes – the Incarnation, the Sermon on the Mount, Jesus's preaching about the kingdom, the Cross and Resurrection and the event called Pentecost – he presented this Jesus to the crowds who flocked to hear him. No doubt some themes were implanted in him at Wesley House, but the way he explained them and distilled their essence was uniquely his own, especially his emphasis on non-violent love.

His Gospel, mediated through the Church, was idealistic but it was also aware of sin. It was not rooted in words like 'paradox', 'ambiguity', 'mystery', but in the cardinal virtues of faith, hope and love. Other great Christian doctrines, the Ascension, eschatology, nature and grace, Donald tended to ignore as he focused on his overriding objective: to preach Christ to this generation, by any means available, if necessary by only talking about a few central Christian themes. Thus his philosophical outlook was transcended by his faith as he persevered and looked for God's kingdom.

Chapter 11

PENSIONER AND PENITENT

DONALD SOPER HAD BEEN 'greatly moved, and not far from tears', at his farewell.[1] Now with Marie, Lady Soper, after a short holiday in Newquay, he was bound for Australia, where in Sydney, for a few weeks he was to replace the Rev. Alan Walker to allow his successor, the Rev. Dr John Newton, time to settle into Kingsway Hall and complete the arrangements for the merger with Hinde Street Methodist Church. It was, of course, not the first time he and Lady Soper had been abroad together. In the 1960s they had twice been to America and Canada, and also to Kenya. They had, too, led some six holiday parties of twenty-five to thirty people, where Marie Soper's eye for detail had given her a vivid sensitivity to her surroundings.

On one trip she had particularly enjoyed the journey up the Empire State Building, the Guggenheim Art Exhibition (the French Impressionists were her favourites) and the bustle of New York.[2] Now, in Sydney – 'a bit of a backwood' – she could look back on the tumultuous years she had lived through since she and her husband had gone to Kingsway Hall in 1936, as well as wonder what Donald would be like as he continued his routine without its specific demands.[3]

There was the period before 1940 to remember, when she had been responsible for work with students, and the time during the war itself when she had helped in the early morning breakfast canteens and supervised the canteen stores.[4] Then there were the Saturday night socials and dances to recall, where she had excelled at the fox-trot and a queue of people wanted to dance with her. Naturally it had been a strain living for a while at the church with Ann and Bridget, but she had survived.

The immediate post-war period had been different, she reflected, with her work on the Executive Committee of the Crèche and of

Emerson Bainbridge House,[5] the opening of annual Christmas fairs and presiding over annual sales. Later, in 1964, she remembered, she had opened Katharine Price Hughes hostel in its new role, as well as taking part in the affairs of Grove House.

She had attended Sunday evening worship with her daughters when possible, for by now there were four to care for ('All those years cooking,' she reflected),[6] one of whom, if Donald preached too long, hung a hymn sheet over the balcony to remind him of the time. Now all four were married, with children of their own ('At forty-three I had become a grandmother,' she had often said) but unlike her they were not having two distinct periods in which to rear a family.[7]

In every house she had made the home a place of beauty and often by a deft placing of their antique furniture, given each room a special style. She had cultivated, too, her garden with great finesse, only on occasions able to persuade Donald, who liked to sit and look at the smaller rather than the ostentatious flowers, to use a rake or trowel.[8]

All four children had gone to the Methodist Girls' Public School, Queenswood, in Hertfordshire, on modest bursaries and done well, she reflected. Ann had studied Zoology at university and Bridget had gone to Art School and then trained as a physiotherapist. Judith had read Botany and Zoology and Caroline Politics and Economics. Children of other Methodist leaders, like Drs Weatherhead and Sangster, had also gone to Queenswood, but Marie recalled she seldom met them, for her school visits had been infrequent. So were Donald's after he had played a syncopated tune on the piano during one of them, an act disapproved of by the school's management at the time!

'Left-winger Lord Soper admits to sending his daughters to a public school because the opportunities and educational facilities are better than those found at state schools,' one Glasgow paper had reported in 1967,[9] but Donald was adamant about the choice, even when accosted by one pupil in a TV debate about whether his socialist views were compatible with private education.

Queenswood had given her daughters she knew the opportunity they needed, though the decision to send Ann and Bridget there, taken by Donald, had been in war-time and was a neat solution to the problem evacuation from London was then presenting. By the time Caroline left, the school had changed substantially but all four girls had been equipped to see their adult life both in terms of career and family. They owed much to her, too, she knew for she had given them love and security, accepting them non-judgmentally and allowing each to flourish and develop gifts as individual as her own.

As the Sopers took part in the life of Sydney there were other things Lady Soper could look back on now. There were the friendships she had fostered in Hampstead Garden Suburb when the children had left home; the golf she had played with her husband, often beating him (she had won twelve silver spoons and a cup);[10] and her interaction with the Deans, as she observed and tangled with her family with both wry amusement and exasperation. She had to admit she had enjoyed all the public events with Donald during the Presidential year and the trip to the Caribbean, as well as the Russian, Turkey and Palestine holidays. She liked, too, the social occasions his life in the House of Lords had brought.

However, she had found bringing up four girls almost on her own a strain, for despite Donald's intellectual appreciation of the family as an ideal, when it came to practicalities, his mind was often elsewhere.[11] He was, she knew, an extraordinary man so it was useless to stand up to him – for 'he always had a strong ego and did his own thing'.[12] Nor had she been able to cure his obsession with time. ('I'm irritated by unpunctuality,' he had commented once. 'It's a form of selfishness . . .')[13] Rather, she had to be complementary to him, creating around him a home, where clearly she was in charge. ('You're not on Tower Hill now, you know Donald,' she had so often said.) Her daughters had been firm with him, too, accepting his faults with 'due aplomb'.[14] 'They by no means regard me as some form of graven image, to be bowed down before,' Donald himself had discovered.[15]

Holidays, like the one now in Australia, were an annual high spot, as were the Christmas gatherings when latterly the grandchildren, and great-grandchildren, came for visits. Then there had been the skiing in Austria and Switzerland, when Donald had not been able to accompany her as he was working, the numerous visits to Cornwall and surfing with the Westons at Newquay. Now and again – and she wished these had been more frequent – there had been trips to the theatre, to the Palladium, for example, to see the Crazy Gang, then at the height of their fame. But overall, she recalled, there had been Donald's need for quiet and privacy, away from the throng, which he had guarded jealously.

The Sopers flew back from Australia via Hong Kong and Singapore, looking over into Communist China from a viewpoint in the colony.[16] Donald was soon in the thick of things as he adjusted to a new office. That autumn there was a service for world peace in Reading, *Any Questions?* from Northern Ireland, a debate from the Oxford Union as well as preaching appointments, including a number in Anglican pulpits. At Christmas there was an appearance on Thames TV and a BBC Watchnight service. Here Donald explained yet again how Christians had to love their neighbours and their enemies. 'It needs an understanding mind as well as a warm heart,' he said. 'It means goodwill on fire, you can't put limits to it – like forgiveness it goes on to seventy times seven; it is an activity which goes far beyond our normal decent behaviour . . .'[17]

Donald was now seventy-six, a pensioner of ten years' standing, yet still eager for battle. He asked John Newton if he could preach a homily and celebrate Holy Communion at 10.00 a.m. each Sunday at Hinde Street and this was agreed. 'When I stretch out my hands to receive the bread and when I lift the cup to my lips I testify to the life which goes beyond the world of sense and time; that world where alone is peace and justice and love,' he had said at his farewell,[18] ever the eucharistic Christian, writing in 1979 that if beginning again he hoped he 'would have the courage to preserve eucharistic worship at all costs' despite changing conditions, but then open the doors of the Church to a new world of music, abandon traditional Sunday observance, develop responsive liturgy and spread devotional exercises throughout the week. He would, he concluded, want to stimulate dialogue rather than sermons, encourage a real economy in theological dogma and the rediscovery of the old Latin tag '*Laborare est orare* . . .'[19]

His year of change from lifelong patterns showed Donald he, too, was a prisoner of the very institutions he had criticized.[20] He had been warned when he left Kingsway Hall as Superintendent he would be as busy as ever though the adjustment would be 'somewhat traumatic'.[21] This had proved the case. Also traumatic was the actual *process* of growing old, as carpel tunnel in his hands developed and curbed his piano playing. He wrote in 1989,

In my experience restriction of various kinds is perhaps the predominant accompaniment of old age. I can't get about because my feet won't let me. I can't hear a conversation, and people think I'm not listening properly. I can't talk as once I did to other people because to quote a hymn – 'my company is gone before'. I feel 'shrivelled' like the lines on my face, as if a kind of lifelessness has happened to me. Of course it need not be as bad as all that but it promotes a kind of loneliness. I don't seem to belong as once I did.[22]

Nevertheless, despite these feelings which developed as the 1980s progressed, Donald found 'a safeguard against boredom'[23] in his preaching ministry and other church activities and visits to the House of Lords. His increasing arthritis was a great burden, but because he had faith in a future which went beyond the planet he remained cheerful. Moreover, he found by trying not to think about his body's problems he could keep going. It was, nevertheless, easy to feel sorry for himself, yet he and his wife were blessed with many grandchildren and great-grandchildren and he found 'being glad for them is a marvellous tonic'.[24]

As he grew older Donald became much more reflective, especially when contemplating his own and Marie's death. The magazine *Care of the Elderly* invited him to write a number of articles. He applied himself to the task with alacrity. 'Old age for me,' he told its readers, 'tends to produce a condition of exasperation', most acute in the realm of sex.[25] There was, too, the inevitability of the process so hope for the future was not an immediate tonic which could be taken. This he felt was particularly so in the moral realm where old people often felt their lives were already decided. Indeed, they became victims of remorse precisely because there was no future in penitence.[26] A vital concern for old people, therefore, was how to discover creative penitence instead of sterile remorse.[27] There was, too, the possibility of selective, creative remembering, a theme he developed in his last book *Calling for Action*, published in 1984.

He did think, he told his readers, that Christianity itself helped, because it taught all were members of God's family. 'The more I have cultivated this good news of "belonging",' he wrote, 'the more satisfactory it has become.'[28] Moreover, for him at any rate, life was not ending because time, space and matter were no more. In addition he suggested old people needed to feel special just because they *were* old.[29]

Calling for Action brought out Donald's reflective capacity to the full. An autobiographical enquiry, it was divided into the three main themes which had preoccupied him – peace on earth; goodwill among men and women; and glory to God. He had, he explained, long been fascinated by Marcel Proust's book *À la recherche du temps perdu*, where 'a certain event or experience, trivial in itself, opens the magic casement on to an otherwise forgotten and lost world'.[30] He therefore decided to use this method to recall events from his own life.

When it came to the third section 'Glory to God' he found he wanted to deal with the question of the world faiths and the fact that they contained mutually contradictory elements within them,[31] a theme which had run through his comments over the decades. He had argued that the West should be prepared to *receive* missionaries from other faiths and ought not to identify Christianity with its earlier manifestations.[32] He himself, he explained, would have been a Buddhist because of its pacifist witness, and the sense of holiness which Buddhists he had met exuded, were he not convinced of the truth of Christianity,[33] but remained open to other truth.

In previous comments he had both commended Christianity for its 'economical representation of what is best in other faiths',[34] and recognized there had been a movement within them towards Jesus Christ. Reluctant to give up his awareness of the differences he yet acknowledged the 'spiritual giants, the Buddhas, the Isaiahs, the Mahomets', had given pictures of God albeit 'each with its truths and its distortions'.[35] Now as he reflected in *Calling for Action* he drew attention to the shrinking globe which meant Christians had examined their beliefs from Buddhist, Hindu and Moslem premises. This had led them to an awareness of the power of non-violence, the role of the body in meditation and the multi-racial implications of Christian belief, 'as going some way to justify the Christian claim to primacy', for these were embryonic elements in Christianity.[36] On the other hand, the impact of Christianity on the non-Christian creeds and practices had been to introduce some new concepts that were Christian in essence, rather than to deepen awareness of their own. This was not, he admitted, the full picture, but pleaded that it might, at least, 'provoke a fellowship of controversy'.[37]

This more reflective Donald Soper was in evidence not only as he considered the external world, but as he looked at himself, too. It had always been latent, of course, as *All His Grace* had shown. 'I am a pacifist, and yet I am by no means immune to the excitement conjured up by military exploits related by military heroes,' he had written in 1958.[38] Now he allowed these off-the-cuff comments to surface more readily. Pride, he had admitted, was his greatest sin, 'putting yourself where only God has a right to be'.[39] He regretted a thousand things,[40] including not explaining enough when he had made comments or statements. He had not found the secret of peace in his own life easily he told BBC's *Silver Lining* listeners in 1958. It had come eventually, however, through the knowledge that all things work together for good to those who love God.[41] As a result he had been content to live from day to day, preoccupying himself with the immediate tasks to hand. It was a discovery he needed now to draw on continually.

Yet he remained something of an enigma, even to himself. His aggression seemed to be channelled into Hyde Park and Tower Hill, as he told Norman St John Stevas.[42] But the aggressiveness was soon replaced by a lively cockney humour, dispelling any hurt feelings or ruffled feathers. 'Shall I be interviewing you when you are ninety?' asked one reporter. 'I don't see why not,' was the retort, 'you look healthy enough to me!'[43] This aspect of Donald's personality had hardly surfaced when another would emerge. He knew, too, as he rang the changes within his complex nature, he was 'not always a desirable person to live with', making it more difficult for those who loved him to 'put up with me'.[44] Indeed, in one candid moment he put it more starkly: 'Those who love me do not know me; those who meet me do not know me.'[45]

Perhaps because Donald knew of his internal contradictions he was always stressing the Christian Gospel related to repentance and forgiveness. He observed,

> As you come nearer to a climax [of your life] . . . looking back you are more prompted to penitence. I have much to regret, and one of the real problems of ageing is that you can't do anything about it. I mean, you can repent, and you can ask to be forgiven, and you can say that your intentions were not as bad as perhaps other people thought they were. But you haven't any time left to put it right. In fact you can't put it right anyhow. There is an irreversibility about time . . .[46]

This need for both repentance and forgiveness stemmed from Donald's sense of sin, both in individuals and groups. He once commented,

> I have never doubted that sin is about the second strongest thing in the universe. And I would make one claim, that I never lost the sense of the need for grace for such a sinner as I am.

And I am very glad about it. If I give an appearance of brazen confidence in the open air . . . it isn't brazen confidence, it is the objectivity of the faith I hold.[47]

'In many respects,' he said in another interview, 'whatever vitality I had and still have I hope is heavily compounded of the realization that that vitality pulls me as much in the wrong direction as it does in the right.'[48]

As Donald travelled he was perpetually reminded of the world's fallenness. 'At present,' he wrote in 1959, 'there is neither penitence nor trust in the utterances of the leading statesmen of either side. For that matter the Nuclear Disarmament Movement here, in Japan, in Germany, in the USA, or in Russia, has not displayed these virtues to any conspicuous degree . . .'[49] He had been in East Germany in 1963, a trip funded through political contacts. 'I could find no-one seemingly responsible for World War Two,' he reflected on his return.[50] In his view both East and West were sinners in the Cold War.[51] Indeed, on the question of Germany's war guilt, she was more responsible, yet 'we are not without sin'.[52]

Was there any hope for relations between the nations, or, indeed, between individuals, he asked and concluded there was. 'There is more penitence for world hunger, and oppression and apartheid than ever before,' he felt in 1963, 'and more determination to do something about it.'[53] Moreover, sometimes the most unlikely people were used as vehicles. So, when Dr Hewlett Johnson, the Red Dean of Canterbury, died, Donald observed, whilst not agreeing with his views: 'It is not blasphemous to say he made a sort of vicarious sacrifice and atonement for the orthodox Christian hatred of communism. While clerics of all kinds and Christians of every denomination were extravagantly treating the Russians as the devil, he was equally extravagantly treating them as angels.'[54] How much, he enquired, is due to the Red Dean that the Communist East was now treated in less black and white categories?[55]

Even to readers of *Tribune* he commended penitence. 'The passion for righteousness is still the fruit of conversion. The penitent form is still more important than any other form in the crusade for socialism,' he suggested.[56] In personal areas also Donald found penitence worked. Speaking to peers on the West London Mission's work with unmarried mothers and their babies he commented: 'To see the awakening of hope, and indeed, the emergence of penitence in many cases, to see the emergence of a new sense of responsibility,' is ample reward. In the House of Lords he also pleaded for a new way of dealing with prisoners involving forgiveness, in his view 'a process by which the past, if not obliterated, is disregarded as having no further impact upon either the present or the future in the life of the man who is forgiven'.[57]

He hoped very much that in the Rehabilitation of Offenders Bill then under discussion peers would not divide miscreants into those whose sins can be forgiven and those who have committed 'unforgivable sins'.[58] He himself was penitent for living in a society which maintained prison institutions he regarded as intolerable. Indeed, his prison work had produced in him 'a condition of humility to which I am not addicted generally',[59] as he had discovered it was almost impossible to sustain the element of penitence 'within the artificiality of prison life'.[60]

For Donald, therefore, forgiveness was the gateway to hope. 'The power of forgiveness that God is exercising makes things become different,' he once suggested.[61] 'In many cases God takes away the tears. But His forgiveness costs God something although it is His free gift to us.'[62] It was, of course, the second stage, coming after repentance. 'The prodigal son would not have been forgiven if he had not come to himself in a far country.'[63] Yet the prodigal *had* returned home: and received a gift which was applicable to all human life.[64]

'Sometimes in this strange and perplexing world,' Donald wrote, 'forgiveness is the only law that makes any sense at all.'[65] And again: 'I believe in the principle of forgiveness and regard it as infinitely more important than consistency.'[66] When he called for a moral revolution, as he often did, it was in the context, therefore, of the need both for repentance and forgiveness. It was, moreover, God's grace alone which could equip human beings to use aright 'the gifts and good things with which He has filled the universe'.[67] 'You must not overrate the spirituality of the human race,' he warned Jill Wallis in an interview. 'We are all a bunch of sinners and it is strange to me that people today are surprised at failure. I am not. I am only grateful when you have a bit of success.'[68]

Outwardly, of course, this was what Donald continued to have as, despite his growing frailty, he went hither and thither. In addition, he continued to see a wide range of people either at Hinde Street or in the House of Lords, from Bob Holman, who was writing a short life of George Lansbury, to the South African M.P., Alex Boraine.

Here in his small office he continued his habit of cat-napping in between appointments after a modest lunch of banana and cheese. His contribution to the church, besides attending most of its main Sunday service and sometimes preaching at it, included meditations during the Three Hours Service on Good Friday, (he took all seven himself in 1985), a Kingsway tradition Hinde Street welcomed, along with the Wednesday Club for those in need, the Christmas Party and a 6.00 a.m. Easter Day service.

Donald also supported the many appeals for WLM social work, though not involved with the day-to-day organization of the various projects, now run almost entirely by professionals. At the start of the merger his presence and support helped the two congregations come together, which was important, for the Kingsway tradition was a shock for the more sedate Hinde Street Christians, who latterly had to get used to homeless people sleeping on their steps. Gradually those from Kingsway who did make the journey to the West End (many, of course, did not) felt at home in a church whose history went back to Charles Wesley, himself buried only half a mile away in an Anglican graveyard bordering Marylebone High Street.

The fire still burned in Donald Soper, even as his body faded. Lady Soper often wished he would stop Hyde Park and Tower Hill ('It's too much for him,' she would say) but Donald's 'addiction' was incurable. That aside, he took almost every opportunity to carry on as one of John Wesley's travelling preachers and contributed one sermon he had preached in St Martin-in-the-Fields on the resolution of fear to a collection of them published in honour of Robert Runcie[69] as he responded to yet another request for a contribution to a book. Numerous other invitations came for him to preach at special occasions like the one for Age Concern in Canterbury Cathedral in 1985. Churches still wanted him for their anniversaries, too, from the Sheffield Mission to the Dome Mission in Brighton. At one moment he would be preaching to the Cambridge Crown Court Service, the next at the Graduation Service of London University in Westminster Abbey. Whether it was at the opening of a united church in Camberley (Methodist and URC) in 1990, or the annual Federation service of the theological colleges in Cambridge in 1993, Donald was there, still lively, with pregnant phrases promoting the theological convictions he had worked out for himself over a lifetime.

He visited schools, too, like Harrow (twice) and his own, to speak at their Assembly. The pupils, who knew only fragments of his life, found him at ninety 'interesting'. It is difficult to imagine the impact on teenagers this man with the strong voice made, for he had become part of the history they studied. Yet they listened attentively to his account of being an Askean in the First World War and then took in his comments about war and peace in the 1990s, especially the need to hope.[70] Perhaps most poignant of all was Donald's visit to the Wesley Day celebrations in the mid-1980s when he attended a service at Nettleton Court by the entrance to the Museum of London, the spot where John Wesley's heart was 'strangely warmed'. Here he sat on one of the seats with a former OCW colleague before speaking about the power of Christ to effect change.[71]

Donald was in his element in 1984 when it was announced both Louis Palau and Billy Graham were coming to Britain to lead evangelical campaigns. In a front page article 'Personally Speaking' in the *Methodist Recorder* (one of the many he wrote for that series) he once again asserted that for him evangelism was a priority. But to 'hitch the wagon of such evangelism to the so-called star "the Bible says" . . . is strictly non-sensical and therefore practically intolerable,' he argued.[72] He was now crusading against Billy Graham as he had in the 1950s. He did not deny campaigns conducted under the banner of 'the Bible says' were, and would continue to be, *occasions* of a converting experience. Yet to swallow the Bible whole meant to take passages of great beauty along with passages of barbarity. If you argued, as some theologians did, for 'a golden thread of progressive appreciation of God's nature which runs through this heterogeneous library of books [the Bible]', this position could not be sustained either, for no woman comparing her status in Genesis and the dignity with which Jesus had invested her would be persuaded that 'St Paul continues that process of emancipation.'[73] For him, therefore, it was still the spirit and teaching of Jesus which mattered, echoes of which could be found in both Bible and Church since the first Easter and in the testimony and experience the evangelists could bring of Jesus as Saviour and 'Lord of His Kingdom'.[74]

During Donald's Presidential year letters often poured into the Presidential office from those opposed to him to which he would reply with urbanity. Now letters of indignation reached the *Methodist Recorder* about Donald's stance. 'Lord Soper's idiosyncrasies sometimes get me down,' wrote Viscount Tonypandy. 'He seems to have an obsessional dislike of everything represented by Dr Billy Graham . . .'[75] Some took Donald to task for his inadequate view of revelation.

Others felt he had missed the point of Mission England, the campaign to which Dr Graham might be coming, if his health permitted. Not all, of course, objected to what Donald said. His former OCW colleague, John Banks, even claimed that Donald was 'the greatest evangelist of our generation'. 'After all,' he explained, 'he has spoken twice a week for fifty years directly to men in the street, while Billy Graham talks most of the time to the man in the pew . . .'[76] It seemed those who wrote for Donald carried more weight than those who were against him, but there was a sharp paragraph in one letter which showed the pros and cons were more complex than had been teased out. 'Would Lord Soper, whose emphasis on the sacraments is well known,' asked the writer, 'refuse to join in mission with the Society of Friends, who acknowledge no sacraments, but with whom I am sure he has many objects in common?'[77]

When in 1993 controversy yet again surrounded the Bishop of Durham Donald recognized in him a fellow evangelist. He had the following advice to offer in connection with the questions and difficulties relating to the historical validity of Christian theology. Christianity was a way of life rather than 'a symposium of thoughts'.[78] Christians knew of Jesus through those who wrote about Him and the continuing experience of His followers. The good news of the Gospel was primarily a moral not an historical one. The ultimate question was how to be saved from evil behaviour and a recurrent sense of hopelessness and meaninglessness to which the Gospel provided the answer and gave access to a world beyond time and space. The overall question was whether people were willing to start an adventure of faith, following in Jesus's footsteps, if necessary on a pilgrimage of grace to the Cross.[79]

As ever the OCW vocation burned in Donald, though his role was inevitably limited. Nevertheless, each year he appeared at the Methodist Conference to take part in a lunch-time open-air meeting organised by Yvonne Griffiths and spoke to the OCW Conference meeting. Even at the Leeds Methodist Conference in 1994, when he was over ninety-one, Donald mounted the open-air stand, supported morally by Dr John Vincent and Dr Leslie Griffiths. Questions were as varied as ever – the fate of animals in the next world; the problem of inherent human evil; the beliefs of Tony Benn; the monarchy and disestablishment. It was the year Prince Charles had proclaimed his intention when King to be defender of all the faiths. 'How,' Donald queried, 'can you be a defender of *all* the faiths?'[80]

His contribution to each Methodist Conference was wider than the open-air gathering of course. At the 1981 Norwich Conference, for example, he supported the National Children's Home and Christian Socialist Movement meetings, shared in an ordination and also spoke to a school and the OCW meeting itself. His ministry as priest continued, too, though in a lower key. His friends from Kingsway Hall died and sometimes he took their funerals. He missed Reg Dobson especially. 'He was,' he wrote, 'the first, when I came to Kingsway Hall to offer what services he could and, my word, what years of co-operation and help he gave to me and to the church.'[81] There were, too, funerals to take from his House of Lords contacts – Lords Llewellyn Davies and Pargiter among them. Weddings he also conducted, sometimes in the House of Commons Crypt, sometimes at Hinde Street. Two memorial services stood out in those years – the one for Lord Caradon in the Central Hall, Westminster, cementing yet again his link with the Foot family, and one in 1987 for Fela Sowande. 'We were having a difficult time at Kingsway Hall,' he told the assembled gathering, 'when a tall, dark, thin man dressed in the uniform of the RAF said: "I can play the organ."' He immediately showed his skill and soon Donald had asked this brilliant Nigerian musician to take charge of the music at Kingsway Hall. 'He was,' added Donald, 'like a great star who came into our firmament and illuminated it.'[82]

By the time of his ninetieth birthday in 1993 Donald had so many incidents on which to look back. He knew on the way he had made some enemies,[83] but it did not trouble him unduly. He knew, too, that he had been 'a selfish young cub'.[84] 'I must have been insufferable because I knew all the answers,' he admitted later.[85] Despite this so many memories were nourishing. There was the sheer fun he had got from reading *1066 and All That*,[86] and the films he had enjoyed, the serious ones like *Gandhi* and all the post-war Hollywood ones, when he and Marie with Bill and Connie Weston would go every Monday night to the local cinema in Hampstead Garden Suburb. Then there were the incidents with people which were lodged in his memory, like his comment in a meeting with Maude Royden that there were too many women present. 'You mean there are too few men,' she had retorted.[87]

Again there were all those late night train journeys coming back from appointments and sleeping in the corridor wrapped in a sheet, hoping it would reach London by early morning. 'It wasn't fair on my wife,' he later admitted, 'and I regret it in this sense. It deprived me at that time of a good deal of the benefits of family life.'[88] He remembered, too, shortly after 1945, his walk along the length and breadth of Blackpool Promenade with Sister Lottie, who could bear her work at Kingsway Hall no more, as he had tried to persuade her to return, which she did.[89]

Abroad there had been the tour of the jazz area of New Orleans[90] and the time in Poland when he and a Russian General had harangued each other on a train journey for three hours.[91] In Japan there was the occasion, after much bowing to each other, he had addressed 700 prisoners, who stood before him and the Governor. And in Zambia he had gone by car into the Zambesi Valley and back to see for himself what nation-building meant at the grass-roots. On the boat trip home from South Africa he had nursed Bridget all the way and on another occasion as he flew to London he had written a limerick about each of his daughters to while away the time. Back home he could remember, too, teaching Ann to wrestle and playing cricket with her and Bridget. More recently, there was the satisfaction he had got from Judith's work for Voluntary Service Overseas and Caroline's work with The Royal Institute for International Affairs to recall. Then there were the visits to Aunt Nellie in the West London Mission home for the elderly in Drury Lane and the half-hour phone calls to Millicent on Sundays, and her funeral in 1991, which he had taken. Above all there was the memory of Sos which came back to him again and again. 'He will have grown,' he commented to Richard Holloway in a radio programme,[92] as he talked about his own experience of sorrow, as he did on other occasions, too.[93]

There were humorous times to recall, too, like when he had made 'Three Blind Mice' into a Rachmaninov Concerto.[94] He had been asked to bring his Wellington boots to Sandringham for his weekend with the Royal Family. 'Catch me going for a walk without a golf club,' had been his instant quip to friends.[95] Golf had been a great addiction[96] but his 'flick' style developed at Cambridge for hockey had been disastrous on the golf course.[97] He had discovered that golf brought out personal reactions which had marked resemblances to original sin. 'Have you ever edged the ball into a more favourable lie?' he had once been asked. 'I have.'[98] As for all the meals he had been given, there was the time he enjoyed salmon after one of the Anniversaries and the Indian (but not the Chinese) meals he had savoured.

He could hardly recall all the Soperisms he had tossed off in the open air and elsewhere, yet he knew some had been really original like 'Christianity is profoundly controversial because it is profound',[99] and 'Wealth is only creative when it is distributed.'[100] He knew, too, he had a tendency to be cavalier with facts as he made off-the-cuff remarks which on closer examination proved inaccurate.

As he looked back there were so many people coming into view. Yet often they were only acquaintances – George Macleod ('same wavelength'), Vera Brittain ('a very considerable influence'), Gipsy Smith ('not my cup of tea') and Russell Maltby ('encouraged me when I was young') – for outside the immediate family circle he had found it 'difficult to find relationships on a personally intimate level'.[101] The names kept crowding in on him – Noel Baker, like him a doughty campaigner for peace at ninety-one, Boyd Orr, Eric Heffer, Frank Cousins, Lord Sorensen (he had spoken at his memorial service), Diana Collins and Emmanuel Shinwell (who had encouraged him when their paths crossed in the House of Lords) and Fenner Brockway. Here there had been more than passing intimacy and with Michael Foot he had been glad to dedicate a statue to him in Red Lion Square.

During this period of 're-treading' Donald kept up his journalistic activity with a regular column in the *Ham and High*, his local paper. Many of his familiar themes cropped up here, including one seldom touched upon – the need for Christians to confess how they had treated the Jews.[102] He wrote in another article,

> I have been especially oppressed recently at the appalling record of human suffering which comes to us almost every news bulletin. As I hear of the heart-rending story of the deaths in Lord Mountbatten's boat, the holocausts in Laos and Cambodia, the sufferings of the Boat people, the carnage in Northern Ireland, I am only too painfully aware of the grim fact of human pain.[103]

Yet all pain was personal. Therefore the key to its alleviation was personal, too.

Donald himself had a number of points where he faced pain. First, there was his physical condition. 'I wish to God the church could do something about arthritis,' he muttered as it took two painful minutes to help him mount the stand at the open-air meeting in Leeds.[104] Yet his bravery in handling his physical pain, as he became more and more dependent on the care of others to get about, and on the chair lift at home, was part of his witness to the Gospel, alluded to by the Rev. Brian Beck, who wrote when Donald was ninety of his 'tenacity' which was 'little short of miraculous'.[105]

Second, Donald was prone to moroseness. Perhaps his hyper-activity was a defence against this. Certainly he met the world as an actor on a number of different stages and only rarely showed his inner feelings. 'Oh, I get depressed all right,' he admitted in 1992. Over the years if he had been able to pin down why he was depressed he would have been happier. But his depressions came and went and he found 'for the life or me I don't know why I am depressed . . .'[106] 'I think,' he commented elsewhere, 'I'm a lonely person. I had one or two men friends whom I've loved, and they died, and one of them I no longer see very much. This I find a burden to be borne.'[107] Part of this isolation lay in his reticence, but partly because he was driven, perhaps obsessed, by his mission. 'I wonder whether I've had as many friends as I might have done had I been a different sort of person,' he once reflected.[108]

How much of his activity was the working out of the work ethic drilled into him in childhood? He admitted in 1993 he had worked too hard,[109] but if each person's task is to integrate internalized parent figures, growing free of them as appropriate, maybe Donald, who seemed to have integrated what he had learned from his mother remarkably well, still stood too much in the shadow of his father?

'I am an old man,' he confessed in 1992 'and we are a long way from the Kingdom of God. And I sometimes look back at all the sermons I've preached about the Kingdom of God around the corner – it isn't. In that respect I think by the grace of God I am more humble than I used to be.'[110] He was, felt Olive Delves, disappointed, for his great attempt to rouse the public against the demon of capitalism as a result of the misery he saw during the 1930s, had hardly succeeded, even in the Labour Party, which, as he always maintained, was not socialist. Yet any disappointment he felt inwardly was not evident for he had, too, a massive resilience and a heart filled with hope.

'I still have some joys,' he maintained in 1992,[111] even though by then his movements were severely curtailed. Above all there were his ninetieth birthday celebrations to enjoy. Lady Soper, too, looked forward eagerly to 31 January 1993, for it had all the makings of a great occasion. By now unwell, she yet determined, with the help of her daughters, to rise to the occasion.

'We were not enough together,' he admitted once in an interview, looking back.[112] He knew, of course, they shared the moral nature of life and the significance of family relationships, but it had been seldom they had crusaded together, as when the Aldermaston marches began, and they had mainly prayed together during times of worship. Moreover, when he had returned home at night he had wanted to be quiet, whereas Marie Soper needed to talk, having been alone all day.[113] 'I have many faults,' he confessed, 'which my wife is very generous in not emphasizing.'[114] Nevertheless Marie Soper was crucial to Donald's life, even though they had their 'ups and downs',[115] and she herself wondered if he really had needed her because he was so self-contained, though quite unable to cook. Often she would keep him in line and be perfectly blunt with him about her feelings. On matters to do with relationships – why marriages failed, for example – she was more perceptive than Donald. 'Time and time again,' he admitted, 'I have been grateful that she has put her finger on the real issue when I have been dithering about.'[116] She had given good advice over abortion, especially when Donald had jumped in with his views too hastily,[117] and could comfort him, too, as latterly he became downcast and she pointed out how many creative ideas he had contributed to public life.

The elements of tolerance and intolerance on moral issues varied in each of them, as did the music they liked, Marie Soper preferring Mozart and Chopin to Donald's Bach and jazz. Their health had often caused the family great concern, for both had bouts of illness, Donald having had hip and shoulder operations to contend with, a severe embolism in the 1970s, which had necessitated his taking warfarin regularly and periodic blood tests at the hospital, as well as a congenital disorder which made a special diet necessary. This was in addition to the consequences for him of the 1938 complications following the appendicitis operation. Lady Soper herself had been in hospital nearly twenty times over the years and was once lucky to be alive after a serious car crash.

Perhaps what she had brought most to Donald's life was flair in relationships, ('She was very much the lady at ease, whether handling Royalty or a local church worker')[118] in dress styles (one of her characteristics was to wear large, flowery hats), or in bringing a sense of distinction to weddings and other celebratory occasions in the

House of Lords and elsewhere. She did, however, at times find the tension of living with a parson almost too great to bear because of the commitment to both church and home.

'I don't like ugliness,' Marie once commented, an indication that her rare spirit revolted against anything which lacked beauty.[119] It was a gift Leslie Weatherhead noticed, observing that 'everything she sees and does she makes more beautiful',[120] and her outstanding feature which had captivated Donald always, though by the 1980s the effects on Marie of her illness were evident.

Did Lady Soper influence Donald, or was it the other way round? It is difficult to be sure. Certainly she introduced him to a world well beyond the Wesleyan Methodism in which he had been nurtured (he never ate sweets in Lent) and her flavour was more Anglican than Methodist, her outlook on the world more debonair than dry. Indeed, latterly she no longer felt it necessary to support Donald's teetotal position. She also retained an independence of her own. 'I agree with most of what my husband does,' she conceded, 'but on the question of pacifism, for instance, one or two of his answers, frankly, are not good enough.'[121]

Now, with the ninetieth birthday about to crown the last ten years, when Donald had received an Honorary DD at Cambridge in 1988,[122] and become a Freeman of the Haberdashers' Company[123] and of the City of London[124] (he had already been made an Honorary Fellow of St Catharine's in 1966), there was much excitement in the family. There was to be a plaque put on a building on Tower Hill near the spot where he had spoken since 1927 and tributes were being made almost by the day. Donald felt distinctly embarrassed. 'Don't overgild the lily,' he said to a colleague, as he came up with another idea for the celebration. On the other hand he knew that if handled well, and the offer of a live *Songs of Praise* to cap the day ensured it would be, the celebration could help the West London Mission.

Even the *Financial Times* ran a spread on Donald's life and work.[125] A columnist in the *Mail on Saturday* called him 'the human photograph of a more idealistic age', after attending a Hyde Park meeting in pouring rain.[126] 'There is in Soper's life,' he wrote, 'so much of an England which is lost or half-forgotten. Joseph Rank's Methodist Central Halls, outdoor meetings, pacifism, ethical social-ism, passionate discussion of issues, working men's missions, and a belief in the perfectibility of men in society.'[127]

Donald was interviewed on an ITV breakfast show the morning of

31 January; and there was an assessment of him on the BBC programme *Sunday*. He even received a mention in *What the Papers Say*, as an extract from the *Sunday Telegraph* was quoted. A number of comments had been pre-recorded for *Songs of Praise* – his daughter Ann recalling the time he had been sent out with four children all linked together with string in case he returned without one. Colin Welland, the actor, spoke of how Donald had helped him to faith and Kenneth Greet spoke of Donald's 'amazing magnanimity'. Sir David Steel felt Donald was a standing rebuke to the argument that Christianity and politics do not mix and Cardinal Hume described Donald as 'a great servant of the Gospel in a very long life'.

Only once did a heckler get the better of him at Hyde Park that afternoon. 'What about reincarnation?' he asked. 'Well, the last thing I would want to be is reincarnated in an environment where I would encounter you all the time,' Donald said wearily, explaining that reincarnation was stuff and nonsense. 'Come off it, Donald,' the heckler retorted. 'You said that in your last life.'[128]

If anything, the tributes were too fulsome, Dr Carey remembering Donald's pioneering in religious television and Leslie Griffiths even finding mention of Donald in an Egyptian novel.[129] The *Big Issue*, too, had a lead story, written by an atheist. 'I leave the West London Mission with my atheism almost intact, but inspired by the idea that one can pick out bits of religion rather than prostrating yourself before a blinding light . . .' he wrote.[130]

For some Donald Soper at ninety was a pundit *par excellence*, who had stood the test of time. For others it was his remarkable perseverance which captured their imagination. One who wrote had started a young wives' club, now forty years old, as a result of a comment Donald once made.[131] Another had become both pacifist and Quaker and worked three years at the Quaker Council for European Affairs after hearing Donald during the 1953 Isle of Man OCW campaign[132] and one Buddhist made her will out to the League Against Cruel Sports after Donald had put her in touch with it. She planted a tree in his honour, too, on the Buddhist Holy Island in Scotland.[133]

Most moving of all the tributes was a letter from a lady in Sussex in which she described how one Sunday four years earlier a man about sixty had sat at the back of her church, then disappeared before speaking to anyone, a pattern he repeated for several weeks. Eventually members of the congregation got to know him and he became a regular worshipper. In a real Sussex dialect he told them why he came to their church:

> 'I heard that Soper man in Hyde Park some time ago,' he said.
> 'I read some of his books – so I thought I'd come down here to
> see what you Methodists were doing – after all he spoke a lot of
> sense and I thought you lot might be following his words.'[134]

> He's been with us four years and now takes communion regularly
> ... How many miles your Hyde Park messages have spread will
> never be known, but to [one person] it has meant a great deal
> and new friends.[135]

It was an incident which stood out because it epitomized all Donald Soper's life and work. And does so still.

Chapter 12

PASSIONATE PILGRIM

'As a pilgrim I am the more certain than I ever was in a reasonable, justifiable and final end,' Donald declared to the Hyde Park crowd gathered round him in 1992.[1] It was a theme which had undergirded his discipleship and was the foundation for all his activities. Indeed, speaking once in the Pilgrim Fathers' Church in Southwark, he had asserted that unless men and women 'became pilgrims – putting God first and dedicating their freedom to Him – in their search for economic justice they will drift into the cages of totalitarianism'.[2]

He remained clear, too, that Christians in the twentieth century had to travel shorn of many supports they had used in previous centuries. 'The Kingdom and the common table may seem like "iron rations" for the Christian pilgrims of this modern age,' he wrote in 1966, 'but they will prove sufficient for the present stage of the journey.'[3] He was equally certain such pilgrims needed to be clear about their destination, as early as 1942 urging 'that which we want to see at the end of the road we must envisage clearly in project and purpose as we continue our journey'.[4]

As he looked back on his life Donald became more aware than ever of his defects. 'If the record of my own pilgrimage is at best a series of desultory forays in the spiritual world, and at worst a series of miserable failures, yet does not hope "spring eternal"?' he had observed in 1955.[5] Now hope became a continuous thread with which he bound together his arguments and presentations, for he knew God's grace could change people and situations, if only he, 'full of egotism' as he was,[6] and his friends and colleagues, would take the first step.

In another mood he recognized the contours of the pilgrimage so set out in front, hoping the troops would follow. Accordingly, from

1978 till well over his ninetieth year, he continued his activities, only giving up driving in his ninety-first year, despite his skirmishes with the law for speeding.

Peace issues came first on his agenda. He remained consistent, as earlier when attacking Joan Littlewood's *Oh What a Lovely War!* because it had been unfair to the Generals![7] He was now disappointed in the pacifist movement, which he felt had failed to gain strength because it involved 'a fundamental change in human relationships, political and economic and people are not ready for it',[8] though CND's membership by the end of the 1970s had gone from 3,400 to 17,000, with 750 local groups with their own network of supporters.[9]

Many peace campaigners died in this period – Peggy Duff, Colin Duff, Colin Winter, Canon Collins, Michael Scott and Sybil Morrison of PPU among them. Nevertheless, Donald himself persisted, attacking the Government's decision to buy the Trident missile system from American for an estimated £5 billion[10] and taking his stand, along with ninety-one-year-old Lord Noel-Baker outside St Margaret's, Westminster, in January 1982, where the World Disarmament Campaign was holding a peace vigil until the United Nations Special Session on Disarmament began that June.[11]

In 1982 Britain went to war with the Argentine over its invasion of the Falklands Islands. On a BBC programme about the war with the Bishop of London and Canon Eric James, Donald argued that the first responsibility of the Church was to represent 'the spirit and teaching of the power of Jesus Christ'.[12] Whereas Bishop Graham Leonard maintained that the Church ought not to pre-empt the political and military leaders, Donald was clear that, though there were just causes, it was wrong to talk about a just war, because now no limitation of violence was possible.

It was the same argument he had used in the House of Lords debate on defence in 1980.[13] Now, despite the provocation, he was still opposed to the use of force.[14] In a subsequent debate he corrected the Archbishop of Canterbury – 'the Most Reverend Primate in his speech was talking about force when he should have been talking about violence. There is a world of difference'[15] and went on to indicate he would support diplomatic sanctions but Britain should consider the helpful role the United Nations Secretary-General might play.[16] 'Today is Ascension Day,' he informed the peers 'and it is for a Christian the proclamation of the victory of the Prince of Peace.'[17] He was arguing his case again in the autumn of 1982 in a debate on

the Address when he took the Bishop of London to task for saying
there was a distinction between 'that which is morally good and that
which is morally acceptable'.[18] He could not, he had to admit, follow
such a convolution, for he thought that, strictly speaking, the only
thing which was morally acceptable was that which was morally
good.[19]

In spring 1983 there was a debate on NATO policy, in which Lord
Carrington was foremost and most generous to pacifists, especially
Donald, though he did not agree with them.[20] There followed weighty
contributions from Lords Home, Brockway, Carver, Gladwyn,
Kaldor, Stewart and Macleod. Donald himself spoke after the Bishop
of Norwich, maintaining, as ever, multilateral disarmament was an
achievement, following upon an activity, whereas unilateralism was
'an activity looking towards an achievement'.[21] There was, he continued, a real distinction between the two. Moreover, it was dangerous to label the Russians the enemy, for many Russians were as
peace-loving as others. For him, therefore, risks must be taken,
principles adhered to and a Jesus, who enjoined Christians to love
their enemies, followed.[22]

The debate among Christians about atomic weapons themselves
had been heightened in 1982 by the Anglican Report *The Church and
the Bomb*, which had recommended British renunciation of the
independent nuclear deterrent, immediate cancellation of Trident
and the phasing out of Polaris missiles and submarines.[23] It was a
course soon to be debated and rejected by the General Synod of the
Church of England in February 1983, under conditions of intense
publicity. Blackwells issued a book that year reflecting the different
positions Christians had taken in that debate, with Donald contributing his views on mass violence. The responsibility of the 'would-be
Christian' was to be obedient 'rather than endeavour to modify the
Gospel in the interests of what he imagines to be practical politics',
for obedience was 'the opening of the door to God's power', he
concluded, for that was what the Sermon on the Mount said.[24]

The following year Donald was one of the signatories, along with
Kenneth Greet and some Methodist M.P.s, to a 'Christians against
Trident' petition launched by the Bishop of Dudley, and backed by
Christian CND.[25] The year 1985 saw him with Bruce Kent at the
head of a Clergy Against Nuclear Arms procession, which marched
through the City of London to commemorate the fortieth anniversary
of the dropping of the first nuclear bomb.[26] That autumn he was

speaking at Hinde Street at the opening of both One World Week and the Week of Prayer for World Peace. 'Those who would pray for peace must regard themselves as starting out on a pilgrimage,' he intimated.[27] For him at any rate prayer was an attempt to put himself on God's side and would lead him to a knowledge of what he must do. His memory ran right back to 1918 and the euphoria of those days when people prayed and looked confidently towards a new order. Things looked very different now, yet radical change was still needed; therefore he committed himself once more to the way of the Cross.[28]

This was also the year Donald went to New Zealand to record a BBC *Everyman* programme with David Lange, by now Prime Minister, and in the midst of the controversy surrounding his refusal to allow American nuclear carriers into New Zealand waters. He felt he needed spiritual encouragement from someone like Donald Soper who, for his part, hoped that Lange's nuclear pacifism would lead to total pacifism.

They met in a Wellington office and Donald readily conceded the complexities politicians in power faced. Lange, of course, knew he could not be a pacifist and assume office in New Zealand: there had, therefore, to be defence security. Donald was adamant, however. It was not possible to baptize some weapons in the context of armed violence in which the world was living. Moreover, in a world contaminated by evil, Christians had to prosecute the Christian life more humbly and ask for forgiveness if they found it impossible to translate the language of faith into the language of programmes.

David Lange was the more realistic of the two maintaining it was not possible to 'hi-jack a whole political party's programme'.[29] Donald was convinced, nevertheless, that an inner assurance was possible through adherence to the teaching and spirit of Jesus, to which Lange responded graphically: 'In the middle of revolving doors you don't think who made them.'[30] Nor did politicians always have a dramatic blueprint on the table. It was, Donald conceded, hard to believe in the kingdom's coming these days, therefore he looked to hope, something which could be generated.

Whenever asked for help, as over the trip to New Zealand, Donald would respond for he knew peace *was* possible because of God's redemptive love. Indeed, there was 'a continuing, redemptive process' alongside the transitory.[31] 'The universe is in travail to bring forth a loving, harmonious world in the way of Jesus – the way of the Cross,' he said elsewhere as, probably without knowing it, he drew on the thought of the Fellowship of Reconciliation, especially as articulated in the writings of Raven and Macgregor.[32]

By now the Sopers were celebrating their Diamond wedding with a party in the House of Lords. Yet Donald still felt driven by his mission and message. In 1990 the House of Lords debated the Nazi War Crimes Bill, when peers were expected to amend the Government's Bill because they were concerned that retrospective legislation would make fair trials impossible. The debate, on 4 June, called forth an unparalleled number of speakers. It was 8.58 p.m., therefore, before Donald spoke, after peers had already heard speeches from Lords Callaghan, Shawcross, Carrington, Hailsham, the Chief Rabbi, Lord Carver, Baroness Phillips and Viscount Tonypandy among others. He knew the House of Commons had already voted three times in favour of the Bill yet intended to vote for the Amendment that the House declined to give the Bill a second reading, he declared. For him, war itself was the crime and the heart of the matter the Christian doctrine of justice, which could never be finalized or completed. 'At what point,' he asked, 'are we prepared to deal with an imperfect process of justice because we cannot finally express it in perfect form?'[33]

Moreover, in the Christian tradition there was the concept of hell. Therefore, he continued, 'those who are indignant we should let bygones be bygones with regard to past enormities by Nazis and others should reflect that it is not a question of letting bygones be bygones but rather a question of letting God be God'.[34] There was, too, the matter of compassion and forgiveness to take into account. Forgiveness in his view was the offering of the hand of re-creation, but it was not forgiveness until the response had been made by those who looked in that direction for redemption.[35]

The debate made *ITN News* that night and Donald was one of those interviewed. TV again highlighted his views when HTV covered his contribution to the MPF Rally at Cardiff during the Methodist Conference. 'We are seeing the demolition of one of the great alternative views,' he told the gathering, as he surveyed what remained of Communist regimes, an attempt to rule which had failed, he felt, because it had not plumbed the depths of human morality on which its projects depended. 'Lift up your hearts and minds,' he therefore urged peace-makers, asking 'how Christians could translate this sense of failure into the instrument of peace'.[36]

By that autumn Donald was again advocating sanctions, this time against Iraq. Supposing, he asked, they do not work, what is the positive alternative to standing up to the aggressor? Surely you cannot merely do nothing? He had to admit he found this 'a formidable reaction to the pacifist case', and regretted that pacifists like himself had tended to leave it unanswered. 'Yet there is an answer and it is embedded in the Christian recognition of the "wages of sin" as having a finality about them when we assert that "the wages of sin is death",' he believed.[37]

He conceded, however, the acceptance of armed violence as a method of social change made it impossible to promote a programme of rejection of 'this total evil'.[38] Yet miracles did occur, like the ending of Marxist regimes 'out of the blue'.[39] Therefore, though the quest for a *programme* of non-violence was out of reach, the *witness* to non-violence was 'a present possibility',[40] though necessarily partial and imperfect.[41]

There was more to be said that autumn as the situation escalated. Donald followed Lords Runcie and Pym, with whom he had debated in Great St Mary's, Cambridge. He said,

I believe that it is sound scholarship to record that the early Christian Church was pacifist in spirit and in action. There is a theological application to that decision which is vital. We believe that the attitude of the early Christian Church was inspired by the pentecostal experience of the grace of God. It is intolerable to think that the first thing that the Christian Church did was to forsake the spirit and teaching as they found it in Jesus.[42]

We need to recognize we are all sinners, he continued. Maybe Saddam Hussein was totally depraved but there was much original sin on the other side, too, which made it an impudence to suggest a conference could not be held with him unless he admitted his sin and repented,[43] for all, including himself, needed the grace of God. 'If we are prepared to turn away from war as the absolute evil, we shall be able to enter into the daylight of a better world,' he concluded. 'That is my testimony. I offer it at this eleventh hour.'[44]

By January 1991, Donald, who was hauled up on to the plinth, was addressing 50,000 in Trafalgar Square, who had marched from Hyde Park to hear the leaders of the No War in the Gulf Movement call for non-violent action to avert the coming conflict. In contrast to Donald's call the Archbishop of Canterbury, Dr Runcie, whom

Donald admired for so many reasons, said on BBC 2's *Newsnight* that there came a point when, for the sake of a greater peace, the military option was the lesser evil.[45] Donald remained firmly against this view, however, and in the centre of a noisy crowd on Tower Hill on 16 January 1991, two weeks away from his eighty-eighth birthday, carefully and patiently explained his feelings as another war began,[46] arguing there was no ultimate justice available anywhere in the Middle East, only grievous evil on both sides. 'I want sanctions to succeed,' he admitted, 'but I would rather have a sell-out than a kill-out.'[47]

Donald was as bullish as ever when, as its President, he had addressed the Fellowship of Reconciliation, in May 1991. Now there was no limit to the capacity to destroy, as the Gulf War had shown, he indicated, an issue not so prominent when the FOR, to which he was as committed as ever, was founded. By its very nature involved in a programme independent of political and economic considerations, it must yet understand that the political and economic were linked, as in America, where vast unemployment would follow when America gave up its arms programme. Nevertheless FOR's role of reconciliation would only be productive if it saw that the over-arching love of God was the prerequisite of its work, so first and foremost it needed to recover the sense that Christians were missionaries of a Gospel.[48]

In 1992 Donald was involved in yet another controversy. News got out that Bomber Harris, who had planned the raids on Dresden and other German cities in the Second World War, was to be honoured with a statue at the RAF Church, St Clement Danes. Pat Arrowsmith and Donald once again found themselves working together, for a protest was being organized by London CND, PPU and others. The idea was to take pre-emptive action at the spot where the statue was to be erected and unveiled by the Queen Mother. Naturally the group had to publicize its plans which the authorities heard about and prevented. However, the group did display a peace dove on an island in the Strand, where it held a ceremony with flowers and speeches from Bruce Kent, Paul Oestreicher and Donald himself.[49] The following year the seventy-fifth anniversary of the founding of the RAF was to be celebrated with an exhibition which concentrated on its strategic bombing in raids on Germany, with the Queen Mother as the opener. 'I wish the Queen Mother wouldn't take part in this kind of ceremony,' Donald commented. 'We must stop celebrating these kinds of achievements in war.'[50]

Two other events drew Donald to the peace movement in 1993, one restrospective, the other prospective. On 1 December he was present with Shirley Williams in St Martin-in-the-Fields for a thanksgiving service for the life and work of her mother, Vera Brittain, whose hundredth anniversary occurred that month. He recalled with pleasure the great Dorchester Peace Rally he had attended in the summer of 1936, a gathering which had led Vera Brittain both to pacifism and the PPU, a commitment which had a quality and depth he cherished. 'It is,' he had to confess, 'a long time ago, but the sounds of trumpets which accompany her ministry still reverberate.'[51]

Donald's prospective meeting took place the previous October in the Central Hall, Westminster, scene of many other gatherings he had attended. Here there was a rally for a nuclear-free world. The banners hanging from its balcony – CND, Greenham Common Peace Camp, Quakers for Peace, Pax Christi UK, among them – gave him an indication of different groups still involved in the peace movement under the National Peace Council, which had co-ordinated the event. After being introduced by Bruce Kent, Donald made the opening speech, commending peace-making not only as a way of thinking but as a way of life. Military arsenals threatened the very continuation of human life into the next century: hence the need for urgent action by all people of goodwill. He was now nearly ninety-one and as his speech ended the whole gathering rose to its feet as he hobbled away.[52]

'Of course I'm a propagandist,' he had said in 1980,[53] re-iterating to Jill Wallis in 1986 he was still one.[54] He continued, therefore, to advocate Christian Socialism and to support the Labour Party, both from his platform in the House of Lords and elsewhere. Donald did not, of course, want a broad-based non-ideological Labour Party. Rather, he continued, even in the 1980s, to plead for a socialist party, espousing therefore the cause of Michael Foot as leader when James Callaghan resigned after the 1979 General Election defeat. He also wanted to see Tony Benn rise in the Party's counsels. But for Denis Healey he had scant regard, declaring once in Hyde Park he ought not to be a member of the Labour Party, doubtless due to the scorn Healey poured on pacifism and utopianism, in his view a substitute for serious thought on foreign affairs in the Labour Party since the 1930s. Needless to say he had no time for the Gang of Four and the founding of the SDP, though he did once say he heard the best exposition of Christian Socialism at one of the fringe CSM meetings at a Labour Party Conference from Shirley Williams.

Donald tried to explain to the *Methodist Recorder* in 1981 what was happening in the Labour Party when in a letter he spoke of the ideological difference between its social democrat and democratic socialist traditions. Such differences were containable, he suggested, especially at a time of crisis when it was necessary to remove a Government which was neither. Yet sooner rather than later the Labour Party must resolve this difference but *not* necessarily then. Secondly, there were issues such as the EEC, disarmament programmes and democratic procedures which divided the Labour Party and historically had vexed, but not incapacitated, it. Thirdly, the Labour Party was not moving left at an ever-increasing and dangerous rate. Squalid elements in the press thought so, of course, and Tony Benn, whose general position was Christian rather than Marxist, lent colour to this view but in principle he was a democratic, not an authoritarian, socialist. Michael Foot himself was no Communist autocrat and his preparedness to accept an electoral college and readiness for some compromises which were necessary to concentrate on the supreme issue of unemployment should commend him to every radical. He was the acceptable leader of the Party and probably the only one who could command general trust. 'I would canvass whole-hearted support for him . . .' he concluded.[55]

The *Methodist Recorder* had a big post bag after publishing Donald's letter, David Mason responding 'with some diffidence', because he hated to cross swords in public with Donald, his friend and mentor for nearly forty years. Yet the debate was too important for him to remain silent.[56] He doubted, he said, if the EEC, disarmament programmes and democratic procedures could be 'quite so airily dismissed' to 'the fellowship of controversy' within the Labour movement, as Donald had done. Indeed, the Labour Party was now committed to withdrawal from the EEC without a referendum and the feeling against the EEC was waxing rather than diminishing. Secondly, the sustained campaign to switch power from the democratically elected Labour representatives, in Parliament or Town Hall, to the local party caucus, was 'a move to the left'.[57] So, too, was the animus against the mixed economy. 'A political party that cannot command the loyalty of a lifelong socialist of the calibre of Shirley Williams is a party that is in a mess,' he concluded.[58]

Earlier, in 1979, Donald had been involved in yet another fracas when he had urged readers of the *Methodist Recorder* not to over-react to the present industrial crisis and the round of strikes. They are merely the 'labour pains in the birth of the only society which can succeed in the modern world – a socialist society'.[59] He added that when people talked about the misuse of union power they ought to reflect on the centuries of misuse of power on the capitalist side, though naturally he did not condone misuse of power from whatever source. Again readers protested though there were also supportive responses. 'The Labour Party should be grateful to Lord Soper,' wrote one. 'I doubt if socialism has ever had a greater champion.'[60] 'It is,' added another, 'a sad thing when a man of Lord Soper's undoubted status, still clings to the now forlorn picture of Utopian socialism.'[61] Donald, however, was not to be diverted from his chosen path by any strictures, so passionately did he feel about his beliefs, even taking the only 'party' line at the annual gathering of Methodist M.P.s and peers in the Speaker's Suite in 1980 when he insisted on expounding his Christian Socialist beliefs to the Conservative, Labour and Liberal M.P.s present.[62]

The year 1983 was a dismal year for the Labour Party for it lost another election. 'Its public image, its political ineptitude, its inbuilt divisions, and the particular behaviour patterns of its principal spokesmen, all these have played a part in the electoral outcome . . .' Donald felt.[63] Moreover, there was an almost total absence of the proclamation of socialism as a creed. Indeed, the story of the Labour Party included unmistakable evidence of 'an increasing indifference to fundamental belief in the so-called interest of electoral success'.[64] 'If more people would read that great apostle of socialism, Tawney,' he continued, 'they could find, as I did, an irrefutable argument for socialism – as the moral application of the Lord's Prayer.'[65]

By now Donald Soper was to all intents and purposes the uncrowned Chaplain to the Labour Party, baptizing the baby of an M.P. in the House of Commons Crypt chapel one minute, presiding at the marriage of a previous Speaker (Lord Maybray-King) the next. By the time his eightieth birthday came (31 January 1988) he had become an English 'institution'. 'All of us in this House are in your debt because of your witness,' said the current Speaker, the Rt Hon. George Thomas, at a dinner in the banqueting room of the Speaker's Palace.[66] For his part, Donald wanted to get on with his work, but he did enjoy celebrating on the day at the West London Day Centre, which benefited by over £1,600 from the birthday fund which had been set up. 'A great deal of the happiness which has come to me has come through my wife,' he made clear when he spoke to the gathering. 'I am profoundly grateful to God for his goodness.'[67]

Two years later, when Neil Kinnock, now Labour Leader, and Eric Heffer had a public row over Militant Tendency and its activities in Liverpool, Donald was the preacher at the pre-Labour Party Conference service at Bournemouth, attended by many M.P.s and delegates, at which the two M.P.s read the lessons. His theme was the same as ever, though the phrases he used were doubtless different: the Sermon on the Mount, the Jesus who was crucified, not for what He said about God, but for His 'revolutionary qualities'.[68] He also stressed the kingdom whose basis was a family relationship. 'The concept of the extended family in the Kingdom of Heaven included one's neighbour,' he explained to the delegates, 'and that was why apartheid was obscene and also blasphemous.'[69]

Another wheel came full circle for Donald at the annual gathering of Methodist M.P.s and peers, when Stuart Bell, M.P. for Middlesborough, paid tribute not only to his Methodist upbringing in Durham, but also to Donald's Tower Hill ministry, which he had attended when working in the City of London.[70] In 1989 a different event took place in Birmingham which involved Donald: a service to celebrate the centenary of the death of John Bright at which he was the preacher. He was met at New Street and, cassocked as ever, walked through the streets with Provost Berry to Birmingham Cathedral, talking to passers-by as he went. The Cathedral was full with people from all over Birmingham to hear Donald describe John Bright as one of the great and outspoken politicians of the city, as he reminded them of its great tradition of dissent and the sharpness and energy of its political life. It seemed, thought Nicholas Gillett, the Quaker descendent of John Bright who organized the gathering, 'as though he was speaking to each person individually'.[71] Also on this visit the Leader of Birmingham City Council hosted a gathering when twenty or thirty Labour Councillors and some church leaders met Donald. Provost Berry was with him as he walked round the room with difficulty because of his arthritis and shook each person's hand. 'It was,' recalls the Rev. Donald Eadie, 'as though some kind of father of the soul of the Labour Party had come.'[72]

In March 1993 Donald chaired the annual Tawney lecture of the Christian Socialist Movement held at Bloomsbury Baptist Church, an occasion when over 400 came to hear the Leader of the Labour Party, the Rt Hon. John Smith, who, along with Tony Blair and others, was a member of CSM, speak on 'Re-claiming the ground: Christianity and Socialism'. As John Smith invoked the memory and witness of Archbishop Temple and R.H. Tawney Donald recalled the times he had met both men and their influence on his own thinking and actions. 'I heard again . . . the dry voice but spiritual clarity of Tawney,' he said in his vote of thanks to John Smith, and also the voice of Temple, 'whose laugh was almost a nuclear explosion'.[73] There was, he felt, a preparedness now to look at other considerations besides market forces and therefore there was reason to hope, though it had been a very difficult ten years. 'Be faithful for a new dawn', he therefore urged the Christian Socialist Movement,[74] afterwards telling *The Week in Politics* 'He's done us good,' when asked his estimate of John Smith's lecture.

Still Donald continued his socialist pilgrimage, now speaking in a House of Commons committee room, with Tony Benn, on Clause Four of the Labour Party's Constitution, now castigating some, like Neil Kinnock, for revisionism, because he did not think Clause Four was 'an adequate presentation of modern democratic socialism' though he used to.[75] When it came to the Labour Party leadership election itself, following the unexpected death of John Smith, Donald declined to comment fully, saying he had yet to read a declaration of principles by any contestant.[76]

Donald, of course, had become President of the Christian Socialist Movement in 1975, so was above the day-to-day life of the movement he had done so much to nourish. He had himself given the Tawney lecture in 1980 and contributed to *Facing the Future as Christians and Socialists*, CSM's first major publication, in 1985. He had also supported CSM's application to affiliate to the Labour Party in 1988 and had been willing in 1990 to launch a one-off appeal for money, Christians for Labour, for the forthcoming General Election. A letter accordingly was sent to all CSM members urging them to support the campaign, with an advertisement in the *Methodist Recorder* and elsewhere. 'My generation looks to Donald Soper as a prophet and an inspiration,' Peter Dawe, one-time Chair of CSM, has observed,[77] adding that one reason CSM was held in good regard was because people thought well of Donald. This had become clear on Donald's eightieth birthday when there had been a GLC lunch for the Sopers, hosted by its Chair, Sir Ashley Bramall. 'It is difficult to think of anyone in public life who has made such an impact on London life for so long,' he commented.[78]

During this latter period Donald was pleased to be mobilized for local political meetings or to attend press conferences like one which launched a CSM book. He once even addressed the Hendon Conservative Association,[79] but mostly attended Labour gatherings like his visit in 1981 to the St Albans Labour Party and the TUC Gala in Durham in June 1985. He also took part with Arthur Scargill in a radio programme about the Miners' Strike. Much of his political activity, of course, still centred on the House of Lords, where he continued to speak on a wide range of topics. He had by now felt vindicated in becoming a member of the Upper House,[80] had indeed come to respect it as a debating chamber, though continued to support its drastic reform. 'I sometimes feel a bit lonely in proclaiming a creed which brought me into the Labour Party and to which I hope to be faithful,' he told peers in 1979,[81] an indication that his brand of ethical socialism was very much in a minority now, yet he refused to be deflected.

In all Donald spoke over seventy times in the House of Lords after 1978. Apart from questions of war and peace, as he continued to speak of the Russians in a positive way, informing peers that the *Journal of the Moscow Patriarchate* was available in their library, he preoccupied himself with social and personal questions, as well as matters related to apartheid and the Third World generally. In 1980, Lord Butler, the architect with William Temple of the 1944 Education Act, and now a dying man, with cross-party support opposed a clause in the Education (No. 2) Bill second reading which would have meant the introduction of charges for school meals and transport. Resistance was led by the Duke of Norfolk, the Bishop of London and Donald. 'I hope,' he said, 'we shall throw out with contempt things which impair not only the welfare of children . . . but the livelihoods of the families in which these children live.'[82] The proposal was rejected 216 to 112, a major defeat for the Thatcher Government.

Always Donald championed the Welfare State, calling the Social Security (No. 2) Bill on its second reading 'ethically ill-natured'[83] on this occasion daring to speak for the churches who 'cherish the welfare state'.[84] It was, he added, a Bill about the monetarist policy of the Government. 'The Bill is wrong,' he said at the Committee stage, when Baroness Gaitskell and Lord Gordon Walker also opposed it, 'and I should have preferred to have cut its throat on a second reading and if that sounds a rather blood-thirsty observation for a pacifist, I feel blood-thirsty about this Bill because it is fundamentally immoral . . .'[85] The Amendment was lost.

In 1981, following the Bishop of Liverpool, Donald expressed the anger many felt at the expenditure cuts in the public services[86] and in a further speech drew attention to the problem of homelessness. Two years later he was making the subject of unemployment high profile. 'The curse of unemployment,' he suggested, 'is not that you have nothing to give. It is that nobody wants you to give anything . . .'[87] He continued, too, to pursue the path he had trod earlier with regard to prisons. Why could there not be a system of bail, like the one in operation at the West London Mission, he asked in 1983, when Lord Kagan asked a question about prison conditions.[88] He was, he said, still in touch with those who suffered the ill-effects of a world in which they were tempted and fell. He did not excuse what they had done; but money should be found to help them. After all it had proved possible to find extra money for the Falklands War.

When Lord Longford introduced a debate on the Probation Service, Donald was quick to support it, again drawing attention to over-crowding and the stress under which the Probation Service in London was operating.[89] He advocated in another debate, again introduced by Lord Longford, the training of prison officers in 'a more friendly and co-operative style of ministry',[90] for he still did not believe society was ever justified 'in preventing the prisoner from seeing a lamp of light, even if it is far away at the end of a long tunnel'.[91] In a debate on inner city problems in 1987, initiated by Lord Scarman, Donald said,

> I was recently sitting on a bus which was caught in a traffic jam near the Elephant and Castle. Through a window I saw a young boy with a hammer smashing a piece of furniture which was adjacent to a window in a high-rise block of flats, and thereafter smashing the window itself . . . What bothered me was that there were a great many people passing by who took not the slightest notice . . .[92]

This disintegration of society, not only in the inner city, was what alarmed him continually now, as ethnic tensions, the clamour of minorities and homelessness increased, along with violence.

For Donald, with memories of the 1930s, unemployment remained a crime, a moral situation 'we ought to find intolerable'.[93] Instead, the Government seemed indifferent and unable to realize the impact of its actions.[94] So, too, over the National Health Service which needed more, not less, money. There was, he felt sure, a basic moral crisis arising from the very action of privatization, and the way it was expressed, and no adequate concept now 'of a united people'.[95] Lord Boyd-Carpenter, however, would have none of Donald's plea for corporate action. The question was what produced better results. 'Certainly as far as nationalized industries were concerned those which had been denationalized had done conspicuously better than under nationalization.'[96]

Donald was always at his best when being an advocate, as in a debate on the treatment of mentally ill offenders in 1988, when he was eighty-five. He had, he reported, been reading about research into mental disease, an area he knew little about. 'We should,' he admonished, 'be grateful to the linguistic philosphers for reminding us that when one has labelled something one has not necessarily described it.'[97] Even with a person recovering from alcoholism one was looking at someone not only rootless and down and out but mentally afflicted. Yet such people were surely to be regarded as members of the community. Indeed, he commented, 'I cannot but reflect that Christianity began with the casting out of devils.'[98]

When Donald reached ninety he found, of course, he could not rely on his memory, so ceased to speak frequently in the House of Lords, but whenever possible attended the 2.15 p.m. meeting of Labour peers on Thursday afternoons, though seldom spoke at it. 'Donald has never been the odd man out anywhere,' observed the former Labour Chief Whip, Lady Llewellyn Davies, 'not even in the House of Lords, which everyone thought he would be.'[99] It seemed he had adapted his style to the place, for the Donald Soper of Hyde Park and Tower Hill, places he still regularly frequented as before, was a very different person from the one Earl Ferrens and many other peers found so attractive to listen to.

Tower Hill, always his first love, because of its importance in his life and ministry, had now declined substantially but Hyde Park maintained well over 100, sometimes many more, each Sunday. Even when latterly he had to be hauled up on the steps by four people, once there and with his adrenalin flowing the years seemed to fall away for him for the hour. 'How much of vanity is there in it?' he was asked when he had left Kingsway Hall.[100] 'A lot, I suppose,' he admitted. 'I have, perhaps, a large sense of *amour propre*.'[101] 'What started as an impulse,' he told one interviewer, 'became a vocation and now I am addicted.'[102]

It was his continued outdoor ministry in a TV and radio age which intrigued the media, always ready to write about what Donald now thought of his listeners and the questions they asked. He would if possible go to Tower Hill an hour before he was due to speak and sit silently in All Hallows, the adjoining church. Now the Tower Hill crowd was small Donald could afford to be more reflective than in Hyde Park, where hecklers did their best to wreck his meeting, indeed, would on occasions have done so had not the police, sometimes mounted, been nearby to intervene when the heckling got out of hand.

Still Donald found people had no argument against Jesus Christ. Rather their complaint was against the churches for failing to live out Jesus's teaching, though for many it was a long time since they had entered one. Donald remained as clear cut as ever, as when he declared that 'Jesus went to His cross to prove the value and ultimate victory of non-violent love.'[103] He continued to come out with striking phrases and sentences which had the power to haunt the mind for a long time after he had forgotten all about them. 'I cannot explain God,' he said once. 'It's like a man who is blind trying to describe the sunshine.'[104] There were Soperisms which he tossed off effortlessly like 'Peace is the fruit of justice', 'Sin is the malignant use of our freedom',[105] and 'The essence of religion is moral not metaphysical.'[106]

Growing increasingly deaf, he could not hear some of the questions and had to have them repeated. Yet nothing seemed to diminish his spirit as he surveyed the world in all its complexity or seemed to have a cogent view of most topics under discussion. One day he would maintain the Quakers were nearer to institutional Christianity than anybody he knew,[107] the next he was extolling the compelling example of St Francis of Assisi.[108] Even a riot in October 1994, against the Criminal Justice Bill, when flaming litterbins were hurled across the road, left him unruffled.

Often Donald's wisdom shone through the arguments: 'One of the most dangerous things in the world is to think you've exhausted the meaning of something when you've described it in words,'[109] and 'a great deal of what before was certainty now comes within the realm of hope',[110] this comment made in relation to the complexities and ambiguities of the natural world. As ever his curious mind drove him on, especially where scientists led. 'Soon we'll be able to stop volcanos,' he declared,[111] and are but a few years away 'from transforming climate'.[112]

Pascal, 'my hero',[113] Bertrand Russell, 'not impressed by his philosophical genius',[114] Nietzsche,[115] too – 'How many of you are acquainted with him?' – were all part of the fireworks of his delivery. Mrs Thatcher had not read Charles Dickens carefully 'or she would not talk about Victorian values', he said in one deft sentence which demolished her.[116] And of America itself, 'The USA is not a country – it's a mass meeting.'[117]

Always, whatever the starting point, Donald reverted to the necessity of faith and the need to treat Christianity as an adventure. 'If you haven't any doubts,' he re-iterated, 'you haven't any beliefs.'[118] 'We shall never come to a final and complete answer,' he commented elsewhere, 'Yet I believe there is a sufficient answer for us pilgrims on this planet.'[119]

It was this capacity to express succinctly and clearly his beliefs and views that made Donald Soper for a decade and more after his official retirement much sought after by TV and radio, still appearing on both popular and serious shows, as well as on *Any Questions?* Gerald Priestland included him in *Priestland's Progress* reports on religion in Britain in 1981, and in 1982 Donald was sent by the BBC to San Diego, in California, to debate with the Creationists. Often he was in arguments and discussions, with Claire Rayner and Mary Whitehouse one year, Sir Immanuel Jakobovits the next.

His views on animals, the Cecil Parkinson affair and vegetarianism, were sought for short items and he also had a number of *Pause for Thought* slots to prepare as well. One of his most interesting assignments was on a LBC radio programme in 1982 called *A Month in a Monastery*. He would, he admitted, be happy to get away from the things he had to do, though he confessed he was no solitary or mystic. Rather, as Marx had taught him, he had a respect for the environment in which human beings had to live.

The programme was interspersed with hymns and Donald started with his favourite, 'When I survey the wondrous cross'. He wanted, too, to hear 'Hail, Gladdening Light', with its confidence in meeting the hazards of life. He was, he said, not particularly loving and faithful, indeed a great deal of his life had been an expression of an imperative – the imperative of hope. He chose now a hymn of peace, with its gloss on the prophecy of Micah – 'Behold the mountain of the Lord'. And the Magnificat.

Had he, his interviewer enquired, ever experienced the dark night of the soul? Donald had to confess he had not, though he had known times of solitude, largely when he had been ill, especially when a severe blood condition had left him on his back for three months. He had suffered, too, from insomnia, one night not losing consciousness at all. But that was not an experience in the realm of spiritual dereliction. He would, he admitted, like the light of certitude, but would it be good for him? The idea of pilgrimage really was what attracted him, or was it compulsiveness? Fortunately the Christian life for its fullness did not depend on isolation from the beauties of the world, so when his month was over, he told his interviewer finally, he would thankfully go home to his wife and family.

The run up to Donald's eightieth birthday was a precursor of his ninetieth. He was one of the few guests invited back within the same week to appear on BBC TV's *Wogan*; the previous week he had been on TV's *Newsnight* and on the *Any Questions?* panel and given half a dozen interviews. Wogan had wanted to discuss world affairs, teetotalism, the account of the marriage of Cana in the Gospel story. On *Newsnight*, they wanted his views on the legislation of Sunday horse-racing, which he was opposing on social grounds. On *Any Questions?* Donald had to give views on the Anderton furore, socialism and pacifism, privatization and personal faith.

During the 1980s and 1990s Donald also continued his interest in minority issues, including the League Against Cruel Sports. He stressed continually his opposition to violence in contemporary society and pointed out because blood sports encouraged such disregard it was essential to abolish them. He did, of course, preside over the League's AGM with courtesy and humour, now and again welcoming people of the stature of Barbara Castle and the Rev. Dr Andrew Linzey to address the gathering, as in 1989. But the two incidents which stood out most were the time he attended court in Winchester Crown Court to defend a League staff member against an allegation which was untrue (the League won the case) and when he went to Somerset for the weekend. Here, in August 1993, a two acre wood was planted in his honour near Dulverton to commemorate his ninetieth birthday. Donald planted a special tree, watched by some 200 members of the League, many of whom bought copies of his aphorisms which had been brought together in a book called *Soperisms*, also for his birthday.

During this time Donald also launched from Lambeth Palace a pastoral handbook for the churches, containing guidance on the services available to help the homeless. There was also the COSPEC initiative, 'Christians for a Change', to support with a letter to the press; and a Vigil for Cedric Mayson, a Methodist minister in detention in South Africa. Donald also addressed 1,000 pensioners at a rally in the Central Hall, organized by the National Pensioners' Convention to protest at the plight of the elderly. He was outspoken as well on matters of sexuality, sensitive to the debate about the age of sexual consent being sixteen, and ready to travel to court to speak on behalf of a minister who had committed an act of indecency.

When the question of homosexual Methodist ministers occurred Donald was clear where he stood. They should not be barred from the ministry, for what they did in their situation made it either a blessing or a curse. How could the Methodist Conference, he asked, turn out the homosexuals who were already ordained? It was a motion he could not support. Certainly there was need for self-control, but that applied to all aspects of life.[120] To show his solidarity with these ministers, therefore, in 1994 he attended a meeting organized by the Methodist caucus of the Lesbian and Gay Christian Movement.[121]

The question of human fertilization (the Warnock Report) was raised in the House of Lords. Donald was similarly sensitive to this issue. Parameters were naturally needed, he argued, but now things formerly attributed to God could be done by human beings. 'There is,' he averred, 'no morality which can be acclaimed as 100 per cent'.[122] As a minister he had to weigh many times the good that could be done to a family against the harm that might be done, particularly to forms of life which 'whatever their potential something at a certain stage', were not to be compared with the value of those fully adult.[123] He therefore found no difficulty in A.I.H. If society were to assist in medical ways to help people bear children, A.I.H. seemed perfectly acceptable and right. In general he would apply the principles of compassion and the provision of happiness to people who would not otherwise enjoy it, and above all 'the retention of the principle of the family'.[124] Surrogacy, of course, would be the problem as the matter developed, particularly if there grew a demand for a bank of anonymous semen, and this could not be tolerated for a moment. Nevertheless, the issue would not go away, so he welcomed the Warnock Report.[125]

Above all, as Donald responded to immediate demands, he pondered the meaning of his own death and grieved for the death of Lady Soper, whose funeral, an occasion which was also a celebration of a life rich in relationships and loving, had occurred in January 1994. He managed to keep his composure as he grieved, but needed his family even more now as arrangements were set in train to support him so he could stay in his own home, and continue his ministry, despite the difficulties in movement his arthritis increasingly brought. He found, in particular, support and friendship from his son-in-law Alan Jenkins, Judith's husband, who lived nearby. In his final sermon at Kingsway he had referred to the 'saints', some of whom were in that very congregation. Now he experienced care from a number of those who over the years he had been able to count on for loyalty and help as they shared in his ministry of reconciliation.

Donald more and more thought about existence beyond the present one of space and time and decided the other world could be known in music, art and mysticism.[126] He, too, would reach out for that experience and, as an adventure of faith, seek eternal life. He summed it up thus:

> For me, I find it increasingly makes sense. In my old age life is not coming to an end because time and space and matter are no more, therefore I am not sitting around waiting for the drift into nothingness. I can be profitably employed in equipping myself for an expedition of which the requirement of effective pilgrimage must be something which already is spiritual rather than temporal. I must try to live a 'good' life now for that is the only equipment that I can take with me when I die.[127]

EPILOGUE

THERE WAS MUCH OF THE Liberal Protestant in Donald Soper, influenced as he was by the historical and scientific scholarship of the nineteenth and twentieth centuries, which robbed the Bible of its absoluteness. Its rock, however, remained solid, amid all the debris around – a Jesus perceived, as one writer said, as 'human, appealing, with a teaching above all the relatives of history'.[1]

In place of the Epistle to the Romans such Liberal Protestants, particularly in America, put the Sermon on the Mount where they felt a Jesus was presented who could captivate any believer. Indeed, faith almost became loyalty to a hero and his teaching, as practical discipleship was set over against academic theology, 'a social gospel supplementing if not over-taking personal piety',[2] and morality replacing 'the long reign of doctrine'.[3] Preachers did, of course, still use words like Incarnation, Atonement, Resurrection or Salvation, but they gave those words an ethical context which made them easier to grasp. In this up-to-date version of Christianity the Church still had a place, too, as the company of those who subscribed to the ideals of Jesus. Indeed it was the society 'called to build the Kingdom of God on earth'.[4]

Donald Soper clearly is a British expression of some of the perceptions of this form of Protestantism, but with a distinct difference – his evangelical upbringing made him always aware of the need to offer Christ and his (later) conversion to sacramentalism ('What I receive in stretching out my hands to receive the bread and the wine – there is the strength and there is the power and the grace')[5] allowed him to have, at least in embryo, a sense of the coming of Christ through the Body of Christ at the Eucharist.

Donald was, of course, not unaware of other theological traditions, especially the cold blasts of a revived biblical theology coming from

Karl Barth on the Continent in the 1930s. But, felt John Stacey, he considered that Barth's outlook 'would not fit in to the Methodist theological outlook'.[6] Donald, with his belief in reason and interest in philosophical theology, was not, therefore, very popular with the Barthians, influenced as they were by dogmatic theology seen in the context of saving faith.

Donald, who was essentially an evangelist, allowed his understanding of Jesus's teaching to be tailored by the needs of his mission: to Christianize the Labour Party and to make socialist the Methodist Church. 'The socialism I believe in is not the fullness of the Gospel expressed on earth,' he once explained in a BBC programme. 'It's the Kingdom of God as far as economics and politics can attain.'[7]

How then did the Labour Party see its ardent recruit? 'Donald Soper's principles are much admired,' Lord Callaghan has observed, 'but is he a practical man? Are his beliefs realistic in the world in which we live?'[8] 'Has he,' wonders another assessor, 'really ever questioned the basis on which his evolutionary optimism can be based?'[9]

Not surprisingly Donald has been called 'the Labour Party's National Chaplain',[10] but was that true? Indeed, would the Labour Party have fared better with a Niebuhrian, one who understood the realities of institutional life, power realities, which Donald disliked intensely, and how to manage change? Perhaps this is what Lord Archer of Sandwell has hinted in his comment that Donald does not 'know how to win',[11] and is only really interested in 'the power of persuasion'.[12] This may be because he sees no compromise possible between the great struggle of good and evil 'yet either option which one chooses contains some evil,' he has added, concluding that possibly 'Donald Soper sees things *too* clearly.'[13]

Some, of course, have considered this a virtue, Len Barnett commenting that 'Donald Soper has made the world listen to him by his consistency and advocacy,'[14] and Bishop Trevor Huddleston that Donald's consistency represents a precious strand in 'the whole tapestry of Christian life through the centuries'.[15] But is this acknowledged consistency only a virtue? Donald himself was once asked how he managed to be so consistent to which he replied: 'By ignoring some of the arguments.'[16]

Donald, it is clear, therefore, sees what he wants to see. In the end, too, for all the charm and humour, the weaving of words and sentences, he is *right*. There has been no time to work out middle axioms, which though not of faith, represent a good cross-section of relevant opinion, and therefore carry the weight of highly informed authority,[17] though Donald was certainly aware, in his Alex Wood lecture on compromise, and sometimes in *Tribune* articles, of the need for provisional policies.

In view of these strictures (even Harold Wilson once remarked that ideals of Donald's order rarely survive the rough and tumble of political life),[18] how did Donald persuade the world to listen to him? Undoubtedly it was because of his oratory. Indeed, Lord Cledwyn of Penhros regards him as 'one of the great public speakers of the century'.[19] Even so, he has admitted, that immensely good as he is, 'he'd lose his deposit in a safe seat in the south of England like any other Labour candidate'.[20]

Society, it appears, needs figures who bear for it its hopes and aspirations which in its better moments it yearns to accept, whilst remaining ambivalent about the consequences of their implementation. Christians and non-Christians alike, therefore, have found in Donald Soper an icon to revere, though he may have disillusioned some when he became a peer. As a *Tribune* staff member once observed: 'Jack Jones, Barbara Castle, Michael Foot, Donald Soper – all were legends we "looked up to". If it helps to believe in Heaven – OK. I can work with him though I do not believe what he does.'[21] Similarly, Tony Benn, who is very aware of the Christian Socialist tradition and indeed that 'socialism wasn't invented in Leningrad in 1917',[22] considers Donald Soper's contribution formidable, and that he will be 'looked on as Wesley was'.[23]

Donald has, he feels, been on parallel tracks in relation to the Labour Party, as a map-maker and as a hiker, going where it goes, even if he does not like all the routes. He is, he considers, really like 'the airborne seeds which fly around – and produce flowers and trees of their own'.[24] It may even be, he adds, with the collapse of Stalinism, a Christian influence on socialism has now become possible.[25]

There is, of course, a further gloss on this. Donald has been a rebel, it is true, but a rebel within a tradition – 'one of the established "characters" that the English public likes to have around like Bernard Shaw, or Cyril Joad or Malcolm Muggeridge',[26] Alan Wilkinson has observed, adding that perhaps Donald should be seen as 'one of the last public heroes of British Christianity ... people whom you could invite to speak at a meeting and virtually everyone would know who they were and would want to hear them'.[27]

Donald Soper's stature, which the world recognized, was acknowledged because of his clarity of thought and the assurance he gave of knowing about the world and its complexities. There was, too, as a Methodist colleague has indicated, an enormous record of achievement – public service for sixty years; open-air work on Tower Hill and Hyde Park, unique to him, as well as his devotion.[28] The world was arrested, too, because he was a 'commanding, intriguing and provocative figure, afraid of nobody',[29] as another colleague has remarked.

This recognition came partly because Donald was rooted in Methodism, not despite it. Indeed, by his practical, controversial and articulate politics, he persuaded the British public 'that Methodism is concerned with people's bodies as well as their souls'.[30] Within Methodism itself he may have been an ambivalent figure, impatient with its structures and outlooks, its congregation and leaders often irritated by his stances, yet essentially he reflected Methodism and its 'Arminian realism', as the Rev. Chris Hughes Smith has noted.[31] By this he demonstrated that Methodism was not a cloistered sect, making raids on a godless world, but a Church eager to co-operate with God's Spirit at work beyond its confines, though found in abundance in the body of Christ. Moreover, Donald's lifelong commitment to human beings in all their complexities had a touch of John Wesley himself, to whom, unconsciously perhaps, he owed his Anglican flavour, and whose brother Charles wrote of giving service 'Till death thine endless mercies seal'.

What Vivian Green has written of John Wesley may well be an epitaph for Donald Soper also when he speaks of 'His charm and grace, cloaked in an iron will; he was granite in aspic.'[32] Like many Christian saints he was, too, 'self-regarding', under God's guidance himself being the real centre of his interest. John Wesley's life, Vivian Green adds, was 'built around his own experience glazed or insulated from the world outside by his confidence in God himself. Completely selfless, yet completely egotistical, he had come to justify himself with his own creation.'[33]

What John Wesley most conspicuously lacked, of course, as Clayton observed in 1738, was 'a spiritual guide', or failing that, 'a religious friend', of the kind that he had hoped for and to some extent found in Oxford.[34] The same comment can be made about Donald, though he did listen attentively to his wife and a few candid friends particularly on specific points, but there was no colleague over the decades close enough to perform this role.

Some Methodists, like Professor Gordon Rupp, feel that in Donald Soper 'the great four square tradition' of Hugh Price Hughes has been renewed, 'like a four-legged table, one leg perhaps a little shorter – for Evangelism, High Churchmanship and Ecumenicity had also for Hughes the wrong belief in German imperialism which was as up to date and as dated and vulnerable as Dr Soper's Labour nonsense'.[35] Yet Donald surely defies comparison with past figures, however much he imbibed from them, partly because none of them really had to grapple with the first secular age in history.

Hugh Price Hughes, by all accounts, was a prophet, one who spoke the Word of God to the people of the day, especially confronting the powers over their iniquity, as Nathan confronted David over Uriah the Hittite. In what sense was Donald Soper a prophet, for many of his views were held by others, and rather than speaking his unique truth he read widely, listened acutely to the accents of leaders like William Temple and R.H. Tawney, and then distilled the essence of what they were saying for wider consumption? This would seem to make him *par excellence* a brilliant communicator, who uses every means available to warn, exhort, cajole, encourage, liberate and guide, in a pioneer ministry of great complexity and originality. This does not mean a belittling of his role. How could a preacher of well over 10,000 sermons and homilies be disregarded? Rather it is to see him using an extremely attractive personality – 'great humanity, enormous sense of humour, no establishment apartness, very truthful, may be wrong, but tells you what he thinks' – with immense intelligence.[36] Part politician, part actor, part dandy and part 'poet' and philosopher, he continually preached Christ 'in our complex, gadget-ridden world'.[37]

It was this gift which drew admiration from people as varied as Salvation Army leaders (on Donald's eightieth birthday the United Kingdom Commissioner sent a party of bandsmen to Hyde Park to play 'Happy Birthday')[38] and the Anglican episcopate. Indeed, as David Sheppard has written, Donald Soper 'was one factor in leading me to believe that God wants to change both human hearts and social structures'.[39] Yet not all have been as captivated by Donald's theology, just as there are many who have had reservations about his politics.

'Donald Soper was supremely a witness to Jesus and His preaching of God's love to His intended world family,' the Rev. Noel Shepherd, an early member of OCW, has written.[40]

> I could understand this message in the open air and on radio and TV, where it was entirely appropriate to the audience. However, when it came to progressing in the Christian faith and understanding I found this version of the Gospel thin and unsatisfying. In the end I yearned for stronger theological meat and a more decisive Gospel to proclaim. Perhaps it was George Macleod's Reformed theology, or his more direct appeal to the individual, but I changed my allegiance from OCW to Iona.[41]

Strikingly, George Macleod and Donald Soper both stood for many of the same things within the Catholic Reformed, and High Chapel Methodist, traditions – socialism, pacifism, frequent celebration of the Eucharist, and mission, especially to the cities, though only Donald Soper was theologically a Republican. But if George Macleod's legacy is the re-built Iona Abbey and its flourishing community, what is Donald Soper's? True the Christian Socialist Movement continues; so does the Methodist Peace Fellowship, the Methodist Sacramental Fellowship, OCW and the social work projects. But is there any distinctive contribution which can be classed as Soperian?

The Abbé Huvelin, comments John Newton, wrote in lives; so, too, did Donald Soper.[42] 'You have, of course, enabled the Holy Spirit to make tremendous changes in the lives of hundreds of people,' wrote Pauline Callard, one of those Donald greatly influenced through OCW.[43] This could not have happened unless there were not something greatly to love in Donald, for all his faults, of which he became ever more conscious, and something, in fact, which appeared to a wide range of groups at a deep level. Moreover, had Donald been more theologically aware 'he would not have been able to give the straight answers to straight questions as he has done'.[44] This is not to say there is no meat in Donald Soper; of course there is; also something healthy-minded in the way he faces up to the role of doubt in faith. So, if at times he seems a latter-day Don Quixote, he also has to be seen as Rodin's *The Thinker*, with head bowed in search of truth, as well as akin to Ignatius Loyola, seeking to fashion disciples for obedience in dark times.

The roles of George Macleod and Donald Soper, therefore, have been parallel. It has not been like with like, but rather a Scottish response, with universal implications, and an English response, also with universal resonance. Both men, too, were ecumenical to the core, Donald, after his Russian visit, deeply aware of Eastern Orthodoxy, as well as the contribution of Roman Catholicism. Perhaps it was its central, organizing face which made Donald feel more at ease than with biblical fundamentalists like Billy Graham, whom he once described as 'a squalid peg on which to hang a few thoughts'.[45]

Certainly, even in his old age, Donald was suggesting that if only the Pope would say that war was wrong this would test the credibility of the Roman claim, as well as be of immense significance. Perhaps, too, because he seemed to be attracted to 'some kind of socialist totalitarianism, rather than to liberal democracy',[46] he wanted the Church to speak out more authoritatively, something on the whole the Protestant traditions were never able to do easily because of their structures and theologies.

Like George Macleod, Donald Soper was full of contradictions. George Macleod was a healer, as well as a man of politics, an aristocrat, as well as a man among the people. Donald, for his part, was deeply rooted in the Puritan tradition, as popularly perceived, though he never wanted to diminish gaiety and enjoyment of life.[47] There was, too, latterly a softening in Donald's approach as he became more approachable, more tolerating, though essentially the views he held in the 1930s he still held in the 1990s. Emotionally, of course, Donald never seemed to be able to resolve the private and the public faces. Nor did he seem to be aware in any significant way that affected him of the psychoanalytic revolution, preferring the Marxist perception about the importance of the outer environment in human affairs. Here was a weak spot in his armoury, going back maybe to unresolved childhood experiences, where intimacy was not the most cherished virtue in an Edwardian family with a strongly moral background and discipline.

Moreover, despite the evidence to the contrary in regimes all over the world that there were deep psychological reasons why some politicians gain power, and certain types of regime retain their grip, Donald believed in the strength of reason – that if things are explained (in as far as they were explainable) there was, to use the Quaker phrase, 'that of God in everyone', which would enable them to respond. It was not that he did not believe in sin, both corporate and personal, rather, as a Methodist, that he had an 'optimism of grace'. And for Christians at any rate, there was the chance to start again once there had been repentance and forgiveness.

As always his mind went back to the family as a model, both for forgiveness and other social matters, though it may be questioned how real this model was in a society in which the whole fabric of the family was crumbling. If anything, however, Noel Shepherd's theological strictures may be too severe, for at the heart of Christianity is a Cross and a man dying on it with words of forgiveness on His lips and Donald seldom strayed far from this Gospel truth. Could there be anything more profound than that? 'When you've said everything,' Brian Duckworth has added, 'my memory of Donald Soper is offering the Gospel at Hinde Street – when each time he returned to the saving power of the Gospel in terms of our personal lives here, and our destiny hereafter.'[48]

After contemplating all Donald Soper's activities there remains the sense that he is original. 'Most truly original characters end up as enigmas to "ordinary" people,' Lady Llewellyn Davies has observed. 'They arouse great hostility, or great admiration.'[49] This was certainly true of Donald Soper, though in old age he transcended much of the hostility. Perhaps people began to see him for what essentially he was – 'a moral revolutionary'.[50] Or perhaps they marvelled that, like Churchill in old age, he seemed to have 'inexhaustible vitality'.[51]

Certainly, too, whatever different groups thought of Donald's unique theological synthesis, it did at least add up to a coherent and cogent Christian position, though John Vincent felt that 'sacramentalism, evangelism, pacifism and socialism, cannot any longer be our resting-places as radicals'.[52] This was a view Donald would not concede. Though the language may need alteration he considered the ideas he sought to express still beckoned 'as goals not yet reached'.[53] Who is right? 'Either Donald Soper has built a great edifice of impeccable logic on a basis of faith long discredited,' David Roberts, formerly of OCW and the City Temple, has considered, 'or he is a prophet whose time has not entirely come.'[54]

John Wesley once asked: 'Who is a Methodist?' and answered the question thus: 'A Methodist is one who has the love of God shed abroad in his heart by the Holy Ghost given unto him.' A Methodist is one who 'loves the Lord his God with all his heart and with all his soul, and with all his mind, and with all his strength'.[55] In all the contradictions people found in Donald Soper, and perhaps he found in himself, he tried to do just that. Indeed, as Brian Duckworth has reflected, 'His life exemplifies Philippians 4:8.'[56]

Moreover, Donald tried to show how love could be interpreted corporately, in the politics of his own country and beyond the nation state. Hence his stress on the need for goodwill. 'The main business of those who believe in goodwill is to seek to increase the amount of it until it becomes a dominant motive for millions of people,' he once wrote in the *News Chronicle*. 'That is surely why the church is right in putting its main emphasis not upon temporary political actions but on permanent ethical ideals.'[57] The question, of course, was not whether or not there could be compromise in Government, but what were the permissible limits of compromise for advocates of goodwill, bearing in mind that even Jesus in His earthly ministry had to compromise. Indeed, He could not have preached at all without the protection of the Roman Empire, 'which His kingdom was to overthrow'.[58]

Donald Soper's life and work stand or fall by how he is seen according to this fundamental conviction of his, for all the stories, talks, interviews, sermons and dialectic, were aimed to convince his hearers that in Christ God had come to show goodwill, to bring peace for a distracted world and invited all to follow the way of the Cross, where only love ruled, beyond which there was resurrection and a new pentecostal community waiting to be born.

NOTES

Chapter 1 Pupil

1. Viscount Tonypandy, *Methodist Recorder*, 7 October 1993.
2. Address to Modern Churchmen's Conference, report in *Methodist Recorder*, 13 August 1964.
3. Lord Soper, *Hansard*, House of Lords, 1969, vol. 306, col. 594.
4. William Purcell, *Portrait of Soper*, Mowbrays, 1972, pp. 40–1.
5. Interview 2, 30 April 1992.
6. Grace Pugh, letter, 23 March 1993.
7. Beryl Watson, letter to Lord Soper, 5 February 1993.
8. Donald Soper, *Calling for Action*, Robson Books, 1984, p. 167.
9. Anne de Courcy, interview with Lord Soper, *Evening News*, 5 October 1979.
10. Donald Soper, *It Is Hard to Work For God*, Epworth Press, 1957, p. 32.
11. *Portrait of Soper*, op. cit. p. 44.
12. *Kingsway Messenger*, February/March 1956, p. 8.
13. *Hansard*, H.L. 1973, 27 March 1970, vol. 340, col. 10045.
14. Interview 3, 7 May 1992.
15. Ibid.
16. *Portrait of Soper*, op. cit., p. 44.
17. *Kingsway*, 1971/2, pp. 2–3.
18. Obituary, *Methodist Recorder*, 19 May 1962.
19. Interview 1, 23 April 1992.
20. C.H. Young, *Methodist Recorder*, 25 April 1957, in connection with the opening of St John's, Wandsworth.
21. *Kingsway Messenger*, October/November 1954, pp. 2–3.
22. Interview 3, 7 May 1992.
23. Interview 1, 23 April 1992.
24. Donald Soper, *Children's Prayer Time*, Epworth Press, 1954, p. 25.
25. *The Times* Saturday Review, 23 March 1991.
26. The Rev. John Wesley, *44 Sermons on Several Occasions*, Sermon 44 on 'The Use of Money', Epworth Press, 1944, pp. 576–88.

27. *Kingsway*, summer 1961, p. 28.
28. Interview 1, 23 April 1992.
29. Ibid.
30. Ibid.
31. The Centenary Year Joseph Malins Memorial Lecture, 'On To The Second Century', The International Order of Good Templars, 1968, p. 6.
32. *The Nineties*, 'Drink Before 1914', BBC 2, 4 April 1993.
33. *Hansard*, H.L., 13 July 1983, vol. 443, col. 416.
34. *Portrait of Soper*, op. cit., p. 44.
35. Ibid., p. 41.
36. Donald Soper, *Answer Time on Tower Hill*, Hodder and Stoughton, 1936, p. 5.
37. Joan Clifford, *Ten of Our Time*, Denholm House Press, 1967, p. 21.
38. Mrs E.B. Green, letter, 27 March 1993.
39. *Portrait of Soper*, op. cit., p. 48.
40. Ibid.
41. BBC interview, *Five to Ten*, 1 April 1965, British Library, National Sound Archive, LP 29671.
42. *Portrait of Soper*, op. cit., p. 41.
43. 'A Childhood: Lord Soper', interview with Judy Goodkin, *The Times Saturday Review*, 23 March 1991, p. 50.
44. Mrs Millicent Lawrence, in *Portrait of Soper*, op. cit., p. 44.
45. *Kingsway Messenger*, June/July 1955, p. 8.
46. Interview 3, 7 May 1992.
47. Ibid.
48. *Portrait of Soper*, op. cit., p. 41.
49. *Children's Prayer Time*, op. cit., p. 27.
50. *The Times* Saturday Review, op. cit.
51. *Portrait of Soper*, op. cit., p. 43.
52. St John's Hill Methodist Church, 1864–1964, Centenary Celebrations, September 1964.
53. Nona Price, 4 June 1993.
54. Interview 3, 7 May 1992.
55. Ibid.
56. Greta Price, (née Reynolds), letter, 23 March 1993.
57. Ibid.
58. Interview 3, 7 May 1992.
59. *Children's Prayer Time*, op. cit., p. 64.
60. Interview 4, 21 May 1992.
61. Interview 3, 7 May 1992.
62. BBC, *Lift Up Your Hearts*, 22 May 1962.
63. *Care of the Elderly*, September 1989.
64. BBC interview, *Five to Ten*, op. cit.
65. *John Bull*, 25 July 1953, p. 13.

66. St John's Hill Methodist Church, op. cit., pp. 2–3.
67. Frank Boysen, letter, 22 March 1993.
68. *Hansard*, H.L., 20 December 1967, vol. 287, col. 1532.
69. *Band of Hope Chronicle*, 1908, p. 167.
70. The Rev. Henry Carter to the Wesleyan Conference at Plymouth, *Band of Hope Chronicle*, vol. 36, no. 412, August 1913, p. 124.
71. The Centenary Year Joseph Malins Memorial Lecture, op. cit.
72. Donald Soper, *The Advocacy of the Gospel*, Hodder and Stoughton, 1961, p. 14.
73. *Calling for Action*, op. cit., p. 137.
74. Ibid. p. 14.
75. G.W. Hawthorne, letter to Lord Soper, January 1993.
76. *Methodist Recorder*, 20 November 1969, p. 2.
77. Ibid.
78. From 'The Methodist Pulse', *Kingsway*, spring 1960, p. 10.
79. *Calling for Action*, op. cit., p. 153.
80. Interview on LBC Radio, 26 December 1982.
81. Contribution for MYP, undated, p. 3.
82. Interview on LBC Radio, op. cit.
83. 'Hit List', Six Records I Don't Want to Hear Again, BBC Radio 4, 6 June 1986.
84. *Calling for Action*, op. cit., p. 20.
85. *Tribune*, 7 January 1966, p. 2.
86. Ibid., 15 November 1968, p. 3.
87. BBC, *Frankly Speaking*, 29 July 1965.
88. *John Bull*, op. cit., p. 13.
89. Interview on LBC Radio, op. cit.
90. *Kingsway Messenger*, December/January 1954, p. 2.
91. Interview 1, 23 April 1992.
92. Interview 3, 7 May 1992.
93. Ibid.
94. Ibid.
95. Interview 1, 23 April 1992.
96. Aske's School, Hatcham, concert programme.
97. *Methodist Recorder*, 30 August 1979, p. 7.
98. *Ten of Our Time*, op. cit., p. 22.
99. *Calling for Action*, op. cit., p. 20.
100. *Hansard*, H.L., July 1982, vol. 333, col. 709.
101. *Calling for Action*, op. cit., p. 26.
102. *Portrait of Soper*, op. cit., p. 45.
103. *The Times* Saturday Review, op. cit.
104. Ibid.
105. BBC Radio 4, op. cit.
106. Donald Soper, *All His Grace*, Epworth Press, 1957, p. 61.

107. Ibid.

108. Ibid., p. 31.

109. *Calling for Action*, op. cit., p. 27.

110. J. B. Bury, *History of the Freedom of Thought*, Williams and Norgate, 1913, p. 232.

111. *Kingsway*, autumn, 1957, p. 20.

112. Donald Soper, *Aflame with Faith*, Epworth Press 1963, p. 130.

113. BBC *Any Questions?*, 13 May 1983.

114. *Kingsway*, autumn, 1957, pp. 18–19.

115. Ibid. p. 20.

116. Ibid.

117. *Tribune*, 20 December 1963, p. 4.

118. *Portrait of Soper*, op. cit., p. 56.

119. The Rev. Eric Fenn, letter, 24 November 1993.

120. BBC, *The Time of My Life*, (1921–6), 5 January 1969, British Library, National Sound Archive, BBC P317R.

121. W.J. Strachan, letter, 25 April 1993.

122. Dr F.S. Marston, letter, 30 May 1993.

123. *Calling for Action*, op. cit., p. 128.

124. Donald Soper, undated and untitled three pages.

125. *Calling for Action*. op. cit., p. 131.

126. Ibid. pp. 125–6.

127. W.J. Strachan, op. cit.

128. Douglas Thompson, *Donald Soper: A Biography*, Denholm House Press, 1971, p. 18.

129. The Rev. Alan Ecclestone, letter, May 1992.

130. BBC, *The Time of My Life*, op. cit.

131. Ibid.

132. *Methodist Times*, 2 May 1935, p. 1.

133. Interview 2, 30 April 1992.

134. Interview, 25 June 1992.

135. *Hansard*, H.L., 12 November 1969, vol. 305.

136. *Hansard*, H.L., (15 June–8 July, 1965), vol. 267, col. 43.

137. Donald Soper, *Question Time on Tower Hill*, Hodder and Stoughton, 1935, pp. 47–8.

138. *Calling for Action*, op. cit., p. 77.

139. To George Hunter 3rd, in *Evangelistic Rhetoric in Secular Britain: The Theory and Speaking of Donald Soper and Bryan Green*, Evanston, Illinois, 1972, pp. 264–5 (unpublished thesis).

140. BBC, *The Time of My Life*, op. cit.

141. Dr Marjorie Sykes, interview, 24 June 1993.

142. BBC, *The Time of My Life*, op. cit.

143. *Portrait of Soper*, op. cit., pp. 57–8. See also BBC, *The Time of My Life*, op. cit.

144. *British Weekly*, 15 May 1952.
145. Vic Baker, letter, 16 August 1993.
146. *Donald Soper: A Biography*, op. cit., p. 16. See also *Methodist Recorder*, 13 April 1972.
147. *Hansard*, H.L., April 1984, vol. 450, col. 7414.
148. *Hansard*, H.L., 11 June 1969, vol. 302, col. 650. Motion in Lord Soper's name on 'Material objectives and social well-being'.
149. The Rt Rev. Robin Woods, letter, 23 July 1993.
150. The Rev. Jeffrey Harris, interview, 25 May 1993.
151. To George Hunter 3rd, op. cit., pp. 60–1.
152. Interview 1, 23 April 1992.
153. *Kingsway*, winter, 1959, p. 12.
154. The Rev. Dr H. Maldwyn Hughes, *The Kingdom of Heaven*, Epworth Press, 1922.
155. Ibid., *What Is the Atonement? (A Study in the Passion of God in Christ)*, James Clarke and Co., n.d.
156. H. Maldwyn Hughes, *Christian Foundations, An Introduction to Christian Doctrine*, Epworth Press, 1927.
157. The Rev. C. Hughes Smith, interview, February 1994.
158. *Donald Soper: A Biography*, op. cit., p. 19.
159. John Lenton, letter, 4 June 1993, based on interview with Lord Soper on Dr Harold Roberts in 1986.
160. *Portrait of Soper*, op. cit., p. 56.
161. Kay Fenn, letter via John Bartlett, 24 November 1993.
162. Lord Soper, interview, 18 June 1992.
163. Wesley House, Cambridge, Minute Book, vol. 1.
164. The Rev. Dr Maldwyn Edwards, chapter on 'The Incredible Soper', unpublished MS, sent to Lord Soper by Mrs E. Edwards.
165. The Rev. Dr Harold Roberts in *Portrait of Soper*, op. cit., p. 56.
166. Donald Soper to David Franklin, BBC, *Cambridge Revisited*, recorded 22 July 1968, BBC T 33217, British Library, National Sound Archive, T11047 WR.

Chapter 2   Parson and Parent

1. Arthur Kelsey, interview, 10 December 1993.
2. Lady Soper, BBC, *Woman's Hour*, 1981.
3. Lady Soper, 'Couples' interview with Sandra Harris, n.d.
4. Lady Soper, to Avril Bottoms, *Methodist Recorder*, 3 September 1992, p. 13.
5. Lady Soper, interview, 20 April 1993.
6. Ibid. 13 July 1993.

7. Donald Soper, interview with Ian Wylie, *Manchester Evening News*, 31 December 1981.

8. Donald Soper, *The Advocacy of the Gospel*, Hodder and Stoughton, 1961, p. 15.

9. Mr C. Bryant, interview, 13 December 1993. I am extremely grateful to this local Walworth resident for reminiscences of his childhood and early manhood in South London.

10. Quoted in John D. Beasley, *The Bitter Cry Heard and Heeded: The Story of the South London Mission, 1889–1989*, SLM, 1990, p. 43.

11. Donald Soper, *Children's Prayer Time*, Epworth Press, 1954, p. 10.

12. *Tribune*, 2 February, 1968.

13. Lord Soper, *Hansard*, House of Lords, 2 February 1987, vol. 484, col. 42.

14. Ibid., 4 December 1968, vol. 298, col. 219.

15. William Purcell, *Portrait of Soper*, Mowbrays, 1972, p. 59.

16. *Methodist Recorder*, 4 May 1933, p. 13.

17. *The Bitter Cry Heard and Heeded*, op. cit.

18. *South London Press*, 3 May 1927, p. 1.

19. Arthur Kelsey, op. cit.

20. Ibid.

21. Ibid.

22. Arthur Kelsey, reflections on Donald Oliver Soper, Minister of Oakley Place, July 1993.

23. Arthur Kelsey, op. cit.

24. Hilda Gent, letter, 2 August 1993.

25. Kay Fenn, letter via John Bartlett, 24 November 1993.

26. Interview, 9 June 1992.

27. Ibid.

28. *Portrait of Soper*, op. cit., p. 63.

29. The Rev. Dr S.B. Frost, letter, 12 April 1993.

30. Arthur Kelsey, interview, July 1993.

31. Donald Soper, *Aflame with Faith*, Epworth Press, 1963, p. 60.

32. Foreword to *The Bitter Cry Heard and Heeded*, op. cit.

33. Ibid., p. 8.

34. Kay Fenn, op. cit.

35. The thesis (unpublished) may be studied at The British Library of Political and Economic Science, The London School of Economics and Political Science, Houghton Street, London, W.C.2.

36. *Hansard*, H. L., 14 November 1974, vol. 354, col. 903.

37. Interview, 4 June 1992.

38. *Aflame with Faith*, op. cit., p. 130.

39. *Methodist Times*, 28 February 1929, p. 1.

40. Donald Soper, *Tower Hill, 12.30*, Epworth Press, 1963, pp. 2–3.

41. The Rev. Reg Frost, letter, 13 January 1994.

42. *Tower Hill, 12.30*, op. cit.

43. Richard Mudie-Smith, *The Religious Life of London*, Hodder and Stoughton, 1904, p. 11.
44. Interview, 25 June 1992.
45. Donald Soper, 'The Man Who Talks on Tower Hill', *Methodist Recorder*, 12 March 1931, p. 7.
46. Reminiscence of Mrs Dorothy Rouse, her daughter, letter 24 March 1993.
47. Donald Soper, *Calling for Action*, Robson Books, 1984, pp. 89–90.
48. Donald Soper, 80th birthday interview with Ronald Eyre, BBC, 1 February 1983.
49. *Calling for Action*, op. cit.
50. The Rev. W.H. Armstrong, *Methodist Recorder*, 27 October 1927, p. 4.
51. George Hunter 3rd, *Evangelistic Rhetoric in Secular Britain: The Theory and Speaking of Donald Soper and Bryan Green*, Evanston, Illinois, August 1972 (unpublished thesis), p. 313.
52. Ibid., p. 314.
53. Theo Stuchbery, letter, 30 March 1993.
54. George Dubock, interview, 11 December 1993.
55. *Calling for Action*, op. cit., p. 87.
56. Hilda Gent, letter, 3 July 1993.
57. *Calling for Action*, op. cit.
58. Len Webb, interview, 9 February 1994.
59. *Methodist Times*, 16 January 1930, p. 14.
60. *News Chronicle*, 17 December 1931.
61. Constance Willis, interview, 11 January 1994.
62. Lady Soper, interview, 20 November 1993.
63. Donald Soper, *Christ and Tower Hill*, 1934; *Question Time on Tower Hill*, 1935; *Answer Time on Tower Hill*, 1936, all published by Hodder and Stoughton.
64. *Answer Time on Tower Hill*, op. cit., pp. 16–17.
65. Alfred Sleep, interview, 13 July 1993.
66. *Islington Gazette*, 30 September 1930.
67. Margaret Fisher, letter, 18 April 1993.
68. *Answer Time on Tower Hill*, op. cit., p. 45.
69. *Methodist Times*, 15 October 1931, p. 1.
70. Interview 8, 17 July 1992.
71. Interview 7, 9 July 1992.
72. Len Webb, op. cit.
73. Laurence Payne, letter, 19 April 1993.
74. *Methodist Times*, 15 October 1931, p. 1.
75. *The Times*, 17 February 1937, p. 11.
76. The *Observer*, quoted in *Islington Gazette*, 9 December 1931, p. 1.
77. Donald Soper, *It Is Hard to Work for God*, Epworth Press, 1957, pp. 44–5.
78. *Kingsway*, winter, 1957, p. 4.
79. *The Advocacy of the Gospel*, op. cit., p. 102.

80. Leslie Irons, letter and enclosures, 23 April 1993.
81. Alfred Sleep, interview, 13 July 1993.
82. Mrs R. Drake, letter, 23 March 1993.
83. Interview 8, 17 July 1992.
84. Interview 7, 9 July 1992.
85. Len Webb, op. cit.
86. Alfred Sleep, op. cit.
87. Ibid.
88. *Islington Gazette*, 1 July 1936, p. 1.
89. *Methodist Times*, 15 October 1931, p. 1.
90. Ibid., 19 November 1931, p. 24.
91. Len Webb, op. cit.
92. *Methodist Times*, 7 November 1935, p. 22.
93. Ibid., 15 November 1934, p. 24.
94. *Kingsway Messenger*, October/November 1954, p. 13.
95. *Band of Hope Monthly Chronicle*, vol. LV, no. 635, 1932, p. 169.
96. Constance Willis, op. cit.
97. *Methodist Recorder*, 13 December 1962.
98. *Islington Gazette*, 10 February 1933, p. 1.
99. Ibid., 17 February 1936, p. 1.
100. Ibid., 13 May 1936, p. 7.
101. BBC, *Voices and Visions*, 7 August 1977.
102. Donald Soper, interview, 25 June 1992.
103. Ibid.
104. R. Ellis Roberts, *H.R.L. Sheppard: Life and Letters*, John Murray, 1948, p. 220.
105. Sheila Fletcher, *Maude Royden: A Life*, Basil Blackwell, 1989, p. 260.
106. Jill Wallis, *Mother of World Peace: The Life of Muriel Lester*, Hisarlik Press, 1993, p. 115.
107. Ibid.
108. For Gandhi's visit see Muriel Lester, *Entertaining Gandhi*, Ivor Nicholson and Watson, 1932, p. 82.
109. Interview 4, 21 May 1992.
110. *Reconciliation*, vol. 10, no. 3, p.60.
111. Ibid., December 1933 vol. 2, no. 2, p. 234.
112. Ibid.
113. Ibid., December 1935, vol. 13, no. 12, p. 324.
114. Ibid., March 1936, vol. 14, no. 3, p. 78.
115. Ibid., vol. 14, no. 5, pp. 117–9. Article 'The Strength of Pacifism'.
116. Ibid.
117. *Islington Gazette*, 1 October 1935, p. 1.
118. Alfred Sleep, op. cit.
119. *Methodist Recorder*, 28 November 1929, p. 4.
120. Douglas Thompson, *Donald Soper: A Biography*, Denholm House Press,

1971, pp. 49–50. See also *Methodist Recorder*, 4 May 1933, 'Methodist Young People and World-wide Mission'.

121. *The Times*, 28 November 1935, p. 8.
122. *Methodist Times*, 2 May 1935, p. 2.
123. *Hansard*, H.L., 12 December 1974, vol. 355, col. 383.
124. Ibid.
125. *Hansard*, H.L., vol. 336, 1972, col. 889.
126. *Methodist Recorder*, 17 September 1936, p. 15.
127. *Kingsway*, October 1956, p. 15.
128. Donald Soper, *Will Christianity Work?* Three broadcast talks, Lutterworth Paper no. 24, n.d.
129. *Answer Time on Tower Hill*, op. cit., p. 74.
130. Interview, 9 July 1992.
131. Alfred Sleep, interview, 13 July 1993.
132. The Rev. C. Hughes Smith, to author, 27 January 1994.
133. 'Couples', interview with Sandra Harris, n.d.
134. Ibid.
135. George Dubock, to author, 12 November 1993.
136. Lord Callaghan of Cardiff, interview, 8 December 1993.
137. Ibid.
138. *Tower Hill 12.30*, op. cit., pp. 33–4.
139. Ibid., pp. 41–2.
140. *Christ and Tower Hill*, op. cit., pp. 95–6.
141. Ibid., pp. 95–6.
142. *Question Time on Tower Hill*, op. cit., p. 40.
143. *Practical Christianity Today*, Ken-Pax Publishing, 1947, p. 99.
144. *Portrait of Soper*, op. cit., p. 39.
145. Interview, 4 June 1992.
146. An ordination charge, *Preacher's Quarterly*, March 1957, p. 71. See also *Aflame with Faith*, op. cit., p. 137.

Chapter 3   Peace-maker and Pacifist

1. Vera Brittain, *Testament of Experience*, Fontana paperback in association with Virago, 1980, pp. 164–6.
2. *Dorset and Daily Echo*, 22 June 1936.
3. *Reconciliation*, June 1936, vol. 14, no. 6, p. 164.
4. Ibid., p. 321. The original paragraph by William Temple in his York Diocesan leaflet in 1935 read as follows: 'Man is incapable of living by love unless the grace of God has both converted and sanctified him; so that the love of God is not applicable to nations consisting in large measure of unconverted or (as in the case of most, if not all, of us) very imperfectly

converted citizens'. Quoted in G.H.C. Macgregor, *The New Testament Basis of Pacifism*, Fellowship of Reconciliation, 1936, p. 70.

5. *Reconciliation*, June 1936, p. 164, under the overall heading 'Dr H. R. L. Sheppard's news'.

6. *Peace News*, 21 November 1936, p. 7. Hugh Price Hughes was against the continuance in public life because of his adultery of Parnell, the leader in Ireland of the party determined to bring Home Rule to his country, a policy Gladstone, as Prime Minister, was espousing. 'What is morally wrong can never be politically right,' Parnell asserted. See *The Life of Hugh Price Hughes*, by his daughter, Hodder and Stoughton, 1904, p. 353.

7. Ibid., 28 November 1936, p. 1.

8. PPU Sponsors Meeting, 22 May 1936, p. 16.

9. Ibid., 14 October 1936, p. 18.

10. See R. Ellis Roberts, *H.R.L. Sheppard: Life and Letters*, John Murray, 1942, p. 290.

11. *Peace News*, 6 November 1937.

12. PPU Sponsors Meeting, 15 September 1937, p. 89. There were *c.* 120,000 members by the autumn of 1937.

13. Ibid.

14. Ibid., 1 December 1937.

15. *The Friend*, 10 December 1937, p. 1169. See also *News Chronicle*, 6 December 1937.

16. *Peace News*, 19 November 1938, p. 10.

17. *Methodist Recorder*, 2 February 1939.

18. Kingsley Weatherhead, *Leslie Weatherhead: A Personal Portrait*, Hodder and Stoughton, 1975, pp. 114–15.

19. *Manchester Guardian*, 5 May 1939.

20. *The Friend*, 10 November 1939, p. 913.

21. *Daily Herald*, 1 November 1939.

22. Ibid.

23. Ibid.

24. *Birmingham Post*, 21 October 1939.

25. *Yorkshire Post*, 21 October 1939.

26. Donald Soper to Frank Unwin, 'The day war was declared', 12 November 1988.

27. Interview on LBC Radio, 26 December 1982.

28. Hensley Henson, *Retrospect of an Unimportant Life*, vol. 3, OUP, 1950, pp. 47–8.

29. William Purcell, *Portrait of Soper*, Mowbrays, 1973, p. 87.

30. Huw Rees, letter and note, 'Donald Soper and Christian Pacifism in World War Two and beyond', 12 June 1993.

31. Donald Swann, interview, autumn, 1993.

32. Stella St John, interview, autumn, 1992.

33. Henry Rutland, interview, autumn, 1992.

34. Reinhold Niebuhr, in *Christian Newsletter*, reported in *Peace News*, 16 February 1940, p. 5.

35. George Matthews, Communist Party Library, (Picture Library and Archive), letter, 15 February 1994.

36. House of Commons Debates, 5th Series, vol. 369, cols. 1148–50; vol. 370, cols. 383–5. See also Neil Stammer, *Civil Liberties in Britain During the Second World War*, Croom Helm, 1983.

37. Melville Dinwiddie, *Religion by Radio*, Allen and Unwin, 1968, p. 42. The internal BBC note at the end of August, 1940, read as follows: 'No one who is shown to belong to an organization the policy of which is inconsistent with the national effort or who has shown to have expressed views inconsistent with the national effort, may be invited to broadcast in any programme or contribute material for broadcasting.' See also Asa Briggs, *War of Words: The History of Broadcasting in the United Kingdom*, vol. 3, Oxford, 1970, p. 205.

38. Donald Soper, *Calling for Action*, Robson Books, 1984, p. 43.

39. Interview on LBC Radio, op. cit.

40. *Peace News*, 24 March 1950, p. 1. Report of an address to Newcastle upon Tyne FOR.

41. *Portrait of Soper*, op. cit., p. 87.

42. *Calling for Action*, op. cit., p. 43.

43. *Glossop Chronicle*, 24 October 1941.

44. *North Wilts Herald*, 6 February 1942.

45. *Methodist Recorder*, 18 June 1942.

46. Donald Soper, *Here Stand I – The Place of Compromise in the Christian Life*, (Alex Wood Memorial Lecture), Fellowship of Reconcilition, 1959, pp. 7–8.

47. *The Christian Pacifist*, December 1941, vol. 3, no 12, p. 198.

48. Ibid., 1944, no. 25, p. 266.

49. *Tribune*, 26 July 1957, p. 9. See also F. A. Iremonger, *William Temple*, OUP, 1948, p. 517.

50. Greater London Records Office, N/M/2/29/ 21 October 1940.

51. *Kingsway Newsheet*, p. 5.

52. *The Times*, 5 February 1943.

53. The Rev. Dr Gordon Wakefield, 2 March 1993.

54. The Rev. David Mason, *Portrait of Soper*, op. cit., pp. 27–9.

55. *The Christian Pacifist*, no. 45, September 1945, p. 673.

56. Ibid. no. 46, October 1945, p. 694.

57. Ibid. no. 49, January 1946, p. 672.

58. *Calling for Action*, op. cit., p. 38.

59. *The Christian Pacifist*, no. 50, February 1946, p. 787.

60. *Methodist Recorder*, 14 December 1944, p. 7.

61. Ibid.

62. *PPU Journal*, August 1947, pp. 8–9.

63. Jill Wallis, *Valiant for Peace*, FOR, 1991, p. 119. See also Fenner Brockway, *Bermondsey Story: The Life of Alfred Salter*, London, 1951.
64. *Kingsway Messenger*, February/March 1947, p. 20.
65. Ibid., June/July 1947.
66. *Peace News*, 11 February 1949, p. 4.
67. *Reconciliation*, April 1950, p. 832.
68. *The Times*, 18 July 1950, p. 3.
69. Robert Kee, letter, 9 June 1993.
70. *Peace News*, 28 July 1950, p. 1.
71. Ibid., 1 September 1950, p. 5.
72. Ibid., 11 August 1950.
73. *Reconciliation*, October 1951, pp. 84–5.
74. E. C. Urwin, *Henry Carter*, Epworth Press, 1955, p. 127.
75. *Hansard*, H. L., 3 December 1980, vol. 415, col. 437.
76. *Reconciliation*, December 1952, p. 236.
77. 8 September 1951, personal diary of trip to America and Australia.
78. Ibid., 10 September 1951.
79. *Peace News*, 19 March 1954, p. 1.
80. *Methodist Recorder*, 1 April 1954, p. 4.
81. Edwin Robertson, *George: A Biography of Viscount Tonypandy*, Marshall Pickering, 1992, p. 140.
82. J.A.D. Adams, *Tony Benn*, Macmillan, 1992, p. 99.
83. John L. Collins, *Faith Under Fire*, Leslie Frewin, 1966, pp. 284–5.
84. *Kingsway Messenger*, June/July 1954.
85. *Peace News*, 16 April 1954, p. 11.
86. *Daily Worker*, 9 April 1954, p. 1.
87. *Peace News*, 17 September 1954, p. 1.
88. Ibid., 22 October 1954.
89. *Daily Worker*, 7 June 1954, p. 1.
90. *Peace News*, 17 December 1954, p. 1.
91. Ibid.
92. Ibid.
93. Ibid., 7 January 1955, p. 1.
94. *Portrait of Soper*, op. cit., p. 140.
95. *The Friend*, 3 December 1957, p. 1252.
96. Interview 5, 18 June 1992.
97. Elnora Ferguson, interview, 6 January 1993.
98. F.W. Dillistone, *Charles Raven*, Hodder and Stoughton, 1975, pp. 372–5.
99. *Daily Worker*, 3 December 1954, p. 10.
100. *Peace News*, 10 December 1954, p. 1.
101. *Daily Worker*, 3 December 1954, pp. 1, 4.
102. Ibid.
103. *Kingsway Messenger*, April/May 1953, p. 11.
104. Ibid., December 1953/January 1954, p. 16.

105. *Tribune*, 9 December 1955, p. 12.
106. *Methodist Recorder*, 19 April 1956.
107. Ibid.
108. Ibid., 26 April 1956, p. 4.
109. *Kingsway Messenger*, June/July 1956, p. 2.
110. *Peace News*, 4 February 1955, p. 1.
111. *Daily Worker*, 7 December 1953. See also 11 January 1954, p. 1.
112. *Tribune*, 2 February 1958, based on interview in *The Times*.
113. *Tribune*, 17 February 1967, p. 11.
114. Ibid., 1 April 1955.
115. *Reconciliation*, September 1955, p. 178.
116. Ibid., July 1956, p. 130.
117. *Edinburgh Evening News*, 5 June 1956.
118. *Peace News*, 10 August 1956, p. 12.
119. *Peace News*, 17 August 1956, p. 1.
120. See Sybil Morrison, *I Renounce War: The Story of the Peace Pledge Union*, Sheppard Press, 1962, p. 82.
121. *Peace News*, 16 November 1956, p. 5.
122. Richard Clements, *Tribune*, 10 November 1972, p. 6.
123. *British Weekly*, 18 October, 25 October, 1 November, 8 November, 14 November 1956.
124. *Peace News*, 14 December 1956, p. 1.
125. FOR Council Minutes, May 1957, quoted in Jill Wallis, *Valliant for Peace*, FOR, 1991, p. 166.
126. *Faith Under Fire*, op. cit., pp. 303–12.
127. *Portrait of Soper*, op. cit., p. 143.
128. *Peace News Supplement*, Easter, 1958, p. 3.
129. *Peace News*, 18 April 1958, p. 7.
130. *Daily Telegraph*, 21 May 1958, pp. 1 and 9.
131. *The Times*, 23 September 1958. See also Christopher Driver, *The Disarmers*, Hodder and Stoughton, 1964.
132. See especially *Daily Sketch, Glasgow Herald, Daily Worker*, 31 August 1959.
133. *The Friend*, 2 October 1959, p. 1123.
134. Pat Arrowsmith, interview, 21 July 1993.
135. *The Disarmers*, op. cit., p. 110.
136. DAC Circular, 17 October 1960, DAC Archive, quoted in Richard Taylor, *Against the Bomb*, Clarendon Press, 1988, p. 150.
137. *Methodist Recorder*, 1 August 1957, pp 3–4.
138. *Scotsman*, 11 September 1959.
139. *Tribune*, 8 November 1957, p. 7.
140. MPF Conference Rally, Gateshead, 12 July 1958, in *Reconciliation*, September 1958, p. 178.
141. *Tribune*, 8 November 1957, p. 7.

142. *Peace News*, 22 April 1960.
143. *Reconciliation*, September 1958, p. 178.
144. *Peace News*, 14 October 1960, p. 3.
145. Bertrand Russell, *The Autobiography of Bertrand Russell*, vol. 3, Allen and Unwin, 1969, p. 112.
146. *Tribune*, 20 January 1961, p. 4.
147. Ibid.
148. Ibid.
149. *Peace News*, 24 February 1961, p. 1.
150. *Tribune*, 30 June 1961, p. 4.
151. Donald Soper interviewed by David Boulton, *Sanity*, November 1961.
152. *Reconciliation*, February 1963, p. 40.
153. Ibid., p. 26.
154. Ibid., August 1963, p. 159.
155. *Tribune*, 24 May 1963, p. 4.
156. Ibid., 26 July 1963, p. 4.
157. *Guardian*, 6 September 1961. The protest was organized by a joint committee of the Federation of Trades Councils and Miners' Union of South Wales.
158. *The Friend*, 27 October 1961.
159. *The Disarmers*, op. cit., p. 238.
160. *Liverpool Daily Post*, 13 November 1961. Also *Guardian, The Times, Glasgow Herald* and *Birmingham Post*.
161. *Peace News*, 3 April 1964, p. 12.
162. Ibid. 30 May 1964.
163. Ibid., 10 July 1964. Also *Reconciliation*, August 1964, p. 163.
164. Kenneth Boulding, *Peace News*, 6 November 1964, p. 1.
165. Pauline Callard, interview, 29 March 1993.
166. *Kingsway*, spring 1968, p. 35.
167. The Rev. John Heidbrink, letter, 11 January 1993.
168. *Guardian*, 12 January 1965.
169. *Tribune*, 12 February 1965, p. 11.
170. *Sunday Telegraph*, 3 July 1966.
171. *Sheffield Morning Telegraph*, 4 September 1966.
172. *Morning Star*, 11 November 1967.
173. *Birmingham Post*, 13 July 1971.
174. *Tribune*, 5 January 1973, p. 4.
175. Ibid., 19 November 1971, p. 3.
176. Ibid., 21 July 1972, p. 3.
177. *Methodist Recorder*, 14 December 1972, p. 12.
178. Ibid., 28 December 1972, p. 3.
179. *Reconciliation Quarterly*, June 1971, pp. 33–7.
180. Ibid.
181. *The Times*, 18 September 1970.

182. The Rev. Dr Colin Morris, *Methodist Recorder*, 20 June 1968, p. 11.
183. *Tribune*, 25 April 1975, p. 17.
184. *Methodist Recorder*, 5 July 1973, p. 16.
185. Ibid.
186. *Tribune*, 26 November 1976, p. 8.
187. Ibid., p. 9.
188. *Peace News*, 16 December 1977.
189. Donald Soper, interviewed by Robert Eddison, *Evening News*, 10 March 1978, p. 6.
190. Ibid.
191. *Tribune*, 27 January 1976, p. 11.
192. *Calling for Action*, op. cit., p. 63.
193. *The Disarmers*, p. 201.
194. William R. Cannon, Chair of the Executive Committee, World Methodist Council, Citation in Presentation of the Peace Award to Lord Donald Soper, *Methodist Recorder*, 2 October 1981.

Chapter 4   Politician and Peer

1. *Kingsway Messenger*, June 1940, p. 84.
2. Ibid.
3. *Daily Herald*, 15 October 1936.
4. *Methodist Times*, 19 March 1937.
5. *Bradford Daily Telegraph*, 28 March 1939.
6. *Ilford Record*, 9 October 1941.
7. *Heckmondwike Herald*, 7 October 1938.
8. *East Ham Echo*, 3 March 1939. Also *East London Observer*, 4 March 1939.
9. *East London Observer*, 11 March 1939.
10. See John C. Heenan, *Cardinal Hinsley*, Burns Oates Washbourne Ltd., 1944, pp. 180–1.
11. *Brighton Gazette*, 1 March 1941.
12. *Mid-Sussex Times*, 10 July 1941.
13. Ibid.
14. *Herts and Beds Express*, 30 May 1942.
15. See *Church Times*, 10 July 1942.
16. *Acton Gazette*, 25 May 1943.
17. *Western Morning News*, 23 March 1942.
18. *News Chronicle*, 9 June 1944.
19. Interview 14, 5 November 1992.
20. Ibid.
21. *Methodist Recorder*, 27 March 1947, p. 12.
22. Interview 14, 5 November 1992. See also *Tribune*, 19 September 1975.
23. *Methodist Recorder*, 12 October 1967, p. 1.

24. Interview 14, 5 November 1992.
25. *The Times*, 16 January 1948.
26. Secretary of the North Staffs Women's Advisory Council of the Labour Party, *Staffs Evening Standard*, 17 February 1946.
27. *Methodist Recorder*, 8 March 1948, p. 5.
28. *Nottingham Guardian*, 25 March 1949.
29. Ibid.
30. *Methodist Recorder*, 21 July 1949. At Linacre Mission on 'The Christian and City Life'.
31. *Canberra Daily Express*, 19 September 1951.
32. *Evening Standard*, 9 October 1952.
33. *Birmingham Despatch*, 13 July 1953.
34. *Christian World*, 1 October 1953.
35. *Methodist Recorder*, 1 October 1953, p. 3.
36. *Oldham Chronicle*, 1 August 1953.
37. *Evening News*, 20 August 1953.
38. *Methodist Recorder*, 12 November 1953, p. 3.
39. *Daily Herald*, 17 November 1953, p. 6.
40. *Methodist Recorder*, 11 March 1954, p. 7.
41. See *Tribune: The First Forty Years of a Socialist Newspaper* (ed.) Douglas Hill, Quartet Books, 1977, p. 3.
42. Michael Foot to Donald Soper, 18 January 1954. In Presidential Papers for 1953/4, Methodist Archive, John Rylands Library, University of Manchester.
43. *Tribune*, 26 February 1954, p. 4.
44. Ibid.
45. Ibid.
46. Ibid.
47. Richard Clements, interview, 2 September 1993.
48. *Tribune*, 4 March 1955, p. 5.
49. Ibid., 18 March 1955, p. 5.
50. Ibid., 25 March 1955, p. 5.
51. Ibid., 29 April 1955, p. 5.
52. Ibid.
53. Ibid., 25 May 1955.
54. Ibid.
55. Ibid.
56. Ibid., 3 June 1955, p. 2.
57. Lord Hailsham, *Spectator*, 8 July 1956, pp. 35–6.
58. Lord Hailsham, *Tribune*, 5 August 1955, p. 3.
59. Ibid.
60. *Tribune*, 22 July 1955, p. 7. and pp. 4–5.
61. Ibid.
62. Ibid.

63. Ibid., 25 September 1959, p. 4.
64. Ibid., 13 January 1961, p. 4.
65. Ibid., 4 March 1966, p. 12.
66. Ibid., 31 January 1958, p. 2.
67. Labour Peace Fellowship bulletin, December 1955, p. 1.
68. 'Make Labour the Peace Party', Statement on Labour's Future Foreign Policy, 1963.
69. *Tribune*, 10 February 1956, p. 12.
70. Ibid., 9 September 1958, 23 September 1960, 22 September 1961.
71. Ibid., 4 March 1960.
72. Ibid., 21 February 1958; 20 July 1958.
73. Ibid., 5 December 1958.
74. Ibid., 2 July 1959, p. 6.
75. Ibid.
76. Ibid., 18 September 1959, p. 4.
77. *Reading Standard*, 18 September 1959.
78. *Kensington News*, 7 October 1959.
79. *Methodist Recorder*, 15 October 1959.
80. *Bromley Times*, 9 October 1959.
81. British Film Institute, National Film and Television Archive, 'Britain Belongs to Labour' – No. 3 Labour Party Election Broadcast, 28 September 1959.
82. *Daily Sketch*, The John Knight Column, 29 September 1959.
83. Barbara Castle, *Methodist Recorder*, 29 October 1959.
84. *Tribune*, 4 December 1959, p. 9.
85. Ibid., 11 December 1959, p. 4.
86. *Methodist Recorder*, 28 January 1960.
87. Interview, 4 June 1992.
88. Interview with the Rev. Len Barnett, Central Methodist Church, Bromley, 1983.
89. Ibid.
90. *Evening Standard*, 2 December 1959.
91. Interview 14, 5 November 1992.
92. Jennie Lee, *My Life with Nye*, Jonathan Cape, 1980, pp. 254–5.
93. *Daily Express*, 16 July 1960.
94. *Darlington Northern Echo*, 16 July 1960.
95. Ibid.
96. *Liverpool Post*, 16 July 1960.
97. Michael Foot, interview, 5 August 1993.
98. *Papers from the Lamb*, Malvern Press Ltd., 1959.
99. Francis Wheen, *Tom Driberg: His Life and Indiscretions*, Chatto and Windus, 1990, pp. 319–20.
100. Maldwyn Hughes, *S.E. Keeble: Pioneer and Prophet*, Epworth Press, 1949, p. 68.

101. See R.H. Tawney, 'A Note on Christianity and the social order', 1937, in *The Attack and Other Papers*, London, 1953, p. 167 note.
102. David Ormrod, 'Christian Socialist Organizations' in *Facing the Future as Christians and Socialists*, Christian Socialist Movement, 1985, p. 29.
103. *New Statesman and Nation*, 20 April 1960.
104. 'Our Public Image', *CSM Bulletin*, no. 1, September–October 1962, p. 2.
105. Ibid.
106. David Hallam, letter, 2 February 1994.
107. Ibid.
108. *Methodist Recorder*, 20 June 1968, p. 2.
109. *Tribune*, 19 February 1960, p. 4.
110. *Tribune*, 7 June 1960, p. 4.
111. Ibid.
112. *Sunday Telegraph*, 5 November 1961.
113. *Tribune*, 7 October 1960, p. 4.
114. Ibid.
115. Ibid., 4 November 1960, p. 4.
116. Ibid., 25 January 1963, p. 4.
117. Ibid.
118. *New Daily*, 4 February, 1963.
119. *Tribune*, 30 October 1964.
120. Lord Archer of Sandwell, interview, 7 June 1993.
121. *Portrait of Soper*, op. cit., p. 107.
122. Interview, 20 June 1993.
123. *Tribune*, 18 August 1967, p. 9.
124. Donald Soper to Illtyd Harrington, 9 December 1986.
125. *Evening News* and the *Star*, 22 April 1958.
126. Lady Serota, *Portrait of Soper*, op. cit., p. 119.
127. *Tribune*, 30 January 1959, p. 5.
128. Ibid.
129. Lady Serota, *Portrait of Soper*, op. cit., p. 120.
130. *Jewish Chronicle*, 29 January 1959, p. 5.
131. Louis Bondy, interview, 7 May 1992.
132. See Greater London Records Office, LCC/Min/657 Agenda Papers, Health Committee, 1958–1960.
133. Lady Serota, interview, 15 June 1960.
134. Betty Vernon, letter, 1 April 1993.
135. Ellis Hillman, interview, 21 December 1992.
136. Mrs Gladys Dimson, interview, 17 August 1993.
137. *Methodist Recorder*, 11 July 1963.
138. *Evening Standard*, 12 March 1962.
139. *Tribune*, 2 July 1965.
140. Ibid.
141. *Sunday Telegraph*, 24 April 1966.

142. The prayer read:

> O God, grant us a vision of our land, fair as it might be:
> A land of righteousness where none shall wrong his neighbour;
> A land of plenty where evil and poverty shall be done away;
> A land of brotherhood where all success shall be founded
> on service, and honour shall be given on excellence alone;
> A land of peace, where order shall not rest on force,
> but on the love of all for the common life and weal;
> Bless our efforts to make the vision a living reality;
> Inspire and strengthen each one of us that we may give
> time, thought, and sacrifice to speed the day of its coming.
>
> > (*Methodist Recorder*, 13 October 1966).

The prayer, with a slight modification, came from Walter Rauschenbusch, *Prayers for the Social Awakening*, published in America in 1918.

143. The Rt Hon. Harold Wilson, *Portrait of Soper*, op. cit. p. 110.
144. Interview, 28 October 1993.
145. *Methodist Recorder*, 20 April 1967, p. 15.
146. Ibid., 1 April 1971.
147. Willi Frischauer, *David Frost*, Michael Joseph, 1972, p. 82.
148. 'Why I Am Labour', Labour Party, 1970.
149. Radio 1 and 2, Party Political Broadcast on behalf of the Labour Party, 21 December 1971.
150. *Daily Telegraph*, 26 February 1974.
151. *Morning Star*, 5 February 1974.
152. *Bishop Auckland Chronicle*, 31 July 1952.
153. Mr. I. Lavery, National Union of Mineworkers (Northumberland Area), letter, 25 April 1994.
154. *Hansard*, H.L., 20 November 1968, vol. 2, col. 97.
155. Ibid., vol. 267, col. 340.
156. Ibid., col. 41.
157. Ibid., col. 43.
158. Rt. Hon Earl Ferrers to Lord Soper, 31 January 1992.
159. Lady Llewellyn Davies, interview, 14 June 1993.
160. Ibid.
161. Baroness Stocks, Douglas Thompson, *Donald Soper: A Biography*, Denholm House Press, 1971, p. 205.
162. Ibid.
163. Rt Rev. David Say, letter, 12 July 1993.
164. Ibid.
165. Richard Crossman, *The Diary of a Cabinet Minister*, vol. 2, Hamish Hamilton and Jonathan Cape, 1976, p. 527.
166. Lord Carrington, *Hansard*, H.L., 21 April 1966, vol. 274, col. 14.
167. Lord Carrington, interview, 23 June 1993.

168. Ibid.
169. Peter McNeal, letter, 5 February 1994.
170. Viscount Tonypandy, interview, 28 April 1994.
171. Lord Bruce of Donnington, interview, 18 October 1993.
172. Ibid.
173. *Hansard*, H.L., 11 June 1969, vol. 302 col. 645.
174. Ibid., col. 647–8.
175. Ibid., col. 750–3.
176. Ibid.
177. Ibid., col. 760.
178. Ibid.
179. Ibid., 21 November 1966, vol. 268.
180. Ibid., 10 May 1967, vol. 252, col. 1527–8.
181. Ibid., 21 June 1972, vol. 332, col. 297.
182. Ibid., 2 February 1972, vol. 327, col. 828.
183. Ibid., 18 October 1973, vol. 345, col. 475.
184. Tony Benn, *Conflicts of Interest*, 1977–80, (ed.) Ruth Winstone, Hutchinson, 1990, p. 14.
185. *Tribune*, 4 April 1980.
186. Derek Willmott, letter, 20 March 1993.
187. Ibid.
188. M.G. Maitland, *Tribune*, 5 May 1967, p. 9.
189. Bishop Colin Winter, *Labour Weekly*, 21 October 1977, p. 13.
190. Ibid.
191. Donald Soper, *Christian Politics*, Epworth Press, 1977, p. 48.
192. Ibid., p. 74.
193. Ibid., p. 33.
194. Ibid., p. 112.

Chapter 5   Polemicist and Pedagogue

1. Joan M. Frayn, letter, 18 October 1993.
2. *British Weekly*, 17 September 1936.
3. *Methodist Times and Leader*, 17 February 1936, p. 6.
4. Ibid.
5. *Methodist Recorder*, 17 September 1936.
6. Ibid.
7. Ibid.
8. *Kingsway Messenger*, 1948, pp. 10–11.
9. Ibid.
10. Greater London Records Office, N/M/81/39.
11. See John McCabe, *Charlie Chaplin*, Robson Books, 1973, p. 16.
12. See Donald Soper, *Christianity and Its Critics*, Hodder and Stoughton,

1937. Also Donald Soper, *Popular Fallacies about the Christian Faith*, Hodder and Stoughton, 1938.

13. Norman Nicholson, *Wednesday Early Closing*, Faber and Faber, 1975, p. 82.
14. WLM Minute Book, Quarterly Meetings, Greater London Records Office, N/M/2/2.
15. Ibid., N/M/81/39.
16. It was the custom of Kingsway Hall to list every hymn sung in the services and the figures have been worked out by consulting the records of the services from 1938 to 1968 in the Archives in the Greater London Records Office and at Hinde Street Methodist Church, London (1948–1968).
17. Donald Soper, *Keeping Festival*, Epworth Press, 1954, p. 25.
18. The Rev. Len Barnett, in Douglas Thompson, *Donald Soper: A Biography*, Denholm House Press, 1971, p. 87.
19. Ibid.
20. *Methodist Times*, 5 November 1936.
21. The Rev. George W. Sails, *At the Centre: The Story of Methodism's Central Missions*, Home Mission Division, 1970, p. 15.
22. See report in *Eastern Daily Press*, 12 July 1945.
23. Ibid.
24. Kenneth Leech, *True God*, Sheldon Press, 1985, p. 1.
25. *Kingsway*, spring 1961, p. 10.
26. *Methodist Times*, 18 March 1937.
27. *Kingsway Messenger*, May/June 1949, p. 16.
28. *Guide and Ideas*, 6 March 1937.
29. Donald Soper, *Aflame with Faith*, Epworth Press, 1963, p. 157.
30. Donald Soper to Stanley Sowton, *Methodist Recorder*, 15 April 1937.
31. *Methodist Recorder*, 28 November 1937, p. 5.
32. Ibid., 11 February 1937.
33. *Methodist Times and Leader*, 11 March 1937.
34. *Methodist Recorder*, 12 May 1937.
35. *The Star*, Johannesburg, 6 August 1937.
36. William Purcell, *Portrait of Soper*, Mowbrays, 1972.
37. *Kingsway Messenger*, vol. 1, no. 8, July 1940, p. 11.
38. Ibid., Feb/March 1956, p. 13.
39. *Methodist Recorder*, 14 October 1937, p. 4.
40. *Methodist Times and Leader*, 14 October 1937.
41. *British Weekly*, 14 October 1937, p. 39.
42. *Methodist Times and Leader*, op. cit.
43. *Methodist Recorder*, 21 July 1938.
44. Betty Tredinnick, letter, 3 November 1993.
45. *Methodist Recorder*, 22 December 1938, p. 10.
46. BBC, *Five to Ten*, 5 January 1969.
47. Greater London Records Office, N/M/2/21.

48. *Kingsway Messenger*, vol. 1, no. 1, January 1940, p. 100
49. Ibid., vol. 1, no. 3, March 1940, pp. 46–7.
50. Ibid., March/April 1949, p. 15.
51. *Evening Standard*, 14 May 1940.
52. *Kingsway Chronicle*, April 1942, p. 3.
53. *Kingsway Messenger*, vol. 1, no. 1, op. cit., p. 71.
54. Ibid., vol. 1, no. 8, August 1940, p. 1.
55. *Methodist Recorder*, 15 May 1941, p. 7.
56. Ibid., 12 March 1942.
57. Greater London Records Office, N/M/2/13, 29 April 1942.
58. The Rev. Kenneth Brown, Notes on Donald Soper, 11 June 1993.
59. *Methodist Recorder*, 8 April 1943.
60. Sidney Kiddell, letter, 28 June 1993.
61. *Christian World*, 15 April 1943.
62. Donald Soper quoted in *Wrexham Leader*, 10 September 1943.
63. *Methodist Recorder*, 1 December 1946.
64. Ibid., 25 November 1943, p. 5.
65. *Evening News*, 23 September 1944.
66. *Methodist Recorder*, 28 September 1944, p. 3.
67. Ibid., 21 July 1946.
68. Donald Soper, *Children's Prayer Time*, Epworth Press, 1954, p. 70.
69. *Kingsway Chronicle*, April 1946.
70. *Kingsway Messenger*, April/May 1947; also Jan/Feb 1948.
71. The Rev. Dennis Lansdown, interview, 19 March 1993.
72. *Kingsway Messenger*, Jan/February 1948, p. 16.
73. Ibid.
74. Donald Soper, *Question Time in Ceylon*, (ed.) The Rev D. Lansdown, India, 1947, p. 83.
75. Ibid.
76. *Methodist Recorder*, 6 November 1947, p. 7.
77. *Question Time in Ceylon*, op. cit., pp. 15–16.
78. *Methodist Recorder*, 24 December 1947.
79. Jonathon Thamber, Secretary, Division of Social Responsibility, Methodist Church, Sri Lanka, via the Rev. Norman Taggart, 12 March 1993.
80. Donald Soper, *Calling for Action*, Robson Books, 1984, p. 146.
81. The Rev. Dennis Lansdown, op. cit.
82. *Question Time in Ceylon*, op. cit., p. 2.
83. Ibid., p. 13.
84. Ibid., p. 1.
85. *British Weekly*, 3 January 1958.
86. *Question Time in Ceylon*, op. cit., p. 6.
87. Ibid., pp. 15–16. See also William Temple, *Readings in St John's Gospel*, Macmillan and Co., 1945, p. 226.
88. Hyde Park, 20 September 1987.

89. Ibid.
90. Ibid.
91. Ibid., 11 July 1976.
92. Ibid. 27 July 1980.
93. *Question Time in Ceylon*, op. cit., p. 3.
94. *The Christian World*, 18 November 1937.
95. *British Weekly*, 23 January 1958.
96. *Question Time in Ceylon*, op. cit., p. 1.
97. Australian Travel Diary (unpublished), 1947.
98. *Methodist Recorder*, 24 December 1947.
99. Australian Travel Diary, op. cit.
100. Ibid.
101. Ibid.
102. Ibid.
103. Ibid.
104. Ibid.
105. *Methodist Recorder*, 20 December 1956.
106. Greater London Records Office, N/M/43/78/2.
107. Kingsway Hall service sheet, 20 January 1940, Hinde Street Methodist Church Archives.
108. Ibid., 4 May 1950.
109. Ibid., July 1958.
110. Ibid., 10 March 1956.
111. *Star*, 19 September 1950.
112. Ivy Dobson, letter, 24 November 1993.
113. *The Friend*, 17 December 1948.
114. *Daily Mail*, 22 December 1953.
115. *Kingsway Messenger*, February/March 1953, p. 7.
116. Ibid., March/April 1953, pp. 12–13.
117. Ibid.
118. Ibid.
119. *Methodist Recorder*, 12 April 1956.
120. Ibid., 21 February, 1952, p. 3.
121. *Calling for Action*, op. cit., p. 107.
122. Olive Delves, interview, 8 March 1994.
123. WLM Staff Meeting Minutes, in Philip S. Bagwell, *Outcast London*, Epworth Press, 1987, p. 127.
124. *Evening Standard*, 24 April 1937, p. 56.
125. *Methodist Times and Leader*, 6 May 1937.
126. Ibid.
127. *Church Times*, 26 September 1941.
128. Heckler to author, Hyde Park, 31 November 1993.
129. *Baptist Times*, 18 March 1937.

130. George G. Hunter 3rd, *How to Reach Secular People*, Abingdon Press, Nashville, 1992, pp. 129–30.
131. George G. Hunter 3rd, *Evangelical Rhetoric in Secular Britain: The Theory and Speaking of Donald Soper and Bryan Green*, (unpublished thesis), Evanston, Illinois, 1972, p. 319.
132. Ibid., p. 321.
133. Ibid., p. 323.
134. Ibid., p. 389.
135. Ibid., p. 391.
136. Ibid., p. 401.
137. Hyde Park, 5 November 1978.
138. The Rev. Professor Gordon Rupp, *Methodist Recorder*, 21 January 1965.
139. *Calling for Action*, op. cit., p. 159.
140. Dr Tony Bradshaw, letter, 29 June 1993.
141. The Rev. Kenneth Brown, op. cit.
142. *Methodist Recorder*, 2 November 1969, p. 1.
143. Ibid.
144. Ibid., 24 February 1977, p. 24.
145. Ibid.
146. Ibid.
147. Hyde Park, 7 October 1979.
148. Ibid.
149. Ibid., 14 October 1979.
150. Ibid., 28 September 1980.

Chapter 6 Pastor, Preacher and President

1. The Rev. Dr Leslie Weatherhead, *Methodist Recorder*, 13 February 1969, p. 11.
2. Ibid., 13 July 1950, p. 9.
3. The Rev. Brian Duckworth, interview, 19 February 1993.
4. BBC, *Voices and Visions*, 8 August 1977.
5. Leslie Weatherhead, *The Transforming Friendship*, Epworth Press, 1928.
6. *Methodist Recorder*, 5 January 1976, p. 6.
7. *The Poetical Works of John and Charles Wesley*, vol. 1, London Wesleyan Methodist Conference Office, 1868, p xxiii.
8. 'The Future of Preaching', *Preacher's Quarterly*, March 1965, pp. 13–14.
9. Ibid., p. 16.
10. The Rev. B. Crosby, letter, 25 March 1993.
11. *Kingsway Messenger*, vol. 3, no. 14, August/September 1955, p. 2.
12. 'The Future of Preaching', ibid., p. 17.
13. Donald Soper, *It's Hard to Work for God*, Epworth Press, 1957, p. 23.

14. The lectures were later published as *The Advocacy of the Gospel*, Hodder and Stoughton, 1961.
15. Interview 10, 1 October 1992.
16. Ibid.
17. Ibid.
18. Interview, 25 June 1992.
19. Rachel Newton, interview, autumn, 1993.
20. The Rev. Kathleen Richardson, recounted at Lord Soper's 90th birthday celebrations at Hinde Street Methodist Church, 31 January 1993.
21. *Kingsway Messenger*, vol. 1, no. 4, April 1940, p. 55.
22. Sermon on prayer, *Kingsway*, summer 1968, p. 28.
23. *The Advocacy of the Gospel*, op. cit., p 68.
24. Donald Soper, *Popular Fallacies about the Christian Faith*, Hodder and Stoughton, 1937, p. 37.
25. Donald Soper, *Aflame with Faith*, Epworth Press, 1963, p. 139.
26. Based on notes made by Pauline Callard at Donald Soper's lectures, 27 September–20 December 1944.
27. Ibid.
28. Quoted in George Streeter, *The Sermon on the Mount, An Exegetical Commentary*, T. and T. Clark, 1988, p. 17.
29. Ibid., p. 180.
30. Donald Soper, *Tower Hill, 12.30.*, Epworth Press, 1963, p. 155.
31. 'The First Word from the Cross', 13 April 1979.
32. Ibid.
33. Ibid.
34. Ibid.
35. *Popular Fallacies about the Christian Faith*, op. cit., p. 85.
36. *Methodist Recorder*, 16 June 1966, p. 2.
37. Ibid.
38. *Kingsway Messenger*, February/March 1947, p. 2.
39. *Kingsway*, summer, 1969, p. 10.
40. The Rev. D. Cleverley Ford, *Church of England Newspaper*, 21 February 1964, reviewing Donald Soper's book, *Aflame with Faith*, op. cit.
41. Ibid.
42. The Rev. Stewart Denyer, *Methodist Sacramental Fellowship (MSF) Bulletin*, 102, 1978, p. 15.
43. *MSF Bulletin*, 91, 1974, p. 8.
44. Ibid.
45. The Rev. Dr J. E. Rattenbury, *MSF Bulletin*, 59, 1960, p. 4.
46. Ibid., 73, 1968, p. 7.
47. Ibid., 23, 1949, p. 13.
48. Ibid., 24, 1949, p. 13.
49. Ibid., p. 3.
50. Ibid., p. 4.

51. Ibid., 27, 1950, p. 3.
52. Ibid., 29, 1951, pp. 3–4.
53. Ibid., 33, 1952, p. 8.
54. Ibid., 36, 1953, pp. 9–10.
55. Ibid., 39, 1953, p. 1.
56. Ibid., 40, 1954, p. 1.
57. Ibid., 43, 1955, p. 11.
58. Donald Soper, *All His Grace*, Epworth Press, 1957, p. 92.
59. Ibid., p. 99.
60. *MSF Bulletin*, 81, 1970, p. 2.
61. *Methodist Recorder*, 8 January 1953, p. 3.
62. Ibid., 16 July 1953, p. 4.
63. Presidential Address, 16 July 1953, p. 1., pp. 3–4.
64. Ibid.
65. Ibid.
66. Ibid.
67. Address to Ministerial Session, *Methodist Recorder*, 23 July 1953, p. 8.
68. *Methodist Recorder*, 25 June 1953, p. 1.
69. Ibid.
70. Ibid.
71. *Methodist Recorder*, 13 August 1953, p. 13.
72. Ibid., 3 September 1953, p. 3.
73. Ibid., 10 September 1953, p. 5.
74. *West Herts Post*, 17 September 1953.
75. May Hewat, *Evening Standard*, 9 December 1953.
76. Ibid.
77. Ibid.
78. *Methodist Recorder*, 31 December 1953, p. 3.
79. Ibid., 'A Year in the Life', 28 January 1993, p. 5.
80. The Rev. F. G. Gill, ibid., p. 5.
81. *Methodist Recorder*, 4 March 1954, p. 13.
82. Ibid., 18 March 1954, p. 10.
83. Ibid., 1 April 1954, p. 6.
84. *British Weekly*, 22 April 1954, p. 11.
85. The Rev. Dr J.E. Rattenbury, *Methodist Recorder*, 18 March 1954, p. 5.
86. Ibid.
87. Ibid., 16 July 1953, p. 11.
88. Donald Soper to Shaun Joynson, for 'Strange Really', 31 May 1992.
89. Ibid.
90. The Rev. David Mason, *Portrait of Soper*, op. cit., p. 30.
91. *It's Hard to Work for God*, op. cit., p. 17.
92. *Aflame with Faith*, op. cit., p. 17.
93. Dr Pauline Webb, interview, 16 November 1992.

94. Douglas Thompson, *Donald Soper: A Biography*, Denholm House Press, 1971, p. 205.
95. Ibid.
96. Interview 11, 8 October 1992.
97. Ibid.
98. Ibid.
99. Ibid.
100. Ibid.
101. Ibid.
102. *Jewish Chronicle*, 5 October 1968.
103. *Kingsway*, autumn 1968.
104. Nauman Neame, *What Men Believe*, Take Home Books, 1957, p. 5.
105. The Rev. Jack House, letter, 15 April 1992.
106. Ibid.
107. *Kingsway*, winter, 1962, p. 23.
108. Ibid., p. 20.
109. 'Ecclesiastical Fascism', in *Pieces of Hate*, edited Brian Redhead and Kenneth McLeigh, Hodder and Stoughton, 1982, p. 69.
110. Ibid.
111. Ibid.
112. *Preacher's Quarterly*, March 1957, p. 68.
113. Ibid.
114. *Methodist Recorder*, 24 July 1958.
115. Ibid., 6 August 1959, p. 8.
116. Ibid.
117. Ibid., 14 July 1960.
118. Ibid.
119. Ibid., 13 July 1961.
120. Ibid.
121. Ibid., 17 July 1980, p. 10.
122. Ibid.
123. *All His Grace*, op. cit., p. 9.
124. Ibid., p. 9.
125. Ibid., p. 13.
126. Ibid., p. 16.
127. Ibid., p. 24.
128. Ibid., p. 32.
129. Ibid., p. 33.
130. Ibid., p. 40.
131. Ibid., pp. 40–1.
132. Ibid., p. 49.
133. Ibid., p. 50.
134. Ibid., p. 52–3.
135. Ibid., p. 55.

136. Ibid., pp. 58–9.
137. Ibid., p. 62.
138. Ibid., p. 63.
139. Ibid., p. 63.
140. Ibid., p. 64.
141. Ibid., pp. 69–70.
142. Ibid., p. 71.
143. Ibid., p. 79.
144. Ibid., p. 80.
145. Ibid.
146. Ibid.
147. Ibid.
148. Ibid., p. 87.
149. Ibid., p. 86.
150. Ibid., p. 119.

Chapter 7 Pressure Group Patron

1. Councillor Arthur Downes, interview, October 1993.
2. Olive Delves, interview, 8 March 1994.
3. *Evening Standard*, 24 September 1953.
4. Sunday Forum, *Bristol Evening Post*, 8 August 1955.
5. *Peace News*, 25 May 1956, p. 1.
6. Ibid.
7. Ibid.
8. Ibid.
9. Ibid.
10. *British Weekly*, 17 May 1956.
11. *Daily Herald*, 8 August 1955.
12. *Tribune*, 9 August 1955.
13. *Picture Post*, 7 January 1956.
14. *Yorkshire Evening Post*, 24 October 1956. *Glasgow Bulletin*, 25 October 1956.
15. *Tribune*, 22 February 1957.
16. *Tribune*, 1 March 1957, p. 1.
17. *The Times*, 1 November 1960.
18. *Socialist Leader*, 25 July 1964.
19. *Daily Worker*, 4 December 1954.
20. *The Times*, 12 April 1954.
21. *Tribune*, 24 September 1954, p. 7.
22. *Tribune*, 25 February 1955.
23. Canon John Collins, 30 December 1954, in Presidential Papers, 1953/4, Methodist Archive, John Rylands Library, University of Manchester.

24. *Tribune*, 8 July 1955, p. 5.
25. Ibid.
26. See *Methodist Recorder* for a photograph of Donald Soper, Trevor Huddleston and Father Raynes, C.R., at a meeting in the Central Hall Westminster, 27 April 1956.
27. *Books and Bookmen*, review of Trevor Huddleston's *Naught for Your Comfort*, May 1956.
28. *Tribune*, 19 August 1960.
29. Ibid.
30. *Tribune*, 6 July 1956.
31. *The Times*, 14 January 1957.
32. *Tribune*, 29 March 1957.
33. Ibid.
34. *Peace News*, 6 December 1957.
35. *Tribune*, 19 September 1958, p. 4.
36. Ibid., 20 March 1959.
37. Ibid.
38. *Tribune*, 8 May 1959, p. 9.
39. *Methodist Recorder*, 14 May 1959, p. 9.
40. *The Times*, 25 November 1959.
41. *Tribune*, 1 April 1960.
42. *Tribune*, 12 February 1960, p. 4.
43. Ibid., 17 June 1960, p. 9.
44. *Daily Worker*, 30 March 1961.
45. *The Times*, 29 May 1961.
46. *Tribune*, 24 March 1961.
47. Ibid., 10 November 1961, p. 4.
48. Ibid.
49. Interview 16, 10 December 1992.
50. *Tribune*, 19 April 1963, p. 4.
51. Ibid., 3 May 1963, p. 4.
52. *Peace News*, 22 November 1963.
53. *Tribune*, 22 November 1963, p. 4.
54. Ibid., 20 March 1964, p. 11.
55. Ibid., 8 October 1965, p. 11.
56. Ibid., 19 November 1965, p. 11.
57. Ibid., 21 January 1966.
58. Ibid., 7 October 1966, p. 8.
59. Ibid., 4 November 1966, p. 11.
60. Ibid., 5 May 1967, p. 9.
61. Ibid., 4 August 1967, p. 3.
62. *Morning Star*, 3 May 1968. *The Times*, 6 April 1968.
63. *Tribune*, 12 April 1968, p. 3.
64. Ibid.

65. *Tribune*, 24 May 1968.
66. *Daily Worker*, 5 July 1968.
67. Ibid., 25 November 1960, p. 1.
68. Ibid., 12 December 1969, p. 3.
69. Lord Soper, *Hansard*, House of Lords, 14 July 1970, vol. 311, col. 530.
70. Jill Wallis, *Valiant for Peace*, Fellowship of Reconciliation, 1991, p. 222.
71. *Jewish Chronicle*, 20 March 1970.
72. *British Weekly*, 4 March 1965, p. 5.
73. Ibid.
74. *News Chronicle*, 18 September 1952.
75. *Methodist Recorder*, 22 March 1956, p. 5.
76. *Tribune*, 13 April 1956, p. 2.
77. *Sunday Express*, 18 March 1956.
78. *Methodist Recorder*, 13 August 1964.
79. *Hansard*, H.L., 8 November 1967, vol 286, col 448.
80. *British Weekly*, 23 May 1940.
81. *Band of Hope Journal*, May/June 1969, p. 7.
82. *Methodist Recorder*, 27 July 1950, p. 8.
83. The Centenary Year Joseph Malins Memorial Lecture, 'On to the Second Century', The International Order of Good Templars, 1968, pp. 15–16.
84. Ibid., p. 9.
85. Reminiscence of the Rev. Christopher Martin, 29 June 1992.
86. *Tribune*, 17 April 1959, p. 4.
87. Ibid., p. 4.
88. *Hansard*, H.L., 21 January 1971, vol. 314.
89. Ibid., 15 December 1975, vol. 336, col. 1268.
90. Ibid., col. 1267.
91. Nick Raynsford, M.P., interview, 23 July 1993.
92. Interview 13, 24 October 1992.
93. *Hansard*, H.L., 16 April 1973, vol. 341.
94. *Morning Star*, 1 July 1975.
95. *Hansard*, H.L., 25 June 1975, vol. 361, col. 1518.
96. Ibid., col. 1519.
97. Ibid., col. 1521.
98. Ibid., 30 November 1976, vol. 378, col. 183.
99. Ibid., 8 March 1977, vol. 380, col. 988.
100. *Voluntary Euthanasia Society Newsletter*, September 1993, p. 10.
101. *Ham and High*, 26 September 1980.
102. *Care of the Elderly*, June 1989, vol. 1, no. 2, p. 95.
103. *Hansard*, H.L., 25 March 1969, vol. 298.
104. Ibid., col. 1195.
105. Ibid., col. 1196.
106. Ibid.
107. Ibid., col. 1197.

108. Ibid., col. 1198.
109. *News of the World*, 25 November 1962.
110. W. R. Matthews, *Memories and Meanings*, Hodder and Stoughton, 1969, p. 354.
111. Ibid., p. 355.
112. The Rev. G. Thompson Brake, *Policy and Politics in British Methodism 1938–1982*, Edsall, 1984, pp. 566–7.
113. *The Times*, 13 September 1980.
114. John Oliver, interview, 22 February 1994.
115. *Care of the Elderly*, op. cit.
116. Donald Soper, *Tower Hill, 12.30*, Epworth Press, 1963, pp. 87–94.
117. *Kingsway*, autumn, 1960, p 26.
118. Interview 13, 24 October 1992.
119. *Tribune*, 23 December 1955, p. 12.
120. Ibid.
121. Ibid.
122. Ibid., 6 January 1956.
123. Ibid., 20 December 1957, p. 9.
124. Ibid.
125. *Tower Hill, 12.30.*, op. cit., p. 91.
126. Ibid., p. 93.
127. *Tribune*, 14 February 1958, p. 7.
128. *Methodist Recorder*, 21 September 1961, p. 15.
129. *Hansard*, H.L., vol. 292, col. 904.
130. Ibid., 2 May 1972, vol. 330, col. 686.
131. *Cruel Sports*, c. 1980, p. 12.
132. James Barrington, interview, 17 December 1992.
133. Nick Raynsford, M.P., op. cit.
134. *The Friend*, 25 December 1959.
135. *The Times*, 11 July 1960.
136. Ibid.
137. Ibid.
138. *Tribune*, 8 August 1961.
139. *Guardian*, 7 August 1964. *The Times*, 7 August 1964.
140. *Jewish Chronicle*, 15 December 1967.
141. *Scotsman*, 17 January 1970.
142. *Hansard*, H.L., 15 February 1973, vol. 338.
143. *Morning Star*, 11 December 1976.
144. *Hansard*, H.L., 18 October 1973, vol. 339, col. 475.
145. *The Times*, 27 November 1959.
146. *Jewish Chronicle*, 15 January 1960.
147. Ibid., 29 January 1960.
148. *Methodist Recorder*, 11 August 1960. *Christian World*, 18 August 1960.
149. *Jewish Chronicle*, 29 April 1960.

150. *Manchester Evening News*, 8 April 1961, p. 21.
151. Ibid.
152. *The Times*, 27 June 1966.
153. *Jewish Chronicle*, 8 January 1971.
154. *Tribune*, 2 June 1969, p. 9.
155. *The Times*, 1 June 1967.
156. *Jewish Chronicle*, 23 January 1970.
157. Ibid., 5 January 1970.
158. Ibid., 28 May 1971.
159. Ibid., 5 January 1973.
160. Ibid., 23 November 1973.
161. Ibid., 2 December 1973.
162. Ibid., 15 June 1973.
163. Ibid., 13 February 1976.
164. Ibid., 14 November 1975.
165. Ibid., 20 February 1976.
166. Ibid., 3 February 1978.
167. Ibid., 10 July 1981.

Chapter 8   Publicist and Panellist

1. The Rev. F.A. Iremonger, letter to Donald Soper, 29 June 1934, BBC Written Archives Centre, Caversham, near Reading, Lord Soper file, 1a, Talks 1933–39.
2. Ibid., the Rev. F.A. Iremonger, to Donald Soper, 3 December 1934.
3. Ibid., 12 April 1935.
4. Asa Briggs, *The History of Broadcasting in the United Kingdom*, vol. 2, *The Golden Age of Wireless*, OUP, 1965, p. 655.
5. *Eastern Daily Express*, 23 September 1936.
6. The Rev. F.A. Iremonger, to Donald Soper, op. cit., 18 December 1935.
7. The Rev. Kenneth Grayston, op. cit., Lord Soper file 1b, Talks, 1940–1952.
8. The Rev. F.A. Iremonger to Marie Soper, 7 October 1938, op. cit., Lord Soper file 1a, Talks, 1933–39.
9. *John Bull*, 2 January 1937.
10. *Daily Herald*, 11 January 1937, p. 10.
11. Ibid.
12. Ibid.
13. The *Sunday People*, 27 March 1938.
14. *Birmingham Post*, 18 July 1938.
15. See *Daily Telegraph*; *Torbay Express*; *Glasgow Herald*; *Daily Mirror*; *Yorkshire Post*; *The Times*, 18 July 1938, for report of the debate.
16. Donald Soper, *Will Christianity Work?* 3 Broadcast Talks, April, 1939, Lutterworth Papers, no. 34, The Lutterworth Press, pp. 1–2, n.d.

17. Ibid., pp. 16–17.
18. Ibid., p. 26.
19. The Rev. Edwin Robertson, letter, 11 May 1993.
20. *Ilford Record*, 9 October 1941.
21. Donald Soper, *Practical Christianity Today*, Ken-Pax Publishing, 1947, p. 26.
22. Ibid., p. 18.
23. Ibid., p. 123.
24. Ibid., p. 124.
25. BBC, *Lift Up Your Hearts*, 27 September 1948.
26. Ibid., 2 October 1948.
27. Ibid., 21 June 1951.
28. Ibid., 11 May 1952.
29. Ibid., 23 May 1952.
30. BBC Written Archives Centre, op. cit., Lord Soper, Personal File, 1947–1952. Talks, TV.
31. Ibid., 29 December 1954.
32. Ibid., 19 June 1955.
33. Ibid., 1 July 1957.
34. The *Tonight* interview was about his visit to Canada and Japan in 1957.
35. BBC Written Archives Centre, Lord Soper, Personal File, 1947–1962, Talks, TV.
36. Ibid.
37. Ibid., 29 November 1962.
38. *Newsnight*, 1 December 1981.
39. *Methodist Recorder*, 18 January 1973, p. 3.
40. *Wogan on Wogan*, Robson Books Ltd., 1987, pp. 28–33.
41. Rhys Williams, letter, 12 June 1993.
42. *Church of England Newspaper*, 26 May 1963.
43. *News Chronicle*, 24 December 1955.
44. Ibid.
45. *Nottingham Evening Post*, 18 March 1962.
46. *Guardian*; *Daily Telegraph*; 5 July 1962.
47. *Evening News*, 6 March 1964.
48. Geoffrey Palmer, interview, autumn, 1993.
49. *Humanist*, 26 February 1964.
50. Interview 18, 25 February 1993.
51. *Evening Post and News*, 5 August 1964.
52. Ibid.
53. Geoffrey Palmer, op. cit.
54. *Radio Times*, 8–14 October 1988, p. 17.
55. BBC Written Archives Centre, op. cit., written record of *Any Questions?*, 13 February 1953.
56. Ibid.

57. Ibid., 23 September 1960.
58. Ibid., 15 September 1961.
59. Ibid., 26 January 1962.
60. Ibid.
61. Ibid., 14 September 1962.
62. Ibid., 22 October 1982.
63. Ibid., 21 May 1965.
64. Ibid.
65. Ibid., 3 June 1966.
66. Ibid., 30 January 1970.
67. The full transcript can be found in British Library, National Sound Archive, LP 36173 bo 1.
68. BBC Written Archives Centre, *Any Questions?*, 2 April 1976.
69. Ibid., 23 December 1976.
70. Ibid., 23 December 1977.
71. Ibid., 11 May 1979.
72. Ibid., 23 December 1984.
73. Ibid., 23 January 1987.
74. Ibid.
75. Ibid., 7 December 1979.
76. Ibid.
77. *Radio Times*, 8–14 October 1988, p. 17.
78. Ibid.
79. *Death of a Young Man, A Good Friday Meditation*, Thames TV. n.d.
80. Ibid.
81. Michael Redington, interview, 8 June 1993.
82. Ibid.
83. Ian Mackenzie, *Vision and Belief in Religious Broadcasting, 1957–1968*, BBC TV, July 1968, p. 2.
84. *TV Guide*, 22 October 1959.
85. Ibid.
86. Ibid.
87. *The Times*, 19 July 1969, p. 10d.
88. *The Times*, 28 June 1982, p. 10g.
89. *Daily Worker*, 7 March 1954, p. 1.
90. Ibid., 3 December 1954, p. 114.
91. *Morning Star*, 30 December 1991.
92. Roger Minshull, letter to Donald Soper, 31 January 1993.
93. *Cherwell*, 1 March 1955, p. 2.
94. *Oxford Mail*, 10 February 1983, p. 5.
95. Ibid.
96. Ibid.
97. *Isis*, 18 February 1983, p. 4.
98. *Oxford Mail*, 28 February 1958. p 15.

99. Ibid.
100. *Newsnight*, 1 December 1981.
101. *Cambridge Review*, 15 May 1954, vol. LXXV pp. 466–7.
102. Ibid.
103. The Rev. Brian Duckworth, interview, 19 February 1993.
104. Interview, 23 October 1993.
105. Councillor John Pennington, letter, 12 July 1993.
106. Roger Minshull, letter, 21 March 1993.
107. Edward Pearce, *Daily Telegraph*, 11 June 1977.
108. *Staffordshire Evening Sentinel*, 22 July 1964.
109. *Birmingham Post*, 3 August 1972; *Manchester Evening News* 4 August 1972; *Church Times*, 11 August 1972.
110. Donald Soper, with Shirley Davenport, *Evening Post*, 31 July 1978.
111. The Rev. J. Neville Ward, interview, 1986.
112. *Southern Evening Echo*, 23 July 1964.
113. Michael Crewdson, interview, 1993.

Chapter 9   Pioneer and Philanthropist

1. *Methodist Recorder*, 28 June 1962, p. 8.
2. Olive Delves, interview, 27 October 1993.
3. Ibid.
4. Derek Walker, *British Weekly*, 28 March 1957, p. 7.
5. Ibid.
6. *Kingsway*, autumn, 1964.
7. *Kingsway Messenger*, April/May 1956, p. 14.
8. Ibid., autumn, 1958, p. 30.
9. Denys Orchard, interview, 25 October 1993.
10. Interview, 10 June 1993.
11. The Rev. Jeffrey Harris, interview, 25 May 1993.
12. Dr A. Bradshaw, letter, 29 June 1993.
13. Olive Delves, op. cit.
14. Ibid.
15. Ibid.
16. *Methodist Recorder*, 10 May 1962.
17. *Kingsway*, summer, 1958.
18. Ibid.
19. *Kingsway Messenger*, January 1949, vol. 1, no. 1, p.4.
20. Sister Marjorie Watson, letter, 20 March 1993.
21. *Methodist Recorder*, 2 May 1957, p. 3.
22. Bill Weston, interview, 31 August 1994.
23. Greater London Records Office, N/M/2/34, 11 October 1950 (Hungerford Minutes).

24. Ibid.
25. *Kingsway*, spring, 1962, p. 31.
26. Ibid.
27. Rachel Squire, M.P., letter, 29 July 1993.
28. Beatrice Holmes, interview, 10 June 1993.
29. Ibid.
30. Ibid.
31. Ibid.
32. *Kingsway*, summer, 1959.
33. Donald Soper, *Calling for Action*, Robson Books, 1984, p. 93.
34. Ibid.
35. *Methodist Recorder*, 20 July 1961, p. 7.
36. *Hansard*, H.L., 22 February 1967, vol. 279, col. 734.
37. Ibid.
38. *Hansard*, H.L., 27 June 1979, vol. 400, col. 1544.
39. *Hansard*, H.L., 20 December 1967, vol. 287, col. 1534.
40. *Tribune*, 25 May 1959.
41. *News Chronicle*, 25 May 1959.
42. *The Times*, 23 May 1959.
43. Ibid.
44. The Rev. Dr Kenneth Greet, interview, 1 December 1992.
45. *Methodist Recorder*, 16 July 1959, p. 4.
46. William Purcell, *Portrait of Soper*, Mowbrays, 1972, pp. 27–8.
47. See David Mason, Geoffrey Ainger, Norwyn Denny, *News from Notting Hill*, Epworth Press, 1967, pp. 12–13.
48. *Portrait of Soper*, op. cit., p. 28.
49. *Kensington News and Post*, 24 February 1962.
50. *Hansard*, H.L., 7 July 1965, vol. 267, col. 1391.
51. *Kingsway*, summer, 1967, pp. 24–5.
52. Lord Soper contribution on 'Leadership, Teamwork and Motivation', (1994) for *Learning from the Leaders*, edited by Humphrey Walters and Paul March.
53. *Kingsway Messenger*, July/August, 1949, p. 13.
54. *Methodist Recorder*, 1 March 1945.
55. The Rev. A.G. Errey, *Experiment in Witness*, OCW, p. 7.
56. Harold Williams, *OCW Newsletter*, 1978.
57. Denys Orchard, *Reflections on the Salisbury Campaign*, 25 October 1945.
58. Based on notes made by the Rev. A. Cartledge, 19 January 1948.
59. *Methodist Recorder*, 14 November 1946, p. 3.
60. The Rev. A.G. Errey, op. cit., p. 10.
61. *Kingsway Messenger*, August/October 1947, pp. 10–11.
62. The Rev. A. Kingsley Turner, *OCW Newsletter*, 1978.
63. The Rev. John Stacey, interview, 17 March 1993.
64. Clifford Sharp, letter, 3 May 1993.

65. The Rev. Frank H. Kelly, letter, 3 March 1993.
66. The Rev. John Stacey, op. cit.
67. *Methodist Recorder*, 21 February 1952, p. 3.
68. The Rev. Kenneth Lawton, campaign organizer, interview, 21 March 1993.
69. The Rev. Alfred Willetts, letter, 28 February 1993.
70. The Rev Dr John Vincent, *Christ and Methodism*, Epworth Press, 1965, p. 77.
71. The Rev. Jim Bates, letter, 27 February 1993.
72. Anne Ord, letter, 26 June 1993.
73. Clifford Sharp, letter, 3 May 1993.
74. Yvonne Griffiths, interview, 7 February 1993.
75. Kathie Wills, letter, 10 March and interview 24 March 1993.
76. The Rev. David Hatton, letter, 8 February 1993.
77. Ibid.
78. *OCW Newsletter*, 16 January 1951.
79. The Rev. Dr John Vincent, *OCW Newsletter*, 37, November 1954.
80. *OCW Newsletter*, Christmas, 1967, p. 4.
81. *Methodist Recorder*, 4 October 1962.
82. Ibid., 12 September 1963.
83. *OCW Yearbook*, 1960, pp. 5–6.
84. *TV Times*, 17 July 1964.
85. Report in local Poole paper, 21 April 1975.
86. *Daily Mail*, 20 September 1979.
87. The Rev. George Thompson Brake, *Policy and Politics in British Methodism, 1932–1982*, Edsall, 1984, p. 634.
88. Ann Bird, interview, 7 October 1993.
89. *Methodist Recorder*, 25 April 1968.
90. Ibid., 3 December 1964, p. 2.
91. Ibid., 7 January 1965, p. 5.
92. *Kingsway*, winter, 1970/71, pp. 17–18.
93. *Guardian*, 20 January 1969.
94. *Methodist Recorder*, 15 July 1965, p. 3.
95. *Policy and Politics in British Methodism*, op. cit., p. 301.
96. *Kingsway*, autumn/winter, 1965, p. 4.
97. Hyde Park, 27 July 1980.
98. Ibid., 19 October 1980.
99. *Punch*, 'Why I am Not A Roman Catholic', 30 June 1965.
100. *Methodist Recorder*, 23 May 1956, p. 4.
101. *The Times*, 19 July 1969. p. 10d.
102. *British Weekly*, 27 February 1969, p. 1.
103. *Methodist Recorder*, September 1969, p. 20.
104. Ibid., 22 July 1971, p. 3.
105. Karen Smith, Pastoral Training Department, Diocese of London, 1993,

Copy of Proposed Sharing Agreement with Holy Trinity, Kingsway, and the Methodist Congregation, formerly occupying Kingsway Hall.

106. Ibid.
107. Denys Orchard, interview, 25 October 1993.
108. Derek Walker, interview, 30 March 1993.
109. *Kingsway Messenger*, October/November 1946, p. 2.
110. Ibid.
111. Ibid.
112. *Policy and Politics in British Methodism*, op. cit. pp. 112–14.
113. Ibid.
114. Ibid. (See also *Guardian*, 28 June 1984, p. 6.)
115. Ibid.
116. The Rev. Jeffrey Harris, interview, 25 May 1993.
117. The Rev. Harry Morton in conversation with the Rev. Dr Colin Morris, BBC, 15 March 1981.
118. The Rev. Austen Williams, interview, January 1994.
119. *Policy and Politics in British Methodism*, op. cit., pp. 409–40.
120. The meeting was held on 26 February 1971.
121. Olive Delves, op. cit.
122. BBC, *Voices and Visions*, 1977.
123. *Methodist Recorder*, 29 June 1978, pp. 14–15.
124. Olive Delves, op. cit.
125. Farewell Sermon, 30 July 1978.
126. Ibid.
127. Ibid.
128. Ibid.
129. Ibid.
130. Ibid.
131. Ibid.
132. Denys Orchard, interview, 25 October 1993.

Chapter 10 Philosopher and Puritan

1. Review of John Pudney, *John Wesley, His World*, Thames and Hudson, *Books and Bookmen*, March 1979, p. 12.
2. Hyde Park, 11 November 1978.
3. *Kingsway*, October 1956, p. 10.
4. F. R. Tennant, *Philosophical Theology*, CUP, 1928–30, vol. 2, p. 259.
5. BBC, *Lift Up Your Hearts*, 1 October 1948.
6. Donald Soper, *Christianity and Its Critics*, Hodder and Stoughton, 1937, p. 62.
7. George Hunter 3rd, *Evangelistic Rhetoric in Secular Britain: The Theory*

and Speaking of Donald Soper and Bryan Green, Evanston, Illinois, 1972, p. 317, (unpublished thesis).

8. Donald Soper, *Calling for Action*, Robson Books, 1984, pp. 123–4.
9. *Tribune*, 14 May 1971, p. 3.
10. BBC, *The Time of My Life, 1921–6*, 5 January 1969, P317R.
11. *Kingsway Messenger*, April/May 1947, p. 27.
12. 'Providence and the Environment', in The Polytechnic of Wales and The Environment Group, *Publication No. 5*, 1978, p. 65.
13. Dialogue with Joan Bakewell, 'Under Bow Bells', April 1976.
14. Tower Hill, 19 September 1979.
15. Ibid.
16. *Kingsway Messenger*, July/August 1951.
17. Hyde Park, 14 October 1979.
18. Lord Soper, *Hansard*, House of Lords, 1965–66, vol. 273, col. 105.
19. Hyde Park, 7 December 1980.
20. Ibid.
21. Ibid., 28 September 1980.
22. *Tribune*, 11 May 1962, p. 4.
23. Ibid.
24. *Kingsway Messenger*, July/August 1951.
25. *Methodist Recorder*, 20 February 1964, p. 2.
26. Donald Soper, *The Advocacy of the Gospel*, Hodder and Stoughton, 1961, p. 36.
27. Ibid.
28. *Methodist Recorder*, 'Personally Speaking', 1 September 1977, p. 20.
29. Ibid.
30. Hyde Park, 28 September 1980.
31. Ibid.
32. Hyde Park, 14 February 1980.
33. *Calling for Action*, op. cit., p. 171.
34. Donald Soper, *Popular Fallacies about the Christian Faith*, Wyvern Books, 1957, p. 13.
35. *Kingsway*, winter, 1967/8, pp. 23–30.
36. Ibid.
37. Hyde Park, 19 October 1980.
38. *Kingsway*, winter, 1967/8, pp. 23–30.
39. Ibid.
40. Ibid.
41. Hyde Park, 7 October 1979.
42. *Methodist Recorder*, 16 September 1976, p. 12.
43. Hyde Park, 27 July 1980.
44. *British Weekly*, 6 February 1958, p. 5.
45. Donald Soper, *All His Grace*, Epworth Press, 1957, p. 71.
46. *Tribune*, 14 January 1955, p. 4.

47. *Daily Worker*, 14 January 1955, p. 3.
48. Ibid.
49. *Tribune*, 14 January 1955, p. 4.
50. A.E. Taylor, *The Faith of a Moralist*, Macmillan and Co., 1930.
51. *Tribune*, 14 January 1955. p. 4.
52. *Methodist Recorder*, 26 May 1966.
53. *Tribune*, 28 October 1955.
54. Ibid.
55. Dr Julian Huxley, *Tribune*, 18 November 1955.
56. *Methodist Recorder*, 18 November 1955.
57. Ibid.
58. *Kingsway*, spring, 1963, p. 28.
59. *Kingsway*, autumn, 1963, p. 24.
60. *Methodist Recorder*, 4 September 1975, pp. 12–13.
61. Ibid.
62. *Methodist Recorder*, 'In My View', 8 October 1970.
63. Ibid.
64. Ibid., 15 October 1970.
65. Ibid., 22 October 1970.
66. Ibid., 29 October 1970.
67. Ibid.
68. Ibid.
69. Ibid.
70. *Kingsway*, winter, 1959, p. 10.
71. *Methodist Recorder*, 9 January 1969, p. 2.
72. Ibid.
73. *Methodist Recorder*, 17 December 1964, p. 2.
74. Richard Clements, interview, 2 September 1993.
75. *Kingsway*, summer, 1957, p. 10.
76. Ibid., p. 11.
77. Ibid.
78. Donald Soper, *Tower Hill, 12.30*, Epworth Press, 1963, pp. 63–4.
79. *Popular Fallacies about the Christian Faith*, op. cit., p. 102.
80. *The Advocacy of the Gospel*, op. cit., p. 77.
81. Councillor Arthur Downes, interview, October 1993.
82. 'Christianity Looks at Communism', *Christian Action*, spring, 1967, pp. 6–8.
83. Ibid., p. 8.
84. John Macmurray, *The Clue to History*, SCM Press, 1938, p. 112.
85. *Popular Fallacies about the Christian Faith*, op. cit., p. 84.
86. *Providence and the Environment*, op. cit., p. 61.
87. Ibid., p. 62.
88. *Methodist Recorder*, 1 April 1976, p. 16.
89. Ibid., 23 September 1965, p. 2.

90. *The Advocacy of the Gospel*, op. cit., pp. 88-9.
91. Ibid.
92. *Tower Hill, 12.30*, op. cit., p. 25.
93. *Methodist Recorder*, 21 November 1958, p. 2.
94. Hyde Park, 14 December 1980.
95. *The Advocacy of the Gospel*, op. cit., pp. 125–6.
96. *Tribune*, 7 July 1972, p. 3.
97. *The Advocacy of the Gospel*, op. cit., p. 119.
98. Hyde Park 6 June 1976.
99. Ibid.
100. *Methodist Recorder*, 9 September 1965, p. 2.
101. See Donald Soper, 'Socialism – An Enduring Creed', Third Tawney Memorial Lecture, Christian Socialist Movement, 1980.
102. *Methodist Recorder*, 16 January 1969. p. 2.
103. Ibid.
104. Ibid.
105. Ibid.
106. Ibid.
107. *Kingsway Messenger*, vol. 1, no. 4, 1940, p. 52.
108. *Methodist Recorder*, 14 June 1962, p. 2.
109. Ibid.
110. *Morning Star*, 27 October 1979, p. 4.
111. William Purcell, *Portrait of Soper*, Mowbrays, 1972, pp. 112–13, quoting BBC, *Frankly Speaking*, with Norman St John Stevas, 18 June 1965.
112. 'Socialism – An Enduring Creed', op. cit., p. 15.
113. Ibid.
114. Donald Soper, *Christ and Tower Hill*, Hodder and Stoughton, 1934, p. 122.
115. *British Weekly*, 1 July 1953.
116. Ibid.
117. Ibid.
118. Hyde Park, 10 October 1979.
119. Ibid., 6 June 1976.
120. *Methodist Recorder*, 19 September 1971, p. 2.
121. *Methodist Recorder*, 7 January 1960.
122. G. J. Heering, *The Fall of Christianity: A Study of Christianity, the State and War*, Allen and Unwin, 1930.
123. *All His Grace*, op. cit., p. 52.
124. Ibid.
125. 'Moral Conflicts', *London Quarterly and Holborn Review*, Epworth Press, April 1962, p. 94.
126. Ibid.
127. Ibid., p. 97.
128. 'Here Stand I – The Place of Compromise in the Christian Life', (Alex Wood Memorial Lecture, 1959), Fellowship of Reconciliation, p. 17.

129. Donald Soper, *Christian Politics*, Epworth Press, 1977, pp. 31–3.

130. Mulford Sibley, *Peace News*, 20 September 1963, p. 5.

131. Reinhold Niebuhr, *Why The Christian Church Is Not Pacifist*, p. 198, quoted in G.H.C. Macgregor, *The Relevance of the Impossible Ideal*, FOR, 1960, first published 1941 as *The Relevance of the Impossible*.

132. *Popular Fallacies about the Christian Faith*, op. cit., p. 112.

133. Ibid., p. 20.

134. Reinhold Niebuhr, *Moral Man and Immoral Society*, Scribner, New York, 1932, p. xii.

135. 'Priorities for the 80s', *Reconciliation Quarterly*, December 1979.

136. Donald Soper, *Practical Christianity Today*, Ken-Pax Publishing, 1947, pp. 107–8.

137. *Kingsway Messenger*, June/July 1966, p. 17.

138. *Western Morning News*, 19 October 1943.

139. *Tribune*, 14 June 1963, p. 4.

140. Trevor Huddleston, *Books and Bookmen*, February 1973, p. 69.

141. *Hansard*, H.L. 1972, vol. 336, col. 1290.

142. Ibid., 21 November 1966, 2R.

143. *Methodist Recorder*, 6 September 1973, p. 3.

144. Hyde Park, 27 July 1980.

145. *Methodist Recorder*, 5 March 1964, p. 2.

146. *The Times*, 7 November 1960.

147. Ibid.

148. *Daily Telegraph*, 21 November 1959.

149. Ibid.

150. *Methodist Recorder*, 13 May 1976, p. 24.

151. *Hansard*, H.L., 13 July 1967, vol. 284, col. 1309.

152. Ibid.

153. *Does Pornography Matter?*, edited by C. H. Rolph, Routledge, Kegan and Paul, 1961, p. 42.

154. Ibid., p. 43.

155. Ibid., p. 47.

156. Ibid., p. 54.

157. Interview with Lord Longford, July 1993.

158. *Hansard*, H.L., 1972, vol. 336, col. 1290.

159. Ibid.

160. Interview 6, 25 June 1992.

161. *Care of the Elderly*, 10 July 1990.

162. *Light*, December, 1948, Report of Donald Soper at the Albert Hall.

163. Joseph Fletcher, *William Temple: Twentieth Century Christian*, Seabury Press, New York, 1963, p. 269.

164. *Kingsway*, winter, 1974, p. 3.

165. 'The Freedom of Non-Establishment', *House of Lords Magazine*, 12 December 1988, p. 92.

166. *Edmond Richer and the Revival of Gallicanism, 1600–1630,* (unpublished thesis), p. 133. Lord Soper's Ph.D. thesis is held at the London School of Political and Economic Science.
167. See Hans Kung, *Does God Exist?* Collins, 1980.
168. *Hansard* H.L., 2 November 1972, vol. 336, col. 192.
169. Tower Hill, 21 May 1986.
170. 'The Oldie Interview', *The Oldie,* 15 May 1992, with Naim Atallah, p. 20.
171. *Calling for Action,* op. cit., p. 15.
172. *Care of the Elderly,* November 1989, vol. 1, no. 6.
173. Blaise Pascal, *Pensées,* translated by W. F. Trotter, Everyman's Library, J.M. Dent and Sons, 1932.
174. *Popular Fallacies about the Christian Faith,* op. cit., p. 23.
175. *Christian World,* 9 December 1948.
176. Hyde Park, 11 July 1976.
177. Ibid., 28 September 1980.
178. Interview 13, 24 October 1992.
179. *Methodist Recorder,* 16 September 1965, p. 2.
180. *Kingsway,* winter, 1974, p. 3.
181. Hyde Park, 7 October 1979.
182. *Popular Fallacies about the Christian Faith,* op. cit., p. 20.
183. *Kingsway Messenger,* August/October 1947, p. 3.
184. Tower Hill, 21 May 1986.

Chapter 11   Pensioner and Penitent

1. *The Friend,* 4 August 1978, p. 962.
2. Lady Soper, interview 2, 21 May 1993.
3. Ibid.
4. Greater London Records Office, N/M/2/29.
5. Ibid., N/M/2/12.
6. Lady Soper, interview 3, 13 July 1993.
7. Lady Soper, interview 1, 20 April 1993.
8. Interview 5, 18 June 1992.
9. *Socialist Leader,* Glasgow, 3 June 1967.
10. Lady Soper, interview 1, 20 April 1993.
11. Lady Soper, interview 3, 13 July 1993.
12. Lady Soper, interview 1, 20 April 1993.
13. *Any Questions?* 20 April 1993.
14. Interview 2, 30 April 1992.
15. Ibid.
16. *Methodist Recorder,* 3 September 1992.
17. BBC Radio 2, 31 December 1978.
18. *Methodist Recorder,* 3 August 1978, p. 3.

19. Ibid., 23 August 1978, p. 10.
20. Ibid.
21. Ibid.
22. *Care of the Elderly*, October 1989.
23. Contribution to a book for Philip Bristow, 1988.
24. Ibid.
25. *Care of the Elderly*, June 1989.
26. Ibid.
27. Ibid.
28. Ibid., October 1989.
29. Ibid., March 1990.
30. Donald Soper, *Calling for Action*, Robson Books, 1984, p. 12.
31. Ibid., p. 146.
32. *Methodist Recorder*, 30 May 1968, p. 19.
33. Donald Soper, *Keeping Festival*, Epworth Press, 1954, p. 19.
34. 'Out in the Open', interview with D. Hanlon and John Coutts, for *R.E. News and Views*. n.d.
35. Donald Soper, *Practical Christianity Today*, Ken-Pax Publishing, 1947.
36. *Calling for Action*, op. cit., p. 148.
37. Ibid.
38. *Tribune*, 12 December, 1958, p. 4.
39. Donald Soper to Henry Kelly, BBC, 28 July 1978.
40. BBC *Midweek*, 'Radio Birthday of the Week', 3 February 1982.
41. *Silver Lining*, 25 February 1958, from transcript in BBC Written Archives Centre, Caversham, near Reading.
42. BBC, *Frankly Speaking*, 29 July 1965.
43. Donald Soper to Michael Brown, *Yorkshire Post*, 31 January 1987.
44. BBC, *Choices*, 16 August 1987.
45. Interview 5, 18 June 1992.
46. Ibid.
47. Ibid.
48. Interview 15, 26 October 1992.
49. *Reconciliation*, May 1959, in MPF News section, p. 989.
50. *Methodist Recorder*, 4 July 1963, p. 2.
51. Lord Soper, *Hansard*, House of Lords, 9 July 1975, vol. 362, col. 871.
52. *Sussex Times*, 15 July 1941.
53. *Tribune*, 20 December 1963.
54. Ibid., 28 October 1966.
55. Ibid.
56. Ibid., 31 July 1959.
57. *Hansard*, H.L., 1 February 1973, vol. 338, col. 783.
58. Ibid., col. 784.
59. Interview 8, 17 July 1992.
60. *Hansard*, H.L., December 1977, vol. 387, col. 2088.

61. *Kingsway Messenger*, March/April 1951.
62. Ibid.
63. Hyde Park, 14 December 1960.
64. *Kingsway*, winter, 1963, p. 24, writing about *God Is No More*, by Werner and Lotte Pelz, Gollancz, 1963.
65. *Tribune*, 11 November 1955.
66. Ibid.
67. *Kingsway Messenger*, September/October 1949, p. 3.
68. Donald Soper, interview with Jill Wallis, 13 March 1986.
69. See *Tradition and Unity*, sermons published in honour of Robert Runcie, edited by Dan Cohn-Sherbok, Bellow Publishing, London, 1991.
70. Based on responses from four pupils, gathered together by Mr Graeme Walker, Headmaster of Haberdashers' Aske's School.
71. Letter to author, 6 April 1993.
72. *Methodist Recorder*, 1 March 1994. p. 1.
73. Ibid.
74. Ibid.
75. Ibid., 8 March 1984.
76. Ibid., 15 March 1984.
77. Ibid.
78. Ibid., 30 March 1993, p. 19.
79. Ibid.
80. *Guardian*, 28 June 1994.
81. *Prospect*, October 1992, p. 10.
82. *Methodist Recorder*, 2 May 1987.
83. Interview 10, 1 October 1992.
84. Interview 18, 25 February 1993.
85. *Daily Mirror*, 25 May 1960.
86. *Care of the Elderly*, September 1989.
87. *Portrait of Soper*, op. cit., p. 126.
88. Interview 9, 24 September 1992.
89. Olive Delves, interview, 27 October 1993.
90. Interview 5, 18 June 1992.
91. *Peace News*, 26 July 1957.
92. Donald Soper to Richard Holloway, 'When I Get to Heaven', BBC, 17 May 1987.
93. British Library, National Sound Archive, BBC, LP 29671.
94. Olive Delves, op. cit.
95. Bill Weston, interview, 31 August 1994.
96. Donald Soper in *One Over Par*, H.F. & G. Witherby, 1992.
97. Bill Weston, *Prospect*, March 1993, pp. 8–9.
98. *One Over Par*, op. cit.
99. Interview 10, 1 October 1992.
100. Interview 9, 24 September 1992.

101. *Portrait of Soper*, op. cit., p. 39.
102. *Ham and High*, 18 February 1982.
103. Ibid., 30 August 1979.
104. *Methodist Recorder*, 7 July 1994, p. 13.
105. The Rev. Brian Beck, letter to Lord Soper, January 1993.
106. Interview 11, 8 October 1992.
107. Donald Soper, 'When I Get to Heaven', op. cit.
108. Interview on LBC Radio, 26 April 1982.
109. Hinde Street Methodist Church, 14 March 1993.
110. Donald Soper, interview with Clive Barrett, 18 October 1992.
111. Interview with author, autumn, 1992.
112. British Library, National Sound Archive, BBC, LP 29671.
113. Donald and Marie, BBC, *Woman's Hour*, 1981.
114. Ibid.
115. Interview, 2, 30 April 1992.
116. Interview 4, 21 May 1992.
117. Donald and Marie, BBC, op. cit.
118. Rachel Newton, interview, 18 April 1993.
119. Lady Soper, interview 3, 13 July 1993.
120. Ibid.
121. *Methodist Recorder*, 3 September 1992, p. 13.
122. *Guardian*, 10 June 1988.
123. 7 June 1988.
124. 5 October 1988.
125. *Financial Times*, 7 November 1992.
126. *Daily Mail*, 7 November 1922.
127. Ibid.
128. *Daily Telegraph*, 1 February 1993, p. 1.
129. The Rev. Dr Leslie Griffiths, *Methodist Recorder*, 21 January 1993, p. 20. The novel was called *Beer in the Snooker Club*.
130. *Big Issue*, no. 27, 2–15 April 1993.
131. Marjorie Savage, letter, 29 March 1993.
132. Angela Kneale, letter to Lord Soper, 28 January 1993.
133. Mrs Elaine Howard, letter to Lord Soper, 5 February 1993.
134. Mrs G. Knight, letter to Lord Soper, 31 January 1993.
135. Ibid.

Chapter 12   Passionate Pilgrim

1. Hyde Park, 26 April 1992.
2. *British Weekly*, 21 September 1950.
3. *Methodist Recorder*, 16 June 1966, p. 2. See also Donald Soper, *Calling for Action*, Robson Books, 1984, pp. 142–3.

4. *Methodist Recorder*, 26 March 1942.
5. Donald Soper, *All His Grace*, Epworth Press, 1957, p. 54.
6. Ibid., p. 49.
7. The Rev. Dr Gordon Wakefield, interview, 23 March 1993.
8. *Methodist Recorder*, 27 July 1978.
9. *Peace News*, 29 May 1981.
10. *Methodist Recorder*, 31 July, 1980, p. 32.
11. Ibid., 28 January 1982, p. 5.
12. 9 May 1982, BBC *Sunday*, British Library, National Sound Archive, LP 40701 fo 2.
13. Lord Soper, *Hansard*, House of Lords, 3 December 1980, vol. 415, col. 439.
14. Ibid., 3 April, 1982, vol. 428, col. 1589.
15. Ibid., 20 May 1982, vol. 430, col. 847.
16. Ibid.
17. Ibid., col. 848.
18. Ibid., 9 November 1982, vol. 436, col. 191.
19. Ibid.
20. Lord Carrington, *Hansard*, H.L., 16 February 1983, vol. 439, col. 276.
21. Ibid., col. 295.
22. Ibid.
23. See *The Church and the Bomb: Nuclear Weapons and Christian Conscience*, 1982, report of a working party chaired by the Bishop of Salisbury, the Rt Rev. J.A. Baker.
24. 'The Heart of the Gospel', in *Unholy Warfare: The Church and the Bomb*, edited by David Martin and Peter Mullen, Blackwell, 1983, pp. 236–7.
25. *Methodist Recorder*, 19 July 1984.
26. Ibid., 25 July 1985.
27. Hinde Street Methodist Church, 20 October 1985.
28. Ibid.
29. David Lange, *Everyman*, BBC TV, 3 November 1985.
30. Ibid.
31. 'Faith in the Future' – A Christian Witness, 13 March 1989, Fulham and Chelsea Adult Education Institute, 'Peace on Earth', Inter-faith series, 1989.
32. *Methodist Recorder*, 27 July 1989.
33. *Hansard*, H.L., 4 June 1990, vol. 519, col. 1164.
34. Ibid.
35. Ibid.
36. Transcript of interview with Lord Soper, June/July, 1990, HTV, Cardiff.
37. *Methodist Recorder*, 27 September 1990.
38. Ibid.
39. Ibid.
40. Ibid.

41. Ibid.
42. *Hansard*, H.L., 13 November 1990, vol. 525, col. 1103.
43. Ibid., col. 1104.
44. Ibid.
45. *Methodist Recorder*, 17 January 1991, p. 18.
46. George Hill, *The Times*, 16 January 1991.
47. Ibid.
48. Fellowship of Reconciliation Seminar, May 1991. Based on notes made by G.V. Clarke.
49. Pat Arrowsmith, interview, 21 July 1993.
50. *Sunday Times*, 10 January 1993.
51. Thanksgiving Service for the life and work of Vera Mary Brittain, St Martin-in-the-Fields, 1 December 1993.
52. Brian Cooper, *Baptist Times*, 21 October 1993.
53. Hyde Park, 28 September 1980.
54. Donald Soper to Jill Wallis, 13 March 1986.
55. *Methodist Recorder*, 19 February 1981, p. 8.
56. Ibid., 12 March 1981, p. 9.
57. Ibid.
58. Ibid.
59. *Methodist Recorder*, 15 February 1979, p. 1.
60. Ibid., 1 March 1979.
61. Ibid.
62. *Methodist Recorder*, 28 February 1980, p. 1 and p. 24.
63. *The Franciscan*, June 1993.
64. Ibid.
65. Ibid.
66. *Methodist Recorder*, 3 February 1983.
67. Ibid.
68. *Methodist Recorder*, 3 October 1985, p. 3.
69. *The Times*, 30 September 1985.
70. *Methodist Recorder*, 21 March 1985.
71. Nicholas Gillett, letter, 9 July 1992.
72. The Rev. Donald Eadie, interview, 29 October 1993.
73. Vote of thanks to the Rt Hon. John Smith, Bloomsbury Baptist Church, 20 March 1993.
74. Ibid.
75. Neil Kinnock, BBC 2, 5 February 1994.
76. *Guardian*, 28 June 1994.
77. Peter Dawe, interview, 31 December 1992.
78. *Methodist Recorder*, 10 February 1983.
79. On 13 March 1979.
80. *Methodist Recorder*, 'Why I Went to the Lords', 14 June 1993, p. 2.
81. *Hansard*, H.L., 13 June 1979, vol. 400, col. 669.

82. Ibid., 25 February 1980, vol. 405, col. 1094.
83. Ibid., 1 June 1980, vol. 409, col. 1162.
84. Ibid.
85. Ibid., 16 June 1980, vol. 410, col. 857.
86. Ibid., 8 April 1981, vol. 419, col. 548.
87. Ibid.
88. Ibid., 22 March 1983, vol. 440, col. 1077.
89. Ibid., 30 June 1983, vol. 443, col. 418.
90. Ibid., 22 March 1984, vol. 449, col. 1344.
91. Ibid., 30 November 1988, vol. 502, col. 236.
92. Ibid., 2 February 1987, vol. 484, col. 43.
93. Ibid., 12 December 1984, vol. 458, col. 312.
94. Ibid.
95. Ibid., 19 November 1986, vol. 482, col. 257.
96. Ibid., col. 258.
97. Ibid., 2 November 1988, vol. 501, col. 514.
98. Ibid., col. 515.
99. Lady Llewellyn Davies, interview, 14 June 1993.
100. Henry Kelly to Donald Soper, a Radio 4 Profile, reprinted in *Listener*, 17 August 1978.
101. Ibid.
102. LBC Radio, 26 December 1982.
103. Hyde Park, Easter Day, 3 April 1983.
104. Tower Hill, 5 May 1982.
105. Ibid.
106. Hyde Park, 20 September 1981.
107. Tower Hill, 1 May 1983.
108. Hyde Park, 17 February 1985.
109. Tower Hill, 10 December 1986.
110. Ibid.
111. Tower Hill, 7 January 1987.
112. Ibid.
113. Ibid.
114. Hyde Park, 23 February 1986.
115. Tower Hill, 2 July 1986.
116. Hyde Park, 8 June 1986.
117. Ibid., 26 June 1983.
118. Hyde Park, 26 April 1992.
119. Contribution in response to the questions 'What is your idea of God?' and 'What happens when we die?' asked by Hayley Mills for *The Good God Guide*, Save the Children Fund, n.d.
120. Dialogue with the Rev. Paul Hulme, Wesley's Chapel, 15 October 1992.
121. *Methodist Recorder*, 7 April 1994, p. 13.

122. *Hansard*, H.L., 31 October 1984, vol. 456, col. 547.
123. Ibid., col. 548.
124. Ibid.
125. Ibid.
126. *Care of the Elderly*, autumn, 1989.
127. Ibid.

Epilogue

1. Theodore O. Wedel, *The Coming Great Church*, SCM Press, 1047, pp. 38–9.
2. Ibid.
3. Ibid.
4. Ibid.
5. Donald Soper to Trevor Beeson, BBC, *The Controversialists*, 30 May 1980.
6. The Rev. John Stacey, interview, 17 March 1993.
7. *The Controversialists*, op. cit.
8. Lord Callaghan of Cardiff, interview, 8 December 1993.
9. Canon Alan Wilkinson, letter, 18 January 1994.
10. Adrian Hastings, *A History of English Christianity, 1920–1985*, Collins, 1987, p. 423.
11. Lord Archer of Sandwell, interview, 17 June 1993.
12. Ibid.
13. Ibid.
14. The Rev. Len Barnett, interview with Lord Soper, Bromley Methodist Church, 1983.
15. Bishop Trevor Huddleston, *Books and Bookmen*, 1972.
16. R. H. Preston, *Explorations in Theology 9*, SCM Press, 1981, p. 40.
17. Ibid.
18. Lord Wilson of Rievaulx in William Purcell, *Odd Man Out*, Mowbrays, 1983, p. 184. *Odd Man Out* was a re-issue of *Portrait of Soper*, with an Epilogue added.
19. Lord Cledwyn of Penrhos, interview, 10 June 1993.
20. Ibid.
21. Sheila Marsh, interview, 26 August 1993.
22. Tony Benn, M.P., interview, 9 June 1993.
23. Ibid.
24. Ibid.
25. Ibid.
26. Canon Alan Wilkinson, op. cit.
27. Ibid.
28. The Rev. Jeffrey Harris, interview, 25 May 1993.
29. The Rev. George Dolby, letter, 13 March 1993.

30. The Rev. Rupert Davies, (ed.), *The Testing of the Churches, 1932–1982*, Epworth Press, 1982, p. 50.
31. The Rev. C. Hughes Smith, interview, 12 May 1993.
32. Vivian Green quoted in Henry Rack, *Reasonable Enthusiast: John Wesley and the Rise of Methodism*, Epworth Press, 1989, p. 544.
33. Ibid.
34. Ibid.
35. The Rev. Professor Gordon Rupp, *Methodist Recorder*, 21 June 1965.
36. Bruce Kent, interview, 14 June 1993.
37. The Rev. Dr Gordon Wakefield, *Epworth Review*, September 1978, p. 3.
38. Major John Crashley, letter, 17 January 1994.
39. The Rt Rev. David Sheppard, letter, 20 July 1994.
40. The Rev. Noel Shepherd, letter, 31 August 1984.
41. Ibid.
42. The Rev. Dr John Newton, interview, 17 April 1993.
43. Pauline Callard, letter to Lord Soper, 21 January 1993.
44. The Rev. Dr Gordon Wakefield, interview, 23 March 1993.
45. Leslie Groves, letter, 31 March 1993.
46. Councillor Arthur Downes, interview, October 1993.
47. *The Controversialists*, op. cit.
48. The Rev. Brian Duckworth, interview, 19 February 1993.
49. Lady Llewellyn Davies, interview, 14 June 1993.
50. Ibid.
51. Ibid.
52. The Rev. Dr John Vincent, *Methodist Recorder*, 27 April 1967.
53. *Methodist Recorder*, ibid.
54. David Roberts, letter, 8 March 1991.
55. 'The Character of a Methodist', from *The Works of John Wesley*, Epworth Press, 1956.
56. The Rev. Brian Duckworth, op. cit.
57. *News Chronicle*, 24 December 1955.
58. Ibid.

DONALD SOPER'S WRITINGS

Christ and Tower Hill, Hodder and Stoughton, 1934.

Question Time on Tower Hill, Hodder and Stoughton, 1935.

Answer Time on Tower Hill, Hodder and Stoughton, 1936.

Christianity and Its Critics, Hodder and Stoughton, 1937.

Popular Fallacies about the Christian Faith, Hodder and Stoughton, 1937.

Will Christianity Work? 3 Broadcast Talks, Lutterworth Papers no. 34, Lutterworth Press, n.d.

Question Time in Ceylon, (ed.) The Rev. Dennis Lansdown, India, 1947.

Practical Christianity Today, Ken-Pax Publishing, 1947, re-published Epworth Press, 1954.

Answering Back, Epworth Press, 1953.

Children's Prayer Time, Epworth Press, 1954.

Keeping Festival, Epworth Press, 1954.

Singing Towards Bethlehem, Epworth Press, 1954.

Pathway to Adventure, (Wensleydale Booklet), New Zealand Methodist Board of Publications, 1956.

All His Grace, Epworth Press, 1957.

It Is Hard to Work For God, Epworth Press, 1957.

Here Stand I – The Place of Compromise in the Christian Life, (Alex Wood Memorial Lecture), Fellowship of Reconciliation, 1959.

The Advocacy of the Gospel, Hodder and Stoughton, 1961.

Christian Socialism, (Questions and Answers), Christian Socialist Movement, n.d.

Tower Hill, 12.30, Epworth Press, 1963.

Aflame with Faith, Epworth Press, 1963.

Christian Politics, Epworth Press, 1977.

Socialism – An Enduring Creed, (Third Tawney Memorial Lecture), Christian Socialist Movement, 1980.

Calling for Action, Robson Books, 1984.

Soperisms, (ed.) Brian Frost, New World Publications, 1993.

INDEX